ko

M,KE +

Glen R Johnson

3-18-12

"Glen, this is Lyndon. I'm supposed to be at Bergstrom Air Force Base tomorrow morning to speak to 12,000 airmen and to raise the Minuteman Flag. I may have to have a Security Council Meeting; therefore, I need you to be there in case I can't make it. And by the way, I need a speech on the White House wire before 4:00 a.m. tomorrow. Thanks, and keep up the good work, Glen."

Lyndon B. Johnson
United States President

"The greatest gift of life is friendship, and this gift I have received in my friend, Glen Johnson."

Hubert H. Humphrey
United States Vice President

"Only my friend Glen Johnson would dare have his feet on my desk."

Walter Mondale
United States Vice President

"I want to especially thank Glen Johnson who has been with the company for 40 years. He was the one who took the money funds into the banks in 1975 and our assets went from $300 million to $30 billion in just five years. Glen has been incredibly important to the growth of Federated."

Jack Donahue
Federated Investors

"In the early 1970s, the United States was beset by double-digit inflation and double-digit yields on short-term debt investments. A problem to some became an opportunity to Glen Johnson. In a stroke of genius, Glen turned idle cash into an asset class for fiduciaries. Money market mutual funds became a user-friendly solution to the liquidity needs of bank trust departments, and an industry was born."

Eugene Maloney
Federated Investors

"Perhaps the best way to tell the story of Glen Johnson's life is to make one thing crystal clear: It was no fluke. Oh, yes, there were some good breaks along the way, but Glen thought all that out in advance. Glen had been climbing the mountains in the vicinity of Lake Lillian in mid-western Minnesota, and it was from that tiny hamlet that he sprouted to become recognized far and wide as a man endowed with a deeply ingrained set of high ethical standards that were an integral part of every quest for success in which he played a role."

Norb McCrady
Minnesota Community Bankers

"Virtually everyone who responded to my plea for memories commented on the great Johnson hospitality, the camaraderie developed, the education received, and the major influence on the formation of the formal CCBA organization. I would add that in my nearly 50 years in and around banking, the meetings on Marco Island, and the allied lobbying efforts in Washington, DC with Glen . . . have been the absolute highlight of my career!"

Milt Klohn
INDEX

"I am not exactly sure what it was that forged our friendship and the relationship we still enjoy today. I just know I'm a better person because of it."

Christopher L. Williston
CAE President and CEO, Independent Bankers Association of Texas

"Glen is first and foremost a person of integrity; honest and true in his dealings with people. He is a loyal and dedicated person. Having been associated with more than a dozen board leaders and scores of board members in the 45-year career in higher education, Glen Johnson ranks at the very top by any measure that is applied. And the same applies to his wife LaVonne as board spouse. It was a privilege to work under Glen. It is a pleasure for my wife, Mary, and me to count the Johnsons as friends."

C. Carlyle Haaland
16th President, Thiel College

"Through hard work and the effective use of his special gifts Glen has become very successful and has achieved an elevated status, but his faith oriented his life around a loving purpose, opened him to the whole world, and in the process enlarged his humanity."

Dr. Louis Almen
17th President, Thiel College

"I first met Glen Johnson in 1978 when I was introduced to him by one of the members of the Pittsburgh chapter of the Family Association for the Youth Services agency I directed. I count that introduction as one of the most fortuitous moments of my life. For 30 years, Glen has been a superlative mentor, business advisor, and caring, generous friend that I came to think of as the chairman of my personal board of directors."

Dan Heit
CEO, Foundation for Abraxas

A Matter of Trust

of Trust

THE PERSONAL MEMOIRS OF
Glen R. Johnson

Taking a $2 Stock to $140,000

KELLER PUBLISHING
Marco Island, Florida

ISBN: 978-1-934002-19-3

Designed and composed in Kepler Std
at Hobblebush Books (www.hobblebush.com)
Printed in the United States of America

Published by
KELLER PUBLISHING
440 Seaview Ct, Suite 1012
Marco Island, FL 34145

KellerPublishing.com
800-631-1952

To my wife LaVonne . . . we are like two volumes of one book.
Thank you for making my story complete.

To the memories of our son David, and our daughter Lori,

and to the lives of the characters still penning our story,
Vicki, Harpo, and Kristianna
David's family: Sheila, Kari, Kora
Katelyn, Eliot, David, and Conor
Lori's family: Miles, Ariana, and Aidan

Contents

Illustrations

Acknowledgments

SPRINKLED THROUGHOUT this text are recollections inspired by the two previous books that chronicle the Federated Investors story: *The Eagle Soars*, and *New Horizons*. However, it is the countless number of people in my life to whom I'm really grateful, for it is they who regularly insisted that I write this book. Without their support, and indeed their powers of persuasion, I would have not completed this task. There are dozens of people who fall into this category, making it impossible to recognize all of them by name. Additionally, the following may only be names on a page to the casual reader, but to me they are each so much more, as they have impacted my life in a significant way.

Dr. Louis Almen—Former President of Thiel College for his contribution.

Cindy Anderson—For introducing me to my publisher, Wade Keller of Keller Publishing.

Andy Bonnewell—For taking over my duties as chief lobbyist. He learned his lobbying lessons well and now is a real political force at Federated.

George Clarke—For helping me remember names of people that worked with me during the Treasury Savings Bond days.

Bill Dawson—For his math calculations regarding the Federated stock, which I found not only interesting, but important as well.

Jack Donahue—For giving me the opportunity of a lifetime and managing to put up with my unorthodox marketing style.

Chris and Tom Donahue—For keeping the ship upright through some very turbulent waters.

Dick and Barbara Fisher—Traveling every day and staying in strange hotels can be a very lonely existence. However, every several weeks when I'd return to the office for a day or two, I distinctly remember looking forward to spending an evening with Dick and Barbara. They would always pick me up from the old Carlton Hotel and take me out to dinner. I will truly never forget their hospitality and friendship.

Reverend David Gleason—Our pastor at First Lutheran Church, Pittsburgh. He officiated at David and Lori's funerals and encouraged us in difficult times.

Dan Goldschmidt—The years he has taken care of the family farm are deeply appreciated.

Ed and Fran Gonzales—Ed, as my associate at Federated and Fran, as LaVonne's business partner.

Robin Guernsey—My secretary who transcribed most of the tapes and continually urged me to write this book. If she had not taken it upon herself to send me a tape recorder, I probably would never have gotten started. She sent me a tape recorder, told me to talk to it, and instructed me to send her the tapes. She said she would do the rest. Without her help, I could never have accomplished this memoir.

Dr. C. Carlyle Haaland—Former President of Thiel College for his contributions during my years on the Board at Thiel.

Dan Heit—Former head of Abraxas Foundation for his friendship and his contributions to this book.

George Hulstrand—My attorney in Willmar, Minnesota. George was not only my lawyer, but also my father's lawyer, and even my grandfather's lawyer. He practiced law into his 90s and retired recently. An incredible person, he was one of the individuals who helped write the charter and establish the bank in Willmar, Minnesota.

Maureen Kennedy—A long time Federated employee who assumed the responsibility of taking many of the photographs and organizing much of the material in this book.

Milt Klohn—Author of the chapter on Community Banking and Glass-Steagall (in the appendix).

Gene Maloney—Without his legal help, marketing would have been much more difficult. He always made my job easier with his fabulous ability to create the legal highway.

Norb McCrady—A long time friend and the past president of the Minnesota Community Bankers. Norb played a major role in 19 years of our work in lobbying. He offered to help me write this book. However, just as he was getting actively involved, Norb suffered a severe stroke, and has recently passed away.

John and Mary Ita McGonigle—For the leadership of John as Head of Federated Legal Department and the warm friendship of traveling around the world with John and Mary Ita.

Mal Newbourne—Fellow car buff who kept reminding me I had a book to write.

Lois Peterson—My cousin whose research into our family history has been invaluable.

Neal Peterson—Neal was a wonderful good friend and was certainly very savvy in political matters.

Ned and Joan Pheifer—For their friendship and ongoing encouragement.

Chuck Wallander—Without his persistence, I would never have found Federated.

Christopher Williston—Although rooted in business, our friendship has certainly grown over the years. As both a friend, and leader of the Independent Bankers Association of Texas, Chris did a wonderful job writing the foreword for this book, and I'm so appreciative of his sentiments.

Of all of the people that have shaped my life over the years, three in particular stand out above the rest:

My mother—For her undying love.

My father—For showing me how to be a leader by the way he lived his life.

LaVonne—For being with me every step of the way. Even when I was away from home for days at a time, she was a pillar of strength. That strength of character shines through, both in all her personal challenges of life and the tasks of assisting me in all my problems and opportunities. Yes, LaVonne has continually inspired me to be the best I could possibly be.

Foreword

Christopher L. Williston, CAE
President and CEO
Independent Bankers Association of Texas
October, 2010

THERE WAS A chill in the Washington, DC air that early October day of 1989 as I walked from the District's landmark Madison Hotel to the Washington Court, a swank new modern hotel near Capitol Hill. There, anxiously waiting at the front door, were two of the most finely groomed and tailored men I had ever seen. They began to make their way toward me and extended their hands.

"Chris, glad you are here. Glen is waiting for you."

It was just six months earlier I had been named the President and CEO of the Independent Bankers Association of Texas, a largely rag tag group of militant and principled community bankers who were looking to expand their power and influence in Austin and Washington. I was no stranger to the world of trade associations nor to banking, having had jobs at another banking trade association and bank consulting firm for the first fourteen years of my young career. But the political process was another thing for me entirely. My previous work was largely administrative in nature. I was a political neophyte, plain and simple.

I had received many a phone call in that first six-month period at my new job. Most all were the usual congratulatory type offering assistance and support for me in my new position. The call from the Twin Cities was different and almost mysterious.

"Chris, welcome aboard. My name is Milt Klohn, and I work with Glen Johnson and Federated Investors in Pittsburgh, Pennsylvania. I am an envoy of sorts for the company, and I work with many of your community bank counterparts across the country on federal legislative issues. I know you are going to be in Washington, DC in a couple of months for IBAA (now the ICBA) meetings. Glen wants to meet you."

I questioned Mr. Klohn about Federated Investors and Glen Johnson. Frankly, I had never heard of either, and I was suspicious of his motives. What did they want from me?

"Just make plans to meet with us when you are in town, and we will explain it all to you," he said. I reluctantly agreed.

I was pretty sure it must have been Glen Johnson sitting at the end of the long table in the boardroom of the Washington Court. Five or six other men, all in dark suits, were fixated on his every word, until we interrupted. It struck me as a scene from "The Godfather." I thought to myself, "Was this Don Corleone and his goons?" I quickly surveyed the room for long black cases that would house an Uzi or shotgun. To my delight, none were evident.

"Sit down, young man. Sit there at the end of the table," said the round man with cherub cheeks and grey hair. "I'm Glen Johnson, and you and I are about to become friends."

For the next hour or so I listened as Glen shared with me the story of Federated and his career of public service in Washington, DC. He explained the Federated business model working with large bank trust companies and the need to partner with the smaller banks to ensure the big banks were not successful in passing legislation that would authorize their entry into the mutual fund business. He never once asked me to do anything other than to keep an open mind in getting to know him and his company. I left the meeting more perplexed than ever.

How strange I thought the meeting was as I made my way back to the Madison Hotel. My mind was full of questions. These guys want to use the grassroots lobby power of the community banks to fight their big bank customers? What could possibly be in it for me? Later I would come to know just how important that meeting was, not only to me personally, but to helping transform the Independent Bankers Association of Texas into a respected Washington player.

———

Twenty-one years have passed since that fateful day in October, and there has not been a single day that I have not thanked the good Lord for bringing this gentle man into my life. I am not exactly sure what it was that forged our friendship and the relationship we still enjoy today. I just know I'm a better association executive and person because of it.

I came to know Glen Johnson as one of the most influential and politically savvy persons on the planet. Over the course of the first ten years as I struggled to learn the ways of Washington he would accompany me and introduce me to Washington's most elite and influential power brokers. He would take me under his wing and mentor me on how to lobby with integrity and purpose, and most importantly, how to win. He would instill in me the importance of never burning a bridge—that your most vehement legislative opponent on today's issue might just be your political ally tomorrow.

But our friendship grew far beyond the banks of the Potomac and the ways of Washington. Glen and I would come to enjoy countless days on the golf courses in and around Marco Island, Florida and DC, and in some of the finest nineteenth watering holes following. He plays the game with the same competitive spirit and integrity and taught me that golf was just a game to enjoy and forget about; it was the fellowship and relationships that the game afforded that really mattered.

Since the day I lost my father in 1999, Glen has filled the void of losing the best friend I had in life. He has been and is like a father to me. He has coached and counseled and has continued to instill in me that despite one's enormous power and influence, we never forget to practice humility and tolerance. He has been the listening ear on the other end of the phone providing solace and advice when things have appeared dismal or insurmountable.

Perhaps it was my immaturity and suspicion that Glen Johnson saw in me that day that he chose to take me under his wing. Or maybe it was that he saw something in me that reminded him of his early days trying to cope, understand and learn the ways of Washington and the political process. Whatever it was I don't really try to understand or care anymore. What matters is that I came to know one of the most positive and influential people in my life; the man I still call "The Godfather" today.

It is my fervent wish for you as you read the pages that follow that it will provide a glimpse into the humility and soul of this great man. A man of humble beginnings, he would rise to the pinnacle of public and private service, never once forgetting and crying out for "the little guy." Everyone should be so fortunate to have sat with presidents or some of Wall Street's most powerful moneymen as Glen Johnson has.

But you won't hear that from Glen. Everyone has importance and is important to him. He never once forgot about this once-young politically-naïve boy from Texas.

Nor shall I ever forget him.

Persistence and Determination

Norb McCrady,
Minnesota Community Bankers

PERHAPS THE BEST way to tell the story of Glen Johnson's life is to make one thing crystal clear: It was no fluke. Oh, yes, there were some good breaks along the way, but Glen thought all that out in advance. As a pre-school youngster on the farm, Glen watched his dad, grandfather, the hired man, and the older children in school in order to learn their skills and figure out how to improve those skills.

Glen grew up as a farm kid near a mid-Minnesota small town due west of the twin cities of Minneapolis and St. Paul. In his early years, family farms were a primary focus of those whose job was to keep track of Minnesota's economic pulse. Frequent updates of the farm market report could be heard on the major Twin Cities radio stations as well as the multitude of local area stations that criss-crossed this North Star of American's upper Midwest. It mattered not whether pork bellies or slaughter lambs were part of your daily vocabulary, if you listened to the radio in this Land of 10,000 Lakes, you were destined to learn how they were doing on the hourly farm market report out of south St. Paul.

Farm kids took an interest in the farm market report from the time they showed their first calf, or pig, or lamb during the 4-H judging at the county fair. Unquestionably, this enhanced their ability to see the relationship between such things as the level of unemployment and the price of farm commodities.

That period in history when our nation made the transition from isolationism to a role of world leadership pretty much coincided with the year of Glen's birth in 1929. The year Glen became 18 was the year George C. Marshall came home from his futile effort to resolve the struggle between the old and the new Chinas. Marshall had gained the respect of the world for his cool-headed leadership in WWII, and he accepted Harry Truman's offer to make him Secretary of State. The Marshall Plan became his theme in this new role and probably generated more worldwide respect than any comparable effort by this nation or any other nation in the history of man. A most deserving Marshall was awarded the Nobel Peace Prize in 1953.

Many mechanical improvements brought about during WWII were adaptable to conversion into non-war machinery and equipment after the war. Tempting as it was, Glen held firm to what he had been taught over the years and that was to repair, not replace, unless there was a measurable gain to be realized by the replacement. Every equipment breakdown called for a careful analysis of the cost versus loss factor. Glen continued to apply this principle throughout his business and political days that were to follow.

You might ask whether raising animals or growing something from seed had an applicable benefit that could be put to use in selling bonds or in creating interest that would lead to massive shifts of money into some heretofore unheard of money market fund. Remember these two words from Glen's 'Blueprint for Success': Persistence and Determination.

These were much more than just words to Glen. They were his 'credo.' They were the nucleus of his *modus operandi* because he knew, by applying these two principles, his likelihood of failing would be remote.

Glen's success story that led him to Washington, DC, New York City, Pittsburgh, Pennsylvania, and Marco Island, Florida didn't start in a metropolis like Minneapolis, or Duluth, or Rochester, or even Willmar.

No, Glen had been climbing the mountains in the vicinity of Lake Lillian in mid-western Minnesota, and it was from that tiny hamlet that he sprouted to become recognized far and wide as a man endowed with a deeply ingrained set of high ethical standards that were an integral part of every quest for success in which he played a role.

Glen's buddies from those days back on the farm knew he would always find a new mountain to climb, and that he would never turn back until he reached the summit. Persistence and determination—they keep showing up throughout his illustrious career.

The following tribute is from Milt Klohn, December 10, 2010:

> The saying goes: "Old soldiers never die . . . they just fade away."
>
> A brave "old soldier" passed on this week. He will be remembered for 660 days of combat in World War II, for the passion with which he met every challenge, for the explosive power and comedy that flew off his pen, for the dedication to community banking that knew no bounds, for the stories he told, the songs he sang, for being a fierce enemy and a great friend, for being truly one-of-a-kind . . . Norb!
>
> We will miss all of these qualities. Just remember, OLD SOLDIERS NEVER DIE . . . THEY JUST FADE AWAY, but the memories Norbert A. McCrady left with us will live forever.

A MATTER OF TRUST

Introduction

UPON REFLECTION, IT is easy to recognize the three major passions in my life: a love of politics, a love of sales, and my love for LaVonne, the bride of my youth. These three passions are the stories of personal memoirs. Finally, after my 80th birthday, I got serious about completing this book, starting the process in 2004.

Certainly the contents of these pages are as factual as I remember. As an octogenarian, my memory is not as good as it should be, but to the best of my knowledge, everything that I have written and dictated here is as it happened.

My father's passion for politics became my passion, shaping my life from the time I was just a young boy. I accompanied my father, a life-long Democrat, to political rallies, meetings, and conventions.

This growing passion led me to become a precinct chairman, a district secretary, a district treasurer, and in 1960, a delegate from Minnesota to the Democratic National Convention in Los Angeles, and again in 1976, I was a super delegate from Pennsylvania at the San Francisco convention.

Along my political path, I had the good fortune to know and work with Hubert Humphrey. He was, and remains today in spirit, my mentor and my hero.

Political campaigning, a form of sales, meant I had to sell my candidate and I had to sell myself. Consequently, sales became the second of my passions. When asked to describe myself, I say simply, "I am a salesman."

My sales career began at age 19 when I became the founder and publisher of my hometown newspaper, the *Lake Lillian Crier*. But my passion for sales evolved even further with three distinct ventures: the sale of government savings bonds and my subsequent position

1

as Assistant Secretary of the Treasury under Lyndon Johnson, a one-year stint with Motivational Systems, and my major and lasting career with Federated Investors. My years of working with Jack Donohue and the Federated family represent the most significant and rewarding years of my working career.

Lastly, but most important, there is LaVonne. None of the politics or sales career would have been successful and certainly not as much fun, if it had not been for my wonderful wife. Her story winds through the pages of this book.

We married many years ago, poor as church mice but that didn't matter. We were united; and the future, whatever it held, we would meet together.

In this Introduction, I have explained the three major passions of my life: politics, sales, and LaVonne. However, the story begins with my early life on the farm near Lake Lillian, Minnesota.

Part 1

Love of the Early Life

BLUEPRINT
FOR SUCCESS

Nothing in the world can take the place of persistence.

Talent will not; nothing is more common than unsuccessful men with talent.

Genius will not; unrewarded genius is almost a proverb.

Education will not; the world is full of educated derelicts.

Persistence and determination alone are omnipotent.

GLEN'S "BLUEPRINT FOR SUCCESS," IS THE ADVICE OF CALVIN COOLIDGE, 30TH PRESIDENT OF THE US (1872–1933), AND IS DISPLAYED ON GLEN'S OFFICE WALL.

1

My Father's Family

ALTHOUGH I GREW up as an only child, I certainly didn't have a small family. My parents had been married a number of years before I was born. May 2, 1929, I was welcomed into their home, a household that in addition to my parents and me also included my grandfather, my grandmother, my aunt, my uncle, my cousin, and the hired man, Jack.

GLEN'S GRANDPARENTS, GUSTAF
AND CHRISTINE JOHNSON, FROM HIS
FATHER'S SIDE OF THE FAMILY.

My Grandpa Gustaf came to America from Sweden with his father when he was 10 years old. He married Christine, also from Dalarna, Sweden, while he was in his 20s.

Investigating on my own, and with the help of a cousin, who has really done a lot of family history research, I started piecing the story together, learning even more of his tale when I went to Sweden.

I visited the house where Grandpa Gustaf was born and raised, as well as the church where I knew my grandparents had attended as youngsters in Gagnef. The church archives had records that were perfectly written. They were penned in beautiful Swedish handwriting. I could see when people were born and when they went to confirmation. My grandfather was included in the records, but his birthday wasn't recorded. Somehow he was born somewhere else, so initially, I didn't have the date of his birth. I did, however, find the date of his father's birth, and through that I was finally able to track my grandfather's birth date.

There were six children in Grandpa Gustaf's family, five boys and one girl. Sadly, Grandpa's mother, my great-grandmother, died of influenza. Coincidentally, the family next door to their house in Gagnef was a family that also had six children. Tragically, the father of that family was killed felling trees to build their log cabin.

During that period in the records, there was an unusual two year hiatus where there was no history recorded. Through a lot of investigation, I found that my great-grandfather had gone to prison. He'd been caught stealing corn from a neighbor's field to feed his starving family.

After serving his time and reuniting with the family, my great-grandfather and the widow from next door apparently had an affair, and they were run out of the country. They each took their youngest child and left, leaving the other children behind. As the youngest child, that is how Grandpa Gustaf arrived in America with his father.

The widow from next door and my great-grandfather were later married, and the two former neighbor kids were suddenly under the same roof. Growing up, I never understood why Grandfather would get upset and say, "She's not my sister," when someone referred to her that way. It wasn't until my grandfather was long dead, and I was in Sweden digging up all this information, that I found out the truth that they weren't brother and sister at all. They had grown up with the same parents, but in actuality she was the youngest biological child of the mother, and my grandfather was the youngest biological child of the father when each emigrated from Sweden. She was his stepsister, siblings only by marriage.

Whatever happened to the older children in Sweden, I don't know. Apparently one of them later came to this country, but I don't know that any of the rest of them did. Digging further, I found a distant cousin living in Stockholm. I wrote him at one time, but I never heard back.

My grandfather was my buddy. When everyone else was too busy, we would sit on the front steps and talk in Swedish about what was going on in the world, what was going on in school, what the crops were doing, and things like that. I was his best friend. I didn't give much thought to that at the time. But, I do remember well all the late evenings when we would sit on the steps outside the house and talk about everything.

My grandfather would wake me up in the morning at 4:45. He would say, "Breakfast is over, milking is done, it's almost lunch time, and you're still in bed." He'd always say that in Swedish. That was seven days a week, and I swore I would never forget that phrase, but yet I can't even begin to say it today. I spoke Swedish to everybody in the family except my dad and mother when I was young.

In the 30s, my grandfather would drive me to school in his 1931 Model A Ford. Our driveway was a half-mile long, and the schoolhouse was a mile away. We had a railroad track to cross just as we turned right to go to the schoolhouse. The railroad workman would have the little speeder carts on the tracks, and I would have to watch for them because my grandfather would never see them coming. Three times he knocked them off the railroad track.

I clearly remember coming home from school in the Model A. It had a throttle that you could pull down and leave down. Sometimes Grandfather would take that corner so fast, the car would just slide. One time we hit the speeder, knocked it off the tracks, and knocked it into a ditch full of water. To this day I can still remember those two guys coming out of the water. My grandfather never stopped. He just kept right on going. It was very funny.

7

Grandfather was healthy all of his life and only slipped at the end. His wife Christine, however, had serious high blood pressure. I can remember the doctor coming when she had problems. That's when they would take a horn to cut her legs and actually bleed her to relieve her blood pressure. It was really weird. I never knew what was actually going on, but I remember that she was in a wheel chair and had to be helped. She died early on, in the winter of 1952. Her funeral is embedded in my memory because it was 30 degrees below zero the day she was buried. My grandfather was very lonesome after my grandmother passed. He lived for many more years, and even had a full head of hair and read the Swedish newspaper up until the day he died at age 91.

GLEN'S GRANDPARENTS, GUSTAF AND CHRISTINE, WITH THEIR CHILDREN. LEFT TO RIGHT: EMIL, HILDA, AUGUST, HATTIE, OSCAR (GLEN'S FATHER), LENA, WILLIAM, AND ALBERT.

The siblings of my father, Oscar, consisted of my Aunt Hilda, Uncle Emil, Aunt Hattie, Aunt Lena, Uncle Bill, and Uncle August.

Uncle Emil never married. His background was interesting. He had worked in the round (railroad) house in Willmar. In St. Paul, he worked on the oil derricks as they drilled for oil near Lake Lillian, and at home he was the one who took care of the pigs. The pigs were considered to be part of his life. We had a lot of pigs—300 on average.

Aunt Hilda was also single. Apparently, she had been quite a good-looking gal in her younger years, but she chose to never marry. Aunt Hilda told me that when she was young, and the Indians would go on the warpath, my grandfather would take his three children, which would have been her, her brother, and her sister, to Fort Ridgley. Although he would then go back to run the farm, they would have to stay in the fort until it was safe. Later on, when the rest of the children were born, the Indians were no longer a threat. However, the three oldest children ended up in the fort many times one summer. I still remember my aunt telling me those stories.

Our hired man was a guy by the name of Jack Adams. Jack had worked for us all of my life. He came to us early on and earned a dollar a day plus room and board. I don't remember what Jack was earning by the time he went into the Army.

Jack was drafted in January 1942 right after Pearl Harbor and was in training for six weeks and then spent the rest of his days on the front lines. Jack had more spearheads and battle stars than anyone could ever imagine. Even though he had no education beyond the eighth grade, he drove a tank in the Army. He went through at least five different crews that were killed along the way in one fashion or another, but Jack survived and returned home.

In less than four years in the Army, Jack made full sergeant. Amazingly, even after seeing the world from the front lines, when he returned and worked for us again, he was the same guy as he was before he went into the service. Jack continued working for us literally until the day he died.

Uncle Bill had a dog with the name "Keno." One day he called my cousin, Martin E. Johnson, "Keno," and Martin became known as Keno from then on. He was Keno to the whole world. No one ever knew he was Martin. Keno lost his mother when he was two years old, and my mother and father raised him as their own. While I don't believe he was ever officially adopted, he had the same rights and privileges as I did, and we grew up as if we were brothers. I even spoke Swedish to my cousin Keno. He spoke only Swedish when he first started school, and then he had to learn to speak English.

Another constant companion was "Sonny" LaVerne Bordie, my Uncle Irvin and Aunt Hattie's child. He was two years older than me, and we spent our summers together while growing up, mainly because his parents were poor and struggling so hard. Sonny literally lived at our house from the day school was out until it started again. That happened all through grade school. He went to school in Lake Lillian at District 110, and I went to school in the country at District 5, but we were together in the summer. We had only eight months of school at that time.

I remember coming home from town one Saturday night during the drought and dust storms of the early 30s. We parked the car in the garage, which was somewhat east of the farmhouse, and shut the lights off. We started walking to the house only to find that we couldn't see our hands in front of our faces. We all got there eventually, although we did that by way of a lot of other outbuildings along the route. We were just lucky to get to the house without wandering around for hours. It really was incredibly dark that night.

My father's first love was baseball. He played 22 years of organized baseball, if you could call it that. It was in a small town, and my father was reputedly one of the best hitters in the business. He was a catcher by trade, but also played the outfield. My father was a line drive hitter, and his whole goal in life was to see his son grow up to be a professional baseball player. While I will admit to being a pretty good ball player, I never made it to that level. After playing baseball for many years, my father umpired for another 10 years. He and the barber in town were both sanctioned Southwest Umpires. They would umpire games all over southwestern Minnesota. Unfortunately, he would even umpire some of my baseball games in high school; it didn't make any difference where the pitch was, it was a strike.

I value the collage I have showing four generations of baseball players.

My father had the greatest laugh in the world. People talked about his laugh. It was just one of a kind. He would roar when he laughed. First of all, he had a great sense of humor, and he loved comedy or a good joke. Then he had the 'burst out' laugh that everyone recognized. They knew when Oscar was laughing.

GENERATIONS OF BALL PLAYERS. FROM TOP
LEFT, GLEN, GLEN'S FATHER OSCAR, GLEN'S SON
DAVID, AND HIS GREAT-GRANDSON, DAVID.

My father was a dedicated Democrat. He had me putting up signs as a young boy while he was running the township meetings that we would all attend. When he attended the county convention, I would go with him. I was too young to participate, but I was definitely not too young to learn. That got me involved in politics, and I believe even more so, got me into the newspaper business. That early involvement with my father laid the foundation for me to become a precinct chairman, a county officer, a district secretary, district treasurer, and eventually in 1960, a delegate to a national convention.

In 1929, the economy was really bad, and it was the start of some terrible years. Dad worked very hard on the farm, and the community regarded him as an outstanding farmer. I know my father struggled. However, it's interesting that in order to survive during those terrible dry years, my father would buy hay in southern Minnesota and haul it to central Minnesota where nothing was growing. He would sell it at a profit in central Minnesota, and that's how he stayed ahead of the game.

If anyone could set a good example, it was my father. He was a leader in everything he did, including many volunteer organizations, or co-ops, in the Lake Lillian area. He was chairman of the bank board, chairman of the creamery board, chairman of the elevator board, and chairman of the District Soil Conservation Committee. He became chairman of the school board when the new school was built.

We would have big parties at the school sponsored by the PTA. Both my parents were very active in the PTA. My mother was always bringing food or some kind of treat. It was the same way with the church. The church would have a mid-summer picnic. This was a big deal in small towns like Lake Lillian, Minnesota. The whole congregation would be there.

Special speakers were often invited to the church picnics. As a matter of fact, Hubert Humphrey, who was mayor of Minneapolis at that time, once spoke at our summer picnic. That was a big day for everyone. The women cooked and brought a wonderful spread of food. It was quite a time.

Lake Lillian was a small town with about 30 business places. It was very active. Today there may be only a few businesses left. An extra "benefit" of running the newspaper was that I was tabbed to be in everything from the fire department, to every fundraiser that came along.

The family used to get together every Christmas at our place because that's where my Grandfather Gustaf was living. We had great Christmases. All the children would come, and it was a fun time. Everyone got along well until my grandfather died without leaving a will.

As a result of no will, each of the children got a piece of the farm. The farm had been 400 acres. Over the years, my father had turned the 400 acres into 800 acres, so he owned the additional 400 acres. After my grandfather's death, each of his children now owned 60 acres.

We never got together ever again because the siblings fought over what the land should be worth and what they were entitled to. Half of them had one opinion, and the other half, an opposite opinion. They didn't want to run the farmland, yet they couldn't rent it out to someone else. My father rented it all until he was finally able to buy it from the rest of the family.

Buying each piece of land was like pulling teeth. Uncle Bill, Aunt Hattie, Uncle Albert, and one other family member were on the same side of the issue. Emil and Hilda, who had stayed on the farm, were easy to deal with.

My father was the one who really improved the farm years before when he started running it. It had been full of rocks. He cleaned the whole farm up and built the roads into it. He did a lot of things and spent a lot of money that he never got paid for. The brothers and sisters just took that for granted. These circumstances totally broke up the family. Overall, the situation was like a war. It was a very sad time. Today, one of the things that I stress with my family is to not let those things tear you apart like it did my family.

∿ 2 ∿

My Mother's Family

MY DAD'S SIDE of the family lived with us, so I knew them very well, but I barely knew my mother's side at all. I do know that they came from Dahlsland, Sweden. My mother was born in the United States, after her father, Sven Anderson, and his wife came to Minnesota from Sweden in 1858. My maternal grandfather was reputed to be the father of the first boy child born in the state of Minnesota, since Minnesota became a state the year they arrived.

My Grandfather Anderson was a guard on the prison wall at Stillwater. Apparently, that is what he did his entire working life. He died before I knew him, but I knew his wife, my grandmother. They'd moved to a farm near Lake Lillian, several miles from where my dad was born.

Later, my grandmother moved to Fosston, Minnesota, about 200 miles north of where we lived. I can remember going there to visit when she was still alive, but I really have little memory of her at all because she died when I was still young. I do know that we have been to family gatherings there. Once we returned for a family reunion, and they had a big sign (the sign had to be 20 feet square) on a tree, which was the family tree. Way over on one branch I found my name, along with the names of my wife and children. You wouldn't believe how many were on this sign, and I don't even know what relation they would have all been to me. They may have been second, third, or fourth cousins, but there were dozens of them. It truly was amazing. My cousin, Lois Peterson, did a lot of research on the family and has much more knowledge than I do. She wrote a story for a Nordic magazine that I have somewhere. It is about growing up, and her father talks about his upbringing.

My family and I have since gone back and helped finance the restoration and replication of the log cabin that my mother's parents lived in. The city of Marine on the St. Croix agreed to maintain the historic home if we would pay for moving the old log cabin from the farm into town. Marine is a tourist spot, and the log cabin is still maintained by the city. All of the tools of the day such as scythes, forks, blades, and planes are kept there. A sign says that this is the cabin where my grandparents were raised.

A PAINTING OF THE HISTORIC CABIN, BUILT BY GLEN'S
MATERNAL GRANDFATHER, SVEN ANDERSON.

THIS CABIN, BUILT BY GLEN'S MATERNAL GRANDFATHER,
SVEN ANDERSON, WAS MOVED TO MARINE ON ST. CROIX,
MINNESOTA, AND STILL STANDS AS AN HISTORIC LANDMARK.

My mother had two brothers and two sisters. Her brother Frank moved to Fosston, Minnesota, where he farmed. Her other brother, Ed, had a farm just outside Lake Lillian. Her sister Edna married and moved to Brooklyn, New York. Esther, the oldest, married and moved to Fosston near her brother and his wife. I remember going to visit them at their farm once a year, and they would come to visit us once a year.

In 1939, I went with my dad and mom to the World's Fair in New York City. We traveled by Greyhound bus for better than 50 hours to get to the Fair. I had no idea where we were in that big city, but once we got to New York, my father went about getting a bus to Brooklyn. When we arrived, we walked about a half block, and we were at my Aunt Edna and Uncle Fred Hitter's house. We stayed with them for an entire week as we attended the New York World's Fair. The Fair was fabulous, and even though I was only 10 years old, I can still remember most of the things I saw there.

An interesting thing happened as we were leaving New York to go to Washington. While in the middle of the Holland tunnel, I had to go to the bathroom. My mother insisted the driver stop the bus, and even though the driver almost had a fit, he actually stopped the bus in the middle of the tunnel, and I stood outside the bus to take a pee.

We then traveled to Washington and visited with my cousin, who worked at the Library of Congress. We visited the Congress, the White House, and several things in Washington. By that time we were tired of riding the Greyhound bus, so we took a train back to Minnesota. Even though we had to change trains in Chicago, the train was a whole lot better than riding a Greyhound bus.

Unfortunately, I don't have memories regarding how my parents met. I know that they went together for a long time. I think that my father was 25 and my mother was 23, or at least they were in their mid 20s when they married. I think they lived close to each other.

My father and I were not close, but I was very close to my mother. I worshipped my mother. She was one of a kind. She and my aunt would be out milking the cows at 3:30 in the morning. Then they would come in and make breakfast.

At harvest time we would get neighbors from maybe eight different farms to come and help thrash the grain and fill the silo. My

GLEN'S MOTHER, RUTH ANDERSON JOHNSON.

mother and aunt would have to fix lunch for everyone. They worked very hard, and it was certainly difficult for them.

Only once did I see my mother cry. It was when the price of eggs went from 11 to 12 cents a dozen. Those were tears of joy when the eggs got to be 12 cents a dozen! It meant they were worth a penny apiece, and depending on the time of year, we always had 30–50 dozen eggs to sell each week at the market in town. When they got to be worth a penny apiece, she thought that was the greatest thing that could have ever happened.

Eggs weren't the only things we took to market. After milking the cows, we'd pour the milk into the separator, and on Saturdays we'd have cream to take to the market with the eggs. The egg cases were long, and they held 15-dozen in each end. I remember that we'd have at least a case and a half of eggs and three of those 10-gallon cans of cream. After we sold our goods, we would go to the store to buy our supplies to take home. For a long time we hauled it ourselves, and then in later years, it was picked up at the farm.

When we cleaned out the house after my parents' deaths, we found that for many years my mother had kept stacks of those store slips. She bought a whole basket of groceries for ten dollars. It was hard to believe.

My mother was a very, very special person, and everybody loved her. She loved to have a picnic. In the summertime on Sundays if there wasn't a ballgame, and sometimes even before or after the ballgames, she wanted to go to the lake and have a picnic. Mother would fry chicken and do all the things to put a picnic together. We would go as a family. That was the highlight of her life. She just truly loved picnics. I also remember on the Fourth of July we'd have big picnics in town. I would get a quarter to spend, and that was a lot of money.

My mother was always on my side for everything. She took care of me for whatever reason. The winter that I was seven years old, I got pneumonia and was very ill. The roads were blocked at the time, and the doctor had to come to our house with a sleigh and horses. The minister was there, and I was in bed. To this day I can remember hearing the doctor say to the minister, "He's not going to live through the night." My mother was quite religious, but very emotional when she thought I was dying. I somehow survived the lobar pneumonia, which was a miracle because it was pre-penicillin days. Lobar pneumonia is the worst kind, and it's what you die from, or at least did in those days.

When I had the mumps, my father came to my bedroom. I was all swollen, and he said, "Oh, you don't look so bad. You'll be alright." Then he left the room. Mother came in and took one look at me, and she screamed. That really scared me. It was horrible, but my mother was just more emotional.

My father would have rather had me stay on the farm then leave for college after I graduated from high school. He was hoping that I would make the baseball team. I probably would have been the starting catcher for Gustavus, the college I first attended, but I got a D in my Swedish grammar class, and they would not let me play. I never told my father. He would have been heartbroken.

When I think of the relationship with my father, I tend to compare it to that of my grandfather, whom I thought of as my best friend. I thought one day, "I never hugged my grandfather." I just didn't do those things. I don't ever remember hugging my father or my grandfather, but I did hug my mother.

When my parents got older, my father's health declined. They came to see us in Pittsburgh when we lived there. I believe he had about eight more years before his mind was gone. In the end, he could relate every inning of a ballgame 20 years earlier, but he couldn't tell you what happened last week.

We had a nursing staff in the house to care for him, and I sort of supervised things from afar. We had three nurses that worked eight-hour shifts, seven days a week. We never put him in a nursing home. My mother took unbelievably good care of him the whole time he was sick, until she died almost two years before him.

I was in Washington, working The Hill, when I got the call that my mother had a heart attack. Since I was in Washington, I called my company to get the company jet to fly home. I took the jet straight to Minnesota, but she was dead when I arrived. My mother died at age 84, and my father died at 86.

GLEN, WITH HIS MOTHER RUTH.

~ 3 ~

Farm Life

FARM LIFE DEFINITELY builds character. As a matter of fact, learning honest, hard work is the thing that is most memorable to me as I reminisce about farm life. I have never regretted the days that I spent on the farm.

The year 1929 was not a very good year, of course. We were at the depths of the Great Depression, and from the time that I was old enough to understand what was going on, I knew how very difficult things were.

There is not a time when I can remember not working. Even as a youngster, from the time I was old enough to lift a shovel I did my part. I remember being about eight years old and standing on a beer keg to harness the horses to go out and mow and rake hay. It was the only thing that I knew, so I grew up working very hard.

My typical day started with my grandfather coming in at 4:45 in the morning and telling me that the day was half gone. My major job was to put down silage from the silo and feed the cows. I would also help gather the eggs, clean the barn, and feed the pigs, before I left for school.

The silage was stored in a big, round 40-foot tall silo. To retrieve what was needed for the morning feeding, I would have to climb up the silo, dig the silage loose, and throw it down. That's called, "putting down the silage," and was part of my daily routine. When I would get a big pile down below, I would climb down and feed it to the cows. First, I gave them each a big pitchfork full of silage, and then I would top it off with a scoop of ground corn. It was their daily fare while they were being milked. I always considered it their reward for being milked.

THE JOHNSON FAMILY FARM, NEAR LAKE LILLIAN, MINNESOTA.

I would go off to school, and then when I came home at night it was the same routine all over again. I did very little milking because my mother and aunt did most of that. We did have milking machines to help the process.

We had roughly 25 cows most of the time, and the amazing thing to me was they all knew exactly where to go. We had long rows of stanchions. I think there were nine in each row, and every single time, every cow went in the right place. On the rare occasion when a cow would go in the wrong stanchion, the one that was supposed to be there would create a ruckus and carry on like crazy until we got the other cow out of there.

The worst time I was ever involved with milking was when my cousin Keno and his wife, Gladys, went to the Black Hills for a week. I volunteered to milk his 10 cows by hand. I want to tell you, I've never worked so hard in my life. What a miserable job! Every morning and every night the cows had to be milked. You cannot believe how happy I was to have Keno home.

Back when I would have been about four years old, our hired man, Jack Adams, brought me an Angora cat. The first cat on the farm, that Angora cat was the beginning of many cats. Before very long, we ended up with about 24 cats. Those were all a result of that one Angora cat Jack brought for me.

With those 24 cats, we obviously didn't have a lot of mice around, but my parents were very good at making sure the cats always had something to eat. My Aunt Hilda, who participated in milking every morning, was also very good about feeding the cats. They would all line up at milking time to get their squirts of warm milk directly from a cow.

In the spring, I cultivated and plowed before Uncle Emil planted the corn. During harvest time, from the time I was probably eight, I rode the tractor, and my cousin rode the binder. We cut all the grain, and then we would shock the grain. We would pitch bundles and thrash the grain. All the farm children grew up having similar obligations.

Thrashing and filling silos was really enjoyable. When we would thrash, my neighbor Donny and I would haul the grain. We were only about 10 years old when we started driving those grain trucks. I drove the cutter when I was 12 years old. That really ran the whole operation. Those were great times.

Filling silos was another kind of project altogether. To get the silage up and into the silo, we would put sections of pipe together and raise it up with ropes. There was a pulley at the top and a big gooseneck, so the silage would blow up the pipe and drop into the tower. The top of the tower had a steel dome roof, and a hole for the silage to go in. It was my job to climb the 40 feet and steer the pipe into the hole. I did that from the time that I can remember. When I was perhaps 14 years old, the people guiding the pipe dropped it, which knocked me off of my perch. I held on to about one inch of tin and managed to get back to the ladder. I climbed down, but I would have probably been killed if I hadn't managed to hang on. Heights have bothered me ever since.

Prior to that, when I was younger, I used to go over to the neighbor's place. They didn't have a roof on their silo and we would actually go up and walk around the 2-inch wide rim when the silo was empty. It was 40 feet down on both sides! There was a tree that we could jump to and climb down. We had done that often, but after my experience with getting knocked off the silo roof, all of that ended.

I was 10 years old when I went to New York with my father and mother to the World's Fair. We also visited the Empire State Building. That was before they put the tall metal guards on the observatory deck that you see today. At that time, there was just a flat concrete railing. My father picked me up and sat me on the edge. I screamed, "Don't do that!" That experience still lingers with me today.

I'm not sure when the happiest times were on the farm. Probably it was just finishing a good, hard day's work. One time when we were small, my cousin Sonny and I went fishing in the Crow River. The river was a five-mile trip one way. We were riding our bikes down Highway 7, and I found a coin purse on the highway. It had $1.74 in it. Boy, did we think we were rich! It was incredible!

We didn't have electricity in the area yet, so we used a light plant, which was our 32-volt generator. It would run as necessary to keep the batteries charged. If you turned a couple lights on it was fine, but if you turned too many lights on, the generator would come on to recharge the batteries. That noisy thing would wipe out the radio broadcast until it stopped. I remember that clearly.

In 1941, when I heard that the Japanese had bombed Pearl Harbor, my folks were out milking the cows. I went out and told them what had happened. They thought I was listening to some mystery show on the radio. We didn't have television yet, but of course, they later found out what I said was true.

Since Jack, our hired man, was drafted 30 days after the attack on Pearl Harbor, it was just my father, my cousin, and me who had to put the entire crop in. It took a lot of long hours of plowing and planting to get the crops in, and by the same token, it took a lot of hours in the fall to harvest those very same crops. I pitched bundles like all the older folks from the time I was 10 years old and was certainly proud of the fact that I could work with the best of them. I even castrated pigs when I was 10 years old.

By the time I was 13, I could traverse the entire half-mile driveway with a 100-pound sack of grain on my shoulder just as Dad, Jack, and my cousin were able to do. Jack came home after the war in one piece, and came back to work for us.

There was always plenty to do on the farm, and we tried to make play out of work. It seemed we all strived to make the work enjoyable.

As a little boy, my favorite job was plowing the snowdrifts soon after it snowed. I had a sled with a snowplow that I had built with my father's help. As soon as it would snow, I would go out and push that plow over all the paths from the house to the barn, the house to the granary, the house to the chicken coop, the house to the hog barn, and any other area we needed cleared. I would have paths running all over the place. Also, during the cold times I would load corncobs and take them up to the water tank to keep the ice off the "ever-freezing tank."

In addition to plowing the snow, I loved to plow the dirt. Turning the ground over was something I enjoyed. Some years I plowed every inch of the whole farm. Of all the work that I did on the farm, that was my favorite.

The work I hated most of all was fencing. We had hogs, and hogs always get out. We had to constantly repair the fence, and that was hard work. There was a big, 80-acre piece of virgin meadow that we would put the cattle on to eat grass until we would corn feed them and get them ready for market. We ran about 100 head of steers.

I'll never forget the day that my dad said, "You're going to build an 80-acre fence." That meant that I had to haul all those posts and dig every post-hole by hand, set the post, tamp it, get it solid, build the gates, and whatever else it took. From the time I got up every morning for six weeks straight, my job was building every inch of an 80-acre fence line that had three strands of barbed wire. Life on the farm was difficult, but other than fencing, I enjoyed it. It was the only thing that I knew.

Almost everything that we ate came from right there on the farm. Any additional supplies were purchased in town when we took our extra eggs and cream to market. For medicinal needs, the Watkins man would come by the farm once a month to check out our medicine cabinet and restore it. We still have the original medicine chest that all of the medicine went into. When the Watkins man came, you would invite him into the house, and he would check the cabinet to see what you were short of. He'd give you a bill for what you needed.

We butchered all of our own hogs and our own steers. We would take the meat and salt it and cure it. We smoked it, then wrapped it in paper and put it in the oats bin. When we ran out of bacon in the house, I would go dig in the bin and get a slab of pork, and we would slice it off. This is how we'd have bacon to last the whole year.

We had a big 2-acre garden with rows almost 100 yards long. My grandfather insisted that we grow at least 100 bushels of potatoes. We would get them out of the ground, put them in sacks, and put them in a big bin in the cellar. That kept us in potatoes for the whole year.

Half the bin was still full of potatoes when the new season started, so we would haul them back out to feed to the cows. By the way, the cows loved potatoes. We would pick the new potatoes and put those into the bin. We always had more than twice as many as we could possibly ever use, but my grandfather was a stickler, and he said, "In Sweden, we had years when we didn't get any potatoes. We have to have enough for a year in case we don't get any potatoes." As a result, we always grew twice as many potatoes as we needed.

Starting back when I was six years old, a job of mine was to pick off the potato bugs. I carried a can of kerosene along with me, and would pick the bugs from the potatoes and throw them in the kerosene can where they would die, of course. The potato bugs would come on about the time that the potatoes were in bloom. If you didn't pick the bugs, they would eat the blooms off, and you wouldn't get any potatoes.

The plow used for the potatoes had a blade with a grate that would shake the dirt off. I would go behind the horse while running the plow by hand and get the potatoes out of the ground. The particular plow that we had was made for just one horse. It had two poles, so you had a pole on each side of the horse. When we started using the tractor, we cut the poles off and pulled the plow with the tractor.

There would be a nice row of potatoes behind you to throw in a sack. Those were 100-pound sacks that we had to pick up and haul to the house. The window to the potato bin in the cellar was just big enough for a 100-pound sack to fit through. One guy would be outside putting the sack in, and one guy inside would dump the sack. Every year I would say, "Can't we plant half as many potatoes?" Every year it was, "No, we have to plant *all* the potatoes."

We plowed with a horse, not a mule. With the horse you used the "giddy up" and "whoa" commands. You could also command "back up," but you rarely backed up. If you were running a mower, or a rake, and had a team of horses you would back up a lot, but not when you were plowing potatoes. So, it was all "giddy up" and "whoa."

Our teams of horses included Dick and Birdie, Cap and Joe, and others. I suppose that we had four teams of horses that were really good working horses. We had maybe 20 more horses that were part of the breeding stock.

When the horses got really old, it was one of my jobs to shoot them. I shot a lot of horses with a shotgun, and I hated it. We would first shoot the horse and then skin the hide to sell. We had 300 hogs, so after skinning it, we'd drag the horse to the pigpen to let the pigs eat the horsemeat. This was not very nice, but I did it more times than I wish to remember.

I can still remember to this day that most of the horses were in the pasture eating the grass on the other side of the fence when lightning struck and killed them all. There were so many, at least a dozen, that we had to dig big holes in the ground right where they lay. Those holes had to be really deep to bury those big horses.

In addition to potatoes we planted cucumbers, watermelon, muskmelons, onions, radishes, and peppers. My mother and aunt would do the canning. We bought peaches, pears, and other fruits from the store to can. We'd have a whole cellar full of 2-quart fruit jars that lasted through the winter.

One of the things that my mother and I did every other Saturday was churn 25 pounds of butter that we put in 5-pound jars. We'd put it down in the well to keep it cool. That was always fun. I would turn the butter churn, and then my mother would turn it. When the cream started to turn to butter, it got very hard to turn. You really had to work to turn it. We never made cheese; it was something we bought instead.

My cousin Keno was very mechanically inclined, and invented a way to put an electric motor on the churn. What a difference the motor made for churning the butter! The churn that my mother and I made all the butter with is sitting in the farmhouse kitchen to this day, as is the washing machine my grandmother used. It's a wooden washing machine, and you push the lever back and forth. We've restored all of it to its original state.

We made most of our own bread. My aunt made several loaves and put them in the oven. The bread would come out, and we'd get big slices of bread with butter. I was probably 10 years old before I had store-bought bread.

Being a farm boy, I was naturally a member of the 4-H Club. We had our 4-H meetings at District 5, which was the same place I went to school. We had a very active group, and had our meetings once a month or more. I can remember there were about 25 people at every 4-H meeting. The different 4-H members had different projects, and it was all tied to the county fair.

The Kandiyohi County Fair was held in Willmar, Minnesota and ran for five days. That was more than the normal three days for county fairs because it was a big county, and there were lots of entrants. People had everything from vegetables, to flowers, to quilt work and animals. I always raised a calf. There was a lot involved with raising a calf. In addition to feeding it, and caring for it, I had to regularly wash it, weigh it, and train it to lead. My calf was a short-horn, a breed chosen because they seemed easier to train and to lead for the parade.

My cousin Keno and I would compete on who could get a blue ribbon, who would get a red ribbon, and who wouldn't get a ribbon at all. One year he had a beautiful white-faced Hereford, and I just knew he was going to get a blue ribbon. When we got to the fair, the one thing we didn't do very well was lead. We were on the racetrack trying to lead our calves, and Keno was just in front of me. A stupid clown came over with a broom and swatted Keno's calf in the rear. Away the calf went. It broke away from Keno and tore through the fairgrounds. It just tore up one side and down the other. I don't recall that it hurt anybody, but it could have seriously injured somebody along the way. The calf knocked down tents and everything else.

The calf was finally cornered, but it was a very traumatic affair. Because the parade was always a part of the judging, Keno never got a ribbon at all for that beautiful animal. I'm sure that was because the calf got spooked.

That year I got a blue ribbon, and the reason I got it was because I had the only shorthorn. The fair was always a great time, and I looked forward to competing with a calf at the county fair every year during the times I was growing up.

We enjoyed the Minnesota State Fair as well. Even as a youngster, I thought like an entrepreneur. I used to swear that there were a million people that attended the state fair every year. I remember thinking, "If I could only get a dollar from everybody who came through that gate, I'd be a millionaire."

Back at the farm, one of the more unfortunate incidents in my life occurred the day after we had gotten 1,000 brand new chicks. Brand new chicks are very tiny and fragile. If anything scared them, or if they got too hot or too cold, they would crowd together and die. When we would get the new chicks, we would have to watch them very carefully. The brooder stove would keep the heat about 90-degrees when the chicks were little.

The large group of new chicks were doing great. The next morning when we came out of the barn, there sat my favorite cat with a circle of 22 dead baby chicks. I was aghast. Thirty seconds later my father arrived. He reached down and picked the cat up by the back legs and crashed it into the concrete. That was the end of my favorite cat. It was a terrible time, and I remember doing a lot of crying for that poor cat. I did understand because times were really tough, and 22 chicks would be a lot of income later on when they would start laying eggs. At any rate, the cat bit the dust, and the chicks were never recovered. At least we didn't lose any more.

The Portingas, Johnsons, and Hedins had farmsteads that were located near each other. The Portinga place was right on Highway 7, we were a half-mile north and a half-mile west of Highway 7, and Donny Hedin was a half-mile south of Highway 7. We were together a good deal all through grade school, and not only at school, but we also worked together filling the silo, thrashing, or doing other farm tasks.

As farm kids, we argued about who had the best tractors. Bud Portinga's folks had a John Deere, we had an Allis Chalmers, and Donny had a Farmall (later he had a John Deere). Every year we argued about who had the best one and which could pull the most plows. It was a running argument about tractors, but it was the same with cars. Of course, since my Uncle Bill owned a Ford dealership, we had nothing but Fords at our place. Bud had a Chevy, and Donny's folks had a Buick. The Buick was probably the superior car, but it was hard for us to admit it.

From the time I was four years old, we would play poker on winter nights. Playing for matchsticks, the players included the hired man Jack, Keno, Dad, and me. When I got old enough to go into town with my dad, I was probably not more than 12, he would invite me to go play poker with his poker friends and him (and he enjoyed that as much as I did). He would give me $25 and say when that was gone I had to quit. These were all older players that were my father's age. Here I was this little kid, but I had grown up playing poker on the farm. Between my dad and me, we won most of the time.

My cousin Keno, who was eight years older than me, would play in town too. There would be seven of us in the game, and between Dad, Keno, and me we would literally wipe them out. We'd go home with $300 or $400 at a time when $1 was a lot of money.

To be a good poker player you have to know the odds, and understand what your chances are with what you have in your hand. Then you figure what the odds are for you to get what you want to get. Poker is typically a seven or five card game. We played Seven-Card Stud mostly. High, low, split, declare.

Later, when I went to college at Gustavus, that's how I paid my tuition. I played poker. If I had not made money playing poker, I would not have been in school.

My friends in Marco Island and I still play poker. In fact, I now play with people who use ten cards. Four of a kind, a big full house, or a straight flush, is not uncommon. You have five cards in your hand, and then five more are turned up. You can use all ten to figure out which five you want to use. I never played that growing up or anywhere along the way. In all the cards I've played in my life, I never played non-poker games. Non-poker games are deadly, and I really shouldn't play, but I do enjoy it when we play on Tuesday nights.

I played poker recently, and I had some great hands; actually five really great hands—every one of them second best. That's when you lose money. There were seven of us playing. We have the high hand and the low hand, and we split the pot. The last hand of the night I had a 6, 5, 4, 3, 2 which is an almost perfect low. I didn't have the Ace.

The guy who won went both ways. He had the Ace, Deuce, 3, 4, and 5 of diamonds. It was a straight flush. He won high, and he won low.

There was $300 in the pot. That would have made me even. I'm not sure whether I will keep on playing or not. There are probably some days when I shouldn't play because I'm pretty foggy. That's why it's important to get this book done; the older I get, the more I forget.

I grew up playing poker and playing baseball. Whenever we would come in from the fields during the summer, we would have lunch, and then we would play catch. Or my dad might hit fly balls to my cousin Sonny and me. My father would hit the ball what seemed like a mile in the air. We actually had a true home plate and bases. We would play baseball even if it were only for half an hour. In the evening if we had time after dinner, we would play baseball.

I never regretted growing up on a farm because that's how I learned to work and how I learned to get up in the morning. Even with all the other jobs that I've had in my life, I've always walked out the door before 6:00 every morning. Even all the years that I was at Federated I was usually at work by 6:00 a.m. When I was at the Treasury in Washington, I was up early in the morning and in the office. Our house was in Reston, Virginia. It was a solid hour from the office, but I was always in the office before 8:00 a.m. and never got home until probably 8:00 p.m. That has always kept me in good stead. I have my thoughts on timeliness, and later in the book you will see I am a real stickler about time.

4

Grade School

I STARTED SCHOOL when I was five years old. The school was about a mile away from our home, and I would go no matter what. In fact, I rarely missed a day except for the time when I had pneumonia and almost died when I was seven. When the weather was really cold and blustery, my grandpa, uncle, or cousin would take me to school. The District 5 School where I went was a one-room country school. When I was in the first grade, there were a fairly large number of students in the school. From fourth grade on, there were only six students in the entire school.

My two best friends were Donald Hedin and Delton (Bud) Portinga. There were also three girls, Lois Portinga, Maggie Flann, and Donna Mae Flann in the school. Bud, Donny, and I were in the same grade. Donna Mae was a grade behind us, and Maggie and Lois were a grade behind her. The small class naturally allowed our schoolteacher the time to spend one-on-one with each of us.

An embarrassing incident happened when I was in the lower grades at District 5 School. It was in the spring of the year, and during the 30-minute noon lunch break Donny, Bud, and I ran down to the bank of the ditch that was about a quarter of a mile away to pick pussy willows.

The ditch was mostly covered in ice. We crossed over the icy water on a tree branch. However, while we were picking the pussy willows, the ice dislodged and floated down stream, no longer resting near our crossing spot. Both Bud and Donny were able to scramble across the branch and to the tree. They took off running back to the school, arriving just as the bell was ringing.

I was the last one to cross. I jumped and caught the branch, but just as I was going to make the grade, the branch broke, and I fell head first into the ice-cold ditch. I ran all the way to the school and arrived looking like a drowned rat. The teacher called my parents, and they came and got me. They took me home, so that I could change clothes, and then I went back to school. It was a very embarrassing incident, but one worth recording.

One particularly good memory I have from grade school is that on every birthday my dad and mother would bring ice cream and cookies to school for all my classmates. That was a real treat that everybody looked forward to, and it still stands out in my mind as a real highlight.

On days when I walked to school I had the choice of walking on our driveway, which was a half a mile running east and west, or walking on the railroad, which ran parallel to our driveway. Actually, if the railroad had gone straight, it would have gone right through the middle of our barn.

The trains came by every single day. There was a passenger train that went to Minneapolis that you could board at 6:30 a.m. in Lake Lillian and be in Minneapolis two hours later. You could then board the train in Minneapolis in the evening and be back in Lake Lillian by 9:00 p.m. We called this *The Passenger,* and you could set your clock by it. I often went to sleep by the sound of *The Passenger* engine in the distance.

Once when I was in grade school, someone gave me a padlock for a birthday gift. As I was playing with it on the way to school one day, I locked the mailbox. Our mail carrier was a guy by the name of Harry Hawkins. He arrived to put the mail in the mailbox and found the padlock. He stopped at District 5 where I was at school, which was right on his route, and asked me if I had padlocked the mailbox. I didn't know it was a federal offense, and he convinced me that I could very well have gone to jail. I want to tell you it scared the hell out of me, but I certainly learned my lesson to never to put a padlock on a mailbox again.

Another experience that stands out as a grade school kid was the winter snowstorm of November 11, 1940. There is actually a book titled, *Where Were You on November 11, 1940?* It was one of the worst snowstorms ever to hit the state of Minnesota, and dozens and dozens of people died in the storm.

November 9, 1940 was a Saturday, and we had been chasing chickens all day. This was an annual event where we rounded up the chickens and put them in the chicken house for the winter, as they had been running loose all summer. It rained all day as we were hunting the chickens. The last dozen or so of the chickens were always very difficult because they would fly away, and we would have to use a hook to catch them and put them in a crate, then finally into the chicken coop.

On Sunday, the 10th, it began to snow, and it just snowed, and snowed, and snowed. I think we probably had six to eight inches by Monday morning.

On Monday morning Keno took me to school in his 1937 straight back 60 horsepower Ford. We had a difficult time getting there and almost got stuck on a number of occasions. By the time I got there the teacher, Doris Goodjohn, was already there, so my cousin just dropped me off, turned around, and went home. No one else showed up at school that day.

It happened to be the first day of duck season, so there were a lot of people out hunting. Our weather had been mild for that time of year, so almost everyone was unprepared for what was to come. The forecast that morning was simply for colder temperatures and some light snow.

Weather forecasting was not very reliable then, and it didn't take long to become evident that the storm was going to be a doozy. It snowed heavily, and suddenly the wind started to blow. And it seemed it would never end. All in all it snowed about 30 inches. The temperature dropped to 25 or 30 below zero, and the wind turned to the northwest at 60 miles per hour and continued to blow for days. The teacher and I were trapped in the schoolhouse with only the lunches we had brought for the day and a few cans of fruit that the school had received as part of a program for "Food for Country Schools."

The storm raged the rest of the day Monday, and all day Tuesday the 12th. Two times on Tuesday my father and Jack got a team of horses out and attempted to take a sled to come rescue us. It was impossible. As soon as they got out of the shelter of the grove that surrounded the farm, they were totally blinded. Each time they had to turn around and go back. The first time they actually had to let the horses go on their own because my dad and Jack couldn't see where they were going, and knew it was better to rely on the horses.

The second time they tried to come get us they had to return because the horses suddenly stopped and wouldn't move, then on their own, had turned to go home. My father discovered they were against the barn wall. The snowstorm was so bad that the barn could not be seen! That was the last time they attempted to come and get us before the storm subsided.

Fortunately, the phone system continued to work, so we were able to stay in touch, but Wednesday and Thursday were just as horrible. By Thursday afternoon, the teacher and I were finally able to walk to Curtis Olson's farm, which was less than half a mile away. We stayed overnight with them, and on Friday, my father and Jack came to get us with the horses and a sled. It was an exciting experience, and we were certainly lucky to escape, considering many of those hunters, who were hunting as close as Kandiyohi Lake, lost their lives. Kandiyohi Lake is less than three miles from our farmhouse.

EXCELSIOR BOULEVARD, WEST OF MINNEAPOLIS AFTER
THE ARMISTICE DAY STORM, NOVEMBER 11, 1940.
COURTESY: MINNESOTA HISTORICAL SOCIETY.

As result of the storm, there was a 20-foot snow bank that was hard as a rock stretching from the school, across the road, and well past the school. For the rest of the winter cars drove over that enormous snow bank until it finally melted away in the spring.

In that infamous storm, known later as the Armistice Day Storm, 49 people in Minnesota were killed, and 150 area-wide.

At our place, we lost 25 white faced Hereford steers that each weighed in the neighborhood of 1100 pounds and were just ready for market. They were in a field west of the home place, and Dad couldn't get to them. When the storm finally stopped, all 25 of them were against the fence like they had gone to sleep. They had frozen to death. One steer was left standing, and he was up where we used to feed them. He was standing on a 20-foot snow bank, looking for something to eat. It was a devastating loss for us because we were just struggling to get ahead after the terrible economy of the Hoover administration. There was no insurance for our loss.

A few final notes about grade school: During grade school, I had a total of three teachers. When I started school at five years old, my first grade teacher was a lady by the name of Alice Erickson. I think she is still alive. She married the inventor of the chain saw, and they became very wealthy.

Many years later, while in California working for Federated, I had about 250 people at some movie studio for a big party. I invited Alice and her husband to come to the party, and they did. At the party I talked about my first grade teacher in front of this large crowd. That was the night we had The Captain & Tennille as the entertainment. Alice never got over that. For the rest of her life Alice talked about the fact they had been invited to this big party. I talked about her because I got an A in all of her classes and remembered her so very well. She was outgoing and very special.

My next teacher was Ethel Berg (who is also still alive by the way). She was very strict, and for most of the time that I had her as a teacher, which was the second, third, and fourth grades, she boarded at our house. Her living with us didn't make my aunt very happy because it meant that she lost her bedroom. Ethel still writes to me at Christmas from a nursing home in Willmar, and I think that she's 97 years old.

The last two years of grade school, Doris Goodjohn was our teacher. She was the teacher I was with when the storm kept us at the school for four days.

In grade school, I got great marks. As a matter of fact, in the seventh grade when we took our state boards, I had a perfect score in geography, which happened to be my favorite subject. The superintendent came to school and presented me with a certificate. I got the highest mark in the county. There were 140 questions, and I got them all right. After graduating from the eighth grade, we had to take four state boards. I did well on all of them.

~ 5 ~

High School

DONNY, BUD, AND I remained friends all through high school. We had a great time. We boarded the bus at 6:30 a.m. every morning to go to school, and had a 2-hour ride on an unheated bus. You can imagine that was certainly miserable. Bud dropped out of high school after his freshman year, so I didn't see as much of him as I did of Donny.

We went to high school at Bird Island, Minnesota where there were a lot of other students. I suddenly understood what an advantage those kids had in attending a larger school. Those advantages were not only scholastically speaking, but athletically as well. We'd played the same sports at District 5 that other children played in school, but it wasn't as organized as it was at the larger school.

High school was a different situation for me scholastically. When I got into Algebra and other subjects, it was more difficult. I had to miss a lot of school, especially my first years, because of spring planting and harvesting in the fall. I never kept track of exactly how many days of school I missed, but I know as a sophomore, it was probably more than 60 days, which of course made it hard to keep up.

The only class I ever flunked was World History when I was a sophomore. I had to take it over again as a senior with a group of sophomores. That was a humbling experience. As I took that World History class over, both Maggie Flann and Lois Portinga, who had gone to grade school with me, were in the class.

Miss Rotier was the principal of the school, and she taught World History. Miss Rotier was badly crippled by polio as a child, and she had a rage comparable to few. She appeared to hate the whole world.

She was one of the toughest teachers I ever had in my life. She was a rabid Republican, and I used to constantly get thrown out of class for debating the Democratic side of the argument. I was never thrown out of the class for any other reason. She would say, "Glen, you're dismissed again." Those were struggling times, but I made it through.

One morning in assembly before class, a friend of mine and I were tossing an orange from front to back. Just as he was throwing it back, Miss Rotier came into the room. I suddenly sat down, and the orange spattered off the blackboard! You can imagine what happened then.

Nonetheless, my high school years were good. The first two years Donny and I rode the school bus most of the time. However, I'd owned my own 1928 Model A from the time I was 12 years old. So finally, as a junior, I would drive the Model A to school whenever I could.

My father had a livestock hauling service. He often loaded the animals and brought them as far as Bird Island. He drove my car home, and I would leave school about 2:30 in the afternoon with the rig. I would do the nine and one-half hour round trip to South St. Paul and back with the livestock several times a week. Obviously, this was after my pre-dawn chores and a full day at school. It was wartime, and everybody had to pitch in and work hard.

Later in my junior year, I got rid of my Model A and got a 1936 Ford that belonged to Jack, the hired man who sold it to me when he went off to the service, expecting not to return. Fighting the Japanese in the South Pacific was so devastating that when he wrote me of his concerns, I bought the car and gave the money to his mother.

The 1936 Ford had an 85 horsepower motor and was blue with yellow wheels. It was wonderful! It was the fastest car in the neighborhood, bar none. It also didn't have very good brakes, so it was necessary to be exceptionally careful. I did, however, drive that car through high school and drove it through my first couple years of college. There will be more on that story later.

With the Great War raging, there was a lot of military focus in high school. During our junior year, we could take a test in "pre-flight." We only had one chance to take the test, but if we could pass all four sections, we could go directly into the service. That would mean we could go into the Air Corp at some higher rank. There were four courses, and I don't remember what each of the courses was, but I passed three of the four. I didn't pass the math section; otherwise, I probably would have ended up in the war.

There were only three senior boys that graduated in the class of 1945 because of the war. The rest had already gone off to the service. The three remaining seniors were all 4F, which meant unfit for service. In 1946, just as the war ended, there were 24 in my graduating class. I could actually go to great length in describing every one of those in my graduating class because I knew them personally. However, for this book that would be too lengthy.

～ 6 ～

Stepping up to the Plate

MY HIGH SCHOOL baseball team didn't have a coach. During the war, there was simply no one available. So I stepped up and coached the team during my sophomore and junior years.

My class had 24 students, and they were our entire baseball team. We actually won the district title in baseball in 1946, beating Olivia by one run. I played second base in that game, but most of my years

A YOUNG GLEN, ABOUT THE TIME HE COACHED
HIS OWN HIGH SCHOOL BASEBALL TEAM.

in high school I was a catcher. During that game I drove in, or had some part of, all three runs that we scored.

When the other team threatened to win the game in the 9th inning, and their player got on first base, I walked in to talk to the pitcher. The first baseman also came to the mound. I said, "Now I'm going to tell the umpire to watch and you take the ball." I gave him the ball and instructed him, "When this guy leads off, put the ball on him."

It happened just like anticipated, and we had the first out. Then the next guy got a hit, and the next guy got a hit. We ended up winning 3–2. I had a lot of exciting baseball games, and I had a lot of fun playing ball.

One boy from our school, Gene Olson (we used to call him Genie boy), signed with the New York Yankees for $7,500 the day he finished the last baseball game in high school. It wasn't uncommon for Genie boy to have 18–20 strikeouts a game.

I will never forget when we had a big league scout there to watch Gene pitch. The big league scout was sitting with my father that day. When I came up to hit, my father said, "He's a pretty good hitter, but he doesn't hit a long ball." I then promptly hit the ball clear over the racetrack, which was in the outer limits of the outfield. That was an easy home run. That actually was one of only a couple home runs of my whole career.

I played baseball all four years of high school, and we had a very good team the entire time. I had an unbelievable batting average of 585 for those four years.

Another one of our players went to play for the Dodgers. I actually signed with the St. Louis Cardinals and went to try out both in 1946 and 1947. I didn't make the cut, however, as I couldn't hit the curve ball. It's probably lucky that I didn't make it, or I'd probably be coaching third base for Newport in some scrub league somewhere in the country.

We also played softball at least two days in between the baseball games. We played some sort of ball almost every day. We had an incredibly good softball team. The first team we had my cousin Keno was a pitcher. We would usually play on Sunday afternoon either at

Lake Lillian or up at Diamond Lake. People would actually gather at the lake and watch us play ball.

It got to be a lot more structured, so we started playing organized ball in Willmar. Myron Flann, a neighboring farm kid, was a snap ball pitcher who could throw the ball in excess of 90 miles an hour. We won a lot of state championships along the way.

Those were glorious years, and there was always a feud between what took precedence—baseball or softball. Obviously, baseball was somewhat more organized, so we had to play softball around our baseball games most of the time. I played both and had a very good time.

One whole season I managed the softball team because we didn't have anyone else. I didn't play during that time, but I actually managed to call the shots on who to pitch, which player to walk, and what our strategy should be. It was very educational, and we had a really great year. We actually went on to win the state tournament.

Later I played on our town baseball team. We were a town of only 300, but we put 4,000 people in the ballpark on any given Sunday. At our peak we played a 48 game schedule (Sunday, Tuesday, and Thursday nights) if you can believe that. Along with the town team, I played organized ball for 10 years of my life.

In addition to baseball and softball, in high school I played three years of basketball. It would have been four years, but I broke my arm playing basketball as a freshman and had to scrap that year. I did, however, play three years as a starter on the B team. I was also the sixth player most of the time on the A team and did start on occasion.

I was not a basketball star, but I played the game at a time when 40 points would have been a lot of points to score in a basketball game. The closest we ever got to compete in a state tournament was when we were seniors, and we played Buffalo Lake in a District 12 game. We lost that game 42–40 in overtime. I tied the score with a second to play with a shot from mid court. Losing was heartbreaking, to say the least.

We always went to see the state basketball tournament in Minneapolis. It was a three-day event and usually wound up with a winner from some small state school like ours.

Unfortunately, we were not a great basketball team, but we all had fun playing the game. In fact, to stay in shape, we used to get off the bus as it was going up and down the country roads and run two miles to meet it as it came by on the other side. We did that when the weather was nice just to stay in shape.

7

Finding My Place

MY FATHER WOULD just as soon have had me stay on the farm and work after my graduation in '46. They really needed my help. Jack, the hired man, was back from the war, but even then it was just the three of us to run the entire farm.

However, I wanted an education.

The County Chairman of the Democratic Party was someone who had a very notable effect on my life. His name is George Hulstrand, and at the time he was Chairman of the Board at Gustavus Adolphus College in St. Peter. I had been to a number of political meetings with George, and he suggested that I go to Gustavus. That's how I wound up applying there in 1946.

Additionally, I felt Gustavus was a good choice of schools for me because it is a Lutheran school, and I am a Lutheran. St. Peter was an hour and 45 minutes from Lake Lillian. It was all gravel roads, and I drove the roads with my 1936 Ford.

There were about 300 returning service men and perhaps 25 kids just out of high school like me who enrolled at Gustavus that year. It was a tough first year because there were so many servicemen attending classes. A group of us lived at the campus in a cold ranch house with about 40 students. At night the water would freeze in glasses that had been left out on the table. We slept in bunk beds and had lockers. It was not the ideal way to begin college.

I had thought it was difficult going from a one-room country school into a big high school like Bird Island High School, but it was doubly difficult to go off to college. The servicemen were all in their mid-20s. They were there on the GI Bill. They were hard drinkers and hard fighters. Mostly they were a really tough bunch.

Between classes, I managed to make enough money playing poker to pay my tuition, but after a year at Gustavus, I still ran out of money. Plus, I went home a lot of weekends to work on the farm. Obviously that curtailed my studies. Feeling the need for a change, I enrolled at the Minnesota School of Business in Minneapolis for the following year.

In 1947, at the end of my first year at Gustavus and prior to starting school at the Minnesota School of Business, I joined the Navy and was in the Naval Reserve. Of course, it was after the conflict, so I didn't go to war, but once a month on a weekend, we were required to go down to the armory in Minneapolis.

I spent eight years in the Naval Reserve. We would go to the armory, and we always marched. Twice we were scheduled to go on a two-week training mission on a destroyer in Alaska. In both instances those training missions were canceled, and I never did get to go on one.

There were several different divisions that were called up, but the 9th Reserve District that I was in somehow never got called, and that was fine with me. I didn't want to go into active service.

The Minnesota School of Business ended up being a good choice of schools for me. I liked the school, and I got good marks. I took classes in sales, advertising, and accounting.

I was able to pass Typing 5, which meant that I could type 80 words a minute with less than five mistakes per hour. That was on an old-fashioned mechanical typewriter. Oddly enough, now I have to hunt and peck on my computer keyboard.

Life at the Minnesota School of Business was enjoyable. I had lunch every day at Herman's Bar because I could get a pork/beef/chicken "commercial," which was two scoops of mashed potatoes and gravy, and one of those three meats for 35-cents. I roomed with Paul Sundin, a student at the University of Minnesota. He was from Lake Lillian also.

On Saturday nights, we went to Hugo's Bar down on Hennepin Avenue where we would go for a steak and all we could eat for $1.25.

Paul and I roomed together for two years. At the start of 1948, we moved to another place out near the university called Dinky Town. I would take the streetcar as I had farther to go to school, but Paul could walk. Our place was just a few blocks from the campus of the University of Minnesota. Of course we went to all the University of Minnesota football games as well as other events. One such event changed the course of my life . . . in a wonderful way.

8

A Tisket, a Tasket, a Green and Yellow Basket

A BASKET SOCIAL is a fundraiser where the gals make baskets, and the guys buy them. Baskets are auctioned off to raise money. It was at a basket social that I first laid eyes on my future bride.

I'd happened over to the social with a friend, and a young lady by the name of LaVonne was there with a friend of hers. Right then and there I decided I was going to try to make her my girl. Somehow my buddy and I took LaVonne and her friend home that night. We struck up a friendship and dated the rest of the year.

All through high school, I had girlfriends along the way. None of them really meant anything to me. When I met LaVonne in college, I was smitten, and I felt as if I could conquer the world.

Our dates consisted of mostly going to movies and to dinner. We listened to records, usually at my house on the farm, and we usually single dated. Having a car allowed LaVonne and me more freedom. I was still driving the blue 1936 Ford with yellow wheels, which was quite sporty. We actually ended up getting married with that car.

In the fall of 1948, my priority was school as I was still attending in Minneapolis. Most weekends I was able to go home. When I got home, LaVonne and I would go out. That was sort of a difficult time because we had already decided to get married in January, and I was still going to school in Minneapolis in December of '48. It was a back and forth sort of courtship.

LaVonne Corley and I were married at Lake Lillian, in her church, Grace Lutheran Church, which was referred to as the Norwegian

Lutheran Church. The Swedish Lutheran Church, where I went to church, was at the other end of town. I bought LaVonne a ring at the time we were married with money I had saved up from mink hunting, something I'd enjoyed from the time I was a kid. We were both as poor as church mice. We didn't have the proverbial pot or the window to throw it out of.

Our wedding was wonderful, but many people predicted that it wouldn't last. That's interesting since we are still married to this day, more than six decades later. And, very happily, I might add.

Prior to the wedding, LaVonne lived with her parents, Christopher and Elphie, and her sister, Byrma. They had a house in the small town of Lake Lillian. During the war, LaVonne's father had been in the Philippines building runways. He was also gone for a long time building the Alcan Highway in Alaska. It was not long after we were married that her parents divorced. That was a difficult time for my wife.

THE CORLEY FAMILY: CHRISTOPHER AND ELPHIE WITH
DAUGHTERS LAVONNE (LEFT) AND BYRMA.

LAVONNE'S
FATHER,
CHRISTOPHER,
WITH HIS
SECOND WIFE
GLADYS.

LAVONNE'S
GRANDMOTHER,
JESSIE RUFFNER
CORLEY ENSOR.

The first year we were married we lived in the home of LaVonne's parents. Later we moved to the summer kitchen on my father's farm, which was three and one-half miles from Lake Lillian. In the old days in the summertime all the cooking was done in the summer kitchen, so the rest of the house wasn't heated. My parents' house was a big house, built in the 1880s. The summer kitchen had three very small rooms.

There was no doubt that the farm could not support the families of my father, my cousin whom my parents raised, and me. I knew that I had to do something else for a living. This was early in 1949 and right in the middle of the Eisenhower recession. The recession started shortly after he was elected.

9

Necessity is the Mother
of . . . Newspapers

AS A 19-YEAR-OLD farm boy at the Minnesota School of Business, I had taken a course in sales and advertising. As part of my school assignment I had to lay out ads for the Dayton Company in Minneapolis. The Dayton Company was a well-established company. Some of the ads that I laid out actually made the big time and were published in the Minneapolis paper.

My instructor was a very dynamic guy, often talking about the possibilities of starting a free circulation paper. The teacher, whose name I can't recall, talked about what a great thing it was to sell advertising and how you could make money by doing so. He stressed it was a good business to be in; a good thought for a kid looking for a good living off the farm.

I had taken many business related classes, so I decided to start a free paper called the *West Central Shopping News*. This paper was going to be published sort of in competition with the *Willmar Daily Tribune* out of Willmar, which was the biggest town nearby. Willmar was about 18 miles from Lake Lillian.

The *West Central Shopping News* did not last long because I had virtually no start-up capital, but I did manage to put out a few issues of the free paper. When we didn't have the funds to publish the paper, the next best thing was to start a traditional newspaper in our hometown.

Pop Jones ran the *New London Times* and the *Murdock Free Press*. We bought the *Murdock Free Press* from him in order to secure his equipment. We actually published the *Murdock Free Press* for a few months until we moved the equipment to Lake Lillian. Not long after, we dropped the *Murdock Free Press* because of its lack of advertisers.

We began our hometown newspaper, the *Lake Lillian Crier*. It was a weekly paper, and was in the mail on Thursday. At our peak, in a town of 300 people, we had a circulation of about 600. Our advertising, which started out at 25-cents a column-inch, eventually went to 40-cents a column-inch.

LAKE LILLIAN, MINNESOTA. ON THE RIGHT, DIRECTLY UNDER THE FLAG IS THE *LAKE LILLIAN CRIER*, WHICH IS IN THE U.S. POST OFFICE BUILDING. GLEN STARTED HIS NEWSPAPER CAREER THERE IN 1949.

The first night we put a paper out in Lake Lillian both Pop Jones and his son-in-law were there to help. We worked all night. The sun was coming up in the morning when we got the first paper out, but we did it. Publication of the *Lake Lillian Crier* had begun!

When starting a newspaper in a town that didn't have a newspaper, it meant that you had to convince everybody that advertising would pay off. Sometimes that was not easy. We did all kinds of things to make extra money. The first year from May through December we grossed $1,800, and there certainly was no profit. We had a job shop, but even that didn't do a whole lot of printing jobs either.

I borrowed $800 from the First State Bank of Lake Lillian just on the premise I was going to start a newspaper in town. I had no collateral. It took a long time to pay that loan off, but we did.

The first year in the newspaper business was really very difficult.

GLEN JOHNSON AT
WORK AT THE *LAKE
LILLIAN CRIER*.

Right off the bat, we were learning the trade and learning on the job. LaVonne and I did a lot of work together. She was my linotype operator, but in the very beginning we didn't even have a linotype, and had to get our type set in Willmar, the neighboring town. When we first started, we had the big old press we'd purchased from *Murdock*. The trick was that I bought paper weekly that was preprinted on one side with national stories. All I had to do was print the four pages on the other side of the paper. We'd set those up, print them, and then we would have to cut and fold them. We did that for probably the first year or so until we got a new press.

The old hand feed Babcock press that had a huge cylinder was replaced by an automatic Kelly B press. Actually at Christmas, we printed color. We printed red, green, and black. That was a real tough job, but we did it.

It was much better once we got the new press. It was really the local news that everybody wanted to read because the paper related everything that had happened all week long. It told who had been at whose house, who in town went where, what someone wore, or some other very localized news.

We also had the job shop and after a time, got some very lucrative jobs to print. There was one job where we printed 20,000 bag tags for an alfalfa mill. We had the contract, and that one job sort of carried us. In the beginning everything was fed by hand. Eventually we got automatic presses to do the job printing as well.

We bought an old 12 × 18 Klugge press that made job printing much easier, more productive, and it was automatically fed. That helped us to make more money. We solicited work in surrounding towns, as well as Lake Lillian. The quality of our work spoke for itself.

Along the way I started a County Newspaper Association. That was where we did tie-in advertising. A person could advertise in four weekly newspapers; our county had five. I ran the association for a long time, and it was productive. We had a good time when all the publishers would get together.

When you are 19, and you start a newspaper, obviously people write stories about you. One of the things we belonged to was the Minnesota Editorial Association. They had an annual meeting where all the editors got together for a three-day conference.

One year I was asked to speak there. Never in my life had I gotten up in front of a group. I made a presentation called, "The First Five years are the Hardest." I was a nervous wreck and just ad-libbed the whole presentation.

First of all, I told the audience how we had begun, and I talked about how we had done certain things. I talked about handling the bundles of papers that weighed 240 pounds. Of course, I talked about how my wife, LaVonne, was the typesetter and how she could set type with the best of them. I included how we had to struggle with printing the newspaper, as well as our struggles in the job shop.

There were 400 editors at the meeting. I probably talked for about 25 minutes. The audience gave me a standing ovation that just went on and on for the longest time. Every one of the editors could relate to our experience. Two of the editors in the next county (the *Rendale County Star Herald* and the *Sacred Heart News*) knew me. They both wrote editorials about the presentation that I made. The editorials really hit the nail on the head of what a struggle it was.

It was a very unique time, and a lot of the newspapers around the state ran articles about me as a young editor. That helped our circulation. People who had been to Lake Lillian or had lived there got interested and subscribed to the paper. At least half of our subscriptions were from out of town people. That didn't do much for the advertisers, but it enabled us to get more for an inch of advertising. We used to run big classified sections.

My job was to sell all the advertising and set all the ads. One of our best advertisers was the biggest grocery store in town. They usually ran a full page, which was a 5-column, by 16-column-inch tabloid. The grocery ad was all set by hand. I had to put all the type on a stick and lock it up. That would be the last ad we put together before printing the paper.

Along the way the *Lake Lillian Crier* grew, and we were often quoted in the Minneapolis paper. At that time there were 400 newspapers in the state of Minnesota. The bulk of them were either Conservative or Independent. We were one of perhaps six newspapers in the whole state considered "Liberal." We were active in writing editorials on any number of topics. That's how we picked up a lot of subscribers. They liked what we had to say. They didn't read that type of editorial in their local newspapers. We were supporting things like the Rural Electric Power. Our biggest advertiser was Northern States Power. I was constantly writing editorials because they were so dictatorial. Our business grew bigger and bigger in time.

A lot of satisfaction was derived from writing editorials about Northern States Power because of how things were when I was growing up. We lived on a farm where we were one half mile from the highway, but in all the years that we were there, even though we offered to pay, the power company wouldn't run a line to our place. It wasn't until 1939 when the REA came in and started to grow that we got power on the farm.

When I wrote editorials, my associates in the county kept saying, "You know they are going to quit advertising with you because you are always on the other side of the fence." The long and the short of it was they advertised twice as much with me and with bigger ads than they did with the other papers in the county who were favorable to them. Why that was, I will never know. I guess they were just showing me they were going to advertise no matter what I said. They did, however, threaten to pull their ads from time-to-time.

Writing the editorials and stories was my responsibility, but I had a couple of women who wrote the social columns, Mrs. Reynold Olson and Mrs. Arleigh Bjur. Those two women provided me at least four columns of news of who was where, and why, and what they did. That was a big part of why the people bought the paper. Sally Olson (Mrs. Reynold) became our linotype operator and in addition, collected local news. Mrs. Arleigh Bjur was another "Local News" writer.

At that time we had five churches in town, so there was always church news. There was PTA news as well. Plus, Lake Lillian's AA baseball team always had at least three ballgames to cover. I did all the sports writing and would include all the box scores in the paper.

Our paper was a good local paper. It covered the news, and we never failed to have the editorial column. I guess that our biggest win was when we started to champion consolidated school districts.

The whole school system area was comprised of small country schools, each with their own board. There were probably 10 or 12 little school districts, each with 6–12 students, plus the teachers. It was obvious to me, because I had been to Bird Island High School and I had been to Gustavus, how important it was to upgrade education. It was easy to see the small rural schools were not that successful. Our newspaper took a survey of the entire community, and the community was 8–1 against a centralized school system.

For a year and a half we wrote an editorial every week. As the debate heated up, I personally spoke at every school district in the area. On at least two occasions, I received letters threatening my life. When the official vote came on redistricting for a centralized school system, it passed by 4–1. That was the power of the press. We had changed the minds of many people.

Getting the centralized school system created more jobs. We had eight new teachers and school bus drivers. It was good for the economy. The advertisers in town reacted to the economic upturn, and our advertising increased.

After 12 years with the *Lake Lillian Crier* I had my eyes on a larger paper. I sold the *Crier* to the publisher of the *Cosmas News,* which had started up long after we started the newspaper in Lake Lillian.

I sold the paper and all the equipment for $9000. That was not a lot of equity for 12 years of work.

The thought of buying a bigger newspaper was a frightening one. After I sold my paper and started to make the offer for the *Elbow Lake News,* I discovered that it was tied up in an estate, following the death of the publisher, and had to stay in the family. I had no idea of that stipulation when I was trying to buy the paper. I had already sold the *Crier,* and as a result, I was at loose ends. As it turned out, it was for the best.

~ 10 ~
Making Ends Meet

DURING THOSE 12 years we published the paper we were blessed with three children, Vicki, David, and Lori. In time, the *Lake Lillian Crier* finally carried itself financially, and we were able to live modestly. We managed to buy a clarinet, on time, for my daughter Vicki. The payments to Sears Roebuck were nine dollars a month. I would go out and collect for the advertising just before the bill was due.

Those were very difficult days, but we managed. To supplement our income while running the newspaper, I worked several other jobs. I literally did all kinds of extra things to make ends meet.

I'll never forget one time after the corn was picked in the fall of 1950. Before the plowing began, LaVonne and I (still dreadfully poor) went out and picked up corn throughout the fields that had been left from the picker. We sold the corn for $137, which was a tremendous boost for us. That particular memory will never be forgotten.

During the summers of 1950 and 1951, I literally had to give up baseball because I took a job at the alfalfa plant for three months in the summer. The alfalfa plant was a cooperative that dried the alfalfa and made carotene, a food supplement for animals.

My first job there was working 12 hours a night running a field cutter that chopped the alfalfa. My wages were 75-cents an hour, which was a good deal more than the workers in the plant who only earned 45-cents an hour.

By the summer of 1952, I was made foreman of the alfalfa plant, which meant I made $1 an hour. For those three months I worked 12 hours a night and 7 days a week. My workday began at 6:00 at night and ended at 6:00 the next morning.

When I was running the field cutter, I could sometimes finish by 3:00 in the morning because with the dew, things got so wet that we couldn't dry the alfalfa. When that happened, we would shut the cutting operation down, but the plant kept operating with the alfalfa that had already been cut.

When I became the night foreman, I had 50 people working for me. We set all kinds of records on the night shift that would beat the day shift by at least 25 percent on any given day. There was a strong incentive to do better than the day shift, and we most always did. Unfortunately (for them), the day crew was often faced with wet hay due to the morning dew. When this occurred, they could not begin work until later in the morning.

Once we finished the process, the alfalfa had become a very fine powder, ready to be used as a food supplement. The powder was put into 100-pound bags, and we had an automated machine that would sew the bags closed.

As night foreman I had a number of responsibilities. First, I had to keep the steam engine running. Keep in mind that I did not have an engineer's license, which is required to run a steam engine of that size. We had two huge boilers, and we needed to watch them very closely.

Many nights the pump failed, so I would quickly prime the pump to get it running again and hope that the water would start to rise in the glass to keep from blowing the place up. When the water didn't rise, I would yell for everybody to get out because I thought the boiler was going to blow. That was one of the pitfalls we had to be aware of all the time.

The second thing to watch was a 500-horsepower diesel engine, which drove the machinery that chopped the alfalfa. The steam heat dried it, and the 500-horsepower motor chopped it up. I needed to watch closely, or we could have a real disaster. The machine would plug up, and we would have to stop everything and start to pull it out spear by spear.

I became very proficient at pulling the spout that put the hay into the machine. I could stop the hay from flowing in, and the engine would keep on running and chop it up. However, if the hay was too tough, I would have to stop the conveyor, so the hay could dry more thoroughly.

On nights when things ran smoothly, I could sit with my back against the 500-horsepower diesel engine and sleep. I would sit on the cement floor with my back against the engine, so that if it started to run down I could hear it and quickly stop the flow of hay. Getting plugged up would slow things down dramatically, and then we wouldn't be able to produce what we were expected to produce in a single night. I slept with a rope in my hand that would stop the flow of hay.

When I wasn't attending the 500-horsepower diesel engine that drove the chopper, I was stacking 100-pound bags of dehydrated alfalfa meal. We would make stairways out of the 100 pound sacks, pick them up, and carry them to the top. We piled them as much as 18 feet high. We always hoped that the people who were to haul the sacks away in big semi trucks would come to get them soon, so the pile wouldn't be as high.

I continued to play baseball when I could, but really it was only when the plant was shut down for some reason that I was able to make a game. The reality was that with all of this going on I only got to go to bed one or two nights a week during the three summer months. I welcomed a day of rain or a shut down for some reason, because that would be the only time I would get a chance to go home and get to bed. Between times at the alfalfa plant I was getting out the newspaper, selling ads, writing copy, soliciting, collecting, and all the things that go with running a small town newspaper.

When 6:00 in the morning came, I had to go and work on my newspaper. When I was getting the type set in New London and in Willmar, it entailed getting copy to them in the morning and then going back and getting the galleys of type at night. We were constantly driving to Willmar and New London.

In the summer of 1955, major repair work began on Highway 7, which ran just past Lake Lillian. This major roadwork started at Highway 71 and extended eastward to where Highway 22 joins Highway 7.

I got a job driving a 6x6 truck. The truck had a double set of dual tires and hauled loads of up to 12 tons. The trucks were dump trucks, and the job paid $2.75 an hour. I thought I had died and gone to heaven. That was more money than I could imagine for an hour of work. I was used to getting 75-cents to $1 an hour. The $2.75 an hour was big-time bucks, for the three months it lasted.

Following the school redistricting, children were bused into Lake Lillian. During that time I was working part-time in the post office and was the 'extra' worker at Christmas time and other heavy mail times. I was fortunate to get a job driving the school bus every morning and night for $90 a month. I did that for six years.

For a time, in the evenings I was part of the local crew that helped build an elevator in town. There were half-a-dozen of us who were good friends, including Laverne Gilhoi, who I referred to as Gilly. We would go down to my newspaper print shop to have our lunch. I remember times when it was cold and raw outside, and we would sit in the print shop and enjoy our half hour break.

———

My good friend, Gilly was an ironworker, and he was very strong. We went through four years of high school together before he went to work on the railroad, and I went on to college. He became our milkman when we were in Lake Lillian.

Gilly and I were fast friends. The sad part of the story is that years later, yet still early in the game of life when he was just 39 years old, he realized he needed a new heart. He was one of the first people to have a heart transplant in California. Dr. Michael DeBakey was the surgeon who replaced his heart.

I visited with his wife Marlene while she was there with him. They had three young girls at the time, and it was a very difficult event for all of them. When he finally got a donor heart and had the surgery, everything went well, and he was doing okay.

As it happened, LaVonne and I were going on one of our first vacations with friends Chris and Zella Soich, on a weeklong cruise to the Caribbean. The day we left, I had been at a board meeting in Cat Key with Federated and got to the ship just in time to set sail. The day we returned to port, I received word that Gilly's heart had been rejected, and he had died during the week we were away. We left and went back to Minnesota where I was a pallbearer at the funeral. It was indeed a very sad event.

His wife, Marlene, has remarried, and we remain friends to this day. She and her husband, Charlie Brown, live in Willmar, Minnesota. We stay in touch with them now and then and consider them good friends.

Part 2

Love of Politics

If

IF you can keep your head when all about you
　　Are losing theirs and blaming it on you;
IF you can trust yourself when all men doubt you,
　　But make allowance for their doubting too;
IF you can wait and not be tired by waiting,
　　Or being lied about, don't deal in lies,
Or being hated, don't give way to hating,
　　And yet don't look too good, nor talk too wise;

IF you can dream — and not make dreams your master;
　　If you can think — and not make thoughts your aim,
IF you can meet with Triumph and Disaster
　　And treat those two imposters just the same;
IF you can bear to hear the truth you've spoken
　　Twisted by knaves to make a trap for fools,
Or watch the things you gave your life to, broken,
　　And stoop and build 'em up with worn-out tools;

IF you can make one heap of all your winnings
　　And risk it on one turn of pitch-and-toss,
And lose, and start again at your beginnings
　　And never breathe a word about your loss;
IF you can force your heart and nerve and sinew
　　To serve your turn long after they are gone,
And so hold on when there is nothing in you
　　Except the Will which says to them: 'Hold on!'

IF you can talk with crowds and keep your virtue,
　　Or walk with Kings — nor lose the common touch,
IF neither foes nor loving friends can hurt you,
　　If all men count with you, but none too much;
IF you can fill the unforgiving minute
　　With sixty seconds worth of distance run,
Yours is the Earth and everything that's in it,
　　And — which is more — you'll be a Man, my son!

Rudyard Kipling, 1865 - 1936

~ 11 ~

Starting off on the Left Foot

ONE MIGHT SAY that I was born a Democrat; I certainly grew up in a politically liberal home. My grandfather and my father were both Democrats that had lived through the Hoover administration. Of course, they blamed Hoover for devastating the farm economy.

My father was chairman of the local township committee. He was also on the county committee, so before I was even old enough to vote, I would go to the polls, put up campaign posters or anything else needed. Hanging campaign signs at 10 years old certainly piqued my political interest early. In fact, no matter my age, I seemed to always be supporting someone, whether it was a local person running for the state legislature, or it was someone running nationally for The Senate or The House. I was active very early in the game.

I even made my own run against a 16-year incumbent mayor when I was editor of the *Lake Lillian Crier*. I turned 21 just five days before the election. My friends didn't think that I stood a chance, so they didn't vote. It turns out I lost by only seven votes! The incumbent had been the mayor since the inception of the town. It was the only run for office I ever made, and I lost.

That year, I became the precinct chairman in Lake Lillian Township where we lived. As precinct chairman I was elected to go to the county conventions, and I attended them faithfully.

While I was involved with the newspaper, I got even more active in politics. We wrote editorials on everything from dogs to foreign policy. There were 400 newspapers in the state of Minnesota at that time, and only 6 of them purported to be liberal. All the rest of the papers were independent or conservative. In fact, when the

Minneapolis Star used to run the "guest editor" columns, they almost always quoted our newspaper because there were so few on "the other side of the fence." We took very liberal positions on everything from public power to education back then.

Becoming more politically active, I attended all the precinct caucuses and the district and county meetings. Early on, I was elected as a delegate from Kandiyohi County to the district. Eventually I served as district secretary to Minnesota's 7th congressional district. I was treasurer for a number of years, and we completely reorganized the old 7th district.

Because I had been involved in politics and had a bit of notoriety, when Clint Haroldson decided on a congressional run, he asked me to take charge of his campaign in 1956. I had written editorials about politics and what I supported. I had clearly stated what I was for and what I was against. Clint agreed with everything that I said. I stayed busy running his campaign, while back at the *Crier*, all of the type was getting set for the weekly issues by Sally.

The campaign for Haroldson included 19 counties. Clint Haroldson was a farmer from Renville, and almost every day I would arrive at his house at 9:00 in the morning. We would set about scheduling the entire day. I made arrangements for all of the speeches and travel, wrote all of the copy for the campaign headquarters newspaper ads, wrote all the copy for the radio ads, got Clint on the radio, traveled throughout the district, set up coffee meetings, set up dinner meetings, and most of all, had to raise money to pay for the campaign.

One of the highlights, of course, was when we brought Harry Truman in from Independence, Missouri, to campaign for Haroldson. It was an outstanding campaign trip.

I decided to call the state office to see if they thought it was a good idea to bring Harry Truman in. After his presidency, Truman had retired to Independence, Missouri after he left office in 1953. The State Central Committee thought it was a bad idea, and I shouldn't do it. I went ahead and called for Harry.

Bess (Mrs. Truman) answered the phone, and I explained that I would like very much to have him come to Minnesota for five days. I told her that I would make arrangements for him to take the train from Independence, Missouri to Sioux Falls, South Dakota. He could open with a speech from the rear of the passenger car in Sioux Falls and then go on to meetings in Pipestone, Luverne, and Marshall. Bess agreed that was something that would work as long as I promised I would have Harry in bed by 10:00 p.m. every night.

President Truman arrived in Sioux Falls, South Dakota to an enormous crowd of well over 100,000 people. It was an absolutely impressive turnout. Without a script, the President made a speech to a cheering throng, and then went on from Sioux Falls to Pipestone and then Luverne. All the schools had let out to see President Truman and to wave to him as he went by. Our little entourage was greeted everywhere. Many farmers came out, stood along the road, and saluted the President as we drove by. It was the most unforgettable event I have ever been involved in.

We made the campaign stops in Pipestone and Luverne and then went on to Marshall where President Truman was to make his most important speech. The hall only held 3500 people, and it was filled by early afternoon. He threw away the script that had been written for him by the Democratic Central Committee in Washington, DC and spoke "from the hip." It was a wonderful speech to a cheering audience. The overflow audience outside the hall was listening through speakers, and there was probably double the crowd outside the hall than inside. They all cheered loudly.

It was a wonderful event, and one I never regretted. I did get to spend an evening with the President, and he told me all about growing up, being a Haberdasher, and how he got involved in politics. It was not much different than the way I, too, had been introduced to the political scene.

The next day we were scheduled to go to Ivanhoe and several more stops along the way. In the meantime, when the State Central Committee saw what had happened in Sioux Falls, they somehow overruled me and took Harry to be with them campaigning throughout the state.

Haroldson's campaign was a great experience, and we did a good job, although it was almost a futile endeavor. The incumbent candidate he was running against, Congressman H. Carl Andersen, was running for his 11th term. Andersen would be going back to Congress for his 21st and 22nd year.

I don't remember the exact details, but I certainly know the outcome of the election. We carried Kandiyohi County, Swift County, and Traverse County, plus some of the more liberal areas, but we lost badly in the very conservative areas like Redwood, Renville, Pipestone, and Rock counties. Those were all Republican counties, and H. Carl Andersen won quite easily. It still was an excellent experience, and certainly broadened my qualifications.

A.I. Johnson, Speaker of the Minnesota House of Representatives, decided to run for Congress in 1958. He asked me to run his campaign. A.I. knew I had been active, and that I knew the district well. This was another opportunity resulting from the editorials in my newspaper. I'd been writing all the things they agreed with.

As we went into the 1958 election, I was Johnson's campaign manager. Because of all the time I was spending on the campaign, LaVonne, once again would have to help set the type and set the ads. I took Wednesdays off to help get the paper out.

The fact that A.I. Johnson was from Swift County, and Speaker of the House of Representatives in St. Paul, made him a very desirable candidate. He was terrific with one-on-ones. However, if you put him on a television spot or put him in front of a crowd, he was not very effective. It was a most difficult campaign, and I had the hardest time trying to keep him "moving within the district." He really didn't want to go out and shake hands with people and have face-to-face interaction. His ads did not sound crisp, and while we could make the newspaper ads look good, it was not an easy sell.

A.I. Johnson was easily defeated, although it was closer than the previous election, and H. Carl Andersen was elected to his 23rd and 24th years in Congress.

～ 12 ～

7th Heaven

HUBERT HUMPHREY WAS one of my father's most admired politicians. My father met Hubert for the first time in the mid 40s, even before he was the Mayor of Minneapolis. Although he might only see my dad once a year, he'd know him instantly. He'd say, "Hi Oscar. How are you?" It was wonderful. Dad was a life-long Democrat and knew all the Democratic candidates, but my father thought Humphrey was one of the great men of the world, and I share that opinion.

In 1960, I ran Hubert Humphrey's campaign for the Senate in the 7th congressional district of Minnesota. As a result of my political involvement, I became a friend of Hubert Humphrey. Beyond my dad's opinion, knowing him personally really had a very major effect on my political thinking. He truly was a mentor of mine.

Hubert Humphrey asked me to run for the post of Minnesota State Chairman because I had been very active in his senate campaign, and he knew my capabilities. Of course, I had run two congressional campaigns in 1956 and 1958 for Democratic candidates, but I believe it was my work at the convention that got Hubert's attention more than anything.

We went into the State Convention thinking we had it all wrapped up. However, the Freeman group had a candidate by the name of George Farr. The Freeman wing was considered the more liberal wing of the party, if anyone could be more liberal than Hubert Humphrey.

We had the votes to win, however, the delegation for the northern Minnesota district left prior to the vote. They left their proxy for us to cast the vote, but the Farr forces caught wind of this. They beat us when the Rules Committee invoked a seldom-used rule denying us the use of the proxies. As a result, neither of the candidates had the votes necessary to win.

There was a first ballot, and it was almost even. There was a second ballot, and we gained a few votes. There was a third ballot, but by that time more people had gone home, and it was obvious that it was going to end in a stalemate. I didn't want the party to have the expense of another convention, so after the third ballot, I convinced Hubert that I should withdraw, and we should throw our support to George Farr.

To be honest, I was actually greatly relieved. Holding the State Chairman position would have taken 100 percent of my time. I would have had to sell my newspaper and make a lot of other changes, which I was prepared to do if it was all going to happen. It did not.

There were many disappointed people, and it turned out to be a very contentious convention. Looking back at my loss as state chairman, I now realize how fortunate it was for me. If things hadn't happened the way they did, I would never have ended up at Federated.

Following the convention, I continued to really work hard with the Humphrey campaign. With an incumbent senator I got a lot more notice than when I was campaigning for a congressman.

Humphrey and I spent hours and hours on the road in my 1960 Ford Falcon making breakfast stops, street stops, dinner meetings, and other events all over the 7th district of Minnesota. It was a joy to campaign with him.

He remembered names of people. We could be driving down the road, and he would seem to be asleep, then he would say to me, "Now, whom do we have to recognize in the next town?" I would pull out my crib sheet and tell him the county chairman is so-and-so, the county chairwoman is so-and-so, and this person and that person are also very important, and they will all be there. Amazingly, he would get to the next stop, stand up, and remember every single name. He never wrote a name down, but he'd get up and make his speech, and he'd recognize every one of them. He had an incredible memory.

He was always great to campaign with, and people would stick checks in his pocket. As soon as we would get in the car, Hubert would take the checks out of his pocket and give them to me. Often he would even say to them, "Why don't you give the check to Glen? He's going to grab it anyway."

I was elected as a delegate to the 1960 Democratic National Convention in Los Angeles. I won that position by a half vote on the 7th ballot. My competition for that post, O.B. Auguston, was the prior delegate and was from the old 7th congressional district. Auguston was the liberal editor of the *Willmar Daily Tribune*. He was a very powerful voice, and a good man. When I defeated him, it was a real victory.

LaVonne and I flew to Los Angeles on an old four-motored prop plane along with the rest of the delegation. I served on the Endorsements Committee. We arrived, and no one went to bed. There were many late nights, and long days, the entire time we were there.

I used to show a whole reel of pictures that I'd taken at the convention and at a memorable Perle Mesta reception. The photos included Mrs. Roosevelt, Jack Kennedy and his brother Robert, Adlai Stevenson, Lyndon Johnson, and other prominent Democrats.

LYNDON JOHNSON AND HUBERT HUMPHREY IN CONVERSATION IN LOS ANGELES, CALIFORNIA AT THE NATIONAL DEMOCRATIC CONVENTION WHERE GLEN WAS A DELEGATE.

During the 1960 DNC our delegation supported Humphrey. He received 41 votes even though he was no longer an active presidential candidate. I will never forget being interviewed for radio and television by a cub reporter. When I suggested that our delegation was going to support Hubert Humphrey, the reporter commented that there was no question we would be casting our votes for Kennedy. However, as I predicted, the delegation cast their vote for Humphrey. That cub reporter was Dan Rather. Dan had to go on the air the next night and admit I was right. It was a glorious moment for me.

The week in Los Angeles was incredibly educational for me, and one of the highlights of my life. I still have the recording when Gene McCarthy made the nominating speech for Adlai Stevenson. It was an incredible speech. Hearing it delivered was an experience of a lifetime. Remarkably, I had a tape recorder on the podium and recorded the address. I still have the original recording. I only regret that I did not have a tape recorder to record everything that took place that week.

The week we went to the National Convention in Los Angeles was the only week of work we ever missed putting out the newspaper. I had to hire a young man from the *New London Times* to put out the paper while I was gone. He did, which was kind of a miracle, but it did happen. He got the paper out.

By the time the 1964 Democratic National Convention came along in Atlantic City, I was a federal employee as State Director of the U.S. Savings Bond Program, and therefore, could not be active in politics. However, my wife, LaVonne, co-chairwoman of Kandiyohi County, was elected as an alternate delegate to the convention. We were in Atlantic City, and were thrilled when Lyndon Johnson chose Hubert Humphrey to run as his Vice President.

Shortly after I was appointed State Director for the U.S. Savings Bond Program, an opportunity arose for a Democrat to capture the congressional seat in Minnesota's 7th district. In the past, running for this seat as a Democrat would have been a disaster because H. Carl Andersen had held it for 24 years. Andersen was so firmly entrenched that it was believed he could not be beaten, though certainly a few had tried. However, times had changed. His party, thinking that he was too liberal, actually ran a candidate against him.

They accused Andersen of nepotism for hiring so many of his family members. Consequently, it was his own party that beat him. The farmers normally voted for him because he was a strong spokesman for them, but other than that, the district was primarily Democratic. The road was paved for a Democrat to be elected.

I could have had the nomination just for the asking. I had been active in the district for years and had been the 7th District Treasurer, plus I knew every county chairman. Getting the nomination to run for Congress would have been a 'no-brainer' as they say.

Had I run for United States Congress and been elected, I can guarantee you I would have stayed there. It's all a matter of keeping in touch with your constituents. I believe I could have been elected in 1962. I felt, however, compelled to continue in the post of State Director of the Savings Bonds Division, which in the long run turned out to be an excellent decision.

I had a very good friend by the name of Alec Olson from a little town nearby. I supported him, and we nominated him to fill the post running against the individual that beat H. Carl Andersen in the primary. In the last four weeks of the campaign, I pulled out all the stops. I got people from Washington who were the most knowledgeable and put together a good finish to Alec's campaign. Alec Olson was elected to the Congress by a very narrow margin.

I worked with Alec again prior to his second term. For the campaign, we got him back to his roots; I got him support from my office in Minnesota as well as Humphrey's office in Washington. It worked. By another thin margin, Alec was reelected.

Alec's problem was that he was so dedicated to legislation, and he was so glued to the Washington demands that he was unable to stay in touch with his constituents back home. He only kept in touch by letter, not appearing often in person in his district. Obviously, he became most vulnerable by not being available.

After two terms as an outstanding congressman, Alec Olson lost to a Republican. It was a bitter pill for the Democratic Party to lose that particular seat. Alec did succeed in coming back, and served as Minnesota's lieutenant governor for a term or two. He was a good friend of mine, and our paths continued to cross over the years in different political spheres.

~ 13 ~
The U.S. Treasury in Minnesota

HUBERT HUMPHREY SAID there was a job open in the Treasury as an Area Manager for the Savings Bond Program in Minnesota, and he would see that it was mine if I wanted it. I had sold the newspaper by now, so went to work there in the spring of 1961.

The office for the Area Manager was in the old Metropolitan Building in downtown Minneapolis.

THE METROPOLITAN BUILDING IN MINNEAPOLIS. BUILT 1888, THIS TWELVE-STORY BUILDING FEATURED A ROOF GARDEN WITH A RESTAURANT PATRONIZED BY MINNEAPOLIS' HIGH SOCIETY, AN OBSERVATION TOWER, AND A SKYLIGHT OVER AN ATRIUM WITH IRON BALCONIES. THE BUILDING WAS RAZED IN 1961. PHOTO TAKEN BY JACK E. BOUCHER, NOVEMBER 1960.

INTERIOR VIEW LOOKING UP TO THE SKYLIGHT IN THE
ATRIUM OF THE METROPOLITAN BUILDING, MINNEAPOLIS,
MINNESOTA. PHOTO BY JACK E. BOUCHER, NOVEMBER 1960.

It was located between 3rd and 4th Street and between Hennepin and Nicolet. There was an open elevator in the middle. You could take the open elevator all the way to the top, but every floor had iron railings around it. You could look down to all of the floors below surrounding the elevator. On my first day on the job, a man decided to go up to the 28th floor and jump. He landed on the sidewalk. Needless to say, that was quite a jolt.

As Area Manager, I had a big area of the state. Not only did I have part of Minneapolis, but also the whole southeastern part of the state; everything from Owatonna to Rochester to Albert Lee, to Winona, to Red Wing, Austin, Rochester, you name it—I've been in all of those towns. I've been in every newspaper and every bank in that whole 20-some county area.

On Monday mornings, I would leave home in Lake Lillian, go to the office, and then travel all week. I stayed in motels all across the district. As a result of all that travel I got to know all the newspaper people and all the bankers. I also knew all the industrialists, pay-roll savings people, and many other businessmen. The only hotel-free nights came when I was in Minneapolis, and I would stay with my aunt, Hattie Bordie. I had grown up with Aunt Hattie and Uncle Irvin's son, Sonny. Incidentally, Sonny and his family had moved to Texas many years before.

There were two other area managers in the state. One was Harry Schmokel. Harry had been in government all his life, even though he had not gone beyond the second grade in school. He was a 20-year veteran and worked his way up to a grade 12 salary. The other area manager was a woman whose last name was Leaber.

When I came to the Treasury, Fred King held the State Director position. He had been the Hennepin County Republican Chairman and had been appointed to this job by President Eisenhower. Quite honestly, he spent more time politicking than working.

Fred was a rabid Republican, as was one of his district representatives. At the time Fred's job was a Schedule-A job and was a political appointment. I decided I would see to the replacement of Fred King. He wasn't much of a State Director. He was a lot of hot air and a very "right-wing" Republican, and he would continue to espouse the causes of the Republican Party. His Republican employees did that as well.

Shortly after I arrived at the Treasury, a man named Bill Neal was appointed as an absolute figurehead. He was the National Director of the Savings Bonds Division and the former President of Wachovia Bank. He spent his time just traveling around the country making patriotic speeches. He never got into the sales end or the guts of the organization at all.

In my first days on the job, Bill Neal came to Minnesota to make the annual pitch for savings bonds. I had never been to one of those big meetings before, which included an audience of about 250 people. All of the key bankers, volunteers, and CEOs were there.

Fred King picked Neal up at the airport and brought him to the office. Harry Schmokel had met Bill because Harry had been there a number of years, so he introduced us. When I stuck out my hand to meet him, he said, "Oh my God! Now they're hiring them, and they aren't even dry behind the ears." He just turned and walked away and never shook my hand. I said to Harry (Harry's dead now, but he would tell the same story), "You know what, I'm going to have that SOB's job before I leave this division." At that moment I knew that

I was going to replace him. I was just an area manager at that time and only 31 years old, but I knew what I needed to do.

Fred King was an ineffective State Director at that time, and he had to be replaced first. After that, I would see about replacing Bill Neal. Fred King worked very hard at being despicable, and he set me up to make a payroll savings call on a company that had never signed up for payroll savings all throughout the war. It was a standing joke at the company that the CEO literally would have nothing to do with savings bonds. The appointment was set for me, and I made the call. While I was making my pitch, the CEO was sitting reading the *Wall Street Journal*.

Finally I said, "Look, if you are through listening before I'm through talking, please let me know." That totally disarmed him, and while the company never did participate in payroll savings, they did do some advertising for us. No one could believe that I had softened that man up.

To be an effective State Director, one has to work hard. It's necessary that the State Director make major calls. Almost immediately, I started work to replace Fred King. I started tracking his activities. He would come to work in the morning, and give orders to everybody, but he never left his office. He never made calls. He was not doing any of that.

It wasn't too difficult to tie him to many political activities that were taking place on his watch as a federal employee. He had been at Farmers and Mechanics Bank and had been the Republican County Chairman. He was still more active in the Republican Party than he was in the duties of State Director.

I got in touch with Senator Hubert Humphrey and Senator Gene McCarthy and told them that Fred was a political appointment, he was drawing a grade 12 salary, but he was still active in the Republican Party. He wasn't working. He was managing the office and giving orders, but his time was spent getting out the Republican vote. I told them that he was simply doing too much work for the Republican Party, and he needed to go. I documented all of that and sent it to both Humphrey and to McCarthy, and then they carried the ball in Washington.

They took the facts to President Kennedy. Fred King had obviously served well into the Kennedy administration and was still very political, and it was his political activities that finally did him in. It had taken me just seven months to get him fired.

The whole Savings Bonds Division had these appointed Republican holdovers. They were to serve at the advice and consent of the sitting president. When President Kennedy came into office, he never made any new appointments; he just left them all in place. Every state had people who had been appointed by the past president.

The job of the area and state directors was to sell savings bonds. The Savings Bonds Division had the greatest cadre of patriotic volunteers who gave their time and talent to sell savings bonds. Every county had a volunteer county chairman. Every bank group had a bank chairman. Every company that was active in payroll savings had a payroll savings chairman. My first payroll savings chairman was the CEO of Minnesota Mining. When there was a meeting planned, all the volunteers were included. The Minnesota state

A TREASURY DEPARTMENT MEETING. SHOWN ARE VOLUNTEERS OF
THE SAVINGS BOND PROGRAM. GLEN AT THE HEAD OF THE TABLE.

A GROUP OF SAVING BOND PROGRAM VOLUNTEERS
WITH GLEN JOHNSON IN WASHINGTON, DC.

GLEN JOHNSON AND THE VOLUNTEER NATIONAL BOND
PROGRAM CHAIRMAN WHERE THE NATIONAL NEWSPAPER
ASSOCIATION WAS HONORED FOR THEIR SUPPORT.

PRESIDENT JOHNSON THANKING VOLUNTEERS FOR
THEIR SUPPORT OF THE SAVINGS BOND PROGRAM.

chairman was Bishop Roland. He was President of the American
National Bank in St. Paul. He was a really good worker. When we
would have a big meeting, he would invite everybody into his bank.
We'd make a presentation to groups ranging from 50 to 100 people.

There were thousands of volunteers nationally, and in Minnesota
every district had a district chairman, and every county had a county
chairman. They were all volunteers. The bankers were important volunteers. They would get people together and help sell the idea that
people should buy savings bonds. That was all patriotic motivation.

The whole division had 950 employees nationwide. We had a
regional director in each region of the country, so there were at least
eight regional directors. There was a state director in every state.
The number of area managers depended upon the population of the
state. Each regional director had an assistant regional director. My
regional director was in Iowa, and his assistant was also in Iowa.

Those assistants were supposed to be experts in getting publicity. They took pictures, and they wrote stories of the events. When there was a big state meeting, either the regional director or the assistant director would be there to cover it. They would interview people, get publicity in the newspapers, and anything else needed to promote sales. The whole goal behind it was to sell savings bonds.

Those were interesting years. We traveled to banks and to corporations promoting payroll savings. Minnesota ranked 50th in the nation in savings bond sales at the time I came on board. Within two years and with some great new reps that I managed to get on the staff, we went from last to first in rank. It was a very rewarding time.

⌒ 14 ⌒

Always the Entrepreneur

WORKING IN THE Treasury Department, my nights were much freer than they had been during the early days when I'd worked two or three jobs just to make ends meet. So, I decided that I would do something I'd considered years before.

Prior to selling the *Lake Lillian Crier,* we also had a fishing and boating paper. That was at the time when we had better presses, better transportation, better linotypes, and just better all around equipment. The *Little Crow Fishing and Boating News* was certainly a success. We published 5500 copies during the summer months. It was a free paper and was distributed by all of our advertisers, which included sport shops, boating places, and hardware stores. This was a big help as far as income was concerned.

When we were going to publish the *Fishing and Boating News,* I went to the local bank, as well as the banks in Willmar, to see if I could get a loan to finance the expanded business. The bank in Lake Lillian had gone as far as it could with the initial $800 loan. Obviously, with a gross income of only $1800, making those payments was difficult at best, so when we tried to finance the *Fishing and Boating News,* the banks simply laughed at us. They said there was no way they could extend us credit.

I distinctly remember telling two of the banks in Willmar, the First National Bank and the Bank of Willmar (one bank was part of the First National system in Minneapolis, and the other was part of the Bremer system in St. Paul) that I would start a bank that would be bigger than either one of them.

Now, in a more stable position at the Treasury, I decided that it was time to start that bank. I started working evenings and Saturdays to put an organization together to compete with the people who had turned me down all those years before.

What do you have to do to start a bank? You have to have a banker, a lawyer, a contractor to build the building and a retailer with money. In my case, I couldn't serve on the board, because of my Treasury position, so my father served on the board in my place.

The first person I met with was Tom Torgeson, who ran a clothing store in Willmar, Minnesota. Tom was very successful. In addition to the clothing store he also ran the Holiday Inn, which was by far the biggest such enterprise in the City of Willmar. He was very interested in starting a bank.

I told Tom that we would need a banker. He suggested a friend, Kelly Forstrom, who ran the bank in Clara City. Late one night Tom and I went to see Kelly and talked about starting a third bank in Willmar, Minnesota with him as the banker. Kelly was very interested, so we now had three of us interested.

We needed someone to be a contractor because we would need to build a building. They said they had a friend, Barney Nelson of Nelson Construction, which was the biggest construction company in Willmar. In subsequent meetings we met with Barney and asked him if he would like to be one of the founders of a bank in Willmar. He indicated he would.

We needed a lawyer and someone to write the charter. I personally asked my friend, George Hulstand, if he would like to be the fifth member of our organization and to write the Charter Application. The charter application was a lengthy document and required documentation of need for establishing a financial institution. At that time there hadn't been but one new bank in the state of Minnesota for many, many years. Charters simply were not granted.

The five of us started to meet week-after-week, and organized how we were going to accomplish our project. I had a good friend, Paul Lindholm, President of the Minnesota Bankers Association that I had worked with. It turned out he was a senior officer at Northwestern National Bank. Northwestern National was the biggest bank in the Twin Cities. I went to see him to ask him how much of the capital we could count on him providing as a down payment to start this bank.

We estimated how much capital we would need, and he said if we were able to put it together, they would lend us 90 percent of the money. We really only had to come up with a few thousand dollars each to start our bank. This was primarily due to the fact that the big bank would be getting a new customer: our little bank. Paul is still a banker in Minnesota. He and his wife, Marlys are close personal friends of ours to this day.

Once Paul agreed to fund our proposed bank, we had to determine how we were going to put up a building that wasn't going to cost us a fortune. We also had to determine how we were going to finance it.

I had done a lot of work with the Lutheran Brotherhood Insurance Company, one of the biggest insurance companies in the state of Minnesota. As a result, I knew a lot of the senior officers. I went to see the senior officer and told him we were going to start a bank in Willmar, Minnesota. I told him we would need a really good, long term, low interest rate loan in order to begin building, and told him we would like for them to be shareholders. The president and vice president, as well as a number of other people in command at Lutheran Brotherhood, eventually all bought stock in this new bank, which was named Citizens' National Bank of Willmar.

We wrote a loan proposal to the "Treasurer" of the Lutheran Brotherhood, and I recall getting the phone call from him after he received the proposal. He said, "There's just no way we can make this loan—30 years at such a low percentage rate, and all the rest you are asking. I'll take this to the board, but I can assure you they are not going to approve it."

Little did he know that I had contacted all the people who were going to make the decision, and sold them on the concept. When the loan came up, it was approved 'just like that.'

He called me and said, "I can't believe this, but the loan has just been approved."

The most important challenge was to acquire the approval of the Comptroller of the Currency in Washington since this would be a national bank. They had not made any new charters for many years, except perhaps one. We needed political pull to make that happen.

While in Washington on Treasury business I went to see my friend, Hubert Humphrey, who was then in the Senate. Hubert and I went to see the Comptroller of the Currency. We sat down and told him we were going to put the charter together in Willmar, Minnesota, and we would certainly like to have the office of the Comptroller of the Currency approve the charter.

The Comptroller really could not easily turn down the senior senator from Minnesota. Without that approval we would never have gotten the charter. I had assured everybody that, if we could put it all together, and could organize it, we would get the charter.

George put together a document on the community, describing the demographics and economy of the area. It was a large, 90-page document, and was extremely well done. We got the charter and started the bank in Willmar, Minnesota. Things ran smoothly for years, until one conversation changed everything.

The man we had hired to be the chief executive officer had said to one of the women at work, "Well, we're not all equal, you know?" In response, eight of the women walked off the job. Pouncing on that comment, they made some incredible demands. They wanted a shorter workweek. They wanted double their pay. They actually went on strike and carried signs outside the bank for literally a year and a half, the longest bank strike in American history. They finally gave up the strike, and we eventually sold the bank 13 years later. A made-for-television movie, *The Willmar 8,* brought increased notoriety and delayed the ability to settle the dispute.

The bank, no longer called the Citizens' National Bank, grew through that entire event. Everyone invested in the project did very well financially because when the bank was sold they made more money than they could have dreamed of. Putting the whole transaction together and making it successful was certainly a challenging, but rewarding sideline endeavor.

⌒ 15 ⌒
Minnesota State Director
Savings Bonds Division

AFTER I BECAME Minnesota State Director in the Savings Bonds Division, I was promoted from a grade 11 to a grade 12 salary. Shortly after my promotion, I'd had a phone call and a letter from Governor Rolvaag asking me to be the State Commissioner of Banks. I wrote him back saying that I couldn't do it because I had already accepted the position as State Director. To have received the offer was fantastic. Now, however, it was time to get to work. I needed to pull together a team. In addition to Harry Schmokel and Andy Henjum, whom I'd inherited, I had two additional appointments that I could make.

I appointed Roland Muller who had been an auto dealer in Windom, Minnesota and Marvin Johnson, a carpenter, who had come out of the labor movement. As new area managers, I sent them to Washington to be trained.

These four reps were all characters in their own right and deserve more explanation than just simply the fact that they were area managers for the Savings Bond Program. All of the reps were dedicated to their tasks and worked diligently at making the payroll calls and the bank calls needed in Minnesota.

Prior to working in the Treasury Department, Andy Henjum was a small town newspaper publisher. He was a hard worker and a good member of our team.

Harry Schmokel had been at every pay grade level in the Agriculture Department before moving into Savings Bonds. He was a wonderful salesman, and he did a great job for the Treasury Department.

Marvin Johnson came out of the building trades and was a carpenter in Willmar. He was very dedicated to his job, and was very influential in developing union support for the Payroll Savings Program.

Roland Muller, a real gentleman, had been a Ford dealer in Windom, Minnesota. He retired from the Ford dealership and made an outstanding area manager. He was a born salesman, and very dedicated to his work.

Mrs. Leaber, also a Republican appointee, was the other Area Manager. She was quite a character. She appeared to be busy all the time, but she never really got anything accomplished. As a matter of fact, she seemed to be visiting all kinds of places, but when I checked them out, she had never actually been there.

It finally all came to light when I was reading her call reports, and I saw that she had called on a man who happened to have been a good friend of mine in the newspaper business. She was apparently unaware that he had passed away three years earlier. As I looked over the records, she noted that she'd called him about nine times. I don't actually know how long she'd been up to this, but when I realized it, I invited her into my office. When confronted with the facts, she resigned on the spot.

After her departure I really started getting my staff in place, and we set an incredible record. The five of us made a great team, and we enjoyed every minute of what we did. I lived in Lake Lillian, Marv Johnson lived in Willmar, and Roland Muller lived in Windom. We all shared an apartment during the week in Minneapolis, which saved some of the travel from our hometowns. Harry Schmokel lived in Saint Paul the whole time and was always near his home.

We came up with many new ideas. We devised the idea of tape recording local bankers and local CEOs for payroll savings advertising. Tape recorders were made available to employees, so they could easily record bankers in their banks talking about savings bonds. They took the recordings to the local radio stations, and we got millions of dollars worth of publicity. That had never happened before, and that was one of my creations. Those recordings did wonders to sell savings bonds, and we were certainly successful. Recording

ANDREW HENJUM, HARRY SCHMOKEL, GLEN JOHNSON,
MARVIN JOHNSON, AND ROLAND MULLER. GLEN JOHNSON
AND HIS STAFF WHEN HE WAS MINNESOTA STATE DIRECTOR,
JANUARY 1962 TO MARCH 1967. THIS PICTURE TAKEN
LATER WHEN GLEN ACCEPTED HIS APPOINTMENT AS
NATIONAL DIRECTOR, U.S. SAVINGS BONDS DIVISION.

GLEN WAS AWARDED THE TWIN CITY CIVIL SERVICE
EMPLOYEE OF THE YEAR, IN THE LEADERSHIP CATEGORY,
APRIL 21, 1965. GLEN WAS ONE OF THREE FEDERAL
EMPLOYEES SELECTED FROM A FIELD OF 16,000.

bankers was a smash hit around the state and took us from 48th in quota sales to 1st in quota sales in two years.

After about five years, Bill Neal was still National Director. He was an Eisenhower appointee, a holdover in a Schedule C position that could have been replaced earlier in the Kennedy administration. He was not being political, but he was also not being very effective. At that time I started making phone calls to Senator Gene McCarthy and Senator Hubert Humphrey from Minnesota.

Both of the Senators heard the story over and over before movement finally got underway to replace Bill Neal as National Director. Gene McCarthy was even more effective than Hubert Humphrey because of his relationship with the Secretary of the Treasury. That was really what made it all succeed.

The ace in the hole I had was Fred Deming, who had been President of the Minneapolis Fed and had become a close friend of mine. He was Under Secretary of the Treasury, and knew of my work with the Savings Bond Program. With Fred at the Treasury and McCarthy and Humphrey in the Senate, I continued lobbying to become the National Director.

As I was campaigning for National Director, I used my letter from Governor Karl Rolvaag asking me to be the State Commissioner of Banks as a selling tool to others to gain support. I knew that it was a good lever.

Every day, for perhaps six months, I would call Hubert Humphrey's office, and I would call Gene McCarthy's office, and try to get them moving to replace Bill Neal. It took several months of pressure to remove Bill Neal from office.

When the word came out that Bill Neal had resigned his post as National Director of the Savings Bonds Division, the rumors started. There were dozens of people named as possible replacements. My name was among those listed; however, with the accumulation of names from people in high places, it looked like an impossible task to get to the top of the heap.

The Assistant Regional Director from Iowa, Ken Glass, really thought he was going to be the new National Director. Arnold Rauen, the State Director in Illinois, had the powerful congressman from

Illinois, Rostenkowski, as a supporter. Arnold Rauen called me and said, "I'm going to be the new National Director."

Alec Olson, a good friend of mine, and a congressman in Washington was very much on my side. Gene McCarthy was outspoken on my behalf. Hubert Humphrey was a consistent supporter of mine, and of course, so was Fred Deming, Under Secretary of the Treasury. With these allies, I was able to become the only appointment to the Johnson sub-cabinet influenced by Vice President Hubert Humphrey. However, even then, I knew I would still have to sell myself to President Lyndon B. Johnson.

Along the way there were 55 names that I heard were candidates to be National Director. A journalist by the name of Anderson, who was nationally renowned, wrote an article about all the people who were candidates to fill the job. Anderson was a syndicated columnist. This article talked about the National Director resigning under political pressure and all of the pressures that were being brought about regarding who would become the new director.

I knew that I was in the mix, but there was lots of competition. I had a trip to Washington with my Minnesota State Volunteer Director for a national meeting that was taking place in DC on January 6, 1967. I remember the date because January 7 is our wedding anniversary, and I was planning to be home for our anniversary as I had always been in the past.

We were having a topflight volunteer meeting at the Madison Hotel for several hundred CEOs and bankers from all over the country. They were there for this big savings bonds meeting when Fred Deming came to my table at dinner on the evening of January 6th.

Fred whispered in my ear and said, "Tomorrow you have an 8:00 a.m. appointment with Joe Barr, the other Under Secretary of the Treasury. You then have an 8:30 a.m. meeting with Henry Fowler." Fowler was the Secretary of the Treasury. He went on to say, "You have a 9:00 a.m. meeting with Marvin Watson (LBJ's Appointment Secretary), and you have a 9:30 a.m. appointment to see President Johnson."

For a small town farm boy, this was mighty heady stuff. I called LaVonne to tell her that I would not be home for our usual get together on our anniversary, and that tomorrow was going to be an incredibly interesting day.

The next day I went through all the interviews. Joe Barr was first, and we discussed the position at length. I next met with Henry Fowler, the Secretary of the Treasury, and we talked about the importance of the position as far as debt management was concerned. Henry wanted to be certain that we were getting the right person for the job. After Henry I met with Marvin Watson. Marvin was completely aware of the positions in the Savings Bonds Division, since his father had been appointed to an area manager position in Texas.

Marvin said that I was to see the President, and I was to meet with him at 9:30 a.m. in "FDR's Fish Room." Marvin said that since the President was in the process of writing his State of the Union message, he wasn't positive that he would be able to keep our appointment.

I waited in the Fish Room, and Marvin Watson came back to check on me. He asked how I was doing, and I said, "Fine."

He said, "Have you noticed the paintings in here?"

I told him that I had noticed the similarities; that the same person was in all six of the paintings. He said they were all Remington's, and that Frederic Remington was in every one of the pictures. Marvin thought I was very perceptive to have noticed.

My wait for President Johnson to show up was a long one, and I was thinking that he possibly wouldn't appear. I was seated facing the door that I had come through when I heard a door opening behind me. I wasn't even aware there was a door there; in fact, it sort of melted right into the wall.

While turning towards the sound, I saw this giant of a man, who looked like he was seven feet tall, come through the door and over to me. I stood up, of course, and reached out my hand, which was totally enveloped in his large hand.

He said, "Hi Glen, I'm Lyndon. Now, you tell me why you should have this job."

For the next 20 to 30 minutes I recounted what I had done in Minnesota to take savings bonds sales from last to first in the nation and went to great lengths and details as to how that was accomplished.

I swear President Johnson wiped a tear from his eye as he said, "My best friend is a department store owner from Fort Worth, Texas, and the only job he has ever wanted from this administration is to be National Director of the Savings Bond Program and Assistant Secretary of the Treasury. It's going to be very hard for me to tell him that he didn't get the job. Congratulations, you are my new National Director." At that point, he got up and left.

What an exhilarating experience! I then proceeded to catch the next flight home to celebrate our wedding anniversary, a day late!

The next few weeks were most interesting as I went through the procedures necessary to obtain the top security clearance, which this job called for. A short time later, I started getting telephone calls from people I had gone to grade school, high school, and college with, and they were asking if I was in trouble because they had received calls from the FBI questioning my integrity! The questions were about what I did, where I went, and what I talked about. Finally, I was told that I had in fact, received the clearance, and that I would be sworn in at a ceremony at the Treasury Department.

～ 16 ～

Going National
National Director—Savings Bonds Division—Washington, DC

IN MARCH OF 1967, I was sworn in as National Director of the Savings Bond Program and Assistant Secretary of the Treasury by the Under Secretary Fred Deming, Secretary of the Treasury Henry Fowler, and Vice President Hubert Humphrey.

GLEN BEING SWORN IN AS NATIONAL DIRECTOR OF THE SAVINGS BONDS DIVISION AND ASSISTANT SECRETARY OF THE TREASURY BY UNDER SECRETARY FRED DEMING. SECRETARY OF THE TREASURY HENRY FOWLER AND VICE PRESIDENT HUBERT HUMPHREY ARE LOOKING ON.

HENRY FOWLER RESPONDING TO GLEN'S APPOINTMENT
TO THE POSITION. VICE PRESIDENT HUMPHREY, GLEN,
AND UNDER SECRETARY DEMING LOOK ON.

HUBERT HUMPHREY DESCRIBING HIS RELATIONSHIP WITH
GLEN FOLLOWING GLEN'S APPOINTMENT AS NATIONAL
DIRECTOR OF THE U.S. SAVINGS BONDS DIVISION. GLEN,
SECRETARY FOWLER, UNDER SECRETARY DEMING, AND
S. J. KRYZSKO, PRESIDENT OF THE AMERICAN'S BANKERS
ASSOCIATION SAVINGS BONDS DIVISION STAND BY.

My family was there for my swearing in. My mother and father were also there and were very proud that I had finally "made it to the top."

GLEN AND LAVONNE, WITH CHILDREN VICKI, DAVID, LORI, AND GLEN'S PARENTS RUTH AND OSCAR, THE DAY GLEN WAS SWORN IN AS NATIONAL DIRECTOR OF THE U.S. SAVINGS BONDS DIVISION IN WASHINGTON, DC.

GLEN AND FAMILY JOINED BY SENATOR HUMPHREY, SECRETARY FOWLER, AND UNDER SECRETARY DEMING COMMEMORATING GLEN JOHNSON "MAKING IT TO THE TOP."

TREASURY DEPARTMENT

WASHINGTON, D.C.
March 23, 1967

FOR RELEASE 12:00 NOON,
THURSDAY, MARCH 23, 1966

SECRETARY FOWLER ANNOUNCES APPOINTMENT OF GLEN R. JOHNSON
AS NATIONAL DIRECTOR, U. S. SAVINGS BOND DIVISION

Secretary of the Treasury Henry H. Fowler today announced the appointment of Glen R. Johnson as National Director of the U. S. Savings Bonds Division.

Mr. Johnson has been State Director of the Savings Bond Division in Minnesota since 1962. Under his direction Minnesota's annual percentage gain in Savings Bonds sales rose from 48th among the states to first.

Mr. Johnson was born in Lake Lillian, Minn., May 2, 1929. He attended Gustavus Adolphus College and the Minnesota School of Business between 1946 and 1949. His first federal job was as a U. S. postal clerk in the early 1950's.

In 1949 he founded the Lake Lillian <u>Crier</u>, a weekly newspaper, of which he was editor and publisher until 1961. He also published <u>Fishing and Boating News</u>, a sporting publication.

Mr. Johnson was appointed Deputy Director and Area Manager of the Minnesota U. S. Savings Bonds Division in May, 1961, and became State Director in January, 1962.

He has been President of the Lake Lillian Chamber of Commerce; Chairman of the Kandiyohi County United Fund and of the county Mental Health Association; organizer and President of the Kandiyohi County Press Association; Secretary of the Congregation of the Lake Lillian First Lutheran Church, and is an Honorary Member of the Minnesota Newspaper Association. He has been active in the Red Cross, March of Dimes and Cancer Drive.

Mr. Johnson was named Twin City Civil Service "Employee of the Year", in the leadership category, in 1965 -- one of three Federal employees selected from a field of 16,000. That same year, he won Treasury's Certificate of Merit Award.

MARCH 23, 1967 WASHINGTON, DC TREASURY DEPARTMENT
NEWS RELEASE ANNOUNCING GLEN'S APPOINTMENT AS
NATIONAL DIRECTOR OF THE U.S. SAVINGS BONDS DIVISION.

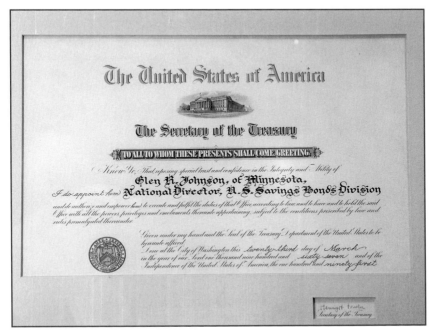

**THE OFFICIAL CERTIFICATE AWARDED UPON THE APPOINTMENT
OF GLEN JOHNSON AS NATIONAL DIRECTOR AND ASSISTANT
SECRETARY OF THE U.S. TREASURY SAVINGS BONDS DIVISION.**

The event made every newspaper in the country, but that was only because Fowler and Humphrey got trapped in the small Treasury elevator for about 45 minutes. The day after that happened the story was carried in all the newspapers, and the story did say they had been on their way to the swearing in ceremony for Glen Johnson.

EN ROUTE TO CEREMONY

Humphrey Trapped in Balky Elevator

From the Tribune Wire Services

WASHINGTON, D.C. — Vice-President Hubert H. Humphrey got stuck in a Treasury Department elevator Thursday while on his way to a swearing-in ceremony for a fellow Minnesotan.

He was freed in about 10 minutes by a mechanic who opened the elevator doors manually. The small private elevator had stopped just short of the fourth floor, and this prevented the door from opening automatically.

Humphrey was delayed in arriving at swearing-in ceremonies for Glen R. Johnson, a native of Lake Lillian, Minn., as national director of the U.S. Savings Bond Division.

The Vice-President cracked that Treasury Secretary Henry Fowler has

Humphrey   Johnson
'The hard way'

"often told me how important it was to come up the hard way.".

Johnson, 37, Minnesota savings bond director for the last five years, was the founder and publisher of the weekly Lake Lillian Crier from 1949 to 1961. In 1965 he was named Civil Service Employe of the Year in the Twin Cities area.

Married, with three children, Johnson will receive $25,890 a year.

TRIBUNE WIRE SERVICES STORY OF HUMPHREY AND
FOWLER BEING TRAPPED IN THE ELEVATOR ON THE
WAY TO GLEN'S SWEARING IN CEREMONY.

VICE PRESIDENT HUBERT HUMPHREY AND GLEN
HOLDING A "SHARE IN FREEDOM" SIGN, THE SLOGAN
FOR THE SAVINGS BOND PROGRAM IN 1967.

VICE PRESIDENT HUBERT H. HUMPHREY BOUGHT FIRST
SAVINGS BONDS IN THE FEDERAL GOVERNMENT'S
1968 "SHARE IN FREEDOM" CAMPAIGN. EDDIE FISHER,
ENTERTAINER, IS PICTURED ALONG WITH VICE
PRESIDENT HUMPHREY AND GLEN R. JOHNSON.

FLAG PRESENTATION MADE AT THE RESTONE ARSENAL
OFFICERS' MESS ON OCTOBER 4, 1967. PRESENTATION MADE
TO U.S. ARMY MISSILE COMMAND AND THE U.S. ARMY MISSILE
AND MUNITIONS CENTER AND SCHOOL IN ALABAMA.

**GLEN PRESENTING A HIGH SCHOOL CLASS WITH
SAVINGS BONDS POSTERS FOR THEIR WORK IN
SELLING SAVINGS BONDS IN WASHINGTON, DC.**

**GLEN JOHNSON, NATIONAL DIRECTOR, PRESENTING
APPOINTMENT CERTIFICATE TO MR. JAMES W. RAWLES,
VOLUNTEER STATE CHAIRMAN, VIRGINIA.**

LEFT TO RIGHT: R. H. O'MALLEY, REGIONAL DIRECTOR
REGION IV, U.S. SAVINGS BONDS DIVISION; GLEN R. JOHNSON,
NATIONAL DIRECTOR, U.S. SAVINGS BONDS DIVISION; JAMES O.
CUMMINGS, UTAH 1968 SAVINGS BOND CAMPAIGN CHAIRMAN;
HONORABLE CALVIN L. RAMPTON, GOVERNOR OF UTAH;
HONORABLE FRANK E. (TED) MOSS, UNITED STATES SENATOR;
MRS. SHIRLEY RILEY, CHAIRMAN, UTAH STATE EMPLOYEES PRS
CAMPAIGN; JAY SANDBERG, PRESIDENT, UTAH STATE PUBLIC
EMPLOYEES' ASSOCIATION; PRESIDENT LYNDON JOHNSON.

GLEN JOHNSON PUTTING AN I.D. BADGE ONTO UNDER
SECRETARY OF THE TREASURY FRED DEMING.

THE SAVINGS BONDS FLOAT IN THE ROSE BOWL PARADE.

When I became National Director, life changed dramatically. The position as National Director involved a much bigger scope than I had dealt with at the state level. It involved dealing with CEOs, including the presidents of Ford and General Motors, and all the airline companies. We'd bring people to Washington, and there might be as many as 500 people at a national meeting. It would include all the volunteers and big industrialists from all over the country. I was definitely swimming in a much bigger pond.

One of the first things that happened after I became National Director was I realized that I had about 15 people on the payroll who didn't work. They were Republican political appointees who had never been replaced. Most of them were former congressmen who had been defeated and then been given a salary.

The first thing that I decided to do was to fire those political appointees who weren't working. I will never forget when Margaret Chase Smith, the Senator from Maine, came into my office just steaming. She said, "You dirty, goddamn, low down, son-of-a-bitch. I'm going to get you. I'm going to call the Secretary, and I'm going

AUGUST 1, 1967—MR. AND MRS. GLEN R. JOHNSON AND
THEIR THREE CHILDREN HAVING DINNER AT THE BALL
PARK RESTAURANT BEFORE ATTENDING THE GAME
BETWEEN THE MINNESOTA TWINS AND THE SENATORS.

to get your ass and get it out of here." I've never heard anyone swear like she could swear, not even a drunken sailor.

I picked up my red phone and said, "This is my hotline to the Secretary. Help yourself." She slammed the phone down and stomped out of my office. She said, "I'll have your ass for this!" She slammed the door on the way out. I never heard another word from her.

This episode was in response to a congressman who had been defeated that she had put on the payroll. The savings bonds position was his income. I had fired that man because he shouldn't be on the government payroll if he wasn't working. In fact I got rid of all of them who were on the payroll, but not working.

Those weren't the only ones cut off in those early days. At the instructions of the Secretary, I had to fire some directors and people in other key positions. Late one afternoon I got a call from Secretary of the Treasury Henry Fowler, and he said, "Glen, tomorrow you have to fire both the regional and the state director out in California. I thought, "Okay."

I requisitioned an airplane at Andrews Air Force Base and flew to California. The regional and state directors were both in the same office. The regional director was over several west coast states that included Hawaii, Alaska, California, Arizona, Nevada; all the bordering states.

The directors had no warning that I was coming. I walked in and told them that I had orders to remove them from the payroll. The way this decision originated is a bit of a story in itself. I didn't know it at the time, but the pressure had come from an area representative in that office. She had political connections just as I'd had in Minnesota. She'd watched what I had done in Minnesota, and wanted to do the same in California. When I was flying there, I didn't know the whole story. I just had orders that I was to contact her, and that I was to fire the two directors.

The meeting was to be kept highly confidential. After my plane arrived in San Francisco, I met with the woman in the wee hours of the morning. Oddly enough, the meeting took place in a topless bar on the day I was to fire the regional and state directors. This was unheard of in Washington or Minnesota, but was somewhat common in California for something so secretive. This dismissal was one of the more interesting things that I have ever done, or at least it had the most interesting prelude.

In Washington I had eight department heads on my staff over areas such as advertising, promotion, and the like. They all had offices with their own staffs. All the employees were 20-year veterans, and they'd been in the habit of coming to work about 9:00–9:30 a.m. and leaving about 4:00 p.m.

To break the previous work habits, I held staff meetings at 7:00 a.m. daily, and at 6:00 p.m. every night for about three months. They 'loved' me. Some left, and the rest got whipped into shape. With the new work ethic, and continued creativity, we signed up 5.5 million new payroll savers in that first year. This new peacetime record earned me a Treasury award for my leadership in this achievement.

One day my Assistant National Director, Elmer Rusted said, "Tomorrow you have a presentation to the Federal Employees. There will be a big crowd there. You had better work on your speech."

As I walked out on the stage and was introduced, I could see the entire Cabinet out in the audience. All of the cabinet members that were with Kennedy and Johnson were there. McNamara, Dean Rusk, and the rest of the Cabinet were in the front row because all the departments reported to them.

That was my first speech. I stressed patriotism, savings bonds, volunteerism, and the fact that we needed their help. I emphasized that they had to set the example, and that I expected every federal agency to be 100 percent invested in savings bonds. They weren't at 100 percent when I arrived, but we got them there. We put pressure on them. You didn't get a federal job until you signed up for savings bonds, and we made certain of that.

Another speech I gave as National Director was in San Diego. The band was playing when I got off the 727. I said, "What's going on?" Someone said, "We're waiting for the National Director." I went back on the plane and got off on the other side as if I was just getting off. It was quite an education for a farm kid from Minnesota.

I enjoyed every minute of what I was doing. I traveled with Dan Houten, the CEO of Lockheed. We flew one of Lockheed's big planes all over the country. We appeared on the *Today Show*, the *Tonight Show*, and several other shows, and visited U.S. Army bases, gave newspaper interviews, and anything else we could think of to promote savings bonds.

Dan was promoting payroll savings. We had industrial meetings in states, and he'd speak. I'd say as little as possible, and he would do all the selling. Those were great times. I made a lot of friends including newspaper people. I don't know how many million inches of space the major publications gave public service ads to the Savings Bond Program. Whatever it was the first year I was there, they more than doubled the amount of space we got. We did a lot of innovative things to bring this about.

GLEN MAKING A PRESENTATION TO A GROUP OF CEOS
AND BANK PRESIDENTS AT THE SHERATON PARK
HOTEL. LEFT IS SECRETARY OF THE TREASURY, HENRY
FOWLER. UNDER SECRETARY FRED DEMING, RIGHT.

POSTMASTER GENERAL AND CHAIRMAN OF THE SAVINGS BOND
CAMPAIGN, LAWRENCE F. O'BRIEN DISCUSS THE SAVINGS
BONDS "SHARE IN FREEDOM" CAMPAIGN AMONG FEDERAL
CIVILIAN EMPLOYEES WITH GLEN JOHNSON, FEBRUARY 8, 1968.

GLEN WITH MRS. U.S. SAVINGS BONDS, 1967.

GLEN R. JOHNSON, NATIONAL DIRECTOR OF THE TREASURY
DEPARTMENT'S SAVINGS BONDS DIVISION, CONFERS WITH
TV DIRECTOR AND COMEDIAN HOWARD MORRIS DURING
THE APRIL 18 KICK-OFF RALLY (1968) FOR THE "SHARE IN
FREEDOM" SAVINGS BOND CAMPAIGN. THE RALLY WAS HELD
AT THE DEPARTMENTAL AUDITORIUM IN WASHINGTON, DC.

GLEN ON A SAVINGS BONDS MISSION TO CAPE CANAVERAL
(NOW KENNEDY SPACE CENTER). TOUR OF THE APOLLO
SATURN "V" LAUNCH COMPLEX, SEPTEMBER 1968.

GLEN R. JOHNSON, NATIONAL DIRECTOR, AT THE KENNEDY
SPACE CENTER WHERE HE ATTENDED A SAVINGS
BONDS AWARDS CEREMONY, SEPTEMBER 1968.

A SAVINGS BONDS MEETING IN WASHINGTON, DC. FROM LEFT,
UNKNOWN, DAN HOUTEN OF LOCKHEED, GLEN JOHNSON, UNDER
SECRETARY DEMING, AND SECRETARY OF THE TREASURY FOWLER.

Drive for Freedom Shares

By WILLIAM DOYLE
Tribune Financial Editor

The n a t i o n 's largest and most aggressive savings bond campaign since World War II is in progress, sparked by a drive to sell Freedom Shares, the newest federal savings instrument.

Glen R. Johnson, national d i r e c t o r for U.S. Savings Bonds, made the point during an Oakland visit yesterday.

Johnson, who took over as national director March 23, is touring the country to promote sales of the Freedom Shares with their return of 4.74 per cent.

He says the new type bonds, which went on sale May 1, are designed to take dollars which might cause inflation out of the spending stream and to finance the U.S. effort in Vietnam.

A buyer must purchase a Series E bond before he is eligible to acquire a Freedom Share and the purchase must be through a payroll deduction or bond-a-month plan, Johnson says.

In addition, there is a limit of $1,350 face value on the purchase of Freedom Shares in any given year.

Johnson says no figures on sales are in yet, but that he anticipates that $5.5 billion will be sold in the combination of Series E and Freedom Share bonds by next May. He is hopeful that the new bonds will account for about $1 billion of this.

Freedom Shares will be sold for two years or the duration

They'll help cut inflation

Banks and S&Ls Cooperate

We'll Sell $5.5 billion

of the fighting in Vietnam, whichever is longer.

The national bond director discussed the effort which was made to make sure that the new bond did not become competitive with commercial bank and savings and loan association savings.

He said the new instrument was designed to pull money out of current income that would not normally be saved.

The 4.74 rate on the Freedom Shares will be realized only if they are held for the full four year and six month term while savings and loans offer a higher rate and both t h e S&Ls and commercial banks provide more flexibility.

In addition, there is the re-

quirement for joint purchase of a Series E bond which in tandem produce a return of 4.39 per cent if held to maturity Johnson points out.

Trade associations in both fields have endorsed the Freedom Share program and more than 50 per cent of the commercial banks have qualified, through the Federal Reserve Bank, to handle the new instrument.

Johnson became state director of the savings bond division in Minnesota in 1962 after a 12-year career on a weekly newspaper.

He increased the percentage of sales in the state, which had ranked 49th in the country, to where it was first.

The y o u t h f u l appearing,

dark-haired national director says there was a lot of luck in this record, but adds that he also utilized a great deal of personal contact with news media and business and industrial leaders to achieve the mark.

He feels that the same enthusiasm for the savings bond program is developing nationally and says that the response of volunteer helpers has been tremendous.

What accounts for this? "A realization that the drive is essential," Johnson says.

His division operates on an administrative cost of slightly more than .1 per cent and he says, "It's the thousands of volunteers who make it possible."

STORY FROM THE *OAKLAND TRIBUNE* ON THE DRIVE FOR
FREEDOM SHARES WITH EXCERPTS TAKEN FROM A SPEECH
GLEN MADE AT A STATEWIDE CONFERENCE IN CALIFORNIA.

SAN DIEGO, CALIFORNIA, MAY 12, 1967 – SEMI-FINALISTS IN THE
MRS. U.S. SAVINGS BONDS CONTEST, TAKEN AT THE CIVIC CENTER.

PRESIDENT JOHNSON ACCEPTS AN AWARD FROM MRS.
U.S. SAVINGS BONDS AS GLEN JOHNSON LOOKS ON.

SAN DIEGO, CALIFORNIA—MAY 12, 1967—CELEBRATING THE
CROWNING OF MRS. U.S. SAVINGS BONDS: LEFT TO RIGHT: JOAN
BERRY, MRS. U.S. SAVINGS BONDS OF 1966; DORIE DAMUTH, MRS. U.S.
SAVINGS BONDS OF 1967; GLEN R. JOHNSON, NATIONAL DIRECTOR
OF THE SAVINGS BONDS DIVISION; MRS. NEW YORK, RUNNER-UP
FOR THE MRS. U.S. SAVINGS BONDS TITLE; AND WILLIAM G. FISHER
OF THE LUTHERAN BROTHERHOOD, MINNEAPOLIS, MINNESOTA.

VICE PRESIDENT HUBERT HUMPHREY, GLEN
JOHNSON, AND MRS. U.S. SAVINGS BONDS.

SAN DIEGO, CALIFORNIA—CARTOONISTS WHO PARTICIPATED
IN THE MRS. U.S. SAVINGS BONDS CONTEST—LEFT TO RIGHT:
BOB STEVENS, *SAN DIEGO TRIBUNE* EDITORIAL CARTOONIST;
GLEN R. JOHNSON, NATIONAL DIRECTOR U.S. SAVINGS BONDS
DIVISION; BUFORD TUNE, WHO DRAWS "DOTTIE DRIPPLE"
AND BERNIE LANSKY, WHO DRAWS THE PANEL "17."

MAY 9, 1967—BURBANK, CALIFORNIA: GLEN R. JOHNSON,
NATIONAL DIRECTOR OF THE SAVINGS BONDS DIVISION,
VISITS COLONEL JACK WARNER AT THE WEST COAST STUDIOS
OF WARNER BROS PICTURES IN BURBANK, CALIFORNIA. MR.
JOHNSON IS PICTURED WITH THE NEW FREEDOM SHARE NOTE.

MAY 10, 1967—OAKLAND, CALIFORNIA—OFFICIALS OF KACC
MEET WITH GLEN R. JOHNSON, NATIONAL DIRECTOR OF THE
PAYROLL SAVINGS PLAN FOR U.S. SAVINGS BONDS AND NEW
FREEDOM SHARES. MR. JOHNSON VISITED THE OAKLAND
HEADQUARTERS AT THE INVITATION OF THE COMPANY.

WILLIAM GWINN, NATIONAL PAYROLL VOLUNTEER CHAIRMAN;
GLEN JOHNSON, UNDER SECRETARY OF THE U. S. TREASURY;
AND SECRETARY OF THE TREASURY HENRY FOWLER.

118

On another occasion we were having a national meeting that included all area reps, regional reps, and state directors. There were 250 people in attendance. Everyone was having a great time since one of their own had finally made it to the top and understood the guts of the organization and what needed to happen to get savings bonds sales to the level that had been expected.

In the middle of the party while everyone was having a good time, my secretary, Hazel Kentz, also at the event, came over and whispered in my ear, "The President is on the phone, and he wishes to speak to you."

Obviously, I was mortified. I grabbed the phone, and the noise level was unbelievable. The President said, "Glen, this is Lyndon. I'm supposed to be at Bergstrom Air Force Base tomorrow morning to speak to 12,000 airmen and to raise the Minuteman Flag. I may have to have a Security Council Meeting; therefore, I need you to be there in case I can't make it. And by the way, I need a speech on the White House wire before 4:00 a.m. tomorrow."

It was already about 10:30 p.m., so I really had to scramble to put things together and to get my speechwriter back to the office. First of all, I had to sober him up and get him straightened out, so he could go back and write the speech. Then he had to get it on the White House wire, which he did accomplish.

In the meantime, I had to make arrangements to get to Bergstrom Air Force Base in Texas. I did that by requisitioning a plane at Andrews Air Force Base in Washington. I was on the platform with 12,000 airmen waiting for the President to arrive.

The entire Congressional Delegation, plus several admirals and generals, were on the platform. There were perhaps a total of 25 to 30 people there when a United States of America Learjet landed. That was the President's plane. I will always remember him coming across the tarmac along with his little dog.

When the President got to the platform and mounted the steps, I was the first one to greet him. He leaned over and whispered to me, "That was one hell of a party you were having last night. What in the world were you celebrating?"

I told him that everybody was celebrating one of their own making it to the top of the division, and Johnson began grinning

PRESIDENT LYNDON JOHNSON GREETING GLEN
AT BERGSTROM AIR FORCE BASE IN TEXAS.

ear-to-ear. He then continued to make his speech and presentation to the airmen. When he left the platform, he just leaned over again, shook my hand, and said, "Keep up the good work."

My next encounter with the President was when he opened the World's Fair in San Antonio, Texas. He was the major speaker that day. He got a column and a half for his speech; the last two lines said that Glen Johnson, Assistant Secretary of the Treasury, had introduced him.

When Johnson needed somebody, he didn't call the Secretary or the Under Secretary, but he called the person in the division that would get the job done for him. As a result, I had five or six encounters in the White House.

Some of the calls were inconsequential, like the President wanting me to have some of the Hollywood people go on radio and television and tout savings bonds. President Johnson was going through some horrible times. The Vietnam demonstrations and the anti-war sentiment were tough. He wanted me to encourage all the Hollywood people to become active and support the Savings Bond Program.

**WITH AIR FORCE ONE AS A BACKDROP, GLEN JOHNSON
LOOKS ON AS PRESIDENT JOHNSON GREETS THE
AIRMEN AT BERGSTROM AIR FORCE BASE.**

Very few of them were supporting the program, and the rest of them were anti-war. The President told me that when he was a young congressman, he and Jack Dempsey traveled the country selling savings bonds. At that time they were war bonds; it was after the war that they became savings bonds.

There were some prominent Hollywood people that went all out to support the bond program, but there were also some who were absolutely opposed. After we discussed it briefly, the President decided Hollywood's involvement was not such a good idea. I convinced him that we could only get limited support, and that I'd rather not do it at all then have it look like we didn't have all out support. We scrapped the idea.

PRESENTATION TO ROWAN AND MARTIN, HOLLYWOOD STARS, FOR THEIR CONTRIBUTION IN PROMOTING SAVINGS BONDS. FROM LEFT, GEORGE CLARK, UNKNOWN, BUD AND MRS. RIDLEY, DAN ROWAN, GLEN JOHNSON & DAUGHTER VICKI, AND DICK MARTIN.

ROWAN AND MARTIN EXAMINING THEIR
AWARD, WHICH GLEN PRESENTED.

ROWAN AND MARTIN ACCEPT THEIR MINUTEMAN AWARD FROM
GLEN JOHNSON. THEY PRODUCED A MOVIE FOR SAVINGS BONDS.

**GLEN PRESENTING AN AWARD TO JACK VALENTI, PRESIDENT
OF THE MOTION PICTURE ASSOCIATION OF AMERICA.
PRIOR TO THE MPAA, VALENTI SERVED AS SPECIAL
ASSISTANT TO U.S. PRESIDENT LYNDON B. JOHNSON.**

While in the Savings Bonds Division, I had the opportunity to work with many Hollywood people, which included Rowan and Martin. I had the opportunity to present them with awards for their performances.

I also met periodically with Jack Warner, the head of Warner Brothers, and others at that level for producing advertising for the Savings Bonds Division. Many Hollywood stars such as Loren Greene,

Raquel Welch, Ava Gabor, Bob Hope, and others gave their full support, which meant that I had the opportunity to work with them.

I traveled throughout the country for a week each with Raquel Welch and Ava Gabor, and the trip was fraught with problems. It was a hectic, but enjoyable week on the road, and we made many television and media appearances. Many of these contacts were very helpful in marketing later in my career with Federated.

GLEN STANDS WITH A GROUP INCLUDING
AVA GABOR, SECOND FROM RIGHT.

GLEN JOHNSON PRESENTS AWARDS TO PHYLLIS
DILLER AND BARRY SANDLER, "BALLAD OF THE GREEN
BERETS" FOR THEIR SUPPORT OF SAVINGS BONDS.

GLEN JOHNSON AND PHYLLIS DILLER WITH POSTMASTER
GENERAL LARRY OBRION. THE POST OFFICE SIGNED 90
PERCENT OF THEIR EMPLOYEES FOR PAYROLL SAVINGS.

There are, however, two other occasions that stand out very clearly in my mind. I got a phone call about midnight one night, and it was the President. He said, "Glen, I need a gold Minuteman Statue. I don't want a bronze one, but a gold one. I want to present it at a ceremony in the White House tomorrow. This ceremony will be proclaiming Bob Hope the Savings Bonds Salesman of the Year. I want it properly inscribed and at the White House by 10:00 tomorrow morning."

The first order of business was to raise money to get this accomplished because there were no government funds available. The first thing that I did was to call my former State Volunteer Director in Minnesota who was the CEO of Minneapolis Honeywell. After getting him out of bed, I informed him in this middle-of-the-night phone call

GLEN R. JOHNSON, NATIONAL DIRECTOR OF THE SAVINGS
BOND PROGRAM PRESENTS KENNETH CLARK, EXECUTIVE
DIRECTOR OF THE MOTION PICTURE ASSOCIATION,
WITH MINUTEMAN STATUE FOR THE OUTSTANDING
CONTRIBUTIONS MADE TO THE SAVINGS BOND PROGRAM
BY THE MOTION PICTURE INDUSTRY, APRIL 4, 1967.

that I needed at least $25,000 to dip this copper Minuteman Statue in order to make it gold for Bob Hope.

The Honeywell CEO asked me what advantage he would get out of that donation, and I told him he wouldn't get any recognition, his name would not appear anywhere. I told him he would be doing this out of the goodness of his heart. He mumbled, "I guess it's all right. Go ahead and do it."

I managed to pull those things together, get everything done, and got the statue to the White House before 10:00 a.m. I was there for the ceremony, but certainly not a part of it. The Minuteman Statue was presented to Bob Hope for being "Savings Bonds Salesman of the Year."

PRESENTATION OF MINUTEMAN STATUE TO TV DIRECTOR
AND COMEDIAN, HOWARD MORRIS, FOR PATRIOTIC
SERVICE TO THE SAVINGS BOND PROGRAM.

**FLAG PRESENTATION HELD AT HEADQUARTERS,
UNITED STATES ARMY GARRISON, ARLINGTON
HALL STATION, ARLINGTON, VIRGINIA, 1968.**

**GLEN AT FLAG PRESENTATION HELD AT HEADQUARTERS,
UNITED STATES ARMY GARRISON, ARLINGTON
HALL STATION, ARLINGTON, VIRGINIA, 1968.**

**GLEN PRESENTING THE TREASURY'S MINUTEMAN
FLAG TO THE GENERAL FOR 100 PERCENT
PARTICIPATION IN THE SAVINGS BOND PROGRAM.**

**NATIONAL DIRECTOR GLEN R. JOHNSON PRESENTS
TREASURY'S MINUTEMAN FLAG TO CHARLES H.
DOLSON, PRESIDENT OF DELTA AIR LINES, INC.,
JANUARY 23, 1968 IN ATLANTA, GEORGIA.**

131

J. M. WASSON, OF SOUTHERN BELL TELEPHONE AND
TELEGRAPH COMPANY, RECEIVES TREASURY'S MINUTEMAN
FLAG FROM NATIONAL DIRECTOR, GLEN R. JOHNSON,
JANUARY 23, 1968. SEATED IS GORDON JONES, PRESIDENT
OF THE FULTON NATIONAL BANK OF ATLANTA.

PRESENTATION TO ENTERTAINER, GEORGE PEPPARD,
IN GLEN'S OFFICE, 1968. MR. PEPPARD DID A
60-SECOND TRAILER FOR SAVINGS BONDS.

PRESENTATION OF MINUTEMAN STATUE TO ENTERTAINER
EDDIE FISHER IN GLEN JOHNSON'S OFFICE, MAY 3, 1968.

SECRETARY HENRY FOWLER (ON LEFT) AND GLEN R. JOHNSON
PRESENTING THE MINUTEMAN STATUE TO JACK VALENTI, THE
PRESIDENT OF THE MOTION PICTURE ASSOCIATION OF AMERICA.

VICE PRESIDENT HUBERT HUMPHREY ADMIRING
EDDIE FISHER'S MINUTEMAN STATUE.

**PRESENTING THE MINUTEMAN STATUE BRANDING IRON.
FROM LEFT, GLEN JOHNSON, SECRETARY OF TREASURY
FOWLER, AND PRESIDENT LYNDON JOHNSON.**

Another time I was at the White House, I needed a branding iron of the Minuteman, dipped in gold, and delivered to the White House for presentation to the retiring chairman of the ABA Savings Bonds Committee, S.J. Kryzsko. The chairman of the committee was from Winona, Minnesota, and he was a good friend of mine.

GLEN WITH S.J. KRYZSKO, PRESIDENT OF THE
AMERICAN BANKERS ASSOCIATION SAVINGS BONDS
COMMITTEE, STANDING IN FRONT OF HIS BANK.

**GLEN JOHNSON AND S.J. KRYZSKO, PRESIDENT
OF WINONA NATIONAL & SAVINGS BANK DURING
INTERVIEW "PROFILE OF A PATRIOTIC BANKER."**

**GLEN JOHNSON AND BANKER S.J. KRYZSKO, PRESIDENT
OF THE BANKERS SAVINGS BOND CAMPAIGN.**

A TREASURY DINNER IN WASHINGTON, DC WITH S.J. AND
MRS. KRYZSKO OF THE ABA SAVINGS BONDS COMMITTEE
(BEHIND RESERVED SIGN). COMMITTEE MEMBER JOE JONES
AND HIS WIFE, SEATED TO THE RIGHT WITH CHARLIE
DOLSON, ON THE LEFT. GLEN JOHNSON AND FAMILY ARE IN
THE FOREGROUND, DAVID, LORI, LAVONNE & GLEN.

The kicker was that I actually had to get 100 cowhides and put
the brand on the cowhides before the iron was dipped in gold. It was
quite a project. The hides were framed and in place, so President
Johnson could give them to each of the heads of the State Banker
Associations as a gift from the White House and as a tribute to my
good friend, S.J. Kryzsko.

—Associated Press

A BRANDING IRON FOR A TEXAN

President Johnson, a Texas. ranch owner, makes a close inspection of a branding iron presented to him in the Cabinet Room of the White House. The gift came from the execu-tive committee of the Volunteer State Chair-men for Savings Bonds. The branding end of the iron is in the shape of a Minuteman, symbol of the savings bond program.

EVENING STAR, OCTOBER 16, 1968. "A BRANDING IRON FOR A TEXAN." PRESIDENT JOHNSON, A TEXAS RANCH OWNER, MAKES A CLOSE INSPECTION OF A BRANDING IRON PRESENTED TO HIM IN THE CABINET ROOM OF THE WHITE HOUSE.

GLEN HOLDING THE BRANDING IRON AND FRAMED,
BRANDED COWHIDE CREATED AS GIFTS TO BE
PRESENTED BY PRESIDENT LYNDON JOHNSON.

S.J. KRYZSKO, RETIRING CHAIRMAN OF THE ABA SAVINGS BONDS
COMMITTEE, BEING PRESENTED WITH A COWHIDE BRAND OF
THE MINUTEMAN STATUE, WHICH LYNDON JOHNSON REQUESTED
THAT GLEN HAVE MADE ESPECIALLY FOR THE OCCASION.

FOR ABA SAVINGS BONDS
COMMITTEE MEMBERS,
ABA STATE CHAIRMEN,
AND STATE ASSOCIATION
SECRETARIES

SAVINGS BONDS BULLETIN

THE AMERICAN BANKERS ASSOCIATION

April   1968

Annual Committee Meeting-Chairman Kris' Trip To West Coast Highlight Spring Activities

A.B.A. Savings Bonds Committee Regional Vice Chairmen and State Coordinators, members of the Executive Committee of Volunteer State Chairmen and Treasury officials pose on the steps of Main Treasury before their luncheon at the Federal Reserve Board.

Much has happened since our October Bulletin and, generally speaking, the news has been good. Efforts to improve Committee efficiency and assure closer liaison between our members and the Savings Bonds Division's Regional and State Directors have resulted in the publication of an updated and expanded version of our organization booklet. Apparently, both volunteers and Treasury staffers are heeding its plea for the development of closer working relationships because our State Coordinators are more active than ever in local promotional activities.

ABA SAVINGS BONDS COMMITTEE REGIONAL VICE CHAIRMEN AND STATE COORDINATORS, MEMBERS OF THE EXECUTIVE COMMITTEE OF VOLUNTEER STATE CHAIRMEN, AND TREASURY OFFICIALS POSE ON THE STEPS OF MAIN TREASURY BEFORE THEIR LUNCHEON AT THE FEDERAL RESERVE BOARD. MARCH 13, 1968. LEFT TO RIGHT—FIRST ROW—JOHN T. WELCH, JR., ABA; A. EDWARD KENDIG, STATE CHAIRMAN; ROBERT C. HUSSEY, ABA; GLEN R. JOHNSON, NATIONAL DIRECTOR; WILLIAM G. DAVEY, ABA; E. M. BLACK, ABA; S. J. KRYZSKO, ABA; RAPHAEL H. O'MALLEY, REGIONAL DIRECTOR; RENO ODLIN, STATE CHAIRMAN.

(CAPTION CONTINUED NEXT PAGE)

Recently LaVonne and I looked at the documentary, *The Ken Burns'
America: The Congress.* While we were watching this episode of the
series, I told LaVonne that if I had a dollar for every mile that I walked
in the Capital, Senate, and House office buildings I would be a millionaire. I covered a lot of time and a lot of miles in Washington, DC.

I had one more very important meeting at the White House near
the end of President Johnson's term. I had worked with both Houses
of Congress and the Administration to make all of the Savings Bonds
personnel Civil Service, so that they couldn't be removed by politics.

My goal when I got to be National Director was to put the whole
division under Civil Service. I achieved that goal on the last day
possible. The Civil Service Commission approved it, and I got both
Houses of Congress to approve it. I sat in the White House for eight
hours waiting for the President to sign it. I knew that if I didn't, it
wouldn't get signed, and it would never happen. That was just one
of the times that I waited for the President.

In the end, I got everybody else's jobs locked in before the change
of administration. However, I didn't have quite enough time to guarantee my own. My position, which was still a Schedule C (appoint-
ive), was of course not covered by the changes, and would be up for
grabs after the transition in the White House.

TREASURY DEPARTMENT

SAVINGS BONDS DIVISION

OFFICE OF PUBLIC AFFAIRS / COMMUNICATIONS ★ WASHINGTON, D. C., 20226

PHONE CONTACT -- 202/964-5775

<u>RELEASE ON RECEIPT</u>   May 16, 1968

<u>TREASURY, IBAA OFFICIALS CONFER ON SAVINGS BONDS PROGRAM</u>

Representatives of the Treasury's Savings Bonds Division and members of the Government Fiscal Policy Committee of the Independent
Bankers Association of America met recently to discuss the Savings Bonds Program.

The IBAA, at its annual convention in Houston, passed a resolu-
tion lending its approval and pledging its continued support of
the Savings Bonds Program.

Left-to-right (clockwise) -- W. F. Enright, Jr., Senior Vice
President, American National Bank of St. Joseph, Mo.; Glenn H.
Larson, President, First State Bank, Thompson Falls, Mont.; Milton
J. Hayes, Senior Vice President, American National Bank and Trust
Company of Chicago; Marshall Barnes, President, Beaver Dam Deposit
Bank, Beaver Dam, Ky.; John A. Jenkins, Board Chairman and Presi-
dent, Pinellas Central Bank & Trust Company, Largo, Fla.; Rod L.
Parsch, Executive Vice President, Lapeer County Bank and Trust
Company, Lapeer, Mich.; Glen R. Johnson, National Director, U. S.
Savings Bonds Division; T. H. Milner, IBAA President and Presi-
dent, National Bank of Athens, Ga.; B. Meyer Harris, President,
Yellowstone Bank, Laurel, Mont.; Carl M. Floyd, Senior Vice Presi-
dent, Fulton National Bank, Atlanta, Ga.; S. E. Babington, Presi-
dent, Brookhaven Bank and Trust Company, Brookhaven, Miss.; Harold
B. Master, Coordinator for Banking and Volunteer Activities, U. S.
Savings Bonds Division; O. K. Johnson, Consultant, Whitefish Bay
Bank & Trust, Whitefish Bay, Wis.; and C. Herschel Schooley, Manager, Washington, D. C., Office, IBAA.

o0o

MAY 16, 1968 NEWS RELEASE FROM THE TREASURY DEPT.
REGARDING THE INDEPENDENT BANKERS ASSOCIATION
OF AMERICA SAVINGS BOND DISCUSSION.

August 27, 1968

SPECIAL MEMORANDUM

TO: All Staff Members

FROM: Glen R. Johnson

When I was named National Director of the U. S. Savings Bonds Division eighteen months ago, one of my major objectives was to get our field staff into the competitive service.

Now that objective has become a reality.

The following official announcement appeared today in the Federal Register:

"Section 213.3105 is amended to show that positions of State Director, Deputy State Director, Regional Director, and Assistant Regional Director, U. S. Savings Bonds Division, will no longer be excepted under Schedule A after September 28, 1968. Effective September 29, 1968, paragraph (d) of 213.3105 is revoked.

United States Civil Service Commission,
     James C. Spry, Executive Assistant
     to the Commissioners."

In effect, this transfers all of our field promotional positions, both in the regions and the states, from the excepted category into the competitive service.

We are indebted to top Treasury officials and the Civil Service Commission for their fine cooperation in making this action possible.

Full details of the procedures we will follow to effect the transfer into the competitive service will reach you within a few days.

AUGUST 27, 1968 STAFF MEMO FROM GLEN JOHNSON ANNOUNCING THE EMPLOYMENT STATUS CHANGE TRANSFERRING ALL FIELD STAFF POSITIONS INTO THE COMPETITIVE SERVICE.

~ 17 ~

Nixonized

NIXON ENTERED THE picture in January 1969. Many CEOs of high caliber wrote the new President and the new Secretary of the Treasury, David Kennedy about my accomplishments. I had received a high honor from the Treasury for signing up the 5.5 million new payroll savers. We had set all kinds of records. When the Republicans came into office, they received letters from Ford and General Motors, the aircraft companies, and other businesses and corporations about my job performance.

TAKEN AT THE U.S. INDUSTRIAL PAYROLL SAVINGS
COMMITTEE MEETING HELD AT STATE DEPARTMENT,
WASHINGTON. PICTURED ARE SECRETARY OF THE TREASURY
DESIGNATE DAVID M. KENNEDY, NATIONAL DIRECTOR GLEN
R. JOHNSON, AND F. CRAWFORD SMITH, STAFF MEMBER.

David Kennedy said, "We want you to stay on and work through the transition with us. You're going to continue to be in your post." Both of the Under Secretaries told me the same thing.

I worked through the transition, and everything appeared fine. I was feeling pretty confident and was even at the Nixon Inaugural. The transition of government required significant work.

Nixon came to see me. There were 13 Assistant Secretaries, and he made it a point to visit each one. This included the heads of the Secret Service, the Mint, the Bond Program, and other assistant secretaries. I had two offices at the time, and he came over to the one at the Treasury.

The President greeted me warmly and said, "I've never received so many letters of commendation for anyone in my life as I have on your behalf." He started naming the writers. Then he spent about 15 or 20 minutes with me; I talked about the bond program and what our goals were for the coming year. He thanked me, and then went on to visit others.

Two days later I got a call from David Kennedy, Secretary of the Treasury, saying that I was going to be replaced. I said, "You just asked me to stay."

He said, "Well, things have changed."

I persisted and said, "Changed, how?"

He then told me that John Ehrlichman, the Counsel and Assistant to Nixon for Domestic affairs, had told Richard Nixon that I had run Hubert Humphrey's campaign for the Senate in the 7th congressional district of Minnesota in 1960.

Two days before Nixon came to visit me he had signed the order that I would be leaving. He discussed the work I had done and all the commendations I had gotten. The discourse was completely phony. I was fired at that time; he'd already signed the notice. All he would have had to do was to tell me that I was being replaced, and he knew it.

I had a big battle with David Kennedy. I said, "You tell me to stay, and now you tell me to go." David said, "Well, I have my orders. You have to go. You have two weeks."

I said, "You know what? I'll make you a bet. I'll bet you are the first one to leave the new administration." He took that as an affront and wasn't very pleasant. He finally wished me well, and I left his office and prepared to leave the Treasury in two weeks.

Not surprisingly, guess who was the first one to leave the Nixon Administration? It was David Kennedy, which I had predicted. That's the Nixon saga. I never had contact with David Kennedy again.

I have a picture with Secretary Kennedy, Secretary Fowler, Secretary Barr, and me. In the group there were three secretaries from the Treasury, former, present, and future. That is interesting because the photo was taken at a bond meeting during the transition, and therefore, both sides were already in place.

R.J. Miller was the CEO at Ford Motor, and I now needed a new car. I called him and said, "I understand that you have a whole fleet of cars that have been driven by officers that you now sell at a big

INCOMING SECRETARY OF THE TREASURY DAVID KENNEDY (1969–71), WITH SECRETARY HENRY FOWLER (1965–68), NATIONAL SAVINGS BOND DIRECTOR GLEN JOHNSON, AND SECRETARY JOSEPH BARR (1968–69).

discount." He said, "Glen, come and pick one out. I'll assign someone to take care of you."

I was still with the Treasury, and in fact, still had a week to go. I flew into Detroit and met the person that R.J. Miller had told me to meet. There were about 2,000 cars in the lot, and I was told to take my pick.

I got a big Mustang, which was one of the 460s. Only a few had been built, in fact a vice president had driven that particular car. He'd actually followed it through the assembly line, so it was welded well, and everything was put together well. It was a beautiful, green car. I bought the car for $2,500, a real giveaway. I drove it back to Reston, Virginia, which was a five hour drive. The car would get up to 120 MPH, and made you feel like you were standing still. When I got home, I called R.J. and said, "Thank you."

◯ 18 ◯

Friends . . . Who Happened
to be Politicians

BACK IN THE days as secretary of Minnesota's 7th congressional district, I had a meeting to attend in the small town of Benson. I received a call from the Minnesota State Central Committee asking if I could give a ride to a young attorney that was to attend the same meeting. On Sunday, as I approached the intended intersection in my 1936 Ford, there was dust everywhere, and someone standing on the corner just as planned.

I opened the door, and he hopped in and introduced himself. He said, "Glen, I'm Fritz Mondale." We have been friends ever since. After the meeting, he got a separate ride back to Minneapolis, and I went back home.

Mondale became Attorney General of Minnesota. Whenever I went to lobby, I would always use Fritz's office. Usually I went there when he was off some other place, so I would sit at his desk with my feet on his desk until he returned. That got to be a real joke. When he would come back, he always said he knew immediately who it was because the only guy who would dare put his feet on his desk was Glen Johnson. That went on all through the days when he was in state government in Minnesota.

When Mondale was in the U.S. Senate, if we had various problems in the mutual fund industry, I would seek him out as a source with questions on what to do and who to see. He was always very good at steering me in the right direction.

FROM THE TOP LEFT, HUBERT H. HUMPHREY, GLEN JOHNSON
AND WALTER MONDALE ARE PICTURED ON THE OFFICIAL
PROGRAM FOR THE ANNUAL MINNEAPOLIS AQUATENNIAL
CELEBRATION THAT BEGAN IN 1939. PICTURED ON THE COVER
ARE MINNESOTANS, EITHER BORN OR MADE FAMOUS IN THE STATE
OF MINNESOTA, THAT WERE FEATURED IN THE 1977 CELEBRATION.
DURING THE 1977 AQUATENNIAL PARADE, GLEN WAS IN THE RUMBLE
SEAT OF A MODEL A FORD WITH TOM BROKAW. RIDING IN THE
FRONT SEAT WAS HAROLD STASSEN, THE PERENNIAL PRESIDENTIAL
CANDIDATE. ALL WERE FROM MINNESOTA, OF COURSE.

When he was nominated for vice president, I was a delegate
from Pennsylvania, and I seconded his nomination in the delegation. There was a nominating speech, followed by three speeches to
second his nomination. I gave the first speech to second him. I had
known him personally for a lot of years before he was recommended
for the position.

During his years as a senator, Mondale served on the bank-ing committee. At one point in his vice presidency, the Minnesota Bankers had a special meeting with him in Washington. There were about 40 of the bankers attending. Vice President Mondale's office was in the Executive Office Building. As vice president he was very busy, and all the bankers were sitting around in his room waiting for him. I went up to his huge desk and put my feet up on it. As Mondale came walking in, he said, "Only Glen Johnson would have his feet on my desk." He went on to talk about our long-time relationship.

GLEN JOHNSON, VICE PRESIDENT
MONDALE, AND NEAL PETERSON.

Incidentally, Federated Investors had a meeting of approximately 200 clients in Washington, nearly every year. Usually we had a sena-tor such as Senator Graham from Florida speaking on subjects that would be of interest to the bankers. I had invited Fritz Mondale to speak, and of course, my Republican friends and more Conservative friends said, "What in the world is he going to say?" Even our lawyer Gene Maloney, my close associate at Federated said, "Do you think that's a good idea?"

Mondale just literally set the place on edge with his address. He gave the most tremendous speech, and the crowd stood with lengthy applause. Afterwards many people came to me saying, "Wow! That was a real deal you put together."

Mondale went on to become Ambassador to Japan after he served as Vice President, which would have been during the Clinton years. He used to call me from time-to-time and tell me what he was doing. When he decided that he was going to resign as ambassador to Japan, he called me and told me that he wanted me to be the first to know his plans.

Both Walter Mondale and Hubert Humphrey were close friends, and I have considered each mentors. I thought the world of both of them. They were honest, and their only concerns were to do the right thing for the people they represented.

Hubert Humphrey and I flew back to Minneapolis on the same plane next to each other after he was diagnosed with terminal cancer. We had two hours to reminisce about all the things that we had

VICE PRESIDENT MONDALE AND GLEN JOHNSON AT A
FEDERATED INVESTORS MEETING IN WASHINGTON, DC
WHERE THE VICE PRESIDENT WAS THE MAIN SPEAKER.

done. We drank a lot of booze on that flight, and they had to pour us off the airplane. He knew at that time that he didn't have long to live. That was very sad.

Politics is a situation of being at the right place at the right time with the right ideas with the right kind of economy and the right kind of businesses and political climate. In politics, timing is everything. Hubert's timing just wasn't meant to be, and if some of the liberal supporters such as McCarthy and other left-wingers had come to his support, he certainly would have been elected and would have been President of the United States. Perhaps I would have ended up as Under Secretary of the Treasury or another position of similar influence.

But, just as Richard Nixon did me a favor by firing me, I was fortunate that I didn't wind up with a new position in government, because eventually I would have wound up somewhere else, and that might not have been with Federated Investors. Undoubtedly, Federated Investors was "the biggest break of my life."

Part 3

Love of Sales

It is not the critic who counts;
not the one who points out how
the strong man stumbled or how
the doer of deeds might have done
them better. The credit belongs to
the man who is actually in the
arena, whose face is marred with
sweat and dust and blood; who
strives valiantly; who errs and
comes up short again and again;
who knows the great enthusiasm,
the great devotions, and spends
himself in a worthy cause; who, if
he wins, knows the triumph of high
achievement, and who, if he fails, at
least fails while daring greatly, so
that his place shall never be with
those cold and timid souls who
know neither victory or defeat.

Theodore Roosevelt

THEODORE ROOSEVELT. HIS SPEECH,
"CITIZENSHIP IN A REPUBLIC," WAS DELIVERED
AT THE SORBONNE, PARIS, APRIL 23, 1910.

~ 19 ~
Will the Real Glen Johnson Please Stand Up?

IN MARCH OF 1969, I did a self-assessment of Glen Johnson. I wanted to know what my strengths were. It was time to decide what type of job in the private sector I should get.

The area of sales was interesting to me. Perhaps marketing is a better word than sales, but when people asked me what I do or have done, I always say I'm a salesman. I've been president of a lot of mutual funds, but what I actually did was sell. It is pure and simple: I love to sell.

When I left the Treasury, I had been in a high level position. I knew that to get a similar job in private enterprise was going to be very difficult. I had many friends in the big companies, but you don't get into big companies at the top, you go in at the bottom and climb the corporate ladder. They all felt for me because I was out of a job and had a young family. I had a mortgage and didn't have a lot of money. We'd been living on the salary of a government employee, which at that time wasn't like it is today.

As I was going through the self-assessment, it was apparent that there were three main areas I'd had experience with: sales and lobbying, management, and the newspaper business.

Because of my previous experience in the newspaper business, I was offered some jobs typesetting right off the bat. I could set two and one-half galleys of type an hour, which is top speed for a linotype. I could have gone back and set type at some place, it's true.

However, once you've run a division of government, and you're at the top at 39 years old, you don't *really* want to go back to setting type.

Outside of being the chief institutional sales person along with my staff, I was also the chief lobbyist. It may not have been hard to replace me in the sales side, but having someone who understood politics as I did would have been hard to replace on the political side. My Treasury days had provided me with numerous contacts. I knew half the members of the Senate and a fourth of those in the House because I had to frequently testify on one side of an issue or the other. Sometimes I would get a call from the Secretary saying that he had to go some place, or he had to be at a Congressional Hearing that day, and he would ask me to take his place.

That can be the most discouraging thing in the world if you are on the opposite side of the issue of the chairman of that particular committee. The whole time you are talking, the chairman is busy visiting with his staff and others. When someone else gets up to talk on the other side of the issue, the gavel goes down, and everybody has to be silent. I've had some horrible experiences with that sort of thing. You learn a lot when you have to learn on the job as I did.

Through these experiences, I'd met many politicians, and they were all friendly and receptive. They were acquaintances, so I thought that I really should look in quasi-government or the lobbying area for some big company. Being a lobbyist was something I was good at. That's what led me to consider Gulf Oil because I knew they had big lobbyists in Washington.

I received an invitation to become second in command to Chairman Bob Dorsey in the lobbying department of Gulf Oil. I had known Bob during my savings bond days, and he was a solid supporter of ours. My interview with Dorsey took place in Pittsburgh, which incidentally was my first time to visit that city. After weighing the opportunity carefully, and being mindful that it wasn't a top position, I chose not to take the job. I chose instead to continue to search for a position where I would be in control.

In hindsight, I learned that I'd made the right decision. Bob Dorsey was later sentenced for bribery of foreign countries to buy certain products. Dorsey was under indictment. Several senior Gulf executives were also affected negatively. If I had been in that administration, it would have been a very difficult situation.

Out of the blue, I received a call from someone telling me about Motivational Systems, a company out of New York. I simply cannot remember who he was or what his title was, but he had read about my background. He was calling to request an interview in New York.

Three Jewish men operated Motivational Systems, Inc. The owner, Morrie Goldwasser, interviewed me and explained what the job entailed. When I took the job, I really took it because I needed to do something, and I needed to do it soon. At that point in life we didn't have a lot of savings, and our children were in school. I took the job thinking, "We'll see how this works."

Credit cards were just exploding in the bank world, and there was great competition to see who could get the most customers. Motivational Systems made money by selling credit card marketing programs to the businesses that would offer credit. They simply printed a copyrighted application for a fraction of a penny and sold them for four or five cents each.

The product was easy to sell because it was a great concept. In this system, if the customer applied and scored 21 points, they qualified for a credit card. It was rather ingenious. The businesses worried that if they didn't buy it, their competition would. Our program was probably the most successful program out there to get people to apply for a credit card.

After taking the job, I was given a secretary and office space in New York. Sixteen states were assigned to me where I would have the exclusive right to sell this franchise product. I was also on a $30,000 a year draw against my sales, which was 10 percent of the billing prices. I was very successful with Motivational.

⁓ 20 ⁓
Being a Good Salesman

OBJECTIONS ARE THE signs that lead to the sale. In order to be a good salesman, it is important that you know your product. I knew my product, and I knew it well and could counter just about any objection. If a potential customer did not want to buy a product because of its expense, I would say, "Look, it's a better price than anybody else is offering. If you need the product, this is the one you should have."

Over the years, I've hired a lot of salespeople. The only elderly salesman I had on my staff was a man from Florida by the name of Jim Page. He would actually put up a checklist of about 15 points when he was selling. He'd go through every one of those points, and that's how he taught the people who worked for him.

Interestingly, I found that the more educated someone is, the harder it is to make a salesman out of him. A person with an MBA will probably be a lousy salesman. Desire to get ahead, however, is so important. When I interviewed someone, I would ask what their goals were. If they responded that their goal was to get my position, they would be the person I wanted to hire.

Two of the best salesmen I have ever known were totally opposite in their approaches. The regional director of the Savings Bonds Division, Jack Kemberly, from Des Moines, Iowa would say, "Now tell me how you would do this?" He would let you sell yourself on the idea.

On the other hand, Morrie Goldwasser with Motivational Systems was the opposite; he was subtle, and he stayed with you until you had no more objections, and you had no choice but to buy.

Most of selling involves having a decent product and something that people want. When we first started selling in the bank industry, a "mutual fund" was a bad word. You did not want to talk mutual funds in a bank. As a result, we just talked about cash management. We called it Cash Management Systems. When we answered the phone, it wasn't "Mutual Fund X," rather we always answered with "Cash Management Department." That worked.

I made 400 calls on banks before I made my first sale of the money market product. Once I sold that first bank trust department, I knew others would fall into place, and they did. It helped to know my product well.

I have probably made over 5000 sales calls, and I think it's more than that, and I've said that I've sold three trillion dollars worth of mutual funds, but it may actually be double that. One time someone did try to figure the dollars out, but I know it's in the trillions.

Anyone who has ever worked with me knows what a stickler I am on timeliness. It's just something inherent to someone who has spent his life as a salesman. Out of all the sales calls I have made in my lifetime, I have only been late for two. Once it was because I was stuck in the Fort Pitt Tunnel in Pittsburgh for four hours, and the second time was when we were delayed at O'Hare Field in Chicago for three hours. Other than that, I can't remember a single time that I have ever been late for an appointment. It would be safe to say that 98 percent of the time I am early. That's one of the lessons you learn in being a salesman: Never be late for a sales call, because the customer doesn't wait for you.

All of the people who sold for me were taught the importance of timeliness, often the hard way. When we had a staff meeting scheduled for 8:00 a.m. I would lock the conference room door at 8:00 a.m. Anybody who wasn't already through that door wasn't going to sit in on the meeting. My sales staff found out in short order that if that happened more than once or twice, and could have been prevented, they would be looking for a new job. The importance of timeliness for a salesman is as important as knowing your sales message.

I do remember a time when I was to meet up with LaVonne, and I said, "Well, I'll meet you at such and such a street in two and one-half minutes." At that she blew her stack! She said, "You aren't running a railroad!" I guess I can't blame her because I was pinning the meeting down to the last 30 seconds. At any rate, even more importantly, it wasn't a sales call.

This personal policy worked to my advantage when I arrived 30 minutes early for a presentation by Secretary of the Treasury Rubin.

To Glen Johnson,

Robert E. Rubin

GLEN'S TIMELINESS EARNED HIM THE RIGHT TO AN
IMPROMPTU PRIVATE MEETING WITH THE SECRETARY
OF THE U. S. TREASURY ROBERT E. RUBIN, WHO SERVED
DURING THE CLINTON ADMINISTRATION.

He had also arrived comfortably early, which opened the door to an unexpected private discussion time. This was a priceless interaction.

Another memory was when I was to meet with a prospective employee to interview him in New York. I set the interview for 8:00 a.m. in the lobby of the Helmsley Palace. Of course, I was there considerably earlier, as was typical for me. At 7:30 a.m. a gentleman came over and introduced himself. He asked if I was Glen Johnson, and when I said that I was, he told me he was the person for the interview. I told him that I wasn't used to people being a half an hour early.

The gentleman shared an interesting story about having played football for Vince Lombardi. He had never met Lombardi before arriving at camp, and he arrived a half-hour early. He walked up to Lombardi and introduced himself, whereupon Lombardi said, "You are only a half an hour early, and with Lombardi that is almost late." I will never forget those words because it emphasizes the importance of being on time.

I recall one night when we were leaving Atlanta after a successful conference day. I'd informed everybody it was wheels up at 11:00 p.m., and that the limo would leave the hotel promptly at 10:30 p.m. At 10:30 p.m. just about everyone was in the limo, when one of the people from administration came over and said, "Just a minute while I go and close up the booth, check out of my room, and let somebody know that I am leaving." At that point I simply said to him, "Goodbye." He learned the hard way, just as many of my salesmen did, that being on time was not only important, but if you weren't on time, you got left behind.

21

The Chance Encounter
That Changed My Life

IN THE MIDST of the hard work, I will say I have encountered many lucky breaks along life's way as well. I worked hard at Motivational Systems and had sold the credit application franchises to literally all 16 states, and most of them were all five-year contracts. That meant that if I never walked out of my office door again at Motivational Systems, I had assured myself $50,000 a year for the next five years. That amount was for commissions on sales I had previously made. At that point I wasn't all that concerned about my future income.

I was in Minneapolis on business to secure bids for the large-scale print job we needed at Motivational Systems. We needed hundreds of thousands and even millions of credit card applications for potential customers. One of the places I called on for a bid was Sorenson Printing. It was through that call that I would wind up affiliated with Federated.

As it happened, the day after I had been there, Chuck Wallander, from Federated Investors was at Sorenson's. While waiting for the print job to be completed, Wallander casually chatted with Ken Sorensen, the owner of the printing company. He mentioned that Federated was looking for someone who had a Treasury background to sell the company's new fund. Ken said, "At the risk of losing a really good customer, I had such a person in my office yesterday."

"Glen Johnson was National Director of the Savings Bond Program," Sorensen told Wallander. "It sold $50 billion worth last year." Wallander was intrigued. Savings bonds were paying only about

4%. "Anyone who could sell so much of something that returned so little had to be a persuasive salesman. What's he doing now?"

"I think he's looking for a job," the printing salesman said. "Nixon fired him because he was a Humphrey backer. Glen Johnson ran his campaign in Minnesota." Wallander's eyes lit up, "A Liberal. The press loves Liberals!"

My secretary in New York informed me someone from Pennsylvania was trying to reach me. I asked my secretary to tell him that Pennsylvania wasn't my territory, that I didn't cover the state, and that he should call someone else. The next day she told me the person had called again, and this time he had said he was with some mutual fund company. She informed me that his calls had nothing to do with what I was selling, and he wanted to talk to me.

I told her that if he called again to tell him that whatever he wanted, I was not interested. On the third day my secretary said the man had called again, and he was very impatient. She said he really wanted to talk to me, and she asked me to please give him a call because he had been calling every hour.

Finally, I called the number in Pittsburgh. It was a direct line to Charlie Wallander with Federated Investors, and he kept talking and talking about the company. He told me about the new fund they had started. It was a fund in government securities, and it wasn't selling well. Charlie said they needed someone to promote it and sell it and asked if I would be interested in looking at the job.

He said the business was located in Pittsburgh, and I told him that I really didn't care to leave Washington because I had so many contacts there. Everyone in Washington was familiar it seemed, and I really didn't want to leave and go to a strange city.

Charlie wanted to come to Washington to interview me. He said he and his chairman would come to see me. I had just returned home from being on the road, and Friday was my day to make appointments for the following week. I did, however, agree to meet with Chuck Wallander and Jack Donahue at the TWA hospitality room at the Washington, DC airport on Friday.

Wallander and Donahue met with me and went through their whole scenario. I gave them some background on myself and told them of some of the recommendations from people in the Treasury and others throughout the country. They seemed very enthused about my joining their company. When I asked where the job was, they again said it would be in Pittsburgh. At that point I reiterated I really had no interest in leaving Washington, and that I thought this meeting was over. I stood and started walking out the door. Jack followed me and asked to talk about it further.

He told me my job would be to travel. I would be traveling all over the country, so he didn't really think it made any difference whether I lived in Pittsburgh or in Washington. At that point I agreed to come to Pittsburgh the following Monday and take a look at Federated.

Jack obviously had assembled Federated's entire board of directors for the meeting on Monday. We had lunch at the Duquesne Club, a very old men's club in Pittsburgh. The dark wood interior was adorned with magnificent artwork, and everything was in order. They were very enthusiastic about the possibility of my coming on board with them, and it certainly looked like an attractive job.

The job would be marketing the fund for the U.S. Government Securities; there was no sales staff at the time. The fund was a product that Federated had designed, and was the first mutual fund that invested in government securities. The fund had a great deal of interest for me because it was very similar to savings bonds, except that it paid a higher return because the money could be invested at a higher rate than savings bonds. Among the things we discussed was the possibility of starting payroll savings. At any rate, when I left the meeting, I agreed that I would get back to them in two weeks.

For the next two weeks I really made an effort to clean up some of the leads that I had at Motivational Systems, all the while thinking about switching jobs. It was literally the afternoon of the final day when I knew I had to tell Motivational I was leaving. I called Jack Donahue at Federated and accepted the job, and then planned to explain to my bosses that I was going to leave.

We were exhibiting at a credit card convention in Chicago when they got a call from Chase Manhattan Bank in New York. Chase wanted to take a closer look at the Motivational Systems product. New York was still open because no one had bought it as a franchise for their credit card operations. It really was huge to have a bank like Chase Manhattan interested.

The Motivational Systems people said they were all headed for New York, and had to be there to see if we could close this account. They asked me to take care of the hospitality suite while they were gone for the next several days. Just as they were getting in the elevator, I told them I was giving two weeks notice, and I was leaving Motivational. They asked me to go with them to the airport, so we could talk along the way.

All the way to the airport they tried to talk me out of leaving. They offered me a set salary plus stock in the company and made me all kinds of proposals. When we got to the airport, they got out, and I was still in the cab. They asked me if I was going to stay, and I answered, "No, I'll be leaving in two weeks."

For the next three days I manned the hospitality suite in Chicago. After that I spent the next week training a new salesman and trying to clean up my orders, because my agreement with them had always been to get paid my commissions upon my billings. The fact was, I had made many sales that were not yet billed.

When I started at Federated on tax day of that year, I informed Jack that Motivational refused to pay me the $5500 in commission I had earned, because it had yet to be billed. Jack simply said, "That's all right, we'll take care of it." That was my first experience with a fantastic company. My work at Federated began on April 15, 1970— over 40 years ago. I was given the title of President of the Fund for U.S. Government Securities. Wallander had pushed hard for me to receive the title, insisting I needed its credibility to sell the fund.

After just three days at Federated it became more apparent just how little I knew about mutual funds. I took the test materials home with me to study, and went back on Monday to take the securities exam. I passed the exam, and thereupon, started my career at Federated. It was time to "sell" Federated Investors.

~⌒ 22 ⌒~
Marketing the Federated Ideals

FEDERATED'S FUND FOR U.S. Government Securities gave the smaller investor a chance to share in the high returns received by large institutions and wealthy individuals. Federated increasingly looked to individual investors, deciding the best way to reach them was through the media. Of course, I knew dozens of financial editors from my savings bonds days, and now that I understood my subject, I could translate the arcane terminology of the financial world into concepts the average reader could understand.

I was persistent with my sales message; yet comfortable with the folks I was trying to help. The investment brokers needed to understand that the banks had taken their savers' money at 3% and 4%, and then made 2–3% by investing in government securities. At the same time, savings bonds holders were being urged to accept 4% on their money the first year.

To get the word out, I often arranged newspaper interviews between sales appointments. Typically, I arrived in a city a day early to sell the local financial editor on the news-worthiness of the government securities fund. Convincing brokers to market the fund to their clients was easier when I could pull out the local paper and say, "Did you see the article on us?"

In one such article, I explained that I thought it really was scandalous that so few mutual funds had arisen to help the middle class earn high yields. "I think it is just as patriotic to loan your money to the government at 7% as at 5%," I told the *Minneapolis Star* one time. "If you aren't getting 7% on your money, someone else is."

We had a press conference in New York where *The New York Post,* who had followed my career at the Treasury, put a big 8-column headline on the story, "Seven Percent Is Patriotic Too." This was when savings bonds were only paying 4%, and the fund I represented at Federated, which was the Trust for the U.S. Government Securities, was paying 7%. A number of newspapers picked up the story.

Some of the news stories were so glowing in their praise of the fund that they made some people at Federated nervous. Tom Donnelly, Federated's attorney and partner, was especially cautious about any hint of regulatory impropriety. None of the readers of these enthusiastic news articles had prospectuses. He told me that I'd better not promise something the fund couldn't deliver. I promised him I'd stop the impromptu interviews.

For the time being, Federated sought exposure through advertisements in publications like the *Wall Street Journal* and *Time* magazine. We also bought space in trade magazines like *American Cemetery* and *Cemetery Maintenance and Management,* between ads for Gravemaster dump trucks and aluminum markers and flower vases. Cemetery associations were perfect candidates for its government fund. These perpetual-care associations typically put their money in banks; every time the lawn was mowed or a grave was dug, someone had to transfer money from savings to checking. Federated's government securities fund could give these groups higher yields, invest the dividends, and wire them money whenever it was needed. The company eventually raised millions of dollars from cemetery associations.

We used brokers to help arrange some of the sales calls for us. The broker got the commission; Federated got the assets under management. A Denver broker once arranged for us to call on the treasurer of a pharmaceutical company in Salt Lake City. The treasurer greeted Richard Fisher and me as he walked in, then sat quiet the entire presentation. Finally he looked at us as if to say, "Are you done?" Then he said good-bye and left.

"What a waste of time," we thought. Yet, when we arrived back in Denver to lunch with our local broker, he almost ran across the dining room to welcome us. "I heard from our man in Salt Lake City," the broker said with a huge smile on his face. "You guys no sooner left his office than he wired $7 million to Federated."

Bolstered by brokerage business, the Fund for U.S. Government Securities was one of the top performing mutual funds in 1970, a disastrous year for the stock market. Of 464 funds rated by Arthur Lipper Corporation, only five closed out the first half of the year on the upside. Federated's government fund was the leading performer at that point and ranked seventh at the end of that year.

By March 1971, fund assets hit $50 million. The fund reached $100 million just nine months later, accounting for nearly a quarter of Federated's $400 million in assets. The fund's average account was $6,000, although one individual had $1 million in the fund. The largest shareholder was a midwestern church's building fund, with $2.3 million.

In the meantime, we just continued to seek publicity. *Nation's Business* told me that it was interested in doing a story on Federated's fund, but in the interest of fairness, only if the magazine also mentioned another government fund.

Immediately I thought of Bruce Bent, a young pension fund manager who had discussed a short-term fund idea with us about a year earlier, so I called him to tell him about the article. "Sounds great," said Bent. "Tell them our fund is called the Reserve Fund."

The article generated a number of leads for Federated and for the Reserve Fund, though it was still not yet eligible to sell shares. Shortly thereafter, the Reserve Fund became effective for sale, expanding its focus from short-term government securities to short-term certificates of deposit. The fund, which put almost nothing into marketing initially struggled, but received a life-saving publicity boost from the *New York Times*. Assets increased from $400,000 to $1.9 million in less than a month. News of the Reserve Fund began to spread quickly by word of mouth among investment counselors, brokers, and corporations. At the same time, short-term interest rates had risen to around 11%, spurred by surging loan demand, inflation, and the Fed's tight money policy. Almost before anyone knew it, the Reserve Fund attracted $15 million.

To Donahue, Federated's course seemed clear. The company had worked like crazy for months and raised $15 million through broker/dealers. It was a solid effort. By contrast, the Reserve Fund had raised the same amount in just a few months with no mutual fund marketing expertise or experience, and almost no effort.

"We're going into the money market business," Donahue decided.

Federated quickly put together its own no-load money market fund in the last half of 1973. Minimum investment was $1,000, and the fund would buy only the instruments that matured in a year or less. The fund declared dividends daily, making monthly cash payments, or reinvesting. A key was that each share's net asset value remained constant.

We registered the fund as the Federated Cash Management Fund, but an SEC lawyer objected. "You cannot manage cash," he said. "Pick a different name, and you can be effective tomorrow." So I thought about it for a moment and asked, "How about Money Market Management?" The SEC approved and the fund, initially paying 8.5%, was launched on January 16, 1974. Money Market Management also launched the widespread use of the term *money market,* giving birth to the generic name of a whole new financial industry.

The fund's initial publicity campaign consisted of two small newspaper ads. The ads generated 2,000 inquiries from almost every possible source: life insurance companies, credit unions, chemical companies, a monument supply firm, a dental school, an anesthesiology group, public school districts, hospitals, a baking cooperative, and fuel companies.

Individuals also flocked to the funds. On a flight to Pittsburgh, I ran into U.S. Congressman (later Senator) John Heinz of Pennsylvania of the Heinz Foods family of Pittsburgh. "Business must be terrible," Heinz said, referring to the stock market, which was struggling again.

"Not really," I told him, "we have this new money market fund." After the plane landed, the congressman made a deposit in the fund.

Federated seemed to make a sale every time one of us talked to someone on the street. Even the florist across from the office (where I was a frequent customer) put the shop's reserves into the fund.

FOR IMMEDIATE RELEASE

New fund provides short-term vehicle

By Eliot Janeway
Consulting Economist
Chicago Tribune Press Service

NEW YORK CITY — Any business is as good as its ability to sell—no better. What's wrong with the mutual funds business is just the condition of the stock and bond markets. Its ability to keep up with the changing moods of America's rich and restless money-using public is as striking as it ever was. Witness its characteristic ingenuity and flexibility in improvising an altogether new vehicle to suit the flight of liquidity into short-term, high-yielding instruments — the instruments smaller savers are anxious to have but don't know how to or are unable to buy for themselves.

"Cash equivalent funds" is the term for them. A number of established managements have moved into this investor service area. Pittsburgh-based Money Market Management, Inc., is one of them. Its president, Glen R. Johnson, explains the whys and wherefores.

JANEWAY: What is your Money Market Management Fund and how does it work?

JOHNSON: It's a no-load, professionally managed investment company, with a diversified portfolio, geared to attract varied corporate and individual investors into the short-term money markets. The higher income yields now available from investment in short-term "money market instruments" maturing in one year or less—bank certificates of deposit, commercial paper, United States Treasury bills, etc.—permit the individual as well as corporate investors to maximize their income by combining their funds with those of many other investors. In other words, the usual advantage of the mutual fund is directed in this case to the desire of investors to stay close to cash.

JANEWAY: What advantages do cash management funds offer?

JOHNSON: In exchange for making a minimum investment of $1,000 in one cash fund, shareholders enjoy full-time, day-by-day professional monotoring and management of their assets, regular payment of dividends, and the important option of complete liquidity when they want to retrieve their capital investment.

JANEWAY: How is dividend income paid?

JOHNSON: Since our portfolio is managed on an exacting daily basis, taxable dividends can be declared daily and either paid in cash monthly or reinvested.

JANEWAY: To what do you attribute your current success with your money market investments?

JOHNSON: Since we established this cash fund in January, 1974, we've increased our assets to $30 million. Higher interest rates on short-term borrowings are netting our shareholders 10 per cent on 11 per cent gross interest rates. We're now issuing investors "safe conduct passes" in a market where there is little or no chance of capital loss and there has been no fluctuation in net asset value. The higher income yields soar, the more more attractive this investment becomes.

JANEWAY: What kind of customers provide the backbone of your business?

JOHNSON: We now have about 5,000 shareholders, most of whom have invested within an average range of $6,000 to $8,000. But we also handle a great number of individual $1,000 accounts, as well as some on the $1 million level.

Our company is receiving about 500 letters a day directly from the investing public. It's notable that all these investors, in search of the highest yields on their capital, are willing to pay a one-half per cent management fee rather than invest independently. Of course, the $10,000 minimum on Treasury bills and the $100,000 minimum on the highest yielding C. D.s make it impossible for many investors to obtain the highest yields in any other way.

JANEWAY: What effect has the current interest rate surge had on your business activity?

JOHNSON: It's been enormously beneficial for our investors because we don't need to take any risks in order to get the highest return. My judgment is that interest rates are now in the plateau range, almost at their peaking point, but they will only level off if the inflationary trend recedes.

JANEWAY: What potential does a cash equivalent fund such as yours have to bolster stock market activity?

JOHNSON: We have been steadily building up a big reservoir of liquidity that will provide a good base for future investing, as well as an antidote for an illiquid stock market. The return of individual investors to mutual funds in any form is definitely a positive, tho gradual, basis for future stock market bullishness.

JANEWAY: What do you feel will spur the public to buy stocks and long-term securities again?

JOHNSON: Renewed confidence in the financial sector and in the market system as a whole is needed to get people from all professions and areas of the country back into a positive attitude toward investing.

CHICAGO TRIBUNE—NEW YORK NEWS SYND., INC.

CHICAGO TRIBUNE: "NEW FUND PROVIDES SHORT-TERM VEHICLE."

The Pittsburgh Press
Business & Finance
Sunday, Feb. 3, 1974

High-Yield Short-Term Issues Inspire New Mutual Fund Here

By WILLIAM H. WYLIE
Press Business Editor

Last year t h e dollar lost nearly 9 per cent of its buying power and prospects for 1974 a p p e a r worse.

R a c e horse I n f l a t i o n makes cash a hot commodity. Investors h a v e to keep their dollars e a r n i n g enough to offset Inflation's greedy bite. They can't let them gather dust.

Wylie

Once a favorite refuge, the stock market has lost its appeal. Now, short-term securities are in favor. But this is a fast-changing market, o n e that requires expertise. However, there are rewards.

If you bought 30-day bank certificates of deposit (CDs) in the current market, they would yield more than 9 per cent — not bad at all. But the minimum purchase is $100,000 — a stumblingblock.

One source said during the last six months of 1973 the yield on 30-day instruments was 7 to 10 per cent.

And Solomon Brothers, a New York investment banking firm, reported that short-term money market instruments outperformed bonds, which in turn did better than stocks.

So much for the advantages of investing in the short-term money market — how does one get into it?

In addition to the $100,000 minimum buy for bank negotiable certificates, minimums range from $50,000 to $150,000 for commercial paper issued by corporations. Even the initial purchase of Treasury bills must be $10,000.

That's no problem f o r corporate, institutional a n d wealthy individual buyers. B u t, obviously, t h e small investor is shut out.

Because short-term instru-

GLEN R. JOHNSON
Flexibility for investors.

m e n t s a r e so attractive, Federated Investors, a financial holding company based in Pittsburgh, has launched a mutual fund that trades in this market.

Called Money Market Management Inc., it is headed by Glen R. Johnson. He is also president of the Fund for U.S. Government Securities, a $100 million fund that deals exclusively in federal securities.

Johnson said Money Market Management also will invest in U.S. Government securities along with bank certificates of deposit, bankers acceptance notes, commercial paper and other money market obligations maturing in one year or less.

"Dividends will be declared daily aind paid monthly in cash or may be reinvested at net asset value," Johnson said.

Flexibility will be one of the fund's assets, he added. "An investor can get in one day and get out the next," he explained.

It would be practical, since t h i s is a "no-load" fund, meaning there's no charge for buying and selling shares.

"Until the first of May the minimum investment will be $1,000," Johnson said. "Afterwards the minimum will be $5,000."

He said the fund will woo corporations, organizations and individuals as investors. In the current market, he talks of an 8½ per cent return. Of course, the yield will rise and fall with the market.

Johnson said the fund will be a useful vehicle for brokerage firms. "This will give a broker an alternative when a customer wants to take his money o u t of stocks a n d bonds," he said.

Federated, which manages a dozen and a half funds, appears to have tapped a new market.

THE PITTSBURGH PRESS
34 Boulevard of the Allies
Pittsburgh, Pennsylvania 15230
(412) 263-1317

THE PITTSBURGH PRESS: "HIGH-YIELD SHORT-TERM ISSUES INSPIRE NEW MUTUAL FUND HERE."

PREPARED EACH WEEK FOR RESEARCH INSTITUTE EXECUTIVE MEMBERS / 589 FIFTH AVENUE / NEW YORK, N.Y. 10017

Items # 58-69
February 6, 1974

58 How to take advantage of today's high short-term interest rates

If you're looking for a place to put temporarily idle cash where it will earn interest and yet be instantly redeemable, you have a new alternative. It's Money Market Management, Inc., a no-load investment fund recently launched by the same group that started the Fund for U.S. Government Securities in 1970. (This is the second no-load fund of its type. ALERT reported on The Reserve Fund last September, #400, 9/12/73.)

Money Market Management is designed to enable individuals or companies to get a good return on their idle funds without becoming involved in the tricky business of buying and selling short-term instruments themselves. Investors buy shares in a portfolio consisting of U.S. Government securities, bank certificates of deposit, bankers acceptance notes, prime commercial paper, and other obligations maturing in less than one year. You receive dividends monthly, or you can have them reinvested automatically.

Net yield was recently about 8½%. Yield will fluctuate with changes in short-term interest rates, of course, but presumably will represent the maximum practical safe return possible at any given time. This is because the Fund's money managers buy and sell with two objectives in mind: 1) to stay invested in the highest-yielding instruments; 2) to maintain a stable asset value. (An idea of how both the yield level and the spread among yields can vary from time to time: On Jan. 1, 1974 a treasury bill yielded 7.4%, certificates of deposit 9.2% and commercial paper 9.2%. A year ago, bills yielded only 4.9% and the other two 5.5%.)

The minimum purchase is $1,000 until May 1, 1974, when it will go to $5,000. There's no sales charge to buy shares nor redemption fee to sell them. The fund takes a small share of earnings as its fee.

Investments can be made for a day, a week, or any number of days. An established customer can put funds in one day and withdraw them the next, earning interest for the day. Transactions are handled by telephone for investors with $25,000 or more in the fund, by mail for smaller accounts. Custodian for the Fund and its Transfer Agent is the State Street Bank and Trust Company in Boston. The President is Glen R. Johnson, one-time Director of the Savings Bond Division of the U.S. Treasury.

For a prospectus and other information, write to: Money Market Management, Inc., 421 Seventh Ave., Pittsburgh, Penna. 15219, (412) 288-1900.

Research Institute 2/6/74

ONE OF THE EARLY STORIES ABOUT MONEY MARKET
FUNDS IN A PUBLICATION CALLED *ALERT*.

I was very optimistic. "Money market funds are going to have $100 billion." My statements were seldom taken seriously; rather they were greeted with laughter from financial experts who insisted that the glitter of money market funds would eventually fade. They really thought I was naïve, suggesting that as short-term interest rates fell, and the spread between passbook savings and commercial paper narrowed, investors would search elsewhere, most likely to a resurgent stock market. The President of Wiesenberger Services, the publisher

The Funds

A Useful Yo-Yo

FOR ALMOST A YEAR, short-term interest rates have been tantalizingly high, as high as 11%, far above what savings banks are offering on their regular accounts. Trouble is, those juicy yields are unavailable for most individual investors. An investor needs at least $10,000, more realistically at least $100,000, to buy Treasury bills, bank certificates of deposit or commercial paper.

Why not a fund that would invest in these instruments? Here is a potentially lucrative market for the flagging industry—at least as long as short-term rates stay up. The answer is that there are already a couple of such funds and others may be on the way.

The first, which came out last month, is Money Market Management, an open-end, no-load fund "limited to money market instruments maturing in one year or less." Money Market is put out by Pittsburgh-based Federated Securities, which manages 16 other funds with total assets of $350 million. The minimum investment is only $1,000 ($5,000 after May 1), and annual expenses come to, at most, 1% of total assets. Thus, a portfolio yield of 8.5% will leave the investor at least 7.5%, still above most savings accounts.

Dreyfus Corp. (assets $2.2 billion), always quick to jump on any bandwagon, is launching its own short-term fund this month, and other fund managements are rumored to be readying theirs.

It's appropriate that Federated was first in this field. Four years ago, it was the first to start a fund for investing in government securities, named, suitably enough, Fund for U.S. Government Securities. Government Securities invests in long- and medium-as well as short-term government paper. As a result, there is no assurance the investor can get out at the same price he came in at. Thus last year, although the fund yielded 7%, the original investors suffered a decline in the market value of their holdings, which reduced the net yield to 4.2%.

The Money Market fund, by contrast, will be almost as safe as a bank. Whatever the investor puts in, he gets exactly that amount out—plus interest—even if he cashes in after a couple of days. How is this possible? Partly because the prices of short-term securities do not fluctuate very much. To the degree they *do* fluctuate, the fund protects itself with buy-back agreements and—if necessary—a slight shading of the dividend yield.

President of both funds is Glen Johnson, 44, an affable, hard-selling former head of the U.S. Treasury's Savings Bond division. "We have had," says Johnson, "the idea on the out of the stock market, the broker can suggest our fund as a temporary place to park his money."

Johnson is hopeful on smallish bank trust departments for much the same reason, ". . . the odds and ends in their trust accounts. I'm told the bookkeeping of putting that money in individual

PROSPECTUS
October 31, 1972

fund for U.S. Government Securities, Inc.

Designed to make it convenient to invest in a diversified portfolio of U. S. Government Securities

Federated Securities Corp.
Distributor

Prospectus
December 3, 1973

FUND FOR INVESTING IN GOVERNMENT SECURITIES, INC.

For investors interested in current income

AMERICAN EXPRESS

AMERICAN EXPRESS
INVESTMENT MANAGEMENT COMPANY
Adviser and Distributor

Imitation may be a sincere form of flattery, but Federated cried foul when American Express' subsidiary gave its new fund a name strikingly similar to Federated's. Federated has filed a complaint with the SEC. AEIMC claims it wanted a title descriptive of its fund's purpose and had no cribbing in mind. Retorts Federated's Johnson, "We pioneered the concept, and people are very confused, taking their fund for ours. When we asked the SEC for a copy of their registration statement, they sent us our own."

drawing boards for a couple of years." By May he hopes to have $100 million in Money Market.

Surprisingly, Johnson thinks only 10% to 15% of that money will come from individual investors. The rest of the money will come from brokers, bankers and corporations.

Why would *they* invest in a mutual fund? Explains Johnson, "It's a good way for brokers to pool all that odd-lot money they have in all their accounts. They don't have to worry about maturity dates. We will send them a read-out each day, and the firm can allocate it to each account. "Moreover, when a customer wants

savings accounts is mountainous. And at the moment, they're getting a far higher yield with us." Johnson also figures that corporate treasurers of small companies will take to the fund as well.

Johnson is aware that his new fund may be quite a yo-yo, losing money when short-term rates fall, pulling it in again when they go up. "We also," he concedes, "expect to lose the guy who wants to go back into stocks when the market recovers."

But yo-yo or not, the fund offers a useful service to investors and will probably return an honest dollar to its sponsors. ∎

STORY FROM *FORBES MAGAZINE* IN 1974 TITLED "A USEFUL YO-YO." A PROSPECTUS OF A COMPANY WHO STARTED ANOTHER FUND FOR GOVERNMENT SECURITIES. THEY COPIED THE FEDERATED PROSPECTUS LITERALLY WORD FOR WORD, BUT HAD TO CHANGE THEIR NAME BECAUSE FEDERATED ALREADY HAD THE NAME.

of mutual fund analyses, told *Time* magazine that money market funds are "a product of high interest rates and not a major trend."

But for the time being, interest rates were high, and interest in money market funds was growing rapidly. Sales of money market funds totaled $176.5 million in July 1974—doubling figures from a month earlier—boosting overall mutual fund sales to their highest level since 1971. Competition was intensifying, too, as many of the established mutual fund companies, such as Dreyfus and Fidelity, introduced money market funds.

Richard Fisher, who was supervising Federated's marketing effort at the office, believed it was time to take the money market message to the public. A Boston public relations company, C. Paul Luongo and Associates, had called Fisher looking for work, and he decided to give them an opportunity (though Donahue and Brown were initially aghast at the cost of publicity).

In the summer and fall of 1974, Luongo scheduled appearances for me in every conceivable major media outlet across the country. Luongo had a knack for stirring the competitive juices of the local media in a given city, thus inducing more coverage for Federated. He also had a sense of flair, enhancing the aura of success by typically booking my first appearance in each city at a press conference in one of the city's posh hotel suites. I was certainly busy. In 16 cities over 16 weeks, I did more than 50 magazine and newspaper interviews, including *Time, Newsweek,* and the *Wall Street Journal.* I appeared on almost 100 television talk shows such as *Wall Street Week* and *Good Morning America*, and was a guest on many radio shows. Fisher and Wallander occasionally made media appearances as well.

As with government securities, I always hammered home the "smaller investor" theme again and again. "Banks have had it their own way for too long," I told a reporter. "Do you realize that last week there was $211 billion in checking accounts throughout the country earning no interest?" I explained that money market funds offered higher returns to people who needed them. In fact, some elderly investors reported they were now able to make their rent payments from their interest.

Such stories helped make the seemingly mysterious, intimidating subject of money market funds a captivating subject even for

Business and finance

World of money

CHICAGO DAILY NEWS, Thursday, Feb. 14, 1974

How the little guy can get rich man's interest rate

Reuters News Service

NEW YORK — For years the little investor has been regarded as being at a disadvantage on the investment scene not only in terms of the lack of funds available for investment but more important from the standpoint of investment opportunities available and the range of professional services at his disposal.

As if these disadvantages were not enough, when it came to finding relatively secure income producing opportunities, the little guy found his hands firmly bound.

Under Regulation Q, the Federal Reserve System set a firm ceiling on his rate of return, which was viable only by severely curtailing liquidity.

At present the Regulation Q ceiling prohibits banks from paying over 5¼-per cent interest on savings deposits of under $100,000, unless the money is put in a time account.

Under time deposits, rates of up to 7½ per cent are permitted if the money is deposited for a period of four to seven years, with penalties for early withdrawal.

AT THE SAME time, though, the wealthy individual or company with over $100,000 to deposit could negotiate with the bank on the rate of return and duration of the deposit.

Furthermore, most of the highly liquid short-term investment avenues, such as certificates of deposits, bankers acceptances and the like, required minimum investments of at least $58,000 and mostly $100,000 or more, again effectively locking out the investor with limited means.

The situation may now be nearing a solution thanks to a new investment approach developed along the classical mutual fund model.

THIS NEW breed of mutual fund permits investors to participate in portfolios made up of high-yielding short-term obligations with minimum investments of $1,000 or $5,000, depending on the fund selected.

Basically, the new breed of funds are income funds and do not differ in their objectives from the traditional income funds. The departure is in the way the funds are invested.

There are three of the new type funds in operation. The largest and oldest is the New York-based Reserve Fund, with current assets of approximately $15 million.

The Reserve Fund spent a number of years in the planning stage before it was opened to the public in January of last year.

The second entry into the field was Money Market Management sponsored by Federated Investors Inc. of Pittsburgh and was followed a few days later by Dreyfus Liquid Assets Inc. sponsored by Dreyfus Corp.

STORY FROM THE *CHICAGO DAILY NEWS* REGARDING INTEREST RATES.

afternoon talk shows that otherwise centered on entertainment and fashion. Kathryn Crosby (Bing's wife), host of a San Francisco TV talk show, threatened to cancel my appearance when she learned the day's topic was money market funds, but I talked to her and convinced her that the audience would love it. Crosby was a fast learner, and the interview went smoothly. Almost 200,000 calls came into the call center during that hour and half long interview.

A funny thing happened in Chicago. After dropping me off at a TV station for a talk show interview, the limousine driver decided to wait inside rather than sit in the car. When the show's host took questions from the audience for me to answer, the first person to raise his hand was the limo driver. It seems that after several days of chauffeuring and listening to Luongo and me talk about money funds, the driver asked me just the right questions, leading to another successful appearance.

One of my primary goals during broadcast appearances was giving out Federated's toll-free Money Market Management telephone number. Many radio stations gave out the number readily, but other hosts made clear that they did not intend to provide Federated with advertising time they should pay for. Of course, this didn't stop me from routinely blurting out the number on radio shows before the host could respond and cut me off. In many cases, however, show hosts were so intrigued by money funds that they asked me to display the number so their listeners could learn more.

The appearances on these shows created leads. A Boston interview generated 3,000 leads; a St. Louis guest spot led to 5,000 more. My appearance on *Wall Street Week* pulled in 8,000 leads. Even when our toll-free number wasn't shown, some shows got so many calls that their own operators gave the number out just to relieve their phone lines.

To handle the leads that inevitably followed the TV and radio appearances, a room was set up at the Federated office with eight desks and eight phone lines. The full-time staff handled the calls during the day. But many shows were at night, sometimes on the West Coast, which could mean an avalanche of phone inquiries as late as 2:00 a.m. in Pittsburgh. To handle the calls, Federated hired part-time workers to answer the phones (some, like Mark Bloss, later became key sales representatives). Several full-time employees even volunteered to help.

Ten minutes before I would go on the air in another city, I would be sure to alert the phone staff in Pittsburgh. I typically had no trouble getting the toll free number on the air. When I did, the calls would start coming, and the phone room would become a madhouse. The staff took just enough time per call to get a prospect's name and address; the next day, they scrambled to send out hundreds of brochures and prospectuses. After my appearance on *Wall Street Week* on a Friday night, so many people called for information about Money Market Management that a makeshift staff worked straight through the weekend to get it out as quickly as possible.

One listener decided to go directly to the horse's mouth. After a late-night appearance in Cincinnati, I finally got to sleep about 2:00 a.m. The phone rang one hour later.

"Were you the fellow on the radio a bit ago?" said the voice on the other end.

"Yeah," I mumbled.

"I want to come down to the hotel and make an investment."

"It's the middle of the night!"

"But I want to meet you."

"Okay, meet me in the hotel lobby tomorrow morning."

The next morning, as I waited, a man wearing coveralls and boots approached me, shook my hand, and handed over to me a paper bag containing $840,000 in cash. "I'd like you to invest this for me," he said.

"I can't take that."

"Hey, I'm sold. Take it."

I escorted the gentleman across the street to a bank, counted the money, and wired it to State Street Bank and Trust Company in Boston, custodian of the fund.

Of course, mix-ups did occur occasionally. Federated's toll-free number, without the 800 prefix, was the same as the home phone of a Fidelity Fund director who lived in Boston. Sure enough, after I appeared on a show in Boston, the director's wife got some 200 phone calls. She patiently explained the mistake to each caller. I was certain to send her a huge bouquet of flowers. Her husband, a business acquaintance of mine, kidded me for years that he had missed his chance to take away Federated business.

Federated's media blitz, the first widespread campaign to take the story of money market funds to the general public, generated 90,000 leads and introduced even more hustle to an already bustling Federated office. Sixteen-hour days and seven-day weeks became common. By late October 1974, Money Market Management had attracted 23,000 investors and $180 million in assets, making it one of the largest funds in an increasingly crowded field of competitors and the hottest financial product of the period.

Earning Power

Cash Balances
Put to Work

F R I FEB 15 1974

By Sidney P. Allen
Financial Editor

PROBABLY YOU regard the money markets as no man's land, territory primarily reserved for international bankers and maybe some of those mysterious gnomes of Zurich. And most assuredly as a reserve for the sophisticated rich.

So it has been, too. For the minimum purchase amount of negotiable bank certificates of deposit is $100,000, and the minimum for commercial paper $50,000.

But now here comes idea man Glen R. Johnson insisting that the little man, too, can get in on those big money rates of return, via mutual funds.

And the little man can even reclaim for himself some good earnings even on his temporary cash balances and cash reserves that now languish in commercial accounts.

Johnson has devised another mutual fund vehicle for it.

This one is called Money Market Management Inc. It's a no-load open-end diversified investment company with very special aims and features.

The investment goal is current income, solely. Investments as small as $1000 will be accepted. The vehicle will declare dividends daily. It will redeem, at any time, all or part of your shares at net asset value, without charge.

Institutions of deposit may shudder at thought of this new vehicle. For millions of dollars of non-teresting bearing deposits now work only for the depository.

Johnson is the man who was "firstest with the mostest" in mutual funds las year, when his Fund for U.S. Government Securities captured the blue ribbon, reminded that there is indeed a time and place for investor interest in interest.

★   ★   ★

MAYBE THE meek will yet inherit the earth. While nobody would be so foolish as to call the Irish meek, Ireland is a comparatively small country.

And it just may outperform all its great big fellow countries this year. Ivor McElveen of the Industrial Development Authority of Ireland paused here the other day with some new evidence. It goes like this:

● Ireland's GNP effectively doubled in the past decade.

● Its real GNP rose 7 pre cent in 1973, despite the world slowdown. And it'll move ahead 4% per cent this year — highest in the European common Market, government calculates.

● New industry increased in the face of political problems. Tourism gained. Exports rose 30 per cent. After 1½ centuries of population outflow, emigration has now ended as a consequence of economic development.

● Demands on Irish agriculture are rising. So is her resource mining. Environment is "conducive to profitability."

A place to do business. .

STORY FROM THE *NATIONAL PRESS* ABOUT THE
POWER OF MONEY MARKET FUNDS.

HIGH INTEREST

... *How you can own a piece*

of a $100,000 certificate.

THE NATIONAL OBSERVER

Week Ending February 16, 1974

By Morton C. Paulson

You've probably seen those alluring bank advertisements that, in Gargantuan type, offer interest of 9 per cent or more on savings and, in much smaller wording, reveal that you have to deposit $100,000 or more to get that rate.

And you may have heard that you can sometimes get 7 or 8 per cent from short-term securities such as U.S. Treasury bills —if you can invest $10,000 or more.

Unfortunately, average bankrolls usually produce small returns when conventionally placed. Thrift institutions, for instance, currently pay between 5

Personal Finance

per cent and 5.25 per cent on passbook accounts and up to about 7.5 per cent on four-year certificates of deposit (CDs). Those were losing propositions last year with respect to consumer prices, which bounded up by a startling 8.8 per cent.

Mutual-Fund Specialists

But it's possible to get in on many of those higher yields. A small number of mutual funds—one is brand new—include high-denomination instruments in their portfolios and pay out most of the proceeds to their shareholders. Usually there is relatively little risk, although there is no guarantee that current payout rates will continue.

The new fund is Money Market Management, Inc., which recently has been paying 8.25 per cent. Others include: the Reserve Fund, 7.4 per cent; Capital Preservation Fund, 7 per cent; Fund for U.S. Government Securities, 8.6 per cent; and Franklin U.S. Government Securities Fund, 8.1 per cent.

Short-Term Specialists

The first three are no-load funds— they impose no sales charge—so the only cost to investors is a management fee which runs about 0.5 per cent of the amount invested. The Fund for U.S. Government Securities and the Franklin fund both have sales charges—1.5 per cent and 8.75 per cent respectively—in addition to management fees.

Money Market Management invests only in instruments maturing in one year or less: U.S. Government securities, CDs, prime commercial paper (unsecured promissory notes), repurchase agreements (instruments that the seller agrees to buy back at specified terms), and similar types. Shares can be bought or sold on any business day, and dividends are declared daily. Shareholders can receive dividends in monthly cash payments or in additional shares. The minimum purchase will be $1,000 until May 1, and $5,000 afterward.

The fund is sponsored by Federated Investors, Inc., of Pittsburgh, which inaugurated the Fund for U.S. Government Securities in late 1969. That fund, which invests solely in Government offerings, now has some 12,700 shareholders and more than $103 million in assets. Its dividend yield has averaged 7 per cent.

Rates Can Drop

Federated's president is Glen R. Johnson, former national director of the U.S. Treasury's savings-bond division.

The Franklin fund also limits its portfolio to Government securities. The Reserve Fund buys CDs and Treasury bills. Capital Preservation is in Government securities and CDs.

As mentioned earlier, there is no certainty that any of the funds can continue to pay, over an extended period, more than individuals can obtain from conventional savings repositories such as banks, credit unions, and U.S. savings bonds. Rates paid by CDs and other short-term money market obligations can fluctuate widely with changes in Government policy, economic conditions, and the demand for money. Lately the returns have been higher than usual because the Government, in attempting to cool price inflation, has cut back on the amount of money in circulation. If inflation abates, the rates should move downward, but not necessarily far enough to render the funds unattractive.

You Can Get Out

Since 1967, three-month Treasury bills have paid as little as 3.5 per cent and as much as 8.6 per cent. Those auctioned on Feb. 4 pay 7.2 per cent, down from 7.7 per cent on bills sold a week before.

Large three-month CDs sold in January are paying an average of 9.2 per cent, up from 5.7 per cent a year ago, the Federal Reserve Board reports. Comparable offerings by New York's Morgan Guaranty Trust Co. ranged from 4 per cent in March 1971 to 10.6 per cent in August 1973.

Of course, if you invest in a fund and the yield diminishes, you can always redeem your shares. If the fund is a no-load you pay nothing to get in or out. The value of your shares could rise if the fund performs well or fall if it falters, but such fluctuations have usually been small with these kinds of income funds. Johnson says that Money Market Management's per-share price of $1 is expected to remain stable because dividends are paid daily and maturities of portfolio holdings are staggered.

Not all investment analysts are enthusiastic about funds that are tied to short-term rates; some regard them as merchandising gimmicks designed to capitalize on public awareness of high money-market rates. "I'd say they kind of take advantage of a current situation," declares the manager of a competing fund. "Buyers may not be happy a year from now. But if short term rates go up, they'll be very happy."

Long-Term Investments

The fact remains, though, that payouts currently are above average. If, however, you're bothered by the volatility of short-term rates, you might elect a fund that invests in long-term corporate bonds, such as Northeast Investors Trust. Also a no-load, Northeast paid 7.2 per cent in 1970, 7.1 per cent in 1971, 7.3 per cent in 1972, 7.3 per cent in 1973, and currently pays 7.75 per cent.

Here are the addresses of the six funds discussed above; purchase applications, prospectuses, and other additional information can be obtained from them:

Capital Preservation Fund, 459 Hamilton Ave., Palo Alto, Calif. 94301.

Franklin U.S. Government Securities Fund, Franklin Distributors, 600 Third Ave., New York City 10016.

Fund for U.S. Government Securities and Money Market Management, Inc., care of Federated Investors, 421 Seventh Ave., Pittsburgh 15219.

Northeast Investors Trust, 50 Congress St., Boston 02109.

Reserve Fund, Inc., 1301 Avenue of the Americas, New York City 10019.

☆ ☆ ☆

STORY ABOUT MONEY MARKET FUNDS FROM *THE NATIONAL OBSERVER.*

THE COMMERCIAL APPEAL, April 26, 1974

Of Mutual Interest—

Money Market Fund Rises Rapidly

By EMMETT MAUM

The Fund for United States Government Securities has enjoyed excellent growth, says Glen R. Johnson of Pittsburgh, president and founder, but its sister fund, Money Market Management, Inc., is even more outstanding.

Launched Jan. 16, Money Market Management's assets have topped $17 million, said Johnson, a former national director of the United States Savings Bonds Division, in a telephone interview. And it already has 2,650 shareholders.

The no-load fund declares dividends daily and payment is made in cash each month or the money is reinvested at net asset value. Johnson said the fund invests in government securities, bankers' acceptance notes, commercial paper, and other money market obligations maturing in one year or less.

Glen R. Johnson

"The key here," he said, "is that the principal does not fluctuate. It always remains constant and the average yield is 8½ per cent to the investor."

Johnson said the fund is attractive to institutions that do not wish to tie up their money for long periods. He said it is designed also for corporations, organizations and individuals with cash reserves.

Meantime, the Fund for United States Government Securities, started in October, 1969, when assets were $100,-000, has risen to assets of more than $107 million. This is the largest fund, he said, whose assets are invested exclusively in United States government securities.

"Seven other funds along the same line are operating, but none comes close to us in size," said Johnson.

This fund was formed to give the "little guy" a chance to invest in this field. Johnson said that in 1970, the Treasury Department eliminated $1,000 and $5,000 treasury bills, and started issuing only a few even at $10,000. The Federal Home Loan Bank offered $5,000 denominations, and other federal agencies followed suit. Johnson says the small investor felt "locked out."

The Fund for United States Government Securities was the first in its field, he added, and it has proved "most successful," now with more than 14,000 shareholders in all 50 states.

MUTUAL FUND INVESTMENT
PERFORMANCE INDEX

(NOTE—In the interest of complete comparability, regardless of a fund's stated objective, Lipper Analytical Services, Inc., calculations include reinvestment of income dividends and capital gains distributions).

No. and Type of Fund	% Cha.(s) Year To 4-19-74	% Cha.(s) Week ended 4-19-74
541 All Funds	—1.25	+1.97
330 Growth	—1.87	+2.19
107 Growth and Income	—0.32	+2.15
22 Balanced	—1.40	+1.70
76 Income	+0.52	+0.90
4 Bank and Insurance	—7.23	+1.38
Median Performance of 541 Funds	—1.82	+2.02
Lipper Growth Fund Index	—4.26	+2.91

UNMANAGED PORTFOLIOS
(EXCLUDING DIVIDEND REINVESTMENT)
Close

	Close		
Dow Jones Industrial			
Average	869.91	+2.24	+2.97
Standard & Poor's 500	94.98	—2.64	+3.11
Standard & Poor's 425	106.31	—2.59	+3.10
NYSE Composite	50.44	—2.66	+2.75
ASE Index	94.92	+5.08	+0.97

a—Averages do not include funds not in existence for full year 1974.

THIS STORY APPEARED IN *THE COMMERCIAL APPEAL* ABOUT
THE RAPID RISE OF MONEY MARKET FUNDS.

82

FINANCIAL

Boston Sunday Globe . October 6, 1974

How the little fellow can fight double digit inflation

By Daniel J. Corcoran
Globe Staff

President Ford has called the greatest economic brains of the country to advise him on the best methods of fighting the nation's No. 1 public enemy — double digit inflation.

So how does the small investor fight double digit inflation?

"Simple," says Glen R. Johnson, double digit interest rates.

"By investing his money to obtain double digit interest rates."

Johnson is president of Money Market Management Inc. of Pittsburgh, one of the first of the new mutual funds which invest exclusively in short-term, high-interest money market instruments.

These instruments include US Treasury bills and notes, US gov-

ernment agency securities, bank certificates of deposit, banker's acceptances and commercial paper which are considered basically safe and currently yield 9 to 12 percent interest.

Johnson was in Boston Monday and Tuesday to meet with officers of State Street Bank and Trust Co. which maintains the share accounts for all shareholders of Money Market Management.

In addition, Johnson was making a sales pitch for his mutual fund at a press conference and in an appearance on the "Good Morning" show on TV Channel 5 Monday.

His 10-minute appearance on video paid even higher dividends than his mutual fund.

The telephone lines at Money Market's Pittsburgh headquarters

started flashing before he got off the air and they never stopped until after 11 o'clock Monday night.

"We don't have a final tally, but there were more than 1000 calls from throughout New England and New York," Johnson said.

From 1967 to 1969 Johnson was national director of the US Treasury Department's Savings Bond Division during which time he achieved a record of five million new payroll savers and $10 billion in Savings Bond sales.

On leaving the Treasury he helped establish the Fund for US Government Securities aimed at letting the "little guy" get into higher yielding government issues than the Savings Bonds without having to put up $10,000 to $100,000.

Johnson is still president of this

fund which now has assets of $100 million.

In January of this year he also helped establish the Money Market Management fund which already boasts assets of about $150 million with an average daily inflow of better than $2 million.

At present the fund's portfolio consists entirely of certificates of deposit of a dozen or so of the largest banks in the country offering yields of 11 to nearly 12½ percent.

While most money market funds require an initial investment of $5000, Johnson's fund has a $1000 minimum, and there is no sales charge.

Interest is computed daily and statements of each account with the

amount of dividends paid are sent shareholders quarterly.

The current dividend rate is about 11.3 percent.

Like many other similar funds, MMM offers almost instant redemption of its shares by a telephone call or by mailed request.

Johnson said he looks for a further easing in interest rates to the end of the year with a prime rate between 9 and 10 percent.

In such an event, he said, MMM might consider placing some of its funds in commercial paper of perhaps six to eight of the top rated corporations in the country if the yield is higher than the certificate of deposits.

Largest of the money market funds is Dreyfus Liquid Assets of New York with assets of about $375

million, closely followed by Reserve Fund of New York, the first such fund, with assets of about $370 million.

Fidelity Daily Income Trust of Boston ranks third having just gone over the $200 million mark and MMM is fourth.

Scudder Manager Reserve of Boston which began operations in August is in fifth place with well over $35 million in sales in date.

Among other recent entries in the money market picture are Oppenheimer Monetary Bridge of New York at $20 million; Anchor Reserve Fund of Elizabeth, N.J., at $17 million; Daily Income Fund of New York at $13 million; Kemper Income and Capital Preservation Fund of Chicago at $13 million and Capital Preservation Fund of Palo Alto, Calif., at $11.5 million.

BOSTON SUNDAY GLOBE: "HOW THE LITTLE FELLOW CAN FIGHT DOUBLE DIGIT INFLATION."

The Philadelphia Inquirer

Oldest Daily Newspaper in the United States—Founded 1771

Daily Home Delivery 75

Sunday, February 2, 1975

He's the Little Man's Middle Man in High Finance

By MARTIN J. SIKORA
Inquirer Financial Writer

As long as money stays in style, Glen Johnson figures he's got a lot going for him.

Johnson virtually functions as a money broker — but with a difference. He's a little man's middleman in the game of high finance.

Johnny always has money to sell — he's already taken in more than $300 million from impressed investors who are pumping a couple of extra million into his coffers each day.

And he always has buyers — 28 of the nation's largest and most prestigious banks who are perennially hungry for the big gobs of cash that Johnson can supply.

His operation, which celebrated its first birthday a week ago, has paid investors an average yield of 10 percent and, even with interest rates trending downward, he believes he can continue to beat most investment returns.

Johnson, former Minnesota weekly newspaper publisher, politician and national savings bond sales director, is president of Money Market Management, Inc., Pittsburgh-based mutual fund organization.

Money Market is one of the more than two dozen funds constructed over the last two years to allow small investors to enjoy the whopping yields offered in short-term debt instruments. But it is, Johnson believes, the only one exclusively staking its millions into large certificates of deposits sold by banks.

Large CD's, are sold for at least $100,000 and their interest rates are not subject to regulation. Because they mean large influxes of cash, which the banks may keep for specified periods of time, they usually command the most generous of yields — up to 12 percent in 1974.

Prior to MMM, now boasting 33,000 shareholders, there wasn't much access to this market for the average investor.

"What we did here was give the average guy the key to a very exclusive club," Johnson said during a recent interview here. "It's a millionaire's game."

Johnson's method may look an easy as falling off a log but, the burly, pipe-puffing money manager insists, it requires hard work to make the system conform to its goals of strict safety and high income.

Through maturities of existing investments and new inflows to his no-load fund, Johnson estimates, he has some $15 million a day to plunk into new CDs. His staff keeps constant tabs on the rates being offered by the 28 selected banks and then the haggling starts to see if a better yield can be obtained.

"The trick is in negotiating rates," he said. "We walk in with $15 million and we can push that posted rate up 50 basis points (half a percentage point)."

Recent slippage of money market rates had depressed the fund's average yield to about 8¾ percent, but Johnson professed to be unworried about the future.

"When the rate comes down, everything else with a fixed income moves down with it, he said. "We'll still pay more than a savings account, more than Treasury bills. The average guy can't find a better home for his money."

Although 80 percent of the fund's investors are individuals, it has proved attractive as well to a growing number of corporations who are consistently hunting for ways to squeeze maximum yields out of spare cash.

MMM got under way after Johnson successfully launched the Fund for U.S. Government Securities, which he still holds.

Like MMM a part of the Federated Investors complex in Pittsburgh, the government securities vehicle now, has $100 million in assets and also faces a bright future despite declining rates, according to Johnson.

The government fund, which carries a load charge to buyers, is averaging an 8% percent yield, which Johnson believes will be maintained because of nimble management.

Such a fund, he says, fares best by buying short-term securities in a rising market and longer-term issues when the rates are coming down.

He says the fund recently invested heavily in 15-to-20-year issues with returns of 8¼ to 8½ percent and "we've locked that yield up."

GLEN JOHNSON
. . . Money Market man

THE PHILADELPHIA INQUIRER: "HE'S THE LITTLE MAN'S MIDDLE MAN IN HIGH FINANCE."

Federated did relatively little advertising after the media blitz, relying instead on word-of-mouth sales. In a typical pattern, Federated might attract one investor in a small town. The investor would tell friends and relatives, and the number of Money Market Management investors in town would grow to two, then four, and often more. Though most of these shareholders were small to medium investors—the average holding was $8,000—several corporations also used the fund. A North Carolina textile company deposited $50,000 a day, withdrawing $850,000 each month for mortgage payments. As short-term interest rates continued to climb to their highest levels ever, Money Market Management ended 1974 with $274 million.

The fund, which accounted for nearly all of Federated's growth during the year, pushed the company's total assets from $340 million to $587 million—an increase of 72%. This growth, the greatest in the company's history, also signaled a major shift in the company's approach. A few years earlier, most of Federated's assets had been in equities. Now, Federated-owned stock funds totaling $100 million, were just a sixth of its managed assets. The rest was in obligations; $50 million in corporate bonds, $110 million in government securities, and $320 million in the short-term money market assets.

As a result, while the stock market suffered through one of its worst years since World War II, and the bond market sustained substantial losses, Federated prospered. Of more than 500 mutual funds in the country, three of its funds: Money Market Management, Fund for U.S. Government Securities, and the Lutheran Brotherhood Government Securities Fund, were among the industry's top 15 performers.

Leads sometimes came from the most unexpected sources. One day I was sitting in the train station in New York waiting for a train to Philadelphia, and The Little Sisters of the Poor, which is a Catholic organization, were collecting money. They were going around asking, "Could you help the Sisters of the Poor?" One of them sat by me as I was waiting. I said, "What do you do with your money when you collect it?" She said, "Well, we have to have a safe place for it." I said, "I've got just the place for it. You should put it in my new fund, Trust for U.S. Government Securities." She just laughed, and we talked a bit more, and that was the end of that. A few days later seven million dollars arrived at State Street Bank from The Sisters of the Poor.

⌁ 23 ⌁

Federated's Trust Management

DURING THE SPRING and summer of 1974, although Federated had successfully sold Money Market Management to individuals and small corporations, we had been frustrated in our attempts to penetrate the market that I thought held the greatest potential: bank trust departments.

The idea was actually conceived during a trip back to Minnesota the previous year. In the course of personal business with my father's trust officer, Mr. Phillips at First National Bank, I made some suggestions to him regarding the government securities fund.

"Sounds good," the banker said, "but I can't use it. The net asset value fluctuates too much. I could never tell customers that I lost some of their cash, no matter how big a dividend they were getting. If you had a fund with a constant net asset value that accrued interest daily, you'd have really built a better mousetrap."

"Why is that?" I asked.

"Because on any given day, in this bank alone, $85 million is just sloshing around in the system uninvested."

"You're kidding."

"Some trust departments put their client's cash in savings accounts. But the bookkeeping is more costly than the profit. A lot of times, the money sits. There's no law that you have to invest cash. Look, I want to make my clients more money. But there's nothing out there to help me do that."

A huge, untapped market had emerged. No one knew exactly how much money was controlled by trust agreements in this country in the mid-1970s, but estimates ran as high as $650 billion. Perhaps two-thirds of that total involved some degree of control by the 4,200 banks that operated trust departments. About $30 billion of it, Federated's research showed, was uninvested.

The concept of property held in trust originated in the social upheaval of the English Reformation. The idea was to separate beneficiaries from the responsibilities of ownership, permitting land or a business left to a widow or children to be managed by an outside party required to act in the interest of the beneficiaries.

Trust was the key word. Held to a code of strict conduct, trust managers wore many hats. Though not required, many trust officers were lawyers as they had to know how to sell new business, invest the assets, understand the complex laws applying to trusts and estates, possess at least a working knowledge of accounting, and for obvious reasons, be tax experts.

Personal service was the trust department's hallmark. One trust officer was called in the early morning to identify the body of a client so despised by his sister she refused to go to the morgue. Another trust manager agreed to fly to Milwaukee with $50,000 in cash to satisfy his client's blackmailers. Yet another, despite his canine phobia, kept a client happy by walking her dogs.

This level of personal service did not translate into greater profits for the trust department or the client. Most trust funds were in individually managed accounts, and investing them was difficult. What could a trust manager buy with a $7,000 cash account that was stable, liquid, and offered a competitive return? Nothing.

Even with the money placed in the bank's passbook account, accumulations of uninvested cash were inevitable. Federal law prohibited the payment of interest on deposits in the bank for fewer than 30 days. Unless the trust department could devise a creative investment medium, interest accrued to the bank. And creativity was often dangerous where trust funds were concerned. If a trust department put a customer's cash into short-term investments and interest rates went up, the principal could lose value. Telling a customer that you had lost his or her cash was a trust officer's worst nightmare. How could you lose cash?

Only a product with competitive returns and a stable net asset value—in other words, Money Market Management—would work for trusts. We were so convinced of this potential market that in December 1973, LaVonne and I packed the car, including our dog, and hit the road to sell trust departments. Of course, we couldn't make any actual sales on this trip, for the fund was still being finalized. However, I brought photocopies of the fund prospectus. For the next few weeks, I made cold calls at bank trust departments throughout the South, and then made a swing through the Northeast.

"I've got this great idea to manage your uninvested cash," I'd say to them. To which the trust officer would respond either, "Get out!" or "Sounds like a good idea. Who else is using it?" When I explained that the concept was new, they said, "Let me know when somebody else decides to try it."

I continued to call on trust departments after Money Market Management was launched, but found no takers. Individual sales boomed, yet still no trusts signed up. I continued to call on trust departments, sandwiching cold calls between media appearances. Still nothing. By late summer, I'd visited 400 trust departments without making a sale.

Even the prospects of increased profitability did not sway trust departments. Some did not even know or care whether they made a profit. They were more concerned about keeping clients happy because they were good customers on the commercial side. If these customers weren't particularly concerned about getting higher returns on trust assets, why should the trust manager be concerned?

Moreover, many trust departments, which stressed personal service over all else, wanted nothing to do with mutual funds, viewing any fund investment as an improper delegation of a trust's fiduciary responsibility. In any case, they had never heard of Federated. Why take a chance on an untested idea with an unknown?

In the summer of 1974, I kept up my efforts and finally convinced John Sullivan to help us out. John periodically sent an audiotape of news and issues to members of the American Bankers Association. He agreed to include an interview about Money Market Management.

Not long afterwards, I received a call. "This is Frank Fulton at the First National Bank in Martinsville, Virginia," the voice said. "I'm on my way to a funeral. I just heard your tape, and I think your product is the greatest thing I've ever heard about. I'd like to invest several accounts with you. What do you suggest?"

Federated immediately arranged a flight for Fulton to Pittsburgh and sent a limousine to pick him up. I gave him a tour of the office, introduced him to almost everyone in the company, and had him check with Pittsburgh National Bank to vouch for Federated's credibility.

When he got back to Martinsville, Fulton wired $3 million to Federated. My first reaction was to get on the phone with all of the bank trust departments that had expressed interest in Money Market Management but wouldn't sign on until someone else took the first step. It worked. In six weeks, Federated had another 22 trust clients and $50 million more in the fund. Ironically, Fulton later called me. The bank president found out what he had done and told him to undo it. Fulton took $3 million out of the fund and put it back in the bank (uninvested). Nevertheless, that was the break we needed. Fulton's bank eventually returned as a major customer, but only after the bank president died. At its peak, there was $55 million invested with Federated.

In the spring of 1975, Federated decided it was time for a major sales campaign to bank trust departments. The only problem was that the company had no sales force. Actually, I was the only one who did sales 100% of the time. Nearly every company officer was assigned to a territory, given a map, pointed toward an airport, and sent on the road. I spent a half-day giving them the highlights of trust and money funds and stayed in my office to handle the calls as our investment people, our lawyers, our accountants, and everybody else hit the road. I believe there were 13 in all.

Chris Donahue, Jack's oldest son who had recently joined the company, was assigned to New Jersey and Georgia. He had no sales training; just a prospectus and a list of trust names and addresses. He made only cold calls, since an advanced letter from a mutual fund would almost certainly result in immediate rejection. Armed with a calling card that proclaimed him "Assistant to the President" (everyone else had the same card), Chris Donahue was nevertheless escorted from some banks just seconds after he entered. His sin— mentioning mutual funds.

On the contrary, John McGonigle, our chief lawyer, was assigned to parts of New England and after his first day of calling on bank trust departments stood in front of the mirror in his hotel room and practiced his pitch. The first bank he entered the next day he mentioned he was from Federated, and the bank trust officer said, "I received Glen Johnson's tape and was waiting for you to come. How do I put my money in the fund?" That was a shock to John, and he had to get me on the phone to ask, "What do we do now?" He had his money before the day was out.

Another lawyer, Dave Dilger, called me from Columbus, Ohio and said, "This trust officer wants to give us $30 million. What do I do now?" I said, "Hold on, I'll be there shortly." Whereupon I caught the next flight to Columbus, met with them, and wired the money to State Street. One of our traders called me after the first day and said, "I can't take this, I can't sleep, I miss my family, and they miss me. I have to come home. I just can't do this." So we did excuse him and he came home. Several of the others did their job and did it well, and we covered the entire industry in just a few weeks. We had planted the seed that would continue to grow.

The rising short-term interest rates that had spurred much of the incredible growth of Money Market Management could not continue forever. From a high of 11.5% in September 1974, its yield fell to 8.5% in early 1975, bottoming out at 4.15% later in the year. The stock market rallied, and individual investors left money market funds in droves. Wall Street gurus began predicting that money funds might become extinct, remembered only as a freak phenomenon of the dreadful bear market years of the early 1970s. Several observers reminded me of my "naïve" predictions about the huge promise of money funds.

Money Market Management, now making two-thirds of its sales to bank trust departments, continued its rapid ascent. What these customers liked best about the fund was not its return—though like any investor, they wanted the highest possible returns for their clients—but the relief it provided trust departments from administrative burdens and operational expense. Trust departments had not only become profitable with Money Market Management, but also had more time to counsel their clients.

Federated made these issues a foundation of its sales strategy to trust departments: "We can streamline your operations, improve your bottom line, and make your life easier." Federated's competitors, on the other hand, emphasized investment performance. The reliability of fund management was certainly a must for bank trust officers, but in an industry where the gap between the top and bottom money fund performers was miniscule; the message of improved operating efficiency resonated more loudly and clearly. Federated sales representatives made more sales when interest rates were low than they had when they were near double digits.

By 1975, bank trust departments had deposited $400 million in Money Market Management, pushing Federated's overall managed assets to $761 million. Federated's assets represented 27% of the money market fund industry's total and virtually all of the institutional markets.

And thus Federated decided to concentrate its resources on the institutional market. Sales to both bank trust departments, and to individual investors did not work anyway, as I had discovered the hard way when a Houston banker greeted me by slamming the *Wall Street Journal* on his desk. "I saw your ad in the paper!" he yelled. "How the hell can you stand there and ask me for my business when you're asking my customers to take their money out of their savings accounts and send it directly to you?"

Federated stopped consumer advertising, a point it further emphasized in subsequent sales calls to bank trust departments. In January of 1976, the company introduced the Trust for Short-term Government Securities, the first money market fund for institutions only. Donahue agreed to cap the fund's total expenses at 45 basis points, about 35 basis points lower than the funds of its major competitors. This lower expense factor, he believed, would be more than offset by larger trust accounts.

The move put Federated in an almost unbeatable marketing position. Through long hours, tenacity, responsiveness, and faith in an idea that most financial experts had dismissed, Federated had created a dynamic new industry—institutional money market funds. Now several competitors were bailing out of money funds altogether or at least discontinuing their advertising.

Federated's profile in the bank trust world had risen markedly since the 1974 American Bankers Association (ABA) National Trust Conference in Miami. The conference was attended by about 1,500 people, yet just six people visited the Federated hospitality suite in those three days. Moreover, for every new client, there were 20 trust departments who knew little or nothing about the company. Clearly, before Federated could make a sale or even a sales pitch, it must make an impression.

The 1976 ABA National Trust Conference was set for Atlanta in the new 66-story Peachtree Plaza. Federated had reserved a hospitality suite on the 65th floor until Bruce Pollock and Bill Dawson, doing advance work in Atlanta, called me and told me that the walls of the 66th floor were solid glass. The view was incredible.

"Get it!" I told them.

"Somebody else already has it."

"I don't care. See the maitre d'. See the clerk. See somebody!"

A few minutes later, Federated's lodging bill had risen substantially, and the company's hospitality suite covered half the top floor. I arrived in Atlanta a few days before the conference to plan our strategy. Because local printers did not have time to work on an invitation for us, I actually found a shop that let me set the type, on the spot; "Come See Atlanta from the Top of the Peachtree Plaza with Crab Legs and Champagne, Compliments of Federated." I hurried back to the hotel where we placed the invitations under the doors of visiting trust officers.

While competitors hyped attractions like "Rudy the Omelet King," Federated hosted more than 500 people enjoying crab legs and champagne from a six-foot-wide silver bucket. The dedicated staff worked night and day during the conference, socializing, and talking about Federated's products. Bankers who were unaware of the company suddenly made time to listen, and when they did, they were usually sold on its funds.

The party created an opportunity, and that was all Federated asked for. Other investment firms often created products they believed had merit, supporting the product until the market wanted it. By contrast, Federated was more prone to wait until the world wanted a certain product, then run like crazy to produce and market it.

~ 24 ~

Crisis Management

POISED FOR A market breakthrough, Federated was suddenly threatened with the loss of its new money market fund altogether. There were five money funds on the scene by this time: Fidelity, Dreyfus, Reserve, Temp, and Federated. In December 1974, Fidelity Daily Income Trust, with $400 million in assets, announced that its shareholders were covered by FDIC insurance, just like bank savings deposits. The FDIC had confirmed, the fund said, coverage of up to $40,000 in each bank in which the fund owned CDs. The bottom line: Some fund shareholders were insured up to $800,000. This was an unbelievable guarantee that many could not believe the government would allow to stand. Obviously, the money started pouring in from all sides.

The next day I got a telephone call from my friend at the Fed, Steve Roberts, who knew that we were very much in the business. On the other end of the line, Steve said, "Glen, the Federal Reserve Board is going to shut down money funds tomorrow. They are going to invoke a little used regulation called Regulation T, which prevents anyone from buying jumbo CDs and selling partnerships in them." I asked him, "Can you get it delayed another day?" "Yes, I can," he informed me. I immediately called the other two funds, Reserve Fund and Dreyfus Fund, and asked them to meet with me right away.

Several months earlier, the *Wall Street Journal* had reported that a few investment firms—among them Merrill Lynch—had been quietly pooling investor money to buy large bank CDs. While FDIC officials confirmed that these pools, offering high returns and insurance protection, were within banking rules, the Federal Reserve was not so sure.

Following Fidelity's announcement in December, the Federal Reserve decided to put a halt to the situation by shutting down all money funds. The weapon, Regulation T, would prevent banks from knowingly selling CDs to get around interest-rate ceilings. A large portion of Money Market Management was in bank CDs and was currently providing top returns. Losing access to these instruments would be a crushing blow.

The Fed had already become accustomed to the fact that money market funds were good for the public, and they weren't about to shut them down because somebody had found a loophole. Through Steve Roberts, we arranged a meeting with the Federal Reserve Board of Governors and the representatives of two money funds: Dreyfus' lawyer, Larry Green, and Bruce Bent, one of the partners in the Reserve Fund.

We made our case that money market funds should be allowed to live because they were a viable entity, they were going to be a part of the future, and the FDIC should change their rules. Instead

STEVE ROBERTS OF THE FEDERAL RESERVE BANK IN
A DISCUSSION WITH A FEDERATED CLIENT, WITH DEE
PETERSON (CENTER) OF WASHINGTON, DC.

STEVE ROBERTS OF THE FEDERAL RESERVE AND GLEN
JOHNSON WITH CONGRESSMAN BRUCE VENTO.

of simply shutting them all down, money fund officials argued, the
FDIC should close its loophole. The Fed agreed, and the FDIC's favorable opinion of Fidelity's coverage was withdrawn. Money Market
Management and the other money funds were safe. It was a major
victory for us, and we went back to work.

GLEN AND LAVONNE JOHNSON WITH FEDERATED
CLIENTS IN WASHINGTON, DC.

BOB HIGGINS AND GLEN JOHNSON WITH A FEDERATED CLIENT.

ED GONZALES, CFO OF FEDERATED, DISCUSSING BUSINESS
WITH FEDERATED CLIENTS AT A WASHINGTON, DC MEETING.

Money-Market Fund Gets FDIC Ruling That CD Holdings Are Federally Insured

By Byron Klapper
Staff Reporter of THE WALL STREET JOURNAL

NEW YORK—In what could be another setback for savings institutions, a money-market fund said its shareholders will be essentially protected from losses by the Federal Deposit Insurance Corp.

Fidelity Daily Income Trust, a Boston-based fund that specializes in short-term investments, said it received a ruling from the FDIC that all the fund's holders are insured with respect to certificates of deposit in the fund's portfolio.

CDs are large deposits left with banks for a specific period. About 75% of Fidelity's holdings consists of CDs and government securities. Its assets are currently valued at about $400 million.

As a result of the ruling, the fund plans to invest entirely in government-insured instruments, William L. Byrnes, a Fidelity vice president, said.

The FDIC also insures deposits at banks and thrift institutions for up to $40,000 in each account.

Under the ruling, each Fidelity holder is insured up to $40,000 in each bank in which the trust's assets are invested. Fidelity holds CDs from about 20 banks. As the fund's policy is to invest a maximum of 5% of assets in any one bank, a holder with up to $800,000 invested in the fund would be 100% covered, company officials aid.

In addition to the investor appeal of federal insurance, the fund's latest return is 9.4%, and investors may make withdrawals by writing checks against their accounts. Money-market interest rates have fallen since last summer, causing the fund's return to decline from about 12%.

Competition Increased

George Kelly, information officer of Savings Bank Association of New York State, said the extended FDIC coverage increases competition for bank deposits.

"It will have an adverse affect so long as the return is substantially above the 5¼% passbook rate paid by thrift institutions," Mr. Kelly said.

Conceding this likelihood, Mr. Byrnes said: "Who'd keep money in a bank at 5¼% when the fund offers liquidity, a check-writing feature and federal insurance coverage."

Money-market funds generally permit shareholders to invest or redeem funds at any time without charge. Interest income is credited daily at prevailing short-term rates. Fidelity charges a management fee equal to 30 cents annually on each $100 of assets, plus a $2.50 monthly service charge on each account.

In 1974's first 10 months, funds specializing in short-term investments posted net sales of $1.2 billion, industry sources say.

Fidelity is believed to be the first money-market fund to get federal insurance coverage for its holders. That's because Fidelity is set up as a trust, under which coverage may be passed through to investors.

Similar Coverage Extended

Similar coverage has been extended to investment trusts operated by Wall Street brokerage firms and others. These are considered "closed" trusts, which don't publicly offer shares constantly. Seven investment trusts specializing in CDs, with $800 million in assets, are operated by Merrill Lynch, Pierce, Fenner & Smith Inc. Begun last August, the trusts sold units of $1,000 each, which are invested in CDs maturing in six months. At the end of the period, the trust matures and investors get their principal back plus interest.

Other money-market funds, organized as corporations, have previously been refused FDIC coverage for individual holders.

An FDIC official in Washington, who confirmed the Fidelity ruling, said an investor in a trust has a beneficial interest in the underlying CDs, and is insured accordingly up to the $40,000 maximum.

Investors whose mutual funds are corporations have an interest in the corporate entity. And while the corporation is insured for the $40,000 maximum, investors aren't individually insured.

The ruling is likely to have a major impact on money-market funds, which have found themselves at a competitive disadvantage because of the insurance issue.

"We'll take whatever steps are necessary to give our shareholders the same type of protection, even if it means changing our organizational structure," Glen R. Johnson, president of Money Market Management Inc., a Pittsburgh-based fund, said. "The funds haven't any other choice but to go the same way."

Jerome Hardy, chairman of Dreyfus Liquid Assets Inc., another money-market fund, said the company "is . . . taking steps to have the bank certificates of deposit in its portfolio fully insured by the FDIC."

WALL STREET JOURNAL ARTICLE: FDIC RULING THAT
CD HOLDINGS ARE FEDERALLY INSURED.

We were just gaining momentum with signing up bank trust departments. The sales force was really involved when, all of a sudden, the Comptroller of the Currency for Trusts, Dean Miller, issued what became known as the infamous Memo #4. The memo essentially said that the investment in a money market fund for a bank trust department was a delegation of authority, and therefore was illegal.

Court decisions centuries before had said a trustee investing in the stock of private corporations was liable for any loss resulting from the depreciation of the account. In 1869, a New York court went so far as to declare that an investment in a common stock was per se imprudent, even without evidence of loss.

By the 1940s, state statutes defining proper fiduciary conduct had begun to use as their foundation the Prudent Man Rule, modeled after a court decision in 1830. This rule, as interpreted by both courts and federal regulatory agencies, required fiduciaries to "exercise the same judgment and care, under the circumstances then prevailing, which men of prudence, discretion and intelligence exercise in the management of their own affairs." Rather than interpret the Prudent Man Rule as expanding the boundaries of acceptable investment options, many bank trust officers did just the opposite. Since few of their peers, under circumstances then prevailing, would not have anything to do with mutual funds, investing in such funds must therefore be imprudent.

This attitude persisted into the 1970s despite scholarly articles arguing that well-managed mutual funds could provide individual trust accounts with diversification unattainable through other investments, as well as lower operating expenses in an industry with traditionally high costs and low profits. By the time I began preaching the benefits of money market funds in 1974, many trust officers had begun to agree. They just wanted someone else to go first. Once Frank Fulton did, dozens followed, but not until being assured by Maloney of the legal prudence of their decision.

Numerous bank trust departments felt convinced enough to place assets into Money Market Management, and many more seemed poised to do likewise, until an Illinois banker called Maloney in December of 1975, "Have you seen Trust Circular 4?" he asked.

Maloney not only hadn't seen it, he didn't even know what it was.

The U.S. Comptroller of the Currency had issued Trust Circular 4. It said that bank trust departments could no longer invest in mutual funds, first, because the arrangement was an unlawful delegation of the trust's fiduciary responsibility, and second, because charging a management fee for both the trust department and a mutual fund constituted a double fee. Federated did not yet have the credibility to convince clients that the memorandum was clearly wrong, and the fears of delegation, fueled by centuries of convention, began to grow again. Bank after bank told Federated they could not do business as long at Trust Circular 4 existed. We watched a promising market, upon which it had planned to stake its entire future, starting to dry up.

Federated kept calling on customers, but competitors started getting out of the business. Needless to say, that caused no end of concern at our company because that was our business. There were calls to get rid of the sales force, although I only had five or six people at the time. People were saying that there was no longer a need for a sales force because we were out of business. However, I refused to roll over and play dead.

Federated lawyers spent hundreds of hours in the law library marshaling evidence against Trust Circular 4. They immersed themselves in the Prudent Man Rule in all 50 states, and where they did not find laws specifically supporting the right of trusts to invest in mutual funds; they sought legal opinions reinforcing that position.

After a significant amount of research with a lot of bankers, I arranged a meeting with the then acting Comptroller of the Currency, Bob Bloom. Gene Maloney and I, in addition to Bob Bloom and one of our bank clients from Ohio, were at the meeting. Bloom also had two young lawyers. Plus, the author of the infamous memo, Dean Miller, was present.

Federated's lawyer, Tom Donnelly, was with us too. The night before we had met in my room at the Madison Hotel to go over the process we planned to use the next day for this once-in-a-lifetime meeting with the Comptroller where we planned to spell out our differences.

In that meeting we all agreed on one thing. We would keep a

GLEN JOHNSON TALKING TO HIS NEMESIS, DEAN
MILLER, THE COMPTROLLER OF THE CURRENCY FOR
TRUST AT A WASHINGTON, DC MEETING.

cool demeanor throughout the entire process. We felt that was of
major importance. We felt fairly confident because we had received
reams of legal documents from lawyers around the country that
Gene Maloney had gathered. We had a lot of evidence to suggest
that they were wrong in Memo #4, and we were right.

Bob Bloom introduced people from his side. Since I had arranged
the meeting, I introduced the people from my side. We got the meeting started. Although we had agreed that we were going to keep our
cool, Tom Donnelly went into a complete rage. He pounded on the
table and said that we had been the victims of the worst bureaucratic
harassment. Tom said we were going to solve the problem legally,
judicially, legislatively, or whatever it took. He went on and on.

In the middle Bob Bloom said, "Wait a minute." When everybody was quiet, and Tom had ceased to rage, Bob Bloom said, "Does

anybody want coffee?" There was dead silence. Some people ordered coffee, and there was a moment of quiet. Thinking that Tom's tirade would be over, we resumed the meeting. It was just like you had left the volume up on a record player and dropped the needle on the record. Tom went right back into his tirade.

We didn't know it at the time, but based on his legal staff's research, Bloom had already arrived at much the same conclusion. At one point, he leaned over to his young lawyers on either side of him and said, "You know, they are right, and we are wrong. Stop what you're saying, and let us talk about fixing this."

Dean Miller, who seemed to slide further and further under the table, spoke up and said, "Look, I'll say whatever I have to say in the memo." Bob Bloom politely said, "Please sit down and shut up. You've done enough damage already." At that point Miller slid so far under the table, we could hardly see him.

We all agreed that we would structure the language for the Revised Memo #4. Gene Maloney, Tom Donnelly, and various others rewrote Memo #4. (See next page.)

Had we not been able to prevail in yet another crisis, we would have been out of business. Some of the people at Federated had already written us off as a business and thought that we would not be able to expand. This was just one of the many times that we did not roll over and play dead, but instead confronted the problem and solved it to our advantage.

We turned our attention back to selling trust departments, having learned a valuable lesson from Trust Circular 4. Legal issues, especially investment delegation, were overriding concerns to the banking industry. Trust officers were not inclined to even want to deal with regulatory problems. At the slightest hint of trouble, they would simply back away from the funds altogether, even if it meant returning to the inefficiency of buying money market instruments themselves.

Trust departments wanted money funds, but they wanted more: a company that would carry them through the inevitable legal and regulatory minefields associated with money market funds, so they could concentrate on the merits of the investment. They wanted a teacher and an advocate. The more Federated proved itself the

Comptroller of the Currency
Administrator of National Banks

Washington, D.C. 20219

Trust Banking Circular No. 4
(Revised)

September 29, 1976

TO: Regional Administrators, Presidents of Banks
           With Trust Powers (Attention: Senior Trust
           Officers) and Trust Examiners

SUBJECT: Investment of Trust Assets in Mutual Funds

NOTE: This Circular revises Trust Banking Circular
           No. 4 dated December 23, 1975, which is hereby
           rescinded

The investment of trust assets in shares of mutual funds may
be authorized and the practice therefore appropriate if
there exists: (A) authority in state statutes or decisions;
(B) specific authority in the appropriate governing instrument
for a given account; or (C) binding consents from all beneficiaries.
In addition, such investments must be appropriate for the
accounts being so invested.

Various "money market funds" are currently being offered for
the short term investment of small amounts of trust cash.
These funds are mutual funds and as such are subject to the
above stated rules. In an earlier issue of this Circular
dated December 23, 1975, we stated that, in our opinion,
"investment of trust assets in shares of mutual funds constitutes
an improper delegation of the trust investment authority
under the common law." After further consideration of this
question, it is the conclusion of this Office that the
little available precedent in this area is insufficient to
permit continued adherence to this statement as a correct
version of the state of the "common law" of trusts throughout
the country. Rather, the courts of many states having either

REVISED MEMO #4, PAGE 1.

expert in these matters, the more it would differentiate itself
from competitors.

After the reversal of Trust Circular 4 when a bank expressed concern about the regulatory ramifications of investing in a money fund,
no company could speak more authoritatively than Federated about
the position of the Comptroller of the Currency. The comfort level of
the bank immediately rose, as did Federated's reputation.

- 2 -

no statute stating fiduciary responsibilities or a statute
merely restating the general "prudent man" standard could
conclude that the applicable standard in that state would
not preclude a trustee from making a responsible, "prudent"
investment in mutual fund shares. Trust Banking Circular
Number 4, accordingly, has been revised to permit national
bank trust officers to obtain the advice of local counsel as
to the state of the law on this question in their state.

This revision in no way relaxes other standards of prudence
and suitability of investment applicable to specific investments
by national bank trust departments. In addition, this
Office has made no determinations that any given fund is
authorized as a permissible investment by national banks for
their trust accounts.

Robert Bloom

Robert Bloom
Acting Comptroller of the Currency

REVISED MEMO #4, PAGE 2.

It also occurred to Maloney that if there was no statutory precedent for what a trust department wanted to do, Federated could
create that precedent, take full credit, and become the expert. No
longer did the bank have to shy away from creative solutions. "If you
have a problem," Maloney said, "we'll do our best to fix it."

Another setback occurred when interest rates skyrocketed, and
Jimmy Carter insisted those money market funds, as well as other
financial institutions, pay reserves. Reserves meant that we had to
put 15% of our assets on deposit at the Federal Bank in Cleveland, and
that money could not be invested for the benefit of our shareholders.

Interest rates were very high at the time, and funds were paying
as high as 16%. It didn't matter to an individual whether he got 14% or
16% because these were rates they could never have realized before
money market funds. However, a bank trust department would go
into the direct market rather than go into a fund. This again would
have put us out of the bank trust business because banks simply
wouldn't invest and take a 150 basis point reduction, which is what
happened when you put 15% of your assets into reserves.

A meeting was arranged with the Federal Reserve Bank, and I suggested that since they had exempted bank short-term investment funds from the reserve requirements, they would indeed have to give institutional funds, such as ours that served the same market, the same type of treatment. Thankfully, they agreed, and we did not have to have reserves on our institutional funds. We had to have reserves on all of our other funds, and we had to start to clone funds in order to continue in business. It was another crisis that we were able to avert because we were able to convince the Fed that we were the same entity as a short-term investment fund in a bank trust department.

The next big crisis came about when the SEC started making noises like they were going to force money market funds into pricing at market, rather than amortized cost. At this point various funds were utilizing different types of bookkeeping. The Reserve Fund was doing something called penny rounding. This meant that a value was replaced by another value that was approximately equal, but had a shorter or simpler representation. An example would be replacing US $23.476 with US $23.45. This was not a very satisfactory arrangement.

Federated was using amortized cost. Dreyfus didn't have a constant net asset value. Federated had a net asset value of a dollar, and the value remained constant. Dreyfus was $10 and went up as high as $10 plus pennies or under $10 by pennies. For a bank trust department, that was a serious problem.

Anne Jones was the head of the Securities Exchange Commission at the time. On her last day in office she sent out a notice that from that day forward all money market funds were going to have to be priced at market. Again, we could not afford to have a fluctuating net asset value if we were to be used as a cash management vehicle for bank trust departments. As far as individuals were concerned, it really didn't matter, but for bank trust departments we had to have a stable net asset value, and we had to protect our amortized cost.

The order came from the SEC, and we told them we were going to defy the order. We took them to court, and a long battle ensued where we spent a lot of money that we didn't have to prove our point. We had days and days of conflict in a courtroom defending our position, but we were prepared for battle. People testified from the banking side, and other fund managers joined in the battle for and against us. The whole industry stood by and watched as we battled the SEC.

It was really no contest when we got into the heart of the matter. In fact, Bob Higgins, who was representing us from the Morin firm in Washington, absolutely destroyed their economist when he tried to explain a scatter gram and how pricing at market would be the thing necessary to do because it would be the only way that you could ever have the true value of the fund.

We had set a new policy level in this industry, and we had again fought a battle we had to win. We couldn't afford to lose this one because we had staked our case on being the fund for bank trust departments.

Although the money funds were very young and fledgling, Federated had the major piece of the market. We fought to stay in the business, which we certainly did with the amortized cost battle. That fight was probably the most severe and was most crucial for us to prevail if we were going to continue in business. That standard still prevails in the industry today.

A common problem for trust departments was dealing with imprecise bond "take-down" schedules. Banks often held in-trust the proceeds of tax-free bond issues for municipal projects such as airports, highways, and even parking lots. The trust invested the money, and then followed a takedown schedule, during which it disbursed proceeds from the bond issue to the contractors as various phases of the project were completed.

Typically, the bank bought Treasury bills scheduled to mature when each phase of the bond takedown schedule ended. But construction might be delayed by bad weather or a strike; as a result, when the trust's T-bills matured, the project might still be several weeks from completion. The bank must make some short-term investment, but such an investment was usually costly to buy and keep on the books. Because trust services for bond offerings were generally bid at very low margins, these unanticipated costs could make the account unprofitable.

This was the concern of an Ohio bank that called Federated in the late 1970s. "It's a pain dealing with imprecise take-down schedules," the trust officer said. "Why don't you build us a fund we can go in and out of on a daily basis? If there's a glitch in the take-down, we just keep the money in place and avoid these other costs."

So Federated started the Trust for U.S. Treasury Obligations, investing solely in short-term Treasury bills. Regulations governing banks assumed that they must buy T-bills directly, raising the question: When a trust invests in this kind of fund, is it buying the legal and functional equivalent of a T-bill? Federated obtained an opinion from an Ohio law firm supporting the concept of equivalence, but the Comptroller of the Currency disagreed.

Led by Maloney, Federated successfully lobbied the passage of laws in 40 jurisdictions supporting the concept of functional equivalency. Maloney quickly became known as the trust industry's problem-solver, its authority on legal issues. He was usually present when Federated made sales presentations. Once called a "whippersnapper" by the counsel to an Alabama bank, he was now the attorney whom trusts called for answers and updates.

In addition to the Trust for U.S. Treasury Obligations, Federated pioneered several new funds in the late 1970s, specifically for institutional investors, to meet nearly every kind of objective. These included the Federated Tax-Free Trust, investing exclusively in securities exempt from federal income taxes; Money Market Trust, investing in CDs, bankers acceptances, time deposits, and repurchase agreements for banks with capital, surplus, and undivided profits of at least $100 million; Federated Tax-Free Trust, its portfolio consisted mainly of short-term, top-rated municipal securities; and the Trust for Short-Term U.S. Government Securities, investing in government agency obligations maturing in a year or less.

Federated developed these funds because the trust market wanted them, but answering the market's demands sometimes involved making decisions that ran against the company's traditional philosophies. Though one bank, Union National in California, offered to place $100 million with Federated if it would start a fund investing in commercial paper—short-term negotiable instruments, such as promissory notes, issued to fund a corporation's activities— Donahue initially balked. "We could get into big trouble," he told the

Comptroller of the Currency
Administrator of National Banks

Washington, D.C. 20219

March 18, 1976

Mr. Glen R. Johnson
Federated Investors, Inc.
Federated Investors Building
421 Seventh Avenue
Pittsburgh, Pennsylvania 15219

Dear Mr. Johnson:

This is in response to your letter of November 24, 1975, in which you request the opinion of our staff as to whether national banks may invest in shares of a Massachusetts business trust designated as the "Short-Term U. S. Government Securities Trust" (referred to hereinafter as "the Trust"). As described in your letter, the investments of the Trust are confined to those securities eligible for national bank investment under Paragraph Seven of 12 USC 24 and 12 CFR 1. In effect, your letter requests that we look through the Trust share to the underlying assets of the Trust to allow the purchase of such shares by national banks.

It is the opinion of our staff that national banks may not purchase shares, units, or participations in entities such as the Trust. By statute and regulation, national banks are authorized to purchase marketable securities for their investment portfolios. A major purpose of national bank investment portfolios is to provide the banks with a source of liquidity to meet the needs of depositor withdrawals. In this regard, it is felt that the officers and directors of national banks best know the liquidity needs of their banks and have been given investment discretion to anticipate these needs. It is our staff's opinion that the officers and directors of a national bank should not delegate this discretionary investment authority to institutional investment portfolio managers who do not possess the knowledge of the individual bank's liquidity needs. This reasoning is considered applicable even when the investment device - here, the Trust - is composed entirely of short-term investments eligible for purchase by national banks.

We trust that this has been responsive to your inquiry.

Very truly yours,

John E. Shockey
Deputy Chief Counsel

MARCH 18, 1976 RESPONSE FROM THE COMPTROLLER TO GLEN REGARDING A MASSACHUSETTS BUSINESS TRUST DESIGNATED AS THE "SHORT-TERM U.S. GOVERNMENT SECURITIES TRUST."

staff. "The Federal Reserve will bail out banks. Bailing out corporations is another matter."

Donahue eventually gave in, and the company started Federated Master Trust, investing only in prime commercial paper and negotiating master notes only with the most select and stable companies. In just a few months, the fund attracted more than $400 million; within a year, it would grow to $1.1 billion.

Despite these achievements, we still continued to promote vigorously to the bank trust market. Doors still were not opening to our reps as quickly as I'd hoped. Clearly, increasing Federated's name recognition required constant and creative effort.

～ 25 ～
Building Relationships

THE FOUNDATION OF the company's marketing focus was relationships; specifically, long-term relationships. Federated's goal was to establish itself as the market's most reliable and credible source. It sought relationships that endured because customers were convinced of the company's quality, skills, and service.

Establishing long-term relationships began with Federated's sales representatives, and these relationships were enhanced at a growing number of regional trust seminars. Like other industry seminars, these events were generally held in warm-weather resorts; however, unlike some other affairs, Federated seminars were not simply excuses for a getaway in the sun. Dinners and golf were mixed with eight intensive hours of information about industry news, regulatory developments, and Federated products. The seminars afforded a chance for trust officers to learn from peers and for Federated to listen to them.

Other organizations offered similar products, but few others offered trust officers the opportunity to spend time with key players, as Federated did. For example, economist Henry Gailliot's speech on the state of the economy was understandable, clear, and when necessary, well argued. His presentation was one of the highlights of every seminar. Gailliot's speeches served as another reminder that Federated was a company of specialists and experts, not simply a seller of goods and services but a valued resource interested in the lasting prosperity of its clients.

Gene Maloney, another Federated regular on the seminar circuit, did not always tell bankers what they wanted to hear, but his seminar speeches on the legal and regulatory trust environment left no doubt that he and Federated were committed to the industry's welfare. The son of an attorney, Maloney grew up on Long Island and graduated from the College of the Holy Cross in 1966. To most Americans, Vietnam was still just five minutes on the nightly news, but the war became real to Maloney when he encountered several classmates on crutches at a Holy Cross-Army football game. They had just returned from Vietnam.

Maloney's own draft status was downgraded while he attended Fordham Law School in New York City, but Vietnam would not go away. The school was near Central Park, and demonstrations became frequent. Shortly after graduating, Maloney met a friend at the airport who had sustained serious wounds in Vietnam. A few days later, he enlisted in the U.S. Army. He trained as a paratrooper, volunteered for duty overseas, and served nearly a year in Vietnam.

Though he had intended to make the service a career, Maloney ultimately decided to practice law instead. His brother, who lived in Pittsburgh and knew Tom Donnelly, suggested Maloney interview with several companies in Pittsburgh. When Federated made him an offer, as did other companies, Maloney asked his brother for advice. He recommended Federated.

"Why?" Maloney asked.

"Well, I'm not entirely sure what they do over there," his brother said, "but they seem to have a lot of fun." On the basis of that analysis, Maloney joined Federated in 1972. At Federated, it wasn't just about client relationships; it was about employee relationships as well.

As we were starting to grow, we had a staff party at our home in Pittsburgh. We called it the MMM Ranch, complete with hay bales and farm paraphernalia. If I remember right, we had about 40 employees, and they were all there. It was an extremely fun evening, complete with an all-girl country western band. Everyone had a great time, and it went well into the evening.

One of our executives had parked on Fernwald Road, which had all trees on the right hand side. Unbeknownst to him, he had backed his car out and pulled a tree, over six feet tall, out by the roots. He had driven several miles to his home before he noticed the tree. Needless to say, he was slightly inebriated. In the morning, when

Glen and LaVonne Johnson's
5563 Northumberland
Pittsburgh, PA 15217
— Casual Attire —
RSVP no later than May 29, 1984
Home: 621-0697   Work: 288-1951

DATE: Saturday, June 2, 1984   TIME: 6:30 p.m.

**SOUTHERN BARBECUE INVITATION TO A GROUP OF
BANKERS IN PITTSBURGH FOR A FEDERATED SEMINAR.**

his wife looked out and saw the tree growing from underneath his car she said, "Now what have you done?"

To add to the fun, as LaVonne and I were eating breakfast that morning, we were shocked when one of our sales reps suddenly appeared. He had gone to sleep in a back bedroom and was rather embarrassed; so much that he tore out of the back door of our house, and up the steps he found near the door. The funny thing was that we had a "stairway to nowhere" out that door. There was a bluff about 12 feet high with a stairway for us to be able to trim the trees, and an eight-foot fence beyond that. The poor guy raced through the door and up the steps only to find he could not go anywhere. He went back down the steps and finally found his car. He was very embarrassed and resigned a few days later. I later heard he went with another company and made over $1 million a year.

By September 1977, Federated had several-hundred trust customers and had reached $1 billion in managed assets. To celebrate, the company threw another party to recognize its employees. Held at the Longue Vue Country Club, overlooking the Allegheny River, the party included about 80 employees.

The next year, during which managed assets grew to $2.3 billion, more than 160 employees and guests attended a companywide party at the Field Club. The annual event became known as "The Bash."

While selling in Los Angeles, Brick Fisher scouted locations for a hospitality suite at the 1979 National Trust Conference. The best option, he reported, was a castle nestled atop a mountain in Beverly Hills. Actor James Garner had recently rented it for his daughter's 16th birthday party, Fisher was told. The location was also used for scenes from the television series, "CHiPs."

It was a serious gamble—and a potentially expensive one. Nevertheless, Ed Gonzales and I believed the possible payoff more than made up for the risk. A decision had to be made quickly, and we told Fisher to pull out all the stops.

The night of the conference, several hundred bankers and their wives were driven to the castle in buses, transferred to limousines, and then taken up a narrow driveway leading up the hill. Eight trumpeters, their horns forming an arch over a long red carpet, met the bankers. Inside the castle, a 27-piece orchestra played songs from *Camelot*, and actors dressed in medieval costumes roamed.

ENTERTAINING MASSACHUSETTS BANKERS AT THE
MARBLE HOUSE IN NEWPORT, RHODE ISLAND.

BACK ROW: GLEN JOHNSON, ROD WOODFORD, ECG;
WALT HELGERMAN, EFM; JOYCE DEASY, AND MARK
BLOSS. SEATED: MRS. JOHNSON, MRS. GONZALES, AND
HER DAUGHTER KIM, IN NEWPORT, RHODE ISLAND.

215

The party was the talk of the conference. "I don't know who you people are," bankers told me as they left the party, "but I'm going to find out." For the rest of the conference, everyone on the Federated staff was inundated with requests for information about our money market funds. One banker was so impressed by what he learned that he promised to put $40 million in Money Market Management as soon as he could.

The day after the event, Gonzales decided to share this good news with the staff back in Pittsburgh and arranged for doughnuts with a flag reading, "Congratulations from Berwinshire Castle" to be placed on everyone's desk.

"New doughnut shop in town?" Jack Donahue asked secretary Joan Jamison when he came in.

"I think it came from the guys in California."

"What?"

The interrogation began, the story unfolded, and so did the estimate of the bill: $25,000. Donahue was upset. Nobody had cleared the costs with him. Federated's assets were increasing rapidly, but the growth of the firm was straining its cash flow.

Moreover, Donahue had always felt uneasy about these events, as did several other members of the executive staff. Regulators tended to frown on such efforts. Although I always defended them as simply another form of targeted advertising, the potential for backlash always existed.

When he returned from Los Angeles, Gonzales lunched with Donahue and Tom Donnelly, who made clear their displeasure despite Gonzales' repeated assurances that the party would bring in millions of dollars of business.

Back in Los Angeles, I was still busy making sales appointments with bankers who had attended the event. The phone rang. It was Donahue.

"I understand you spent $25,000 on your party."

"That's not true," I informed him, adding, "In any case, the money's just a drop in the bucket compared to the money we're going to make."

"Thank goodness," Donahue said. "We don't have $25,000 right now. Before you set up these events, I wish you'd talk to me first. How much did it cost?"

"Oh . . . $88,000."

I heard a crash on the other end of the line and a long silence. "Jack, are you there?" For a moment, I thought Donahue had suffered a heart attack.

"I want to see you in my office when you get back."

I informed him that I wouldn't be back for a couple of weeks. In the meantime, Donahue called a friend at a local bank that had attended the Berwinshire Castle festivities. "How did you like the little party we threw?" he asked cautiously. The trust officer raved about the event, and Donahue began to cool down.

A few days later, I called Gonzales. "You won't believe what just happened!" he said. "Remember that banker who promised us $40 million? He called. The money just arrived at State Street Bank." Gonzales instantly calculated the management fee on $40 million: $160,000, nearly twice the cost of the party. He rushed to Donahue's office with the news.

Federated later estimated that the Berwinshire Castle party had led to contacts that produced up to $800 million in new business. From out of nowhere, Federated had demonstrated its ability to gain attention, but more important, it had proven its skill and commitment to creating valuable products for bank trust clients and removing the regulatory obstacles to using them. As a result the trust industry no longer wondered who this company from Pittsburgh was. Neither did the mutual fund industry wonder.

After our huge success at Berwinshire Castle and the trust companies getting more and more aware of what money funds could do in managing their cash and trust accounts, I started planning early for the conferences that would follow. I made many calls, not the least of which was the manager of the Maza Galleria in Washington, DC. I convinced them to stay open on the Sunday night we'd be in town, as that was always the big night at bank trust conferences. We got out a beautiful invitation and called it an American Golden Gala.

FROM TOP LEFT: TRUST ADMINISTRATOR CONVENTION
IN NEW ORLEANS; FEDERATED'S GOLDEN GATE GALA IN
WASHINGTON, DC; NATIONAL TRUST CONFERENCE IN LOS
ANGELES, CA; AND GLEN JOHNSON'S TRUST STAFF.

We had 36 buses going from the downtown DC hotel where the trust officers were staying, and taken to the Galleria, which the road went right down Embassy Row. It was during the Iranian Crisis, and every tree was wrapped with yellow ribbons. We had a Federated employee on each of the 36 buses.

When they arrived, I greeted every single person as they came in. We had entertainment of a different type on every one of four levels, as well as different food on each of the four different levels. Our seafood bar alone was more than 75 feet long. Hundreds of trust officers attended, and they were treated to a first. The Navy Sea Chanters, who had never in their 275 years performed for a private for profit group, sang for us. (I was a personal friend of the admiral in charge, and had convinced him to do it). The Maza Galleria is a wide-open center, so everyone on all four levels, which had food and entertainment, could sit by the rail and watch the performance. We had at least six senators, a half-dozen congressmen, and people from the Office of the Comptroller of the Currency, SEC, NASD, and the Investment Company Institute. It was a party of all parties. The world's largest caterer had over 100 men and woman maintaining the stations and serving food.

In a letter following the performance, the caterer wrote me and said they had served kings and queens, senators and congressmen, governors, and representatives, but never in their 60-year existence had they served a party like ours.

While the Galleria was open, all the clerks were available so that people could try on all the various items of clothing; including the $75,000 lynx fur coat and other valuable items. Dozens of people were seen trying them on while having their pictures taken professionally, although they could not purchase them on the spot. I understood from the Galleria that many of these people came back when the store was open for business and made purchases. I don't know how much they were charged, but I understood it was a "substantial" amount.

At the close of the evening I had a small mountain of Godiva chocolate that I passed out to every person as they left. To this day I cannot remember how many assets came in as a result of the Gala, but it totaled in the millions of dollars, and paid for that party many times over. So that Jack Donahue was to be aware of what we were doing this time, he and the senator from Pennsylvania were invited and had dinner together. They, too, thought it was the best experience they had ever seen.

All of the 36 people from Federated, whether they were in sales, accounting, management or investment, performed admirably. To this day it remains the biggest event we ever held. This party was in advance of having a staff to organize parties, and I had to make all the arrangements myself. I had an 88-page portfolio of contacts and events in order to pull it all off.

The following year we took over the entire Bishop Museum in Hawaii, and although the attendance was not as high because of the location, it too was a huge success. It was extremely important for us to mix our clients with our non-clients. That means they did all the selling for us. They were marvelous events.

One major national bank trust department event was at the Lincoln Center in New York. There were literally thousands of people there, because after our trust officers were seated in the primary part of the Center, the public was invited. That night, after a tremendous opening by our daughter's group Con Spirito, the group was treated to a concert by Crystal Gayle.

The Omni in Atlanta was another smash hit. We had Johnny Cash entertaining for "Cash Management." We had planned an 8:00 p.m. preferred seating for our trust officers prior to opening the doors to the public. However, on that cold and windy evening there were already hundreds of people waiting to get in by 6:00 p.m. We let them in shortly thereafter, and more than 8,000 people enjoyed the night with Johnny Cash. He did a beautiful job and entertained for literally two hours or more. Prior to the show, I spent an interesting hour and a half visiting with him. That was quite memorable.

Connections continued to open doors for Federated. One day, I received a call from my friend, Steve Roberts at the Federal Reserve. He had been present when the American Association of Retired Persons (AARP) had lobbied the Fed to intervene on behalf of the older generation. They were hoping to receive higher rates, as the interest rates at the time were particularly low. Following the testimony, Steve told the CEO of AARP that he should call me about starting their own "money market fund."

Upon receiving the call from the CEO, I spent about 30 minutes explaining Federated Investors and their role in managing money market funds. I went on to describe how we had joint ventured with the Lutheran Brotherhood and produced funds for them. I instructed Chuck Wallander, head of the Lutheran Brotherhood Funds to give him a call to follow up on our conversation. Chuck immediately went to visit with them in Washington and put the partnership together.

It was the first time in history that anyone had prepared such a major mailing as we did to announce the new venture. We mailed 10 million members four different mailings, and raised $400 million almost instantly. It was a "one of a kind" transaction that had never happened in the history of money management before. After a number of years, they bought out our share of the management, but it had been a very successful venture.

As its managed assets passed $5 billion in 1979, Federated remained dominant in one of the nation's fastest growing financial markets—institutional money market funds—and one of the leaders in a mutual fund industry driven totally by money funds. Five years after being derided as a passing fancy, money market funds were nearing $30 billion in assets and shooting higher, while stock funds, with about $34 billion in assets, were falling. By the end of the decade, money market funds accounted for the majority of mutual fund assets. Although rising short-term interest rates were responsible for part of the money fund upswing, Alfred Johnson, chief economist of the Investment Company Institute noted, "The potential for money funds disappearing is zilch, no matter what the stock market does."

The efforts of Federated and other money fund pioneers did more than simply shore up the sagging mutual fund industry in the 1970s. Money funds were *the* catalyst that fueled the dramatic increase in mutual fund assets that continues today. Money market funds allowed Americans to get their feet wet by investing in stable-asset funds, and helped convince them to put their money in fluctuating-value funds, especially equities. Federated's Money

Market Management—and before that its Fund for U.S. Government Securities—was the genesis of that growth.

The explosion of new bank trust assets placed unprecedented demands on Federated's administrative capacity. Trust departments had made clear that what they liked best about Federated's funds was not the return but the service. Federated's sales force could sell all the product it wanted. If the office couldn't keep up, it was for naught.

Much of the responsibility for accelerating Federated's service capability fell to Gonzales. In recent years, he had moved away from an exclusive accountant role and became involved in the bigger picture: building Federated's administrative relationship with Lutheran Brotherhood and enhancing Federated's connection with its custodian, State Street Bank of Boston.

Gonzales had drawn on his accounting background to solve a critical challenge early in the development of the bank trust market. The problem: money transferred into a mutual fund could not be invested until the close of the business day and did not start earning income until the next day. This hardly mattered to the trust departments whose money hadn't been earning any interest or was in lower-yielding savings accounts.

But it was a major concern for large trust departments that already owned U.S. Treasury bills and other money market instruments. Many recognized the value of Federated's funds, not for the yield, for their own money market instruments paid a comparable rate—but for convenience, liquidity, and service. But were these advantages worth losing a day's interest? The larger the investment and higher the interest rate, the more likely a bank trust department would answer no.

Federated had been examining the problem for several months, with no apparent solution, when a large trust department at Washington National Bank in Washington, DC told me it was ready to sell $40 million in Treasury bills and invest the money in Federated funds, but only if it did not lose a day's interest—in this case, between $11,000 and $12,000.

I called Dick Hastings, head of Federated's operations depart ment. Hastings called Gonzales, then vacationing in South Carolina. Hastings said, "Ed, we've got a bank that will give us $40 million if we can get them first-day interest."

Gonzales responded, "We've been through this a hundred times already."

"Okay," Hastings said and started to hang up.

"Wait," Gonzales said, "Let's try to figure this out. We've always made this a complicated problem. Maybe there's a simple answer. Where does this bank want to put its money?"

"Treasury notes."

"How does a bank get first-day interest on a Treasury note?"

"They buy it in the morning, get Fed funds, and the government gives interest the first day."

"What's a Fed fund?"

Hastings didn't know. He called back the next day with the answer. Unlike a personal check, Fed funds, from the Federal Reserve Bank, were credited instantly to the purchaser's account, thus producing income immediately.

Gonzales had his solution. Federated would simply act as a conduit for the bank, buying the same instruments the bank would have bought using Fed funds.

Gonzales discussed the plan with McGonigle. "The SEC says money that comes in today doesn't get priced until the close of the day," McGonigle explained. "That's too late to do us any good."

"What if we price earlier in the day?" Gonzales asked. "We get the money, price it at 2:00 p.m., invest it immediately, and start collecting interest. Then we price again at the close of business, like the SEC wants."

McGonigle checked with the SEC. The plan seemed unorthodox, but the agency couldn't find anything wrong with it. Federated started pricing its funds twice a day (eventually three times a day for West Coast banks). Federated's solution, developed in response to client needs, soon became the industry standard.

As trust assets rolled in, demands on the home office became heavier. I asked our trust customers what they needed and promised Federated could do it. When I returned to Pittsburgh, I would inform the staff what I'd promised. It was their responsibility to figure out a solution, and sometimes within 24 hours. Gonzales compared his challenge to that of a logistics officer trying to keep up with General George S. Patton as he rolled across North Africa during World War II.

⤳ 26 ⤶

Infrastructure Evolution

WHILE FEDERATED WAS perceived as a giant computer center, the reality was something else. The wizardry occurred elsewhere. Every month Federated employees flew to Kansas City, picked up computer tapes from the company's shareholding agent, flew to Pittsburgh, and delivered the tapes to Buzzy.

Buzzy ran a computer business in his basement. At one time Federated's 1,000-plus customers used 240 different systems. Buzzy accomplished the formidable task of translating information to all of these systems in just four days, every month. Often working nights and weekends, Federated employees placed each accounting medium into an envelope with a check—and sent them by express mail to each trust department client.

The tidal wave of new trust clients and the inevitable demand for solutions to their problems became so great that it became obvious Federated needed more employees. The company, founded in 1955 had grown slowly over the years, and continued to do so. With 58 employees in 1973, the number increased to 92 by 1977. However, as the number of trust clients climbed near 1,200, Federated's employee count increased to 131 in 1978 and 200 just one year later.

It became clear that the company needed computers. No longer could Federated rely on the Buzzys of the world to fulfill its skyrocketing information processing needs. While all of Federated's leaders agreed on this critical point, none of them wanted anything to do with choosing the system until James Dolan volunteered for the job.

Dolan quickly began looking for a computer system. An intriguing option was the Apple personal computer, which was smaller than a portable typewriter, yet capable of the same feats of the much larger computers then dominating the industry.

Dolan bought an Apple, studied it at home, and even used it at work. On the advice of others he ultimately decided against personal computers for Federated because many computer experts considered them more a toy than a business tool.

Instead, Federated decided to go with a computer system developed by Tandem, a Silicon Valley company. Tandem's product was targeted to on-line computer operations, like bank transactions, requiring a system that would not stop operating or jumble data if any single component failed.

Federated developed its own application on a Tandem system for $500,000 and installed terminals and printers in 300 client banks for a few million dollars more in 1979. The staff named the application EDGE (Electronic Data Gathering Extension).

EDGE solved a number of problems. It transferred the responsibility and control of entry orders back to bank clients, while dramatically reducing Federated errors in receiving information. As such, EDGE greatly boosted the company's reputation for doing the job right. No competitor had anything like it, and Federated heavily promoted EDGE advantages in sales presentations and marketing literature.

Thanks in large part to EDGE, which soon served almost 1,300 banks, Federated was able to stem the rising tide of customer-service jobs and focus again on meeting clients. The company's workforce increased from fewer than 200 in 1979 to 450 in 1981, most of them in jobs involving direct customer contact. In the same period, Federated's managed assets rose meteorically from $5 billion to $24 billion, making it the fastest-growing financial institution in the country. Federated was the 40th on the list of mutual fund companies in 1971. Just one decade later, Federated had become the nation's second largest mutual fund manager, with only Merrill Lynch ahead.

Firms that had ignored the bank trust market could no longer ignore Federated's results, and they started scrambling to gain a foothold in the early 1980s. But while competition and market both multiplied rapidly, Federated continued to hold more than 70% of the bank trust market. In several states, every trust department

Pittsburgh Money Fund Rescues Banks In Battle For Deposits

By William H. Wylie
Press Business Editor

It's no secret that banks have their backs to the wall in the bitter battle with money market funds over deposits.

At this point, the money funds have the edge. Nearly $160 billion has been pumped into these mutual funds whose main lure is a high yield — currently around 16 percent — and flexibility. That means a depositor can move his money in and out freely and collect interest daily.

JOHNSON

The flow of money into the funds has put a sizable dent in bank and savings and loan deposits. So far bank and S&L investment products have been overshadowed by the money funds.

"But the banks will win the war," says Glen R. Johnson, president of Federated Cash Management Funds. These are subsidiaries of Federated Investors Inc., the Pittsburgh-based firm that manages more than $19 billion through its various money market stock and bond funds.

"Banks will win because they have all that brick and mortar."

What Johnson means is that there's a bank on almost every corner, that banks have great exposure to the public. On the other hand, brokerage firms, which manage many of the money market funds, have much less exposure.

Banks have another edge: individuals are more accustomed to doing business with them than with brokers.

To win the war, banks must fight fire with fire, Johnson told an interviewer. That means providing customers with the same advantages offered by money market funds.

"Already 200 banks in the United States are doing this," Johnson said. "They are using us (Federated) to compete with the funds."

The irony of this is that a money fund is offering banks relief from their worst enemy — money funds. Federated's service, called Automated Cash Management Systems, is being marketed aggressively by a subsidiary, Federated Administrative Services Inc. Federated also provides the computer know-how needed to actuate the program.

"One of the big Pittsburgh banks is going to jump pretty soon," Johnson predicted. "Five hundred banks are talking with us now."

While he wouldn't be more specific, speculation centered around Union National and Equibank as possibilities, although neither has indicated it might launch a cash management program for its customers.

When a bank does this, it is providing, at least in part, the same kind of services available at many brokerage firms. The idea is to keep a customer's money working for him constantly at the highest available return.

The ability of computers to "sweep" thousands of accounts makes cash management possible. It works like this: Once a day account balances are monitored automatically. All dollars above a predetermined balance, say $2,000,

are switched to a Federated cash fund where it earns the market rate of interest. Funds below the $2,000 level would be used for bill paying and other typical checking account functions.

Although the bank doesn't get the customer's deposits above $2,000, it collects a management fee and retains some influence over them.

Johnson said cash management functions ultimately could be extended to stock acquisitions and other kinds of investments.

Both MasterCard and Visa have announced plans to launch cash management programs. Each has said it is waiting for authorization from the Securities and Exchange Commission.

Meanwhile, Federated has established a strong beachhead in the market and feels it is far ahead of the competition.

"We already have the computers and software to run the program," Johnson said.

To handle its rapid growth — the funds it manages have soared from

$8 billion on Jan. 1 to an expected $20 billion Nov. 1 — Federated has beefed up its computer arsenal and expanded its office space. More than 600 employees are on the payroll, forcing an overflow from the firm's six-story building on Seventh Avenue into 3½ floors of the Chamber of Commerce Building next door.

Federated is an old hand at managing cash for individuals and banks. It had one of the first money market mutual funds and has five funds (totaling $14 billion) for banks. Of the 1,800 banks that use funds, Federated manages cash for 1,250 of them, Johnson said.

Federated's computers can handle 120 phone calls a minute and 10,000 investment transactions a day, he said.

Recently when a U.S. agency, Housing and Urban Development, announced a $250 million offering, Federated bought all of it.

"By the end of next year we expect to be managing $35 billion," Johnson said. Federated already is the largest financial institution in the state, he added.

The Pittsburgh Press

BUSINESS-LABOR

Sun., Sept. 27, 1981

STORY FROM THE BUSINESS SECTION OF *THE PITTSBURGH PRESS.*

that used money market funds was a Federated client—and many of them declined even to hear proposals from other companies. When competitive proposals were entertained, Federated won almost every time.

Federated had maintained its dominance because it recognized the simplest yet most important rule of the high stakes game in which it competed: The contract renews every morning. Unless it did the job right today, all its fund assets could be liquidated the next morning. Federated was setting industry standards for service.

While the company's trust events got the client's attention, its sales staff communicated their needs. Federated's lawyers cleared legal obstacles, and its customer service experts—backed by computer technology—solved the client's administrative problems.

No one department was solely responsible for Federated's sudden, stunning rise. Each, working together, was the reason it was so successful.

Just as internal relationships were critical in serving Federated's clients, external relationships were also important, and none more so than that with State Street Bank. As custodian of Federated's funds, the bank was responsible for safeguarding shareholder securities, in physical form or in computer entries, and it accounted for them daily, receiving new deposits and distributing income.

To coordinate its activities with State Street Bank, Federated started an office in Boston headed by Ralph Alexander. He died in 1961 and was succeeded by V. William Efthim, a former State Street employee. Assisted by Helen Magoon, Efthim kept records for a growing number of Federated funds, including its Income Foundation Fund, Federated Growth Fund, Empire Fund, and several other exchange funds. Efthim ran a tight ship, always asking himself how a serious regulatory slipup would read in the *Boston Globe* or *New York Times*.

Federated's involvement with State Street Bank increased in 1969, as the Lutheran Brotherhood Fund and the Fund for U.S. Government securities were launched. A new area at the bank had to be set up for the huge bags of mail coming from Lutheran Brotherhood's direct mail campaign; it soon became known as "The Chapel."

The explosive rise of assets in Federated's money funds required even closer liaison between the company and its custodian. Instead of paying quarterly to yearly dividends, Money Market Management declared daily dividends. No other mutual fund did this at the time, and Gonzales met with the State Street Bank staff to explain what Federated wanted. The bank did not have an accounting system to handle daily dividends but said it would have no problem creating one.

A few months after Money Market Management was launched, Gonzales paid a visit to State Street Bank. "I'd like to see the fund records," he told the manager in charge of the project.

"Don't worry, Ed," he said. "Everything's working just fine."

"I know. I just want to see the records."

"To tell you the truth, my secretary is keeping those records."

They walked to her desk, and she opened the right-hand bottom drawer. Inside were 300 cards, one for each shareholder, on which she had handwritten all the transactions.

When Gonzales, the manager, and his secretary finished laughing, Gonzales said, "This fund is going to grow. You really need to do this on a computer."

State Street agreed, and as Money Market Management assets skyrocketed, so did the assets of the bank. In 1975 State Street had custody of $14 billion in mutual funds, about 20% of the industry's assets. State Street eventually became the largest custodian in the world, holding 52% of the country's mutual fund assets.

While Federated's insistence on state-of-the-art custodial services for its clients helped State Street develop capabilities critical to the bank's growth, the bank also played an essential role in Federated's success, ultimately starting a division devoted strictly to the company's funds (housed in its own building). About the same time Federated started the 'Bash' for its own employees, the company began sponsoring an annual Christmas party for State Street employees who worked on its funds.

Pleased but bewildered, the State Streeters often asked Gonzales why Federated bothered to wine and dine them. After all, Federated was the client. "Actually," Gonzales would reply, "The ultimate clients are our shareholders. We both have to keep them happy, and we just want to thank you for the part you play in helping us do that."

I really viewed Federated's alliance with banks as a long-term strategy. Banks would ultimately win the battle against money funds because of "bricks and mortar." A bank sat on nearly every downtown corner. If the banks offered comparable services, it seemed that most people were more comfortable doing business with local banks than with money funds headquartered in distant sites.

I regularly preached Federated's commitment to banks. I was quoted in *Forbes*, "If someone calls us and wants to put money into a money market fund, I ask them where they live and send them to the local bank." I cautioned against legislation that would hinder that effort. "Sure, you have some legitimate gripes, but by the same token, you must view us differently from other money funds," I told banking representatives. "We're not taking money out of banks because we're serving banks."

To counter criticism that it was sucking savings deposits from small and medium-sized banks, Federated started buying several million dollars of certificates of deposit from small banks around the country. The Independent Bankers Association applauded these efforts but reiterated its desire that reserve requirements and other restrictions be imposed on money funds.

One of our "Friends of Federated" had promoted the idea of "prepaid tuitions" that would accumulate tax-free, and we thought it was a great idea. It needed to have federal legislation in order to be able to do it countrywide. A close friend of ours, Phil English, a congressman from Erie, Pennsylvania, agreed to write and introduce the legislation in Washington. We saw it as a great "business expander," and I proceeded to lobby to make it happen. I visited countless colleges and had more than 150 colleges write to their congressman to support the legislation. Obviously, it took a couple of years to get support for the program, and there were countless things that happened along the way.

The Clinton Administration said they would probably veto it because it was a perk for the wealthy. I finally convinced Al Gore to talk to the President. He explained that this was not the case at all, and had the opportunity to really get support for what would eventually become known as 529 plans. We received word late one evening that the bill had passed the Congressional Committee and that it would automatically pass the House and Senate. The Clinton Administration was quick to take credit for it the next day, and released it to all the media. It wasn't until Wednesday afternoon after the Monday announcement that we realized that part of the bill had not passed at all. Untouched by congressional hands, it had been removed when the staff directors of both parties had a discussion late into the night and removed the language from the bill.

In the meantime, we had already inserted an ad in the *American Banker* (that I had to later remove when we found the bill did not pass). We had the support of all the Lutheran schools, all the African American schools, and many southern colleges. I know that Vanderbilt University was also a strong supporter, as was the Heritage Foundation in Washington.

After a great deal of effort, we finally gave up. Five years later, the bill finally passed, and it was the original bill that we had written and had been introduced by the congressman from Erie, Pennsylvania. I have always been able to say that we authored the 529 Plan that was eventually approved by Congress and today is a huge success in educational circles.

Not everyone at Federated had the same positive feeling about the program as I did; however, the huge success of the 529 plans

GOLDEN TRIANGLE—DOWNTOWN PITTSBURGH.
PITTSBURGH IS HOME TO FEDERATED INVESTORS.

shows how successful the program has been as billions have now accrued in 529 plans all across the country.

We worked long hours, long days, and long weeks. Most weeks were 100 hours or more as we traversed the entire country, spending 2 ½ days in as many as 26 locations. The sole requirement of Federated's senior managers was that they get the job done. How they accomplished this was essentially their own business. "You can paint your own painting." Donahue liked to say. "Just make sure you stay on the canvas."

FEDERATED BOARD OF DIRECTORS. FRONT ROW: WESLEY W. POVAR, JOHN A. STALEY, JOHN F. DONAHUE, JAMES E. DOWD, WILLIAM COPELAND, AND J.JOSEPH MALONEY. BACK ROW: EDWARD L. FLAHERTY, J.CHRISTOPHER DONAHUE, MARJORIE SMUTS, LARRY ELLIS, GREGOR MEYER, GLEN R. JOHNSON, EDWARD C. GONZALES, AND RICHARD B. FISHER.

27

On Board the *Queen Mary*

IN THE FALL of 1981, the discussion by Federated's executives centered on whether the company should seek a buyer. A few, especially Staley, were not so sure. He argued that the company ultimately would realize more value by staying on its own. But while Donahue wanted to hear all opinions, he was nearly impossible to move once he had made up his mind. He was convinced that Federated should be sold to a large corporation while continuing to operate nearly autonomously in Pittsburgh.

By the spring of 1982 the executive team included Jack Donahue, Dick Fisher, Ed Gonzales, John McGonigle, John Staley, Chuck Wallander, myself, Chris Donahue, Henry Gailliot, Gene Malone, controller David Taylor, and James Dolan, who oversaw the company's computer operations.

Federated hired an investment banker to contact companies that might be interested in buying Federated. Several were contacted, including General Electric and Mellon Bank, but nothing came from those discussions with Federated. Donahue also broached the possibility of a sale with Bob Kirby, Chairman of Westinghouse, during a golf outing, but the company was not interested.

About this time, Jack Truschel, who ran an insurance agency in Pittsburgh, read an article in the *Pittsburgh Post Gazette* that I had been interviewed for, chronicling Federated's accomplishments. Truschel had been one of Donahue's closest friends for nearly 40 years, and they golfed together frequently.

Truschel clipped the Federated news article and sent it to Dean Wolcott of Aetna Life and Casualty, one of the 15 largest corporations in the country. Wolcott, Senior Vice President of Aetna's Personal Financial Security Division, had served as an Aetna general agent in Pittsburgh during the 1960s. Whenever a story mentioning Federated appeared in the Pittsburgh press, Truschel passed it along to Wolcott with a note: "Here's the latest on Dick and Jack."

As it turned out, Wolcott's interest in Federated went beyond old friendships. Aetna, the country's largest investor-owned insurance and financial services corporation with assets of $44 billion and 50,000 employees, was seeking to level the cyclical peaks and valleys in earnings that affected it and every significant player in the property-casualty insurance industry. The industry was in its "sale market," competing vigorously to hold market share by severely reducing prices after having lost $6.5 billion in 1981.

Hoping to counteract Aetna's cyclical casualty losses, Aetna Chairman John Filer pushed the traditionally insular corporation into a number of non-insurance businesses, including real estate, consumer credit, oil exploration, computers, and a British merchant bank. In that vein, Wolcott was seeking to diversify Aetna's individual insurance line. Marketing Federated's mutual funds with these other products, through Aetna's massive distribution network, seemed a promising connection. Adding Federated's mutual fund assets would also help Aetna's annuity business.

Wolcott responded to Truschel's note with one of his own. "Next time you see Jack Donahue," the letter read, "ask him if there's any interest in getting together." Truschel wrote Wolcott's telephone number on the note and sent it immediately to Donahue. Donahue was perplexed. Federated's investment banker had already checked with Aetna's top officer in charge of diversification. He had said Aetna was not interested.

Wolcott's note sat on Donahue's desk for several weeks before he responded: "Our investment banker already talked to someone in your company, and he said you weren't interested."

Wolcott was not surprised. Running Aetna, a massive company, required multiple layers of bureaucracy, and messages were not always relayed quickly. "That doesn't matter," he told Donahue. "I'm thinking about this from a different perspective." They talked, Donahue making clear his unease with Federated's lack of diversification, and his own desire, as Wolcott put it, to "monetize" his holdings.

Several other Aetna officers, including Philip Roberts, who headed the company's annuity and pension operations, and the company president, William O. Bailey, soon joined the negotiations. Bailey, especially, was impressed with Federated. He also got along well with Donahue.

Bailey's questions had increasingly centered on the prospect of bank deregulation. If Regulation Q was revoked (allowing banks to offer higher rates on passbook savings), or the Glass–Steagall Act would change, Donahue admitted that Federated's business would change dramatically. But Federated had faced similar challenges before, and it had always landed on its feet. The company, Bailey believed, was creative, profitable, well managed, and was likely to succeed no matter what the obstacle.

Donahue had questions too. Federated's culture was different from Aetna's. Federated changed on a dime. Promising ideas were implemented quickly; when unsuccessful, they were dropped just as fast. But Aetna had 50,000 employees. Before ideas could be implemented or abandoned, studies must be commissioned, committees convened, and superiors consulted. Could Federated still function as Federated?

On the other hand, the possibilities for synergy were endless. Aetna had 24,000 agents and access to markets Federated could only dream of. Few companies had more name recognition. Most important, even in its worst year since 1976, Aetna still had almost boundless capital reserves, and stock analysts continued to respect its "mighty" earning power. Gailliot described the situation like this: Federated was like a rowboat in the middle of the Atlantic Ocean. The small boat was accelerating, but the waves might suddenly become overpowering. Might it not be more prudent to board the *Queen Mary*? The answer was yes, Donahue decided, provided Aetna's offer was right.

Meetings between Federated and Aetna were delayed for several weeks during the summer of 1982. But, on July 28, Donahue's 58th birthday, he got a call from Bailey: Aetna had reason to believe that news of Aetna's interest in Federated was about to be leaked to the press, undoubtedly driving up the price of its stock.

"Can we make our offer in Pittsburgh tonight?" Bailey asked.

"That would be fine," Donahue said, and then spread the word among Federated's executives that they would be working all night (I was on the way to Newport, Rhode Island for a Massachusetts bankers meeting).

Negotiations were straightforward. The companies had talked often, and Bailey had a good estimate of what Donahue believed his company was worth. By 4:00 a.m. the companies had reached an agreement in principle about the deal's structure. The only obstacle was the price: Aetna offered 1⅛ shares of its stock for each share of Federated stock, and Federated wanted 1½ shares. The companies finally compromised at 1¼. The time was 5:30 a.m. Federated had boarded the *Queen Mary.*

Aetna acquired 4.4 million shares of Federated stock, or about 86 percent of the company, by exchanging 1¼ shares of Aetna common stock, then selling at more than $40 per share, for one share of Federated. Total value: $256 million. Donahue jokingly told Aetna's officers that if Aetna had paid the same rate that Federated paid for its first successful fund 27 years earlier, the price would have been $5 billion.

Under the deal, Federated executives retained 14 percent of the company through 1987. Aetna could purchase the remaining shares using a formula based on Federated earnings and Aetna stock performance. Donahue would continue as Federated's President and CEO, reporting to Bailey, and the company would continue to operate from Pittsburgh as a separate Aetna subsidiary.

Aetna was willing to grant Federated its "space" because the company produced. Bailey would later say Federated was the best acquisition Aetna ever made. At a time when the casualty insurance business was hurting and Aetna profits were down, Federated supplied Aetna with operating earnings well beyond its size, growing steadily from $22 million in 1983 to $55 million in 1988.

Still, despite the mutual benefit and the good personal relationships, Federated and Aetna had been unable to find synergy. Hopes for cross selling had been high. Federated mutual funds would not have access to a vast market while the company's banking relationships seemed an ideal way to distribute Aetna annuities. In 1983, Aetna's blanket commercial property policy was introduced to Federated's trust department clients. Federated tried to offer its Multi-Trust products to Aetna's 401K marketing force. But for many reasons—not the least of which was the companies' divergent operating styles—it simply hadn't worked. By 1987, Aetna basically left Federated alone, content to collect its steady earnings.

As a result, Jack Donahue began to wonder whether Aetna might be better off finding a more suitable buyer for Federated. His rationale was primarily financial. In an overconfident market, the mutual fund industry was booming. A competitor's stock was selling in the market at a price-to-earnings ration of 23. At that rate, Federated, which had earned $49.4 million in 1986, was worth more than $1 billion—an unbelievable price. He took his plan to new Aetna CEO James Lynn and President William Bailey. By selling Federated, which was overvalued, and buying Aetna stock, which was undervalued, Donahue argued, Aetna could make a significant profit. But Lynn and Bailey were not interested. Aetna buys for the long term, they said.

Any hopes Donahue might have had for his plan ended in April 1987 when the U.S. bond market turned hysterical after the dollar plunged against the Japanese yen. Investors responded frenetically to every report about inflation, trade, and exchange rates. Bond prices alternately dove and skyrocketed as much in that one day as Wall Street veterans were used to seeing in a year. When the April carnage was over, holders of government, municipal, corporate, and mortgage-backed bonds had lost an estimated $100 billion.

From April to December 1987, Federated's managed assets fell from $48 billion to $40 billion. Federated's business projections for Aetna hoped to rebound slightly, to $41.5 billion. Instead, the company's assets ended 1988 with $37.8 billion, down 6.2%.

In a similar situation, some business people might have moored their ships more securely in Aetna's vast harbor, but Jack Donahue had become more convinced than ever that Aetna and Federated no longer were a good fit.

And so by 1988, Jack Donahue, age 64, having diversified his personal wealth by selling Federated, having reached a point he could not have dreamed of three decades earlier, decided he wanted to do it all over again. He wanted to buy back Federated.

The deal was announced to the public in March 1989. Aetna received $345 million—$35 million of it from Donahue's management group, $235 million in loans from the PNC syndicate, and $75 million in loans from Westinghouse. The loans were to be paid in 10 years. Aetna also received preferred stock that could be converted into 27.5 percent of Federated's common stock. The stock was valued at $61 million, which brought the total that Aetna received to $401 million. In addition, Aetna retained about $80 million in Federated cash, receivables, and marketable securities.

Federated ruled out cutbacks in its workforce of 800, noting that they did not present their offer until they were sure they would not have to cut jobs. "This is a people business," McGonigle told the *Pittsburgh Press*. "In a people business, the last things you can cut are the people. They are the ones who produce income; they have the contact with the client base."

Federated's lawyers and proxy solicitors spent the next four months getting approval from the shareholders of each of Federated's more than 60 funds. The deal was finalized on July 28, 1989—the date of Donahue's 65th birthday and seven years to the day that he had agreed to sell Federated to Aetna. Afterwards, the Federated employees went next door to the Vista Hotel for a celebration, complete with laser lights, and red, white, and blue balloons. They called it "Independence Day."

28

It Takes a Community to
Beat a Regulation

FEDERATED HAD GROWN significantly and was firmly entrenched in the bank trust business, and I knew from the start that banks were pressing for mutual fund powers. The first real threat came when one senator proposed that banks be allowed to get involved with the mutual fund business. We knew we had to squelch that proposal.

Fortunately, we had a powerful friend in a high place. I had befriended Senator Heinz way back when he was a congressman, and we used to share travel space on plane rides to Washington, DC from Pittsburgh. Now he was a Senator and happened to be Chairman of the Senate Banking Committee.

I spent an entire evening in Senator Heinz's office on strategy that we might use in order to defeat this first run at the banks getting into the mutual fund business. The long and the short of the deal with Senator Heinz was that he said, "Look, as chairman of the Senate Banking Committee, I can take out any parts of this proposed legislation." The next morning, on every member of the House Banking Committee's desk, sat the new agenda. The new agenda had nothing about mutual fund powers, and the senator who had raised the issue was literally never heard from again. Senator Heinz saved the day for us, and we did not have to go to battle with Congress. At least not yet.

In the early days of the company, we were not large enough to withstand the big banks getting into our business. I began to think, "Who out there has the same concerns as we do?" Obviously, it was the small community banks. I decided I would try to put together a lobby group of community banks. This decision would bode well for us for many years to follow.

The first ever gathering was at my home on Marco Island in Florida. Our committee meetings were held at a local hotel. I think that five heads of community bankers associations represented us, including Minnesota, which was under the auspices of Norb McCrady. There were other people from the community banks present as well. This coalition was the key to our survival when crisis struck again.

The Assistant Comptroller of the Currency, Dean Miller, issued a question and invited comments regarding proposed Regulation 9. The plan was that in 60 days they were going to allow banks to take their stiff funds and essentially turn them into mutual funds. They would be able to advertise them and charge fees for them.

This would have let banks walk into the mutual fund business through another door. It would have been a total disaster for us. Federated would have probably lost all of our business because this was the one thing that banks had wanted for a long, long time.

We decided we were going to defeat the Regulation 9 proposal. We geared up all of our community bankers, had conference calls and meetings with them, and did a lot of preparation. This culminated with Congressman Markey from Massachusetts holding hearings with people from the Investment Company Institute, the Office of the Comptroller of the Currency, and others.

We had people come and testify on our behalf, and we made a real case for the proposal's defeat. It seemed every bank in the country got involved. We had many consumer groups on our side, including the Consumer's Federation, AARP, and Labor Unions. Even the Chinese Bakers of America were in our corner on this battle.

We advertised our opposition in the *Roll Call Newspaper,* the *Congressional Newspaper*, and we did direct mail to all congressmen. We made an all out effort to kill the Regulation 9 proposal (see page 242).

The Markey hearings were fantastic. Congressman Markey put the Comptroller on the spot and made him back down on his position. We had made contacts through our community bankers, and they had their representatives keyed up for this particular hearing.

U.S. considers proposal to allow banks to advertise trust funds

By JOHN M. DOYLE
Associated Press Writer

Washington — A federal bank regulator was urged Thursday to delay a plan that would ease rules governing bank trust funds and lead to competition with the trillion dollar mutual fund industry.

The proposal marks another effort by banks to branch into businesses dominated by the securities industry and, not surprisingly, has met stiff opposition from mutual funds.

Under the proposed change, the Office of the Comptroller of the Currency, which regulates 4,000 national banks around the country, wants to allow banks to advertise collective investment funds separately from their other services.

Bank trust departments are allowed to combine individual trusts, like those maintained for wealthy widows and minors, into collective funds for administrative purposes.

The comptroller's office wants to lift a ban preventing banks from advertising the availability and performance of those combined funds, in effect, letting them be marketed as ersatz mutual funds.

Mutal funds, small banks and some members of Congress have criticized the proposal as risky after the savings and loan debacle and reports of underfunding of the Federal Deposit Insurance Corp., which guarantees bank deposits.

There also is concern that financial products sold in banks will give customers the impression they are federally insured, which they are not. That was a problem arising out of the failure of Lincoln Savings and Loan, where some investors lost their life savings in securities sold at the thrift.

"Without appropriate safeguards in place the potential for investor confusion is substantial," Rep. Edward J. Markey, D-Mass., said at a hearing before the finance subcommittee of the House Energy and Commerce Committee. Markey is chairman of the panel.

But Robert L. Clarke, the comptroller of the currency, said that while the negative reaction is large, the issue is small.

"The revisions we are contemplating would not expand bank powers," Clarke said. He said banks already are permitted to advertise the service along with others but not separately.

"The government doesn't tell supermarkets that they cannot advertise carrots unless they advertise all the other vegetables in the produce section," he said. "Why then should the government keep banks from advertising common trust funds services separately from other trust services?"

Markey suggested that since Congress is trouble-shooting the country's banking laws, the comptroller's office should wait to implement the change until the Bush administration presents its opinion.

Clarke said that he had no timetable for making a decision.

The Securities and Exchange Commission doesn't oppose the change, but SEC Chairman Richard C. Breeden told the panel it would impose its own regulations on banks if they are allowed to market their collective trust funds.

Clarke said he neither supported not opposed that move, and had informed banks of the SEC's plans. But he said banks are exempt by law from other SEC restrictions to which mutual funds are subject.

The SEC would be unable to regulate the sales practices of banks vending funds as it now can for mutual fund salesmen. That would deny investors the protection of those laws, Breeden said. "In our view, the commission believes these statutory exemptions for banks are no longer appropriate," he said.

THE DAY (NEW LONDON, CONNECTICUT), OCTOBER 6, 1990.

Each of them did an absolutely marvelous job of talking about Regulation 9 and what its effects would be. The effects were that the huge banks would be making significantly more money, and the little banks would again be on the outside looking in.

We won hands down. It was a major victory, and it was one more time that we did not roll over and play dead. We met the opposition, and we proved that we were prepared for the battle, although there would be many more power struggles along the way.

Clearly, our lobby group turned out to be tremendously effective. The group met at Federated's expense, and the 19 annual meetings were very worthwhile. At our peak we had 26 state community banker associations in attendance. The head of the association and his wife and/or any other legal people involved in that particular

February 22nd, St. Paul, Minnesota. This was the day! Glen Johnson called to say that Senator Heinz office had confirmed that the Comptroller of the Currency had no plans to implement Reg. 9! The following obituary tells it all. After discussion, it was decided to distribute this message only to our friends. Any public display would rub salt in Clarke's wounds and might come back to haunt us. The victory was unprecendented, but carried with it the cautions mentioned in the obituary! Rest in peace!

OBITUARY?

An obituary is the report of a death - death is usually final!

**Reg. 9 reportedly drew its last breath on February 22, 1991,
just over one year after its birth.**

But, will it, like Frankenstein's monster, be resurrected should Congress fail to legislate similar powers? Unless concrete assurances can be obtained of the withdrawal of this rule, we must assume that it may rise again to add risk, unfair competetion and inappropriate charges to the banking system and the public.

And what of the Administration's banking proposal? My intention during attendance this week at both the Senate and House hearings with Treasury Secretary Brady, was to search for some benefit to independent/community banks in the proposal, but I came away empty handed! Every "big bank initiative" that we have fought for the last 50 years has been incorporated into this plan.

We must do more than "circle the wagons" to prevent such legislation, we must gather all possible allies and establish positive offensive and defensive positions to wage a battle that may go on for several years. Change will happen, but we must play a role in that change to protect not only banking franchises, but the public interest as well.

E. Milton Klohn
INDEX
February 28, 1991

CIRCLING THE WAGONS AGAINST REGULATION 9.

association would attend. Sometimes there were 90 or more in attendance at the events, and they turned out to be bigger and better each time. As a matter of fact, at the Marriott Hotel on Marco Island, we did a skit on Regulation 9, and it was absolutely hilarious. The skit told the whole story of how we won the battle and how we were able to put in place all the support for the hearings.

Some time later, we had one other tremendous rush from the banks trying to get into the mutual fund business. The problem was that our opposition forces and the banking community had become rather ho-hum. The interest was not there like it had been before. It seemed as if they thought that every time this situation came up nothing happened anyhow, and it was getting harder and harder to get people aroused against it. There were even many people who were starting to think that maybe it was time that banks should get into the mutual fund business.

At one point it became such a major issue in Congress that they were determined to pass this legislation, and the discussion to allow banks to get into the mutual fund business started in the House of Representatives.

Early in March I ran into Congressman Dingell from Michigan at the Willard Hotel in Washington, DC. I asked him what the chances were of us defeating this legislation that by now had a full head of steam. I will never forget his answer because he said, "Little or none." He told me that the only two people he could say were honestly against it were Congressman Markey from Massachusetts and himself. Congressman Dingell said that it would take an absolute miracle to turn this legislation around. I asked him if it would have any impact if we could get thousands of letters to the congressmen from their constituents from all over the country. He said, "Go to work on it. It can't hurt, and it can only help."

We had an all out blitz. We contacted all of our community bank presidents. They contacted all of their members, particularly those who were actively involved in legislative affairs. They told them of some of the consequences that would happen as big banks got into the mutual fund business and how the uneven playing field would become even more unleveled if this were to happen. It is pretty hard to get a handle on exactly how many letters were written, but we had sent sample letters out to the community bank presidents to pass along to their members.

Once we had our support team in place, Paul Riordan and I actually took our staff and set up shop at the Washington Court Hotel. We worked tirelessly on the Hill, talked to members, got information to them, and ran ads in *Roll Call.* All in all, we waged a full attack.

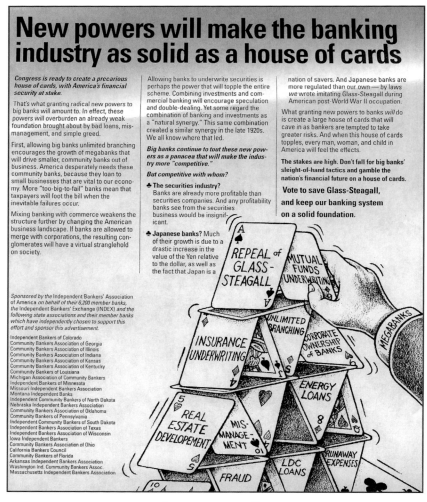

INDEPENDENT BANKERS' ASSOCIATION: "NEW POWERS WILL MAKE THE BANKING INDUSTRY AS SOLID AS A HOUSE OF CARDS."

WANTED!

Congressional Heroes -

to protect the public from the repeal of the Glass-Steagall Act. There were not enough heroes that came forward when Garn-St. Germain was foisted on the American taxpayer. The result is that the taxpayers will still be paying on the bonds for the $250 billion thrift debacle until the year 2020, in addition to the cost of a new federal agency, the Resolution Trust Corp. The RTC is scheduled for extinction, however, if Glass-Steagall is repealed, the RTC should be retained - *it will be busier than ever!*

Americans for the Protection of Glass-Steagall

1827 North St. Paul Road, St. Paul, MN 55109

Reprinted from the June 5, 1995 edition of Roll Call Newspaper

WANTED!
CONGRESSIONAL
HEROES!

A message to the members of Congress...

The American public will be paying for the thrift debacle created under Garn-St. Germain with higher taxes for years to come!

Changes being proposed for
THE GLASS STEAGALL ACT

might well prove to be even more costly!

It took the full faith and assets of the United States Treasury in 1933 to bail out commercial banks because of their deep involvement in investment banking and it can happen again!

This is a high budget, heavily propagandized campaign aimed at diverting your attention from the risks to the safety and soundness of the banking system. Those risks far outweigh any possible benefits! There is no grass roots support for this proposal and the scales of justice must fall on the side of consumers, small business, community banking - or just about everyone except the mega banks and investment company proponents.

America needs
"THE PROTECTION - NOT THE DESTRUCTION" of GLASS STEAGALL!

Independent/Community Bankers Associations representing 5,285 banks

Ind./Community Bankers Ass'n. of Alabama - 124, Arkansas Community Bankers - 195
Independent Bankers of California - 200, Community Bankers Ass'n. of Colorado - 162
Community Bankers of Florida - 170, Community Bankers Ass'n. of Georgia -326,
Iowa Independent Bankers Ass'n. - 300, Community Bankers Ass'n of Illinois - 500
Community Bankers Ass'n. of Indiana - 113, Community Bankers Ass'n. of Kansas - 146
Community Bankers of Kentucky - 127, Community Bankers of Louisiana - 97
Michigan Ass'n. of Community Bankers - 131, Ind./Community Bankers of Minnesota -320
Missouri Independent Bankers - 190, Montana Independent Banks - 47
Nebraska Independent Bankers Ass'n. - 170, Independent Bankers Ass'n. of New York - 94
Ind./Community Bankers of North Dakota - 100, Community Bankers Ass'n. of Ohio - 160
Community Bankers Ass'n. of Oklahoma - 100, Pennsylvania Ass'n. of Community Bankers -276
Independent Banks of South Carolina - 67, Ind. Community Bankers of South Dakota - 52
Independent Bankers Ass'n. of Texas -780, Virginia Ass'n. of Community Banks - 95
Ind./Communty Bankers Ass'n. of Wisconsin - 205, Ind./Community Bankers of Washington - 38

A MESSAGE TO
THE MEMBERS
OF CONGRESS.

And you thought the S&L crisis was bad...

...Don't make the big banks' problems bigger

"The real problems," says **FDIC Chairman William Seidman,** *"are in the big banks."*

We agree.

Bad loans. Massive credit exposure. Woeful neglect of the fundamentals of good bank management. Together with grossly ineffective federal supervision, these are quickly sending our big banks the way of the S&Ls.

The answer?

From the big banks:
A page out of the S&Ls' playbook. Massive increases in PAC contributions and lobbying to strongarm Congress into deregulation.

From the regulators:
News of a tidal wave of red ink, amassed on their watch. With warnings of more to come—unless the big banks get their way.

And from the Bush Administration:
More voodoo legislation. For big banks that can't manage banking, a plan that gives them new powers, puts them in speculative new lines of business and pushes them to take new risks. More rope for the big banks and the regulators to hang themselves — and us.

THE REAL PROBLEMS ARE IN THE BIG BANKS.
Let's not make them bigger.
That's what will happen
—if Congress repeals Glass-Steagall and sets the big banks loose to "get well" in the securities business.
—if Congress opens their doors to new abuses, conflicts of interest and manipulative practices.

—if Congress foists new responsibilities on the regulators when they can't handle the ones they've got already.
—if Congress disregards the interests of consumers, small businesses and local communities and the independent banks that serve them.

Congress must decide. To bet the system on the promises of the big banks. Or avert another S&L disaster, by refusing to compound the damage ~~they've~~ already caused.

We believe the choice is clear.
SAVE Glass-Steagall.

Sponsored by The Main Street Coalition to Save Glass-Steagall

AND YOU THOUGHT THE S&L CRISIS WAS BAD.

246

Banking Reform Means WALL STREET VS. MAIN STREET

Reducing your deposit insurance, moving capital out of your community, merging big banks and business, and allowing banks to enter the risky securities business are all parts of the banking proposals now being considered by Congress.

Now is the time to let your Senators and Congressmen know how you feel about cuts in deposit protection and big new conglomerates that will have a major effect on *all* of the citizens of the community by siphoning local deposits from Main Street to Wall Street.

The Big Banks and Wall Street want this badly.

SAVE MAIN STREET by writing today!
Send the attached coupon to your Senator and Representative in Washington today! Or call us for more information.

I am concerned about the threat that proposed banking legislation has on our community banks. I urge you to vote to keep FDIC insurance coverage at its current levels, to preserve the laws that separate banking and securities underwriting, to prohibit the merging of banking and commerce, and to protect my community.

Name: _____

Address: _____

City: _____

State: _____ Zip: _____

WALL STREET VS. MAIN STREET.

The bill was finally debated in the House of Representatives. On the day of the debate I spent the morning talking to congressmen before they went on the floor. We knew it was going to be a close vote. We had kept Congressman Dingell in the loop on our efforts. We thought we had gotten 300,000 letters to congressmen from their constituents opposing the mutual fund powers for banks.

Paul Riordan and I were in seats in the gallery of the House listening to the debate when finally they did the roll call vote. Just watching the board was so amazing because it stayed almost even both for and against. When it came to the end, it was a tie vote. The Speaker of the House, Foley, could cast the deciding vote, but he had to allow five minutes for people to change their votes.

The minutes were closing down, and Foley was about to vote. We knew that he would vote with the people who were in favor of the big banks getting the powers, and we knew that he would vote against us. Just before he was to cast his vote to break the tie, a congressman from Texas, who I had talked to in the hallway that morning going into the session, changed his vote, and we won the battle by two votes. Nobody, and I mean nobody on earth, could believe we had won this battle, and nobody ever figured out how it happened.

The media surrounded John Dingell after it was over, and with the media watching, Dingell broke through the crowd, came over to me, threw his arms around me and said, "It's a miracle you won this battle. It would never have happened without your effort, and we have prevailed. Perhaps this will be put to rest for a long, long time because they really felt they had every chance to win this battle." They had put everything they had on the line, and the big banks had lobbied for it for months. In three months we had taken it from a no-win situation to a solid victory.

That was the closest call we had in our days of fighting big banks against getting legislation to have mutual fund powers. It certainly strengthened the close friendship between John Dingell and me.

This story ended with a huge success and much to my delight, a footnote that brought me pleasure. I attended a $25,000 per plate President's Dinner that was also attended by representatives from the big banks in the country. I attended from Federated. Seated at the table with me were nine major New York bank CEOs. The conversation led to them trying to figure out how they had lost that battle. They couldn't figure it out.

The attendees from the major banks couldn't put their finger on us because Federated never once surfaced. The community bankers were active, and they were expected to be opposed to it, but no one had any idea who orchestrated the battle. The big bankers concluded it was the community bankers who were responsible for the win. They were still puzzled how the community bankers could have snatched victory from the big bankers. That topic was the entire conversation at the table that night. I had a hard time keeping a straight face. Incidentally, most of those large banks no longer exist.

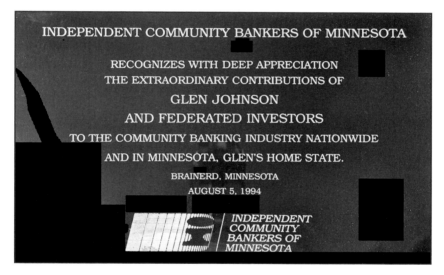

AWARD PRESENTED TO GLEN AND TO FEDERATED
INVESTORS BY THE INDEPENDENT COMMUNITY BANKERS
OF MINNESOTA AT THEIR STATE CONVENTION.

∿ 29 ∿

Miscellaneous Memorable Moments

AT THE END of 1974 I had my first 22 bank customers, and I didn't know what I should send them for Christmas. I didn't want to send them booze or anything like that. At the time I was a member of the New York Athletic Club. They made a mincemeat pie, which was huge. It weighed more than five pounds and was in a big tin. That year I sent 22 mincemeat pies to my customers. The next year I sent 150 mincemeat pies to my customers.

When it got to where we were ordering 2500 mincemeat pies from the New York Athletic Club, extra employees had to be hired just to handle our order. When the price of their pies increased to over $25, we made the decision to get a bunch of empty pie tins from the New York Athletic Club, which had the flying foot logo on them, and we sent our clients an empty pie tin, along with the pie recipe from the club. We also committed to give $50,000 a year to the Children's Hospital in Pittsburgh for the next three years. That's how we got out of sending out any more mincemeat pies.

But we had a lot of fun through the years sending our customers mincemeat pies. Obviously, we became famous for our holiday gift. Customers sometimes started calling us long before the pies were sent out, asking if we had forgotten them because they hadn't received them yet. To this day, I still send, on my own, a number of mincemeat pies.

I had a particularly interesting competitor who worked for Dreyfus. Every time he would call on a different bank, the bank would tell him they were already a Federated customer. He decided to go to his hometown, Bar Harbor, Maine, because he thought I had probably never gone there. Unfortunately for him, I had gone there and sold both trust departments in town. When he got 'home' to sell to his own trust departments, they gave him the same answer, "Well gee, if I leave Federated, they won't send me a mincemeat pie." As a result, he lost the sales because of the mincemeat pies. We thought that was humorous.

In many of my early interviews with magazines and newspapers about money funds and money market management, journalists would chide me over the fact that when interest rates went down, people would abandon such funds, just as they had embraced them initially. To some extent, that was true. However, for bank trust departments who found that this relieved them of a tremendous amount of work, it was good for the client because the money was invested. It was good for banks because they could get income. It was good for the operations side of the bank because they didn't have to do much work to keep their cash invested. We did all the bookkeeping for them.

Every month we would run a punch card. We had punch cards for any system, and we would send banks a check for the income. Our system was a savior for bank trust departments. We consistently found that the easiest sale to make was clearly not the head of the trust department, but rather the person who was in charge of operations. His life would become a great deal easier.

We had a lot of things happen along the way. For instance, in Iowa, I had sold a big bank on the fact they ought to use money market management for their bank trust cash. After they finally agreed and gave us a lot of money, they couldn't get the account to balance. When we would send out the punch cards and the checks at the end of the month, the balances were always incorrect. I got a call one day that said we either straighten this out, or the bank was just going to pull their money out. They said they just couldn't do it anymore because their accounts never balanced.

There was a woman in the operations department named Eileen Dagenheart. Eileen was a petite lady and had never been out of the city of Pittsburgh. I sent her to Iowa on the next flight to visit the bank. When she got to the bank, it turned out that the head of operations was a big Russian girl. This girl was more than six feet tall. When Eileen came in to straighten things out, the girl quickly took Eileen across the street for a cup of coffee. She then confessed that she had been cooking the books; she thought as long as they had found a new way to manage their cash, she wouldn't have a job.

Eileen convinced her she would only have a better job if she made this work, and that the sum and substance of it was that the bank had a product that worked perfectly. This story ended well; the bank never knew that one of their internal employees was at fault. This is an example of one of the many pitfalls that we ran across along the way.

———

There was another occasion at the Southern Trust Conference in Mobile, Alabama. I had been looking for someone to entertain the clients, and I was going to have a hospitality suite at the Southern Trust Conference in Mobile. I asked one of my client banks if they could come up with an entertainer. The head of that particular trust department was a client of ours, and he suggested somebody he knew who was a very good pianist. He recommended that as good entertainment and suggested that it would be perfect to have somebody off playing in a corner for an event such as we were planning. People would be coming through and could enjoy the music. I said to go ahead and hire him.

When I arrived on the scene and was setting up the hospitality suite, my client took me over to introduce me to the piano player. He introduced us by saying, "Glen, this guy used to manage our cash before we were able to utilize your money fund. We didn't need him anymore, so now he has a job playing the piano." That was a rather embarrassing time, but the guy assured me that he was making a better living playing the piano than he did managing the cash for the bank, so everything turned out okay.

———

Another funny incident took place in New Orleans where we were setting up to entertain the bank operations officers. I had told one of my staff members to arrange something that would be different and would capture the entire audience. It turned out that he got permission to do a fireworks show, and he leased the *Natches* for the evening. The *Natches* is a very large riverboat. It was the hit of the conference.

There were other vendors that did things on the same night that we did the fireworks show, and they literally had no attendance. Everybody wanted to go on the *Natches*. We had can-can girls and crab cakes galore. We also had all kinds of hors d'oeuvres. It was a really beautiful trip.

It turned out the captain of the *Natches* was a grizzled old captain who was very displeased that the Russians were always parking in the boat parking places, although boats were ordered to stay in their berths,because of the upcoming fireworks. As we were cruising up and down the river, it was exceptionally foggy. We were about to start setting off the fireworks, so we parked under a bridge and requested that the first of the fireworks be shot. Fog was so thick that we couldn't see a thing. We could hear the fireworks, but we couldn't see anything.

We decided we would wait for fireworks until we got a little closer to land. We got a little closer and shot off another rocket. We were able to see it, but it was still not clear. We traveled perhaps another hundred yards and just stopped there in the middle of the river. We stopped all the riverboat traffic. Nothing could move until we finished the evening.

Everybody was complaining, but they couldn't leave their berths. The captain was happy as a clam. We sat there and watched about 35 minutes of unbelievable fireworks. Through the fog it was absolutely amazing.

What we didn't know was that no one had expected what happened, and the rumor was that somebody had invaded the French Quarter. Hundreds of people had been there to observe the fireworks. The next day's newspaper carried a big story about all the fireworks that took place. No one could figure out who was responsible for our fireworks, so they decided it was a celebration in honor of the first Republican governor elected in more than 100 years.

It turned out that the fireworks in the fog had caused so much pressure that it had broken dozens of windows in the county building. We were delighted they never figured out who the culprit was because we probably would have ended up paying for a lot of windows.

All of our customers thought the whole event was absolutely fabulous. Another first had been pulled off for Federated.

We might have as many as 200 in attendance when we entertained clients at Federated events. We would bring our clients in to listen to our story and be entertained. People who were good at golf played golf, the people who were good at tennis played tennis, and the people who were good at shooting could shoot. Many of the places didn't have a range, but if they did, I headed the delegation that went to the range. I was a much better shooter than golfer.

I never played golf as a kid, but later I did play tennis. We had a tennis court in our backyard in Pittsburgh. One duty of my secretary was to schedule players, all summer long, on the other side of the net at 6:00 a.m. to play tennis with me. As a result, I played a lot of tennis.

When we went on the road for group meetings, out of 200 people in the group, there might be 25 that played tennis, and 50 that played golf. I'd always play with the tennis group.

Some of my experiences were really very interesting. I was in West Virginia, and was heading the group to play tennis. We had a woman client who said she had been dying to play tennis against me. As it turned out, she was the city of Charleston's tennis champion. It was one of the most humiliating experiences I ever had. I never scored a point and never hit the ball back.

Later, after Aetna acquired Federated, I played tennis with the Chairman of the Board of Aetna. When I was serving, I hit him in the back of the head and knocked his hat off. He didn't think it was too funny. That was my first game with our new boss.

Although I continued to play an occasional round of golf, I was never very good at it. Later, when we moved to Florida, I played a bit more. I would ride my bike over to the club and play golf before anyone else in the morning. It took me an hour to play 18 holes. Although I did improve, I was certainly not great.

Federated's client events were always top-notch. Once, a group of 200 enjoyed steak dinners that were cooked on a big open pit. I will never forget when I went up to get my steak, the bank trust officer ahead of me was asked how he wanted his steak cooked. He responded, "Very rare!" The chef questioned him, "Very rare?" To which he replied, "Yes, I want one so rare that a good vet could bring it back!" I have never forgotten that.

We entertained at the National Trust Conference in Hawaii where, as was typical, we stole the show. We certainly had fun. Everybody at the Trust Conference came to our event. In fact, for five straight years everybody at the American Bankers Association Trust Conference came, much to the chagrin of other advertisers and trade groups.

Clients were always treated as first class citizens, and that was part of our secret in developing the tremendous trust business, which in today's world is still the Federated Franchise, Bank Trust Departments.

———

At one time an employee of the Morin School of Banking at Boston University published a book called *The Duties and Responsibilities of a Fiduciary.* I got the American Banker's Association and the ICI, which is the mutual fund companies association, both as contributors to the book. That was putting two enemies in the same camp. I raised a quarter of a million dollars for the publication of the book. It has been used widely throughout the country on the duties and responsibilities of a fiduciary.

As soon as we got into the trust business with Federated Funds, we really got involved in making a difference in the local market. Minnesota was the first state where we got a bill passed where school districts and municipalities could use the fund for their excess capital. That got to be a big market for us. However, to make that possible I had to go in and get a senator to sponsor the bill, followed by a representative from the House. Having a lot of friends in Minnesota, this wasn't too difficult.

A few weeks later I got a call one night saying, "Glen, you've got to come tomorrow. We're having a final vote on your bill. We're doing the final reading, and it'll be going in for passage. You have to be here." By that time we had a corporate plane, so I flew to St. Paul and was there for the start of the session.

The representative stood and read the wrong bill. It had nothing to do with us, and the bill passed unanimously. The title of the bill was the right one, but the contents of the bill were something totally unrelated. That shows you what can happen in government. It's incredible.

We went on from there and passed laws in Kentucky, Kansas, and various other states. I would find a banker who was a customer who could introduce me to somebody in the House or the Senate. I would explain to them how this was going to work, and that we needed to pass a bill.

I went into Nebraska where the bill would require the approval of the state treasurer. When I finally got to meet him, he asked why I was there. It took about a half hour to explain this fund. He then said to me, "Well, tell me. What's a mutual fund?" We never did get the bill passed in Nebraska. It turned out that the treasurer was a local farmer who had backed the governor. The job as treasurer was his reward, but he didn't know a thing about finance.

We were very successful, and with our lawyer Gene Maloney, we passed legislation in almost every state. We've been very effective in passing legislation statewide and nationally. We've been very successful in sponsoring bills. And more often we've been successful in beating down bills that would have put us out of business. If the banks had gotten in the mutual fund business about the time we were starting to grow, we'd have been dead in the water.

A piece of legislation I did not like was the Garn-St. Germain bill. It gave savings and loans new powers they didn't have before. In my opinion Garn-St. Germain was the worst piece of legislation ever written. Freddie St. Germain was Chairman of the Boston University

Banking Law School, so he was a good friend. The night of the final meeting on the bill, I said, "Freddie, the last thing you ever want to do is pass this legislation. It will cost the American taxpayers hundreds of billions of dollars."

He said, "Oh, no, no, don't worry about me."

When he came out of the meeting, he tried to avoid me, but I stopped him and said, "What happened?"

He said, "Well, I put my name on a piece of very famous legislation. It's called Garn-St. Germain."

That's what led to his downfall. Garn-St.Germain cost the American taxpayers 500 billion dollars. I made speeches all over the country predicting what would happen if that piece of legislation passed, but they passed it anyhow. Garn-St.Germain called for 3700 new regulators, but they never hired a single one. If you read the legislation, it's all there.

The Pittsburgh PRESS

SCRIPPS HOWARD

Thursday, April 18, 1991

Singel hasn't given up hope for Heinz appointment

By Dennis B. Roddy and Don Wolf

The Pittsburgh Press

Lt. Gov. Mark Singel says he still has hope that Gov. Robert P. Casey will appoint him to the Senate seat left vacant by the death of John Heinz, but he won't break with the governor over it.

"My understanding is that he has not made a final decision and that he is still looking for a candidate who has name recognition, who is ready to go and is preferably from the west," Singel said yesterday.

Earlier this week, Singel met with Casey to make his case for the appointment, but Casey has said he wants Singel to remain in the lieu-tenant governor's office.

After a day of suggestions that he might challenge Casey's Senate appointee when the Democratic state committee meets to nominate a candidate for the Nov. 5 special election to fill the balance of Heinz's term, Singel said yesterday: "I want the governor to know that his lieutenant governor will not cause him any great consterna-tion."

Singel left the door open to a last-minute change of heart by Casey, saying he still considers himself the best candidate for the appointment, but had little hope of winning the appointment.

Until Heinz died April 4 in an airplane-helicopter collision out-side Philadelphia, Singel had been

exploring a possible challenge to incumbent Sen. Arlen Specter, R-Philadelphia, in 1992.

Yesterday, Singel said he was resuming his exploration of a Sen-ate run next year.

Casey was in Philadelphia yes-terday and had no immediate reac-tion to the lieutenant governor's announcement. The governor still is sorting through names of possi-ble appointees.

Among those under consider-ation is Arthur J. Rooney II, grand-son of the late owner of the Pittsburgh Steelers, who has re-ceived the written endorsement of Allegheny County Commissioners' Chairman Tom Foerster. Foerster urged Casey in a letter to appoint Rooney to the seat.

"I have known Art Rooney for his entire life. I know him to be a person of high integrity," Foerster wrote.

Foerster's letter, according to an aide, indicates that the politically influential commissioner is strong-ly backing Rooney as the selection.

"He's not recommending anyone else," said Harry Kramer, Foer-ster's chief deputy.

Another potential appointee is Glen R. Johnson, 61, of Squirrel Hill, a former confidante to the late Sen. Hubert Humphrey of Minneso-ta and now an officer with Federat-ed Investors of Pittsburgh. Johnson today said he would be available for an interim "caretaker" appoint-ment but would not be inclined to run in November.

FEDERATED—Managed Asset History

Year-End Managed Assets 2010
$400,000,000

1955	Company founded.	
1962	Introduced one of the first exchange funds in the industry.	$78
1969	Created the first government bond fund.	265
1972	Introduced one of the first high yield bond funds.	402
1974	Provided small investors access to the U.S. money market by offering one of the first money market funds. Entered bank market for management of trust customers' cash.	575
1976	Created the first institutional-only money market fund and one of the first municipal bond funds.	824
1977	First $1 billion under management.	1,146
1979	Started marketing private label money market funds through broker/dealers.	5,255
1980	Affinity group relationship established with America's largest association of retired persons.	8,631
1982	Aetna purchased Company. Began to market equity and fixed-income funds to bank trust departments through Multi-Trust product line.	29,258
1986	$3 billion raised in offering of GISI fund through Merrill Lynch and other broker/dealers.	44,163
1987	Began to market mutual funds through broker/dealer affiliates of commercial banks.	40,067
1988	Established administrative services to banks through proprietary private label mutual funds.	37,348
1989	Management re-acquired control of the Company from Aetna.	38,948
1991	Introduced offshore funds for non-U.S. citizens and institutions.	47,740
1993	Formed institutional sales force to market products to investment advisers, government entities, insurance concerns, and other corporations.	57,628

1995	Began Federated Global Research, a New York-based investment management unit to develop global equity and fixed-income products.	61,713
1996	Acquired the remaining shares (approximately 25 percent) held by Aetna. Completed acquisitions with Lehman Brothers ($5 billion managed assets) and ARM ($230 million managed assets).	74,842
1997	Passed $10 billion in domestic equity fund assets. Completed acquisition of William Penn Funds ($550 million managed assets).	92,540
1998	Completed initial public offering of FII on May 14 on the NYSE. Launched venture with German insurer LVM-Versicherungen to manage and market funds in Germany and other parts of Europe.	111,553
1999	Offshore, global, and international managed assets exceed $7.0 billion.	124,820
2000	Launched six retail funds in Germany with LVM-Versicherungen. Completed fund acquisition from Investment Advisers, Inc. ($346 million managed assets). Record sales of $10 billion of equity fund products.	139,584
2001	Money market managed assets exceed $100 billion. Integrated Federated Kaufmann Fund ($3.2 billion managed assets) into equity product line.	179,687
2002	Awarded $13.2 billion in money market assets from TexPool, Texas' local government investment pool. Added to the S&P 500, Standard & Poor's widely regarded index that includes leading companies in leading industries.	195,353
2003	Increased equity assets to a record high of $26.6 billion, up 28 percent from Q2 2003.	197,917
2004	Acquired $19.3 billion cash management business from Alliance Capital.	179,269
2005	Money market managed assets increased by $36 billion to reach an all-time high of $160.6 billion.	213,423
2006	Federated Kaufmann managed assets reached $10 billion. Completed acquisition of MDT Advisors totaling approximately $6.7 billion in quantitative equity assets.	237,440

2007	Managed assets exceeded $300 billion with record highs for equity assets, money market assets and total assets. Launched the Federated Inter-Continental Fund.	301,616
2008	Completed acquisitions of Prudent Bear and Clover Capital. Won mandate to manage Florida's local government pool. Paid $3.69 per share in dividends, including a $2.76 special cash dividend.	407,310
2009	Launched Federated Clover value equity mutual funds. Completed acquisition of assets from two Touchstone Advisors mutual funds.	389,316[*]

* As of Dec 31, 2009

～ 30 ～

The 200 Million Dollar Kitchen

THE SUCCESS OF Federated Investors has persisted over many years. At no time was it more dramatic and beneficial to investors than the 30-year period from the mid-1970s through 2008, when malfeasances and significant errors at the rating agencies threatened the world of finance and nearly created a worldwide depression.

This was a period of generally lower lows and lower highs in both interest rates and inflation. The stock market also rose during this period. The creative forces of financial innovation were in full bloom, as the money market funds and money market securities, in particular, allowed the banking system to progressively transform itself into more of a capital market system.

Ironically, Jimmy Carter and Paul Volker ushered in Ronald Reagan and a golden age of investors. During this dynamic period, Federated Investors thrived. This chapter will chronicle how this very well led and innovative company created wealth for those who stayed the line and invested in its stock over the long term.

Indeed, it is startling and even glorious just how an accommodating economic environment and good leadership were able to create wealth over this period. While many are familiar with how entrepreneurs and investors made fabulous fortunes in technology companies during the 80s and 90s, there are relatively few who realize a similar story of success was experienced by those invested in the growth of the financial system.

When I arrived at Federated, there were many early investors who had a stake in Federated stock, not all of whom shared Jack Donahue's conviction or intuition of pending growth and

GLEN JOHNSON AND PAUL VOLKER, CHAIRMAN
OF THE FEDERAL RESERVE BOARD.

opportunity. Notably, in 1976, Jack allowed a very large percentage of the company's employees to purchase restricted stock at approximately $2.00/share. I am happy to say several of my key salesmen were able to buy 5,000 shares each in 1978. When Federated tendered for 252,611 outstanding shares (over 20 percent of outstanding stock) in 1979 at $6.00/share, my own daughter and her husband sold the 5,000 shares they had bought back in 1970. One senior portfolio manager in the money market funds sold shares, and even one of my colleagues on the senior staff sold 5,000 shares of FII that year in order to remodel a kitchen. As you will see, these were very unfortunate decisions.

Under the terms of the merger, every four shares of Federated stock were exchanged for five shares of Aetna stock and given $\frac{2}{10}$ shares of Federated Development Corp. stock (Federated's ill-fated Oil Development Company, which was worth about $1/share). So what were five shares of Aetna stock worth on October 21, 1982, the day of the merger? Would you believe $216.25 (i.e. 5 × $43.25)?

Further, on July 31, 1989, the day Federated's executives, the profit sharing fund, and several Donahue family members, bought the company back from Aetna, those same five shares of Aetna were $297.50 (i.e. 5 × $59.50). Notably, the cost of those 5,000 shares was now approximately $1,487,500 (i.e. 5000 × $297.50). Also, the dividend on that stock was a little under $70,000 per year.

The new company was capitalized at $2.50/share. Those five shares of Aetna could now be swapped, tax-free, for 119 shares of the new Federated Class B common shares.

While the company was now a private corporation, it was able to pay down its debt and pay back shares retained by Aetna before it once again went public in May 1998.

Also, between July 1989 and May 1998, the stock split three times; two for one in 1996; two for one in 1998; and three for two in early 1998. Those 119 shares of Federated stock were now 714 shares.

After it went public, the stock split one more time in 2000; three for two shares: you now owned 1071 shares of Federated Class B stock. At its high point in late January 2008, the stock was trading at over $40/share. At this price, that $2 share of Federated stock purchased in 1977 was now worth $42,840.

The math of it all takes your breath away. If you bought 1000 shares of the stock at $2/share in 1977 and were able to hold it all the way through this process, your investment was now worth over $21 million.

Notably, my colleague on the senior staff who sold 5000 shares in 1979, in order to refurbish his kitchen still did okay. I am told he actually sold 400,000 shares at approximately $40/share in 2008, in order to purchase a $16 million vacation home. As exorbitant as that may seem, it was a fraction of what that kitchen cost him in retrospect (i.e., over $200 million).

Needless to say, as Benjamin Franklin once said, "A penny saved is a penny earned," or in this case, $42.84.

	Early Federated Stock	
8/27/59	Heck & Co. took public 42,000 shares @$4.75/share	= 1 share = 5 shares = 4.75 = 2.375
3/1970	2 for 1 stock split	= 5 shares = 10 shares
	1977 to 2010	
1977	One share of Federated stock	= 1 share (FII) × $2 to $3 (est. market value) = $2 to $3
1979	One share of Federated stock	= 1 share (FII) × $6/ share = $6.00
1980	4 for 1 stock split	= 4 shares (FII) × 2 ⅜ at low = $9.50
10/21/1982	1.25 shares of Aetna @ Merger	= 5 shares Aetna × $43.25/share = $216.25
7/31/1989		5 shares Aetna × $59.50/share = $297.50
(1) 1989	$297.50 divided by 2.50 /share of FII	= 119 shares of FII (B) (5000/shares = $1,487,500)
(2) 1996	2 for 1 stock split = 2 × 199 shares	= 238 shares FII (B)
(4) 4/15/1998	2 for 1 stock split = 2 × 238 shares	= 476 shares FII (B)
(6) 4/30/1998	3 for 2 stock split ⅔ × 476 shares	= 714 shares FII (B)
(9) 2000	3 for 2 stock split ⅔ × 714 shares	= 1,071 shares FII (B)
(10) 2008	High point in FII stock value	1,071 shares × $40/ shares = $42,840
	Cost of Federated Senior Executive's 1979 kitchen 5000 shares × 42,840 /share	= $214,200,000
	Sold to Federated Senior VP for $7/share	= $35,000
	Same executive's vacation home in 2008 400,000 shares × $40+ /share	$16 million

~ 31 ~

Banking on Boston

THE OUTSIDE COUNSEL at Federated Investors was Charles Morin, a prominent Washington lawyer. He was the lawyer to the Teamsters and was the lawyer who had bailed Federated out in their early years. Interestingly, Charlie was a law partner with Chuck Colson in Boston before Colson went to the White House. Charlie Morin was famous in his own right. He is deceased now, but when the company was struggling to get certain funds out of the SEC, Charlie was instrumental in making all that happen.

A graduate of Boston University, Charlie gave money to Boston University to start what he called the Morin School of Banking. His main goal was to be sure that mutual fund companies were kept up to date with the 40 Act and other significant legislation. The Morin School had sponsored a couple of seminars before I came to work with Federated. The seminars were financial in nature where bankers and lawyers were invited to talk about current rules and regulations.

One of the main attractions of these seminars was that Charlie brought people from Washington who were at the top of their game in the administration. I had not only been to a couple of the seminars, but being considered successful, I had been asked to speak at one of them. Shortly after that, when he was looking for a board of advisors, he approached me and I was placed on the board right out of the gate.

I helped organize some of the meetings that included both bankers and mutual fund companies. Freddie St. Germain, well known at that time and chairman of the House Banking Committee, was named chairman of the advisory group. Today I am the only member who has been on the board since its inception.

One of my prior complaints was that when I wanted to hire a

JERRY HAWKE, COMPTROLLER OF THE CURRENCY,
U.S. TREASURY. CHAIRMAN OF BOSTON
UNIVERSITY'S MORIN SCHOOL OF BANKING, WHERE
GLEN JOHNSON WAS ON THE BOARD FOR 22 YEARS.

lawyer to look at the trust side of banking, which involved securities and security selection, I couldn't find a lawyer who knew both sides of the issues. They didn't know both the security side and the commercial banking side. Lawyers typically were either experts on one side or the other. It was my belief the Morin School could make a fortune if they started a degree in banking law.

My thoughts were that an MBA and a law degree should be required in order to enroll. I also felt we needed to get people from law firms in Boston and Washington. My lawyer at Federated, who was an expert in trust law, could teach the course. He's now taught trust law since the day we started. We started with the domestic program and met with success. Later we expanded the degree in banking law to a global program.

Two separate programs became somewhat complicated, so we scaled back to a single course, which includes both domestic and global. The program still attracts people from all over the world. In 2009, we had people from 27 countries. In fact the program has

267

exceeded our expectations, and we have had to restrict it to 60 students per year. The quality of applicants has improved dramatically. I can't tell you how many applicants we have to turn away every year, but we've become very selective.

People who complete the course are normally key figures in their local banking industry when they return to their country. Having been taught by Gene Maloney, our inside trust lawyer, the benefit for us is obvious. Often those banks have become our customers.

It's a huge assist to us. When we have to make law, which we often do, we lobby. This means when we have people within the banking and legal fraternity who understand who Federated is and what our goals are, it makes passing laws that much easier. Many of these same people have become members of the Legislature. If we go into a state to pass a certain kind of law, we have friends there from the beginning.

The program nets the school $1.6 million annually. It could net them a lot more. The teachers receive a stipend of $5,000 a year. Boston law firms teach most of the courses, with a few taught by Boston University teachers. The individual who heads the ICI taught there for years. Our lawyer, Maloney, has taught there for many years as well. All of the instructors are already in industry, and they are now a part of a very successful program. They make friends, and friends make more friends and now have a "global law firm," as the instructors keep in touch with the attendees who are from all over the world. Such a program appears to have significant potential, and I hope I am around long enough to see it succeed. What a fantastic idea!

Another challenge we faced created another asset. We found that even though individuals were lawyers and MBAs, they really didn't know much about the inner workings of finance. For example, many were unfamiliar with what the SEC or the Federal Reserve Bank does, what an exchange-traded fund is, and what a stock or a bond is. The book, *Guide to Money & Investing,* by Virginia Morris and Kenneth Morris helped with that deficiency. Now available to the public, a two-day seminar in Boston covers every topic in the book. At the end of the course participants are tested, so we can tell which ones out of the 60 students in the group will surface to the top and who will not.

When we first started accepting foreign students, many didn't speak English very well, and we found they were not successful in our program. Now, in order to qualify, participants have to be proficient in English, and this has benefited the program participants greatly.

Boston University School of Law is honored each year to present its outstanding alumni and friends with Silver Shingle Alumni Awards. These awards, a tradition at the School of Law since 1967, are presented in recognition of notable contributions to the legal profession, leadership within the community, unfailing service to the School of Law, and superlative contributions to society.

Presented at a dinner of over 500 people, I was privileged to receive the Silver Shingle Award. I was honored for serving on the board and for my idea to create a degree program in Banking and Financial Law at the school. Interestingly, the other award recipient that year was Geraldo Rivera!

Charlie Morin and I became very, very close friends. We did a lot of work together, and we were at Federated board meetings every three months in some part of the world.

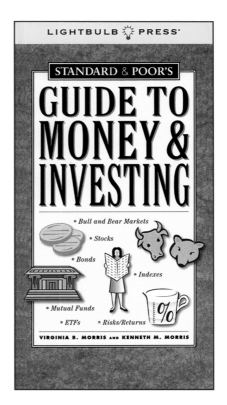

GUIDE TO MONEY & INVESTING, BY VIRGINIA MORRIS AND KENNETH MORRIS, OFFERS CONCISE EXPLANATIONS OF FINANCIAL PRINCIPLES FOR BOTH NOVICE AND EXPERIENCED INVESTORS.

~ 32 ~

Air Traffic (out of) Control

WITH THE TREMENDOUS amount of business travel I've experienced, there has been more than one close call over the years. Some were funny and some had tragic endings.

At the U.S. Treasury Department, one of my regional directors was Ray Morvant in Louisiana who, as I understand it, had been adopted by or cared for by Senator Russell Long. Senator Long had tremendous political sway over the people in Louisiana. I used to stay in his private apartment when I was in New Orleans. On one of those occasions there was a knock at the door at 3:00 a.m., and a female voice said, "Russell, are you in there?" Needless to say, I did not answer.

Ray, my director, was a character of sorts, and one of the things he always did was to have six martinis at lunch. Once while in Louisiana for a regional meeting, we went bar hopping. Ray would stop his car in the middle of the road, would tell a cop to watch it, and the car would be sitting there in the middle of the road when we returned. This was always the case. It appeared Ray held some kind of sway over the police force.

During my stay there, I had spoken to a large group of industrialists and bankers that even included a future governor who ended up spending some time in jail. I don't remember what his crime was, but I remember him being a pleasant individual when I met him.

The key to this part of the story was that on the way to the airport, we had a flat tire. We arrived at the airport late, and as we were approaching the gate, the plane was just being pushed back. No matter how hard we pleaded that I needed to be on that plane, they just kept pushing it back, and of course, it took off. I didn't know it yet, but that was one close call. As it turned out, I was grateful to have missed the flight because the plane was hijacked and spent a week in Havana, Cuba.

Another close call occurred when I was to make an appearance in Texas. I was called to testify at a congressional hearing. Unable to attend, I had to get a replacement speaker. I called the Secretary of the Air Force who was a very good speaker. He wasn't a friend of mine but rather an acquaintance. On his way to make the speech for me, his plane was involved in a mid-air collision over Tell City, Indiana. Tragically, everyone in both planes was killed. That was a bit of a shock, and another close call.

With savings bonds we had a meeting of top-flight volunteers in the Pocono Mountains of Pennsylvania, and in order to get there, we had to take a small 2-engine prop plane. This was a 10-passenger plane that would take us from Philadelphia to the airport at the resort. I had nine bankers and industrialists from Minnesota on the flight, including my State Volunteer Chairman, Roland Bishop. As we were getting ready to take the flight, a young man got into the co-pilot seat of the plane. I felt greatly relieved that we had two pilots. It was a rather stormy, overcast day, but we took off.

On the way to the Poconos we ran into a really terrible rainstorm. Shortly after takeoff, the pilot notified us that he had lost all radio contact. We bounced all over the sky and got struck by lightning, which cracked the windshield. Water started coming through the windshield, and smoke began appearing in the cabin. Needless to say, everybody on the plane was praying that we would get some-where safely.

We did not make the Poconos. We landed in a town quite a long distance from there. Once on the ground we were all invited to either take a six-hour bus ride or get back on the plane and fly there. As soon as we hit the ground and stopped, one of the passengers demanded to get off the plane. He laid flat on the runway, and I thought he had totally flipped out. Another of my passengers had a half-pint of booze and drank it almost straight down. We had a planeload of terrified people. I got back on the plane for the balance of the trip, but several people took the bus. We finally got to the planning meeting for the Treasury Department.

A friend of mine, Joe Jones, had been playing golf when that storm rolled in. His clubs were in a pull cart, and as the thunder and lightning got nearer, he left his cart in the middle of the fairway and ran for cover. Lightning hit his golf cart, and it was the most twisted, melted piece of garbage you can imagine. Luckily, he wasn't with his clubs.

Other than that we had a rather uneventful time, although one of the golfers backed up and dropped into a six-foot concrete viaduct, which scared all of us. We did continue with our planning session and eventually left after the three-day stay.

I went straight to Atlanta where I had to make a payroll savings speech. My payroll chairman was Charlie Dolson, chairman of Delta Airways. As we were sitting at the head table of the 200 or so CEOs and bankers, I was telling Charlie about my adventures on Pocono Airways. He said, "You know, last week I went to the Poconos for a planning session, and was flying Poconos Airways on the return flight when the door or hatch where you get into the plane blew off right beside the seat where I was sitting." We both decided flying Pocono Airways was perhaps not the safest thing to do.

Once, when flying out of Grand Rapids, Michigan, we were about four feet off the ground when we took a pheasant rooster in the right engine. I happened to be looking out the window when it went in. The pilot immediately put the plane back on the ground, and we ended up in the beginning edges of a swamp. They couldn't get the plane out of the swamp, and we all had to walk a mile and a half back to the airport. That was just another of the many exciting adventures I had while flying around the country.

There was another flight to remember when Tom Madden of Federated Investors and I attended a regional meeting in Colorado. It so happened to be at the time when Federated was considering buying a company airplane. We had actually bid on this particular plane as a test to see if it was the kind that we wanted. We arrived at Eagle Pass with no problem and attended the meeting.

However, things got interesting when it was time to leave. One of the two pilots explained to us that the plane had an oil leak. Apparently they had blown a seal and the oil was just pouring out of the engine. He announced that we could continue the next leg of the trip with the risk of losing an engine, or they could take the bus several hours back to Denver to get the part, bring it back, and install it before continuing. The last option seemed like the safest thing to do, but time was always critical.

We decided, or at least I decided, we would fly to Denver, which was only a 15-minute flight. We could have the part installed and continue home from there. If you have ever taken off in Eagle Pass, you know there are sharp canyons on every side, along with high mountains. We took off, and it was the roughest flight I had been on in my entire life. Even though we had seat belts on, we had to hang on for dear life. Tom Madden said, "If my wife ever finds out what kind of a flight I was on here, she would never let me fly again."

We landed safely in Denver, got the part, had it installed, and flew back to Pittsburgh with no problems. I found out later that Gene Maloney was coming to the same meeting and was told when they were 12,000 feet over Eagle Pass the plane he was on had no possible way to land, so he wound up having to take a bus for several hours to get to the meeting.

Perhaps my scariest flight was a trip into Houston, Texas. We were stacked up with a couple hundred airplanes because of bad weather, and we were flying at 22,000 feet. I was the only passenger on the plane. After two hours of circling, I was standing in the cabin when the pilot said that if we couldn't land in the next 15 minutes, we would have to go on to the next destination, which was Albuquerque, New Mexico. Just as we were about to do so, the pilot got word that we had been cleared to land.

The sky was full of planes as we started our descent. I sat down, and had just fastened my seat belt, when suddenly "My God! We hit another plane!" was all I could think. What we had actually hit was the top of a tornado at 22,000 feet. We plummeted through the sky, which was loaded with planes, and it was so overcast and heavy with clouds, we could not see around us. It seemed like it took forever to right the plane, but we dropped and came out at 1800 feet.

Things were scattered all over the cabin, and my suit coat, which was hanging behind the pilots, was thrown around. I had a gold, Cross pen in my pocket, and six weeks later, the pen was found in the baggage compartment, which was behind the back seat of the plane.

There was a big FAA exam with questions and answers about that particular incident. The pilot said that he had black and blue shoulders for six weeks after that trip from hanging upside down in the seatbelts. It was the scariest time I have ever gone though in my life.

These by far are not all of the interesting airplane trips that I encountered, but bear in mind, from the time I started at Federated in 1970, my task was to sell the trust for U.S. Government Securities. In doing so, I traveled almost constantly. I have traveled more than seven million air miles in my lifetime, and I actually stopped counting the miles a long time ago. There was a time when I flew almost every single business day for years, and have probably been to every state at least ten times.

If the city was large, I would stay for a few days, but in most cases I would work the day calling brokerage firms, entertain for lunch, do a dog and pony show in the afternoon, entertain clients at night, and catch the last flight out to the next city—all well planned. Of course, I always flew tourist class and used airport limos instead of taxis.

Airport limos are a special item; they differ greatly from city to city. In the early 70s, most of them were old used limousines, panel trucks, or small busses. The experiences could be so entertaining that I decided that if I ever wrote a book it would be about my life in limos; airport limos, that is. I can't tell you how many wild and unbelievable circumstances that I ran into. In the interest of brevity, I will mention just one.

I left Chicago one night and arrived in Toledo, Ohio around 10:30 p.m. With a number of other people, we caught the local airport limousine. It turned out to be a very old vehicle designed to haul people, but it was very, very ancient. It had four rows of seats and storage in the back behind two full sized doors. After the typical 45 minute delay as everyone was loaded, the 70-some-year-old driver positioned himself in his "loaded" vehicle, and off we went.

It was obvious that it had all kinds of problems, including a very sticky clutch. We started out with a big jerk, and the two doors in the rear that were holding the luggage opened up and spread the luggage for at least 200 feet down the street. He went back and patiently picked up each suitcase, some of which had fallen open, piled them back into the vehicle, and shut the very rickety back doors. By now, everyone was somewhat concerned, perplexed, and annoyed, if not amused.

He climbed back in to the vehicle, put it in gear, let the clutch out, and took off down the street. Once again, he spread the suitcases another 100 feet. Again, he got out to find that some of them had opened again. He patiently closed them all up, and piled them back in. By now another half-hour had gone by. It was approaching midnight. At this point, everyone was getting short tempered and starting to complain. I was too tired to care, but noticed my suitcase had suffered some wide gashes from the road.

After piling the suitcases back in, he took off and the door flew open for the third time. This time the suitcases spread even farther down the road, because he had problems stopping the vehicle due to poor brakes. Now, everyone was clearly grouchy and the complaining began to crescendo. We were out in the country, not near any humanity, and had no other choice. We were headed out of the airport, but on a very small road. The airport had closed down by now, yet people were still threatening to go back there. The poor guy picked all the suitcases up, put them back in the vehicle, and finally was able to take off without jerking the doors open again. He delivered us to our hotels, and I checked in about 1:30 in the morning. That was the time I decided if I ever wrote a book I would be sure to share a little bit about my life in airport limos.

During my first few years at Federated I was on a commercial flight almost every day or at least every other day. I flew all over the country. Because of my extensive travel, I said to Tom Donnelly and Jack Donahue in a meeting one day that I really needed a jet. It was my belief that the time had come for us to buy one. I was told in no uncertain terms the company would never own a jet because of all the terrible things that happened to a company when they owned one.

Tom Donnelly said, "Once this company gets to 20 billion dollars, you can buy any airplane you want." With our spectacular growth that time arrived in the not too distant future. It was actually only a couple of years later.

Again I went to see Tom and Jack, who ran the company, and reminded them I had been told when we passed 20 billion dollars of revenue; I could have any airplane I wanted. Now that we were at 22 billion dollars, I expected that to happen, and it did.

When we finally got our own plane, it was a huge relief and a much better way to fly. I must have been the only one who flew on the Citation we owned during the first year we had it. We had some adventurous times in that Citation, including getting struck with a bolt of lightning upon takeoff from Allegheny County Airport. When that happened, a ball of fire rolled through the cabin. It came in one wing and went out the other. That was definitely one of those things that we hoped would never happen again. We owned the Citation for a couple of years, and then we got a Learjet. We later bought a second one. Not long after, I bought my own personal Learjet.

The first Learjet I purchased had only been flying for about five and one-half months and was doing a really good job. We had secured a contract to deliver spare parts (actually hearts, livers, kidneys, or other vital organs) whenever the UPMC Hospital in Pittsburgh had an organ on location. The crew would take as many as five doctors, go to the location, harvest the organ, and bring it back to Pittsburgh. It was a very lucrative business, to say the least. However, one day

GLEN'S LEARJET ON A FLIGHT OVER PITTSBURGH.

on a training mission, the plane crashed into a slag dump just off the airport.

We will never know what happened, but it's been theorized that both the pilot and the trainee each shut off an engine, and the plane dropped like a rock. The plane was loaded with fuel, and it exploded on impact.

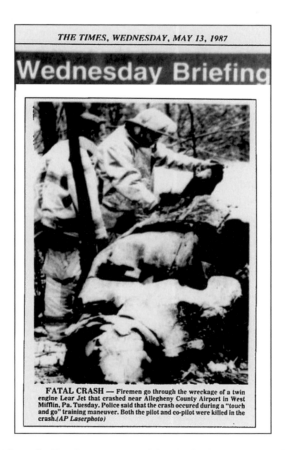

THE TIMES, WEDNESDAY, MAY 13, 1987

Wednesday Briefing

FATAL CRASH — Firemen go through the wreckage of a twin engine Lear Jet that crashed near Allegheny County Airport in West Mifflin, Pa. Tuesday. Police said that the crash occured during a "touch and go" training maneuver. Both the pilot and co-pilot were killed in the crash.*(AP Laserphoto)*

GETTYSBURG TIMES—FIREMEN GO THROUGH THE WRECKAGE OF A TWIN ENGINE LEARJET THAT CRASHED NEAR ALLEGHENY COUNTY AIRPORT IN WEST MIFFLIN, PA TUESDAY. POLICE SAID THAT THE CRASH OCCURRED DURING A "TOUCH AND GO" TRAINING MANEUVER. BOTH THE PILOT AND CO-PILOT WERE KILLED IN THE CRASH. (AP LASERPHOTO)

NTSB Identification: **DCA87MA031** .
The docket is stored on NTSB microfiche number **35569.**
Accident occurred Tuesday, May 12, 1987 in WEST MIFFLIN, PA
Probable Cause Approval Date: 11/29/1988
Aircraft: LEARJET 35A, registration: N100EP
Injuries: 2 Fatal.

The copilot (dual student) was to get a professional check on the first leg of the flight with a simulated single engine power loss on takeoff. According to witnesses, the takeoff was normal, until lift-off approximately 3200 feet down the runway; but after lift-off, the aircraft climbed only about 50 feet and didn't seem to accelerate. They reported the nose pitched up and the aircraft went in a steep bank attitude near the departure end of the runway. Subsequently, it descended and crashed in wooded terrain in a right wing down, nose high attitude. A by-stander tried to get in the aircraft to rescue the pilots, but the door was jammed and he was unable to break the cabin windows. A fire erupted and engulfed the aircraft. Due to rough terrain, there was a delay in getting firefighting equipment to the accident site. No pre-impact mechanical failures were found. The gear, flaps and spoilers were found in the retracted position. For takeoff the flaps should have been extended to the 8 or 20-degree position. The stall speeds for 20 deg, 8 deg and no flaps were 104.5, 109.0 and 119.5 kts, respectively. The captain was an FAA designated flight examiner and a certified flight instructor (CFI).

The National Transportation Safety Board determines the probable cause(s) of this accident as follows:

Raising of flaps: premature, copilot/second pilot. Airspeed: inadequate. Stall: inadvertent. Supervision: inadequate. Pilot in command: (CFI)

THE NTSB FINAL REPORT ON THE CRASH OF GLEN'S LEARJET. THE TRAINING MISSION TRAGICALLY CLAIMED THE LIVES OF THE TWO PILOTS.

The bank that had the loan on the plane called me the very next day after the crash. Of course, with the collateral now gone, they were wondering how they were going to get paid. I have no idea how the insurance company found out about the accident because I had not called them yet, but there on my desk was a check for the full amount left by a messenger. I was able to tell the bank that I could send them a check for the whole amount of the loan.

The plane was gone, but for me, the flying continued. I believe the most I have ever flown in one week was due to an incident that occurred while I was still working for the U.S. Treasury. I had a call on Sunday from Secretary of the Treasury Fowler saying that he was scheduled to make a speech in San Diego sometime on Monday, but that he had been called to a Security Council meeting. He said I would have to go and make the speech for him.

A plane was requisitioned. As a Grade 18, I was ranked equal to a three star general. That meant I had to be met by two staff cars and at least one colonel. The plane I requisitioned was an F86 with the armament taken out. It actually had two pilots and three passenger seats. We flew to San Diego where I made the speech, and we flew back to Washington. After exiting the plane, while walking across the tarmac, the announcement came that I had to go back to Los Angeles to make another speech the next day. The Secretary of the Treasury was still working on the Security Council matter, and that took precedent over anything else he was doing. We turned right around and flew back to Los Angeles.

As I returned to Washington after the second Los Angeles trip, I got the same notification that the Security Council meeting was still going on, and I had to fly back to Sacramento to make another speech the next day. Back to California we went for the third time in three days. I actually had to go back to California a fourth day, and on Friday I had to go to Denver. I made five speeches in five days and crossed the country five times. It was a long week.

Eventually, Jack and I wanted a plane with a stand up cabin and a sit down bathroom. In order to meet those requirements, we had to purchase a Hawker Sidley. The Hawker Sidley is an eight-passenger plane, and it does have those two important amenities.

The time came when one wasn't enough. Our latest purchase was a brand new Hawker, a 14 million dollar airplane. It is in the air every day. In a company of our size and with all the people who must travel, the only way to go is to have a jet. It is costly, but in terms of time saving, it is a necessity.

~ 33 ~
Secretaries in My Career

BY DEFINITION, A secretary is a position of administrative support. The title is given to a person who performs routine, personal and most importantly, administrative tasks for a senior position. A secretary keeps a track of the executive's schedule, including meetings, appointments, commitments and reports. Typing letters and accessing important data are certainly paramount tasks, in addition to keeping a record of all incoming and outgoing phone calls in the office. The responsibility of taking effective messages when the executive is unavailable falls to the secretary as well.

Without question, a secretary is a personal organizer for a manager and performs a very important job. An effective secretary is a valuable part of an executive's team, helping build bridges with clients and facilitating a more effective and efficient work environment.

After spending 12 years running a newspaper and serving as editor, publisher, and secretary myself, I suddenly found myself at the U.S. Treasury Department in Minnesota with a secretary to assist me!

Well, she really wasn't a secretary, but an office manager, and her name was Mrs. Zierman. She was "all business" and rarely smiled, but was as efficient as she could be. My having taken shorthand in business school gave me a better insight into dictating. That was a new experience, but one that I certainly became accustomed to.

Arriving in Washington, DC as National Director, there was a secretary already in place. Her name was Hazel Kentz. I remember that she was 6'2" tall with blazing red hair, and was a retired colonel in the women's U.S. Air Force. Hazel was from Georgia and had a Southern drawl that could melt you in your tracks. Since she was required to talk to lots of CEOs across the country, she was a godsend. They could call and be irate about anything under the sun, and when she got done talking to them they were as tame as a lamb. Hazel had a hard time getting to work at 9:00 a.m., and usually arrived by 9:20 a.m. For someone like me who was a stickler for time, that was a little difficult; however, she made up for it by working as late into the evening as I cared to stay, which was sometimes 9:00 or 10:00 at night.

When I transitioned into Motivational Systems, the only thing furnished to me by the company was a secretary in New York. The office was located on 46th Street, just off 5th Avenue, and even then, it was in a bad area and a "tough place to work." I didn't spend much time in the office. I barely remember my secretary, and I certainly don't remember her name, but she was efficient in doing all of my follow-up letters, which were always dictated over the telephone.

At Federated Investors, I shared a secretary with Dick Fisher. Her name was Alexis Maas, and she was a ravishing beauty. I think she worked for us for a couple of years. Since I spent 99 percent of my time on the road, most of my dictation was on the phone, and after a short period of time she graduated to Wall Street in New York. Sometime after that she moved to California, was attracted to Johnny Carson, and they were married. They would return to Pittsburgh at least once a year, and at times I ended up riding an exercise bike right next to him in the hotel's health club. At any rate, we all agreed Alexis made it "big time."

The next few years were very hectic as we were going through unprecedented growth. I remember my secretary for a year or two was Joanne Minyo. Her husband ran a denim shop in Oakland. They left and moved to California, and the next thing I heard, Joanne was the personal secretary to billionaire, Jack Cook Kent, who among other things was the owner of the Washington Redskins. I remember her telling me she had to fly back and forth from Los Angeles to Washington many times. Obviously she also made "it big."

We moved our headquarters into the Chamber of Commerce building where I had a very large office on the second floor on the front corner. Just outside my office were three secretaries: Fern Brown, Paula Chicowicz, and one other whose name escapes me. I kept them all very busy. Unfortunately, I was traveling every day and arrived back in Pittsburgh late one night, only to find that I was to be in Chicago for a television appearance the next morning. This meant I had to catch a very early morning flight. I got to the appointed television station only to be told, "Didn't you hear we canceled this early yesterday?" Upon hearing this I called Paula and asked her if she had received that message and she said, "Yes." She was immediately transferred to another department. After that Fern left to go to the American Association of Associations in Washington, DC where she served as their conference coordinator.

My next secretary was Jeannie Emerick, who worked for me for 11 years and finally left to have a family. She was extremely efficient, and I do not know how I would have survived without her outstanding service.

After Jeannie left, Robin Guernsey became my new secretary. Robin has worked for me for 17 years, and continues to do so. She is the best secretary I ever had. Robin typifies the idea that an effective secretary can also help an executive build bridges.

∿ 34 ∿
Highs and Lows of My Career

TALKING ABOUT THE highs and lows of my entire career is very difficult because my career has been so varied and has encompassed so many people, places, and things. Taking up this challenge, I will do my best. It is hard to know where to begin.

Of course your career and your personal life are closely intertwined. Perhaps it is appropriate to say that my highest high and my lowest low have involved my family.

Obviously, my highest high was my marriage to LaVonne. Without her, many of my accomplishments would not have been possible. Life would certainly not have been as pleasurable or rewarding. That makes LaVonne the highest high.

The lowest low was the deaths of our children David and Lori. Just as it is impossible to comprehend the anguish of loss until death comes to someone you love, it has been equally impossible for me to write of my sorrow before now.

As far as my career goes . . .

Working with Jack Donahue and Federated was definitely a high. Jack didn't want you to be bothered with anything other than knowing your product, meeting your client, and making the sale. It's simply been an absolute privilege to work with someone who thinks like I do, who handed me the ball and said, "Go do it!" It has been the ultimate experience.

Watching those you mentor succeed is a satisfying high. John Fisher now heads Federated's investment department, which is a $400 billion dollar company, and Tom Terrate heads the entire sales department. Both young men came to work for me in sales just out of college. I am very proud of them.

Working with the stars in the entertainment industry was another high. All the glitter and glamour of the entertainment world was at my fingertips. Traveling with Raquel Welch and Eva Gabor added to the excitement.

Equally exciting were my associations with CEOs from all over the country. Not only was I able to work with many of the Fortune 500 CEOs in this country, I got to know many of them personally.

My years working in the Treasury Department and meeting with the presidents and secretaries of the agencies were certainly a high note. These contacts proved invaluable throughout my career.

Gustavus President Axel Steuer granted me a full degree from Gustavus. The degree had to be signed by every member of the faculty and every member of the board of directors. Fifty years after I was a freshman there, I received a full undergraduate degree from Gustavus Adolphus College. That was certainly one of the major highlights of my life.

One of the thrills of my career was doing public relations work in 16 cities in 16 weeks for Money Market Management. C. Paul Luongo organized the public relations campaign. This blitz created tens of thousands of leads for money market funds across the country.

Staying at the finest hotels in the country while we entertained our clients was especially memorable. As a result of our travel experiences, C. Paul Luongo wrote a book called *America's Best,* which was well received.

We once had 200 clients out in the Arizona desert that we entertained in a tent. To get there you had to walk over a hill, and when you arrived, there was a big sign that said, "Black Tie Only." Of course, everyone would stop with some concern when they saw the sign. We had a tee shirt that looked like a coat and black tie that we gave the guests as they arrived. As a result, we had an audience in black tie apparel. Hosting creative events was certainly a lot of fun.

A career low was when I was summoned to New York by the President of the Bankers Association. I was told if we continued to dominate the trust conferences, we were going to be banished from the American Bankers Association. That slowed down entertaining our clients at many of the finest resorts. Some five years later, when that president was no longer head of the Association, he confessed to me his story was contrived. There was no way they would have put us out of business or even tried. They would not have revoked our membership. He said at that time he was just reacting to the advice of others who wanted recognition at the trust conferences, where we continued to dominate.

One of the lowest points of my career was when I was fired by President Nixon. In retrospect, however, that turned out to be a high since I probably would not have ended up at Federated had Nixon not done this unintended favor for me. As a result, this low turned into a high.

Another United States President was responsible for one of my many career highs. This was Lyndon Johnson. I was able to sell myself and convince him that I was the person who should be the National Director, although he had someone else in mind for the job.

Winning a Treasury award for breaking the prior peacetime record when we enrolled 5.5 million new payroll savers in my first year at the Treasury was certainly a high point.

The development of Money Market Management allowed hundreds of thousands of individuals to receive more income on their money. In terms of dollars received, that amounted to billions. What a gratifying high in my career!

Another high occurred at a press conference in New York where *The New York Post,* which had followed my career at the Treasury, put a big eight-column headline on the story, "Seven Percent Is Patriotic Too."

At one time we had over 100 cemetery associations as our clients in the U.S. Government fund. I'm not sure if that's a high or a low!

Another lifetime high was working with Dan Heit, the head of Abraxas, to bring Abraxas out of the woods and into the city.

Another Fortune 500 financial group offered me a job, at more than double my salary (up to $4 million), to switch from Federated. Obviously that was a thrilling offer, but I was having much too much fun at Federated.

Throwing out the first pitch at a Washington Senators game, and throwing out the first pitch at a Pirates game are certainly included as high points in my life.

Giving Christmas mincemeat giant pies from the NY Athletic Club, not only became a Federated Family Tradition, they even helped retain clients. We were always amazed by that.

Another high of my career that I am pleased with is the financial security afforded to me. Without this, the endowed Charitable Remainder Trusts listed in Appendix C would not have been possible.

Life is often described as a seesaw, with many ups and downs. As you can see, my ups, or highs greatly exceeded my downs, or lows. For that I continue to be grateful.

GLEN JOHNSON AND A NUMBER OF BOSTON RED SOX BASEBALL TEAM MEMBERS PRIOR TO THE GAME WITH THE WASHINGTON SENATORS—A GAME SALUTING THE BOND PROGRAM. GLEN THREW OUT THE FIRST PITCH.

BUSINESS

E

SECTION

PITTSBURGH POST-GAZETTE ■ FRIDAY, SEPTEMBER 12, 1997

Money market mogul

Glen Johnson cashed in 24 years ago by making bank trust officers feel special.

By Steve Massey
Post-Gazette Staff Writer

The news slipped by most people. This newspaper didn't even take note of it.

But for 68-year-old Glen Johnson, the recent report that U.S. money market fund assets topped $1 trillion for the first time was cause for reflection and quiet celebration.

Johnson, after all, is as responsible as anyone for the popularity of money market funds. And money market funds, in turn, are responsible as much as anything for the explosive growth of his company, Federated Investors.

It was Johnson who coined the phrase "money market fund" in late 1973 to describe a new mutual fund he helped create for the relatively small Pittsburgh money manager. The fund would pool investors' money to buy jumbo bank CDs, thus allowing small fry in on a higher-yielding investment that heretofore only wealthy or institutional investors could afford.

As the money poured in, Wall Street took note and soon, everyone was offering money market funds.

The rest, as they say, is history. Money market funds became a fad with staying power. Federated rode the boom to become the nation's sixth-largest mutual fund company. It now manages or administers $127 billion of investments, including $56 billion in money market funds its bread and butter.

"We developed a product that not only built a company, it built an entire industry," says Johnson, cracking into a good-natured laugh, something he does often during an interview in his 27th-floor office atop Federated Investors Tower at Liberty and Grant, overlooking the Golden Triangle and North Shore.

"And it all started right here."

Well, not exactly here.

Johnson is the first to admit an even smaller investment concern out of New York created the first money market fund in the fall of 1973, a few months before Federated. But that concern didn't call it a money market fund and never did much to promote it.

Johnson, on the other hand, did everything to promote Federated's money market fund.

Initially, Johnson and his wife, LaVonne, took to the highways calling on bank trust officers. They started in West Virginia and worked their way down to Florida, then to Arkansas where they had relatives, and then back north, all the way to upstate New York and eventually Bar Harbor, Maine.

The pitch: The fund would let the banks make money on their excess trust cash by investing it in attractive interest-bearing instruments. At the time, most banks didn't invest spare cash — the amount left over after investing their clients' money in stocks, bonds and other investments. They just sat on it.

While some banks were intrigued, none bit. So Federated, using a well-connected publicist, did a 16-city, 16-week blitz aimed at individual investors.

Johnson did 55 newspaper and magazine interviews, from smaller regional publications to the biggies — the Wall Street Journal, New York Times, Forbes, Fortune. He appeared on 127 radio and 88 live television shows, including Today, Tonight, Tomorrow with Tom Snyder; and a New York station with a fresh-faced correspondent named Stone Phillips. Repeatedly.

In every interview, Johnson would mention Federated's toll-free number. Repeatedly.

Back in Pittsburgh, at Federated's old 421 7th Ave. offices, Johnson's wife, the wives of other executives, and lower-level staffers (including founder John Donahue's son, J. Christopher, now Federated president) would man the phones as inquiries flooded in.

The marketing blitz generated 90,000 leads and $400 million from individual investors. And, Johnson is quick to note, Federated did it without one paid advertisement.

"That's what launched us," he says. "We brought money funds to the world." Ever the salesman, Johnson wasn't finished.

There still was the matter of the

SEE **MONEY,** PAGE E-

The birth of money market funds

U.S money market fund assets' growth since their inception in 1974
(in $ billions)

Growth of the value of Federated Investors' money market funds and total investments
(in $ billions)

Federated —
Total —

Money funds made a reputation

MONEY FROM PAGE E-1

lucrative bank market. It was esti-mated on any given day, U.S. banks were sitting on about $40 billion of cash. (And this, remember, was 1974, when a billion dollars was still real money.)

Johnson turned to a bit of trick-ery. He made a video outlining the benefits of putting cash in a money fund, called it "For Effective Trust Management," and hired the voice of a long-time American Bankers Association narrator.

"The ABA used the same guy for all their tapes in their education series," Johnson says. "So when this tape arrived on your desk and it said, 'For Effective Trust Manage-ment,' it almost looked like it came from the ABA. And it talked about how you could invest your trust cash."

The ploy landed Federated its first bank customer, First National in Martinsville, Va.

That broke the logjam. By the end of 1974, Federated had attracted 22

bank trust departments to its fund service.

That number grew over the years to 1,800 as Federated expanded its array of funds and services, and devoted itself to serving banks, a change made in 1976 when it stopped selling directly to the public and became a wholesaler.

Federated didn't just target bank trust officers, it wined and dined them. It befriended them.

It threw them some of the best parties the industry has ever seen — so good, in fact, that the ABA in 1980 ordered Federated to tone it down or it no longer would be welcome at the ABA's annual conventions.

The first big bash came at the ABA's 1976 convention in Atlanta. Determined to get Federated's name out, Johnson rented the top floor of the newly opened 66-story Peachtree Plaza and personally printed hundreds of invitations.

"All the fliers said was, 'Come see Atlanta from the top of Peach-tree Plaza. And enjoy champagne

and crab legs,'" Johnson says. "We had 500, 600 people show up. We couldn't chase them out of there."

Federated solidified its party rep-utation the next year. It rented a castle atop a hill in Beverly Hills. Party-goers walked across a moat and up a 200-foot red carpet into a hall where a 26-piece orchestra was playing Camelot and the waiters were dressed as monks.

It cost $88,000, enough to make a few top officers back home swallow hard. But it generated almost $400 million of new business, including a coveted Ohio bank whose top offi-cer wired Federated $30 million the day after the party.

The next year was Federated's biggest blowout of all. It transported 1,600 trust officers from Downtown Washington, D.C., to the Mazza Galleria in the suburbs, using 36 buses. There was a fish bar stretch-ing 100 feet, 150 entertainers, and the U.S. Navy Sea Chanters.

It marked the only time the elite group of singers performed at a private, for-profit event, says John-son, who as a former Capitol Hill insider, used his connections to book them. In the mid-1960s, John-son served as assistant treasurer in the Johnson administration, pedal-ing U.S. savings bonds.

As the guests left the Galleria, Johnson personally handed each a one-pound box of Godiva chocolates and thanked them for coming.

"We made heroes out of trust officers, who were at the bottom of the barrel before we came along," he says. "We taught them that they weren't the lowest on the totem pole."

There were other parties over the years. A big fireworks show and steamboat cruise in New Orleans. A museum gala in Hawaii. Johnny Cash. Al Hirt. Pete Fountain. Crys-tal Gayle.

It was after a Lincoln Center show that the ABA laid down the law. Other vendors, unable to com-pete with Federated, were threaten-ing to stop coming to the convention.

"They'd have beer and peanuts, and we'd have Pete Fountain and champagne," Johnson laughs.

Johnson lives in Pittsburgh, in an

Fund primer

Money market funds are pretty much what they sound like: funds that invest in money market instruments, such as U.S. Treasury bills, bank certifi-cates of deposit, commercial paper issued by corporations and tax-free municipal notes.

They allow the small investor to buy into these short-term, low-risk investments without having to put up the large sums that would be required if they were to buy the investments individually.

Investors buy shares in the fund, typically valued at $1 a share, and the money from the share purchases is pooled and used to buy money-market in-struments. Investors make their money on interest and other income generated by the fund's investments, and receive the payout when they sell their shares.

— By Steve Massey

Oakland townhouse, and serves as president of Federated's 28 money market funds and directs its legisla-tive affairs.

But he spends an increasing amount of time away from the office, at opposite ends of the coun-try. The couple has a winter home in Marco Island, Fla., and a family farm near Lake Lillian, Minn., 90 miles west of Minneapolis.

Johnson grew up on the farm, homesteaded by his great-grandfa-ther in 1873, and in many ways his heart remains in Lake Lillian, where for 12 years he published the Lake Lillian Crier, serving a com-munity of 300.

The fact Johnson's a liberal Dem-ocrat — he ran former Vice Presi-dent Hubert Humphrey's U.S. Senate campaign in Minnesota in 1960 — stands out at Federated, where Republicans rule and conser-vativism is a way of life.

But given the business he's brought to the company, no one's complaining about his leftward leanings.

Relishing his role as the in-house liberal, Johnson likes to joke that, "My associates are so far right that they thought Ronald Reagan was a flaming liberal."

PITTSBURGH POST-GAZETTE: "MONEY MARKET MOGUL," PAGE 2.

LAVONNE AND GLEN JOHNSON WITH
PRESIDENT GEORGE W. BUSH.

Part 4

Love of Adventure

"THINGS WORTH WHILE" BY LUDVIG S. DALE.

～ 35 ～

College Boards and the Royal Roundtable

EARLY IN THE book I talk about attending Gustavus as a freshman and spending one year there. I talk about how many servicemen were there at the time, compared to a handful of students like me, who were just out of high school. Two of the freshmen attending at the same time as I did, were John Kendall and Paul Granlund. I didn't know them as a freshman, but John Kendall went on to become President of Gustavus, and Paul Granlund became a famous sculptor and artist-in-residence at Gustavus.

Years later, we commissioned Paul Granlund to create a sculpture, "Resurrection," for the front of First Lutheran Church in Pittsburgh, Pennsylvania (see photo next page). The Mayor was there for the dedication, along with many others. That was a really special event, and the sculpture provides a landmark for the church. Paul has since died, and I believe that John Kendall, who was president at the time that Paul was sculpturing there, has also passed away.

John Kendall got in touch with me and asked if I wanted to serve on the Gustavus Board. I told him I was on the board at Thiel College, which he knew. The president of Thiel College had told him of my involvement there, and the fact that I had attended Gustavus. One thing led to another, and I agreed to serve on the Gustavus Board, so at one time I was on both the Thiel and Gustavus Boards. I was on the board at Thiel for 14 years, but only served half of the six-year term with Gustavus because of my time constraints as Federated grew.

For about 12 consecutive years we entertained the Gustavus

"RESURRECTION," BY PAUL THEODORE GRANLUND AT THE FIRST
LUTHERAN CHURCH, IN PITTSBURGH, PA. THE SCULPTURE
REPRESENTS THE RESURRECTION OF MAN, NOT GOD. TWO
DEDICATION CEREMONIES WERE HELD. ONE FOR THE CONGREGATION
ON OCT. 20, 1985; AND ANOTHER FOR THE CITY, ON OCT. 21, 1985.

alumni at our Marco Island home. On one occasion we had about 250 guests, which included about 70 members of the choir. That was very exciting and culminated with an outing on the *Marco Princess* and the *Naples Princess*, each boat carrying 125 of our guests.

Over the years the alumni met in Marco annually, with small groups of successful professionals often attending by special invitation to present an informative seminar on various subjects, such how to set up Charitable Remainder Trusts, and other pertinent information.

Axel Steuer, the President of Gustavus that granted me the full undergraduate degree, really wanted me to stay on the board and become chairman. He was quite disappointed when I did not accept. In the end, he became the victim of a coup, so-to-speak, and had to resign as president. I am certainly sorry I was not in a position to prevent that action.

Axel went on to be president of Illinois College where he has been extremely successful. I have not stopped supporting Gustavus, although I was unhappy with some of the circumstances that occurred. Axel was really an excellent president.

In all of my years of traveling I called on numerous CEOs for Federated to encourage them to invest their corporate money in our Money Market accounts or investments that fit their needs. Through those endeavors I met Curt Carlson, who was in the banking business when he invented Gold Bond Stamps. Eventually, Curt owned the Radisson Hotels worldwide, T.G.I. Friday's restaurants, car leasing companies, and one of the world's largest travel companies. The headquarters for Carlson Companies is just outside of Minneapolis, and they hire thousands of people. He has endowed Gustavus as well as other educational institutions.

Curt invited me to join the Swedish Council. Once I joined the Swedish Council, he suggested I join the Royal Roundtable. The Royal Roundtable consisted of approximately 30 Swedish CEOs and 30 American CEOs. Their purpose was to advance and maintain the culture and the connection between Sweden and the U.S.

To further trade between the two countries, Federated was investing large amounts of money at one time. At the time I was visiting there, Federated owned 300 million dollars of Sweden's debt in one of the funds.

Connections with Sweden were very rewarding. We would meet every other year in Sweden, always in Stockholm, and alternate a year in the U.S. at various locations. We met in Washington, DC, Jamestown, New York, San Francisco, Chicago, and other cities.

Each year we would come up with a *Swede of the Year*. I distinctly remember that the *Swede of the Year* at one time was William Rehnquist, 16th Chief Justice of the Supreme Court. They studied his ancestry, and found a judge or jurist from the 1200s had been accused of some crime and was beheaded. That was the only connection they could find, but we made the most of it and had a lot of fun. We sat at a lunch table with his daughter, and the emcee did a marvelous job of building up this story about the Supreme Court Justice's ancestor.

LaVonne and I both enjoyed the years with the Royal Roundtable, especially the trips to Sweden. On one of the trips to Sweden, I was able to find the house where the family of my grandfather, on the Johnson side, originated. We also visited Dalsland, where the Anderson relatives on my mother's side of the family lived.

In Dalsland, we found a cousin about 30 miles outside of the area. He ran the bank in town, which I found interesting. We spent the day there, and I was able to see the church where my great, great, great, great grandmother had been the organist 500 years ago. The records of my mother's family were all listed in the church records, as was common in that era.

✺ 36 ✺
Lutheran Church

BAPTIZED BY THE age of seven, my Lutheran parents saw to it that I always went to Sunday school. That was mandatory; I didn't miss it, even on the days my parents had to take me the three miles to church with horses and sleds. My parents were more concerned about getting me to Sunday school and Confirmation then they were about being in church themselves.

However, when times weren't too busy, we went to church on Sundays together. My mother went much more often than my dad because my dad often had ballgames to umpire.

GLEN'S FATHER OSCAR
PLAYED BASEBALL FOR
22 YEARS AND UMPIRED
FOR 10 YEARS.

When I was going to Sunday school, Pastor Bergstrand was the minister. He had been there for years and years when I started Confirmation with him. Confirmation was two years, but he died in the middle of my Confirmation study. Upon completion of the study, his son, Wilton Bergstrand, confirmed me.

One of my more vivid memories stem from a time when I was visiting my cousin's house, and the elder Pastor Bergstrand came over to see them. I don't know the reason he was there, but we boys were sitting behind the door playing cards, and he asked us what we were doing. I told him we were playing cards, and to this day, I remember saying, "And this is the ace of spades." Why I did that I have no idea. Everyone joked about my remark from that time on. I had told the minister what the ace of spades was. In those days, some people considered playing cards a sin.

My dad believed in God, but didn't go to church much. He always supported the church financially. I'd say that was probably due to my mother being so involved in the Ladies' Aid and other church activities.

LaVonne and I were always Lutherans. We married in the Norwegian church that LaVonne attended. After our marriage, we attended the Swedish church where I was a member. When we moved to Reston, Virginia, we went to a Lutheran Church in Herndon. We also go to a Lutheran Church on Marco Island, although we are still members in Pittsburgh. We keep the Pittsburgh membership. Our daughter is interred in the Columbarium in Pittsburgh, and we are destined to be there as well.

In my first year at Federated (1970), we attended the Lutheran Church located right in the middle of downtown Pittsburgh, across from the U.S. Steel building. The church, built in 1837, looks very small surrounded by the city's skyscrapers.

The congregation needed to raise some money to fix the organ at the church. After discussion of hiring a fundraiser to assist in the project, I said, "Look, I'll do it." We needed to raise $60,000. I raised it in a couple of weeks from the congregation. Eventually the church needed a new organ and a new slate roof, so we went on to raise further funds as those and other needs arose. It is a very generous congregation. I was involved in most of the fundraisers.

The Lutheran Church in America had an office in New York where there were three people in the hierarchy of the church. The treasurer had some kind of a conflict and was forced to resign. The Lutheran Church was looking for someone to fill that post. Unknown to me, I'd been recommended by my local pastor, and I was called to go to New York to look at this job. I thought it was entirely about managing the church's money, but there was more to it than that, so I didn't accept.

As a result of the meeting, however, I was appointed to the Pension Board of the Lutheran Church of America (LCA). We met four times a year, and we managed the pensions of all the church employees. We had millions of dollars to manage. There were five board members on the pension fund as well as a paid director.

Two of the people on the board were unbelievably staunch in their opinions of investing in "sin stocks." These were stocks from companies that are associated with products or activities widely considered "sinful" in one way or the other, such as tobacco, liquor, gambling, or armament. They were unyielding in their position and would debate for hours and hours about which companies were connected with "sin." At one point I told them, "If you want to put it that way, you can't even invest in Treasury bills because we use that money to go to war." I was livid. Finally, I introduced them to the book, *The Duties and Responsibilities of a Fiduciary*, so we could better focus on fiduciary responsibility.

When there was a merger of three synods, the pension board had to be dissolved. To have a more balanced board the new group chose to expand the board to 15 people. Our former five members oriented the new members of the board.

Some new board members had no knowledge at all. The first question one of the women asked me was, "What's a Treasury bill?" I thought, "God help this organization." I was off the board, but the members continued to struggle for years.

After the new board functioned for about six months, a woman from Des Moines, Iowa asked me to come back on the board. I said, "I wouldn't go back on that board for all the money in the world." That group of people had no idea what was going on. The biggest necessity was trying to teach the new board members what it took to manage money. Suffice it to say, my three years on the Pension Board proved to be another interesting experience.

Clearly, the Lutheran church has been very important to our family, but also to LaVonne and me, individually. LaVonne served on the Education Committee, the Call Committee, and Church Council at the church in Pittsburgh. We are not official members of the local Lutheran church, but LaVonne serves on the Foundation Board. The church has a sizable endowment and funds grants each year.

Our pastor in Pittsburgh, David Gleason, officiated at both our daughter's and our son's funerals. We will always be grateful to God that Pastor Gleason was our shepherd at that time.

~37~

Flying

ABOUT A YEAR after I started the newspaper in 1949, I developed incredible headaches. I went to the doctor to see what was wrong, and he told me it probably was the 18-hour days I was working. He said I simply had to find an outlet; something else besides work to think about. So in 1950 I took flying lessons.

I convinced my friend, Bud Portinga, to take lessons with me. At that time it was quite reasonable. It cost only $2.50 for an hour lesson in an Aeronka Chief, later to become an Aeronka Champ. It cost $6.50 to take lessons in a Stinson Station Wagon, which later was replaced by the Cessna 140.

After six hours of dual flight time, I was able to solo. I really enjoyed flying. It took my mind off other things I had to do, and I must say it truly made my headaches go away.

Over my flying years I logged about 310 hours, most of it flying little planes around the state. Much of that time was in the wintertime when I could land on lakes with skis; this made everything simpler for landing.

One of the more precarious adventures ocurred when Bud and I were out flying in the winter of 1951. It was a warm day, and I actually landed in one of Bud's cornfields where the stalks had been chopped. The whole cornfield was covered with snow. It was a good landing spot. The snow was soft and slushy and the plane's skis slid fairly well. We stopped the plane and went to Bud's house to listen to a Minnesota Gopher football game.

When we returned, the wind was fierce, and the temperature had dropped to about 20 degrees. We got in the plane, and the skis were frozen to the ground. In order to get the plane loose, I told Bud to jump up and down on the skis while I revved up the motor in hopes of getting us out of there.

The wind was blowing about 25 miles an hour out of the northwest. I had landed the plane to the northwest. I'm not sure I was perceptive enough to think that the wind would be blowing from that direction when we took off, but fortunately we were headed in the right direction. As I revved the engine louder and louder, giving it more and more revs, Bud was jumping up and down on the skis to crack them loose. Suddenly they came loose, and the plane went straight up in the air. Bud was hanging on to the skis, and we were taking off. We were several feet in the air before he was able to scramble in through the door. It was one of those incidents where we could have had a terrible accident, but we were fortunate, and it was a memorable day to say the least.

Bud had about six or seven hours of dual time in, and he decided that he wanted to solo, but he had to have a licensed pilot with him. Since I had received my private pilot's license some weeks earlier, I decided I would fly with him. Bud took off from the Willmar airport, and we flew around the area including the farms. We then flew back to Willmar. Try as he would, he just couldn't get that plane back on the ground. He was simply too scared to land.

Unfortunately, I had learned to fly with the stick in my right hand, and the throttle in my left hand. In order for me to fly from the other side of the plane I had to do just the opposite, and that was extremely difficult for me. I was able to bring the plane in, but it was a very bumpy landing. To my knowledge Bud never flew again, which was very sad.

Another friend of ours from Lake Lillian, Duncan Flann, joined the club with us and learned to fly. He kept getting into trouble. He landed the wrong way in a cornfield and ended up in a slough; the plane had to be hauled out. Another time he landed at Hub Field in Chicago, but landed "down wind" and almost crashed. He was just constantly getting into trouble, but for all intents and purposes, he was a "member of the club."

One Saturday morning Dr. Gilman, the physician who had recommended I take flying lessons to help deal with my migraine headaches arrived at the airport, and I had just finished flying around the airport and making takeoffs and landings in the Aeronka Chief. The other plane we owned was a Stinson Station Wagon. The Stinson was a much bigger, heavier, and more powerful plane that glided like a brick. Dr. Gilman said he was going to Minneapolis that morning and asked me to go along. He said he knew I needed to get some more dual time in, and as far as he was concerned, he thought I could fly the Stinson.

Although I explained to him that I had never flown that particular airplane, he said that it flew just like the other ones, and I shouldn't worry about it because he'd be right there. We taxied down to the end of the runway and turned around to take off.

It never occurred to me how many feet of runway were needed to get that big old crate off the ground. We were getting closer and closer to the end of the runway, but he never touched the wheel. When I took off, I realized there was no way I was going to make it over the telephone wires, so I flew under the telephone wires instead. The telephone wires weren't any more than 20 feet above the ground, and there was a road between the wires and us, so we just sort of scraped on through. Dr. Gilman said, "Whew!" and he never said another word.

I flew the plane all the way to Minneapolis and landed it. We were there for a few hours, and then we were scheduled to turn around and come home. We still had skis on, and in order to take off, we had to cross a concrete runway to get to the other side where the snow was. The runway had been totally cleared and was solid concrete. We got right in the middle of the runway and couldn't get any farther. The plane stopped, and no matter what we did it just sat there.

We suddenly realized there was a big four-engine flying fortress coming down the runway. It was barreling down on us, so Dr. Gilman revved the thing to the top. It giggled, and we got loose just as the plane shot right behind us. I said, "We had a close call coming, we might as well have a close call going." I looked at him, and he was white as a ghost. He was a lot more scared with the close call going home than he was when we took off under the telephone wires.

⌒ 38 ⌒

A Collector (of Sorts)

I SAW AN ad in the *Wall Street Journal* for a 1971 Mercedes-Benz 280SE 3.5 Cabriolet Convertible. It piqued my interest because I had always wanted a convertible, and this looked like a good one. I asked one of my reps, Chris Fives, to check it out. He called me and said he had "kicked the tires," and the car really looked great. The car was in Kansas City, Missouri. I bought the car sight unseen for $30,000 and had it shipped to Pittsburgh. It looked as great as I thought it would, and it only had 50,000 miles on it. I drove it every year in the Pittsburgh Grand Prix, which is an event that attracts 125,000 people for a weekend of antique car racing in Schenley Park.

After several years, I had put a for-sale sign on it at the Grand Prix, and an individual became extremely interested in it. He informed me that he had taken the car's serial number, tracked it, and found it to be the car Baron Hilton had bought for his wife's birthday in 1971. It had only been driven between the Hilton Ranch and Las Vegas and never driven in the rain. With all the new information I decided not to sell it. I had it partially rebuilt and restored to like new.

As we began to spend more time in Florida than Pittsburgh, I didn't drive it as much as before. However, I didn't sell it after John Olson, the editor of *SL Market Letter* in Minneapolis, Minnesota, convinced me that it was a good collectible and it would only go up in value. Only 1100 were manufactured.

John also convinced me that buying a 1979 6.9 would be a good investment because as the "bankers hotrod," a limited number had been built, and they too would only go up in value. I found one in

Minnesota and had it shipped to Florida. It was my family car for a couple of years. It was a great car, but very heavy on gas.

I began to collect other cars along the way. There was the Mercedes 280 SL, a Mercedes 380 SL, and a 600 Mercedes, which was the very large 4-door with a 6-liter engine and a refrigerator for champagne between the two front seats. LaVonne bought me a 1936 Ford for my birthday because it was what we had when we were married (a car which I still own).

One day in Pittsburgh, shortly after I had back surgery, our son-in-law, Miles Wallace, called to say he was going to a car company in Aspinwall that had a number of "old" Mercedes for sale and wanted to know if I would go along. LaVonne was going shopping, and urged me to go. Although I still had a hard time getting around, I agreed. We got there and of the six old cars, the one that I was most interested in had been shipped back to Austria for rebuilding and was no longer there. The other cars were rusty and old, and I had no interest.

After looking at them for about an hour, and walking through the showroom I saw what looked like a brand new Rolls Royce and questioned the salesman, "What's this?" He informed me he had taken it in on trade the day before from an old couple from Palm Beach that drove it back and forth from Pittsburgh twice a year. It was a 1990 Silver Spur, and it was still under warranty and had only 19,000 miles on it. When I inquired of the salesman what he was going to do with it, he said they would ship it to Florida and look to get between $75,000 and $100,000 for it. It looked fabulous and you could not tell it from new.

I kidded the salesman, asking what his boss would say if I handed him a check for $50,000, and he informed me that the boss would laugh. So I did it! He was right, his boss did laugh, then the salesman returned the check. Fifteen minutes later we were about to leave when the owner came out behind us and said, "I'll take it." So, I was now the owner of a Rolls Royce, although I have to admit it was an accident.

When I got home, LaVonne was showing me the new boots she bought and asked me if I had bought anything. I said, "I bought a Rolls Royce." She said, "Of course you didn't buy a Rolls Royce," and promptly called Miles to see if I was kidding. He informed her that I had in fact bought the Rolls.

"What are you going to do with it?" she asked. I informed her that I planned to "drive it in Pittsburgh for a couple months then ship it to Florida and sell it." Once we got it to Florida we started using it on occasion. Ed Gonzales had bought me a chauffeur's hat (as a joke) and once when we went to the Philharmonic, Fran, Ed, and LaVonne sat in the back seat, and I chauffeured them. Everyone got a charge out of it, and it was a really good time. I still have the Rolls Royce.

The only other car that was an interesting investment was a convertible "Bitter" that I had seen in a showroom in Los Angeles. It had 28 coats of candy apple red paint with leather interior from the back window to the windshield. I bought it on impulse and had it shipped back to Pittsburgh. Everyone who saw the car thought it was amazing! After it was shipped to Florida and we didn't use it a great deal, I finally advertised it on eBay and did sell it. The ad attracted attention from a collector in Germany who came and bought it from me at one-third the price I had paid for it, which wasn't bad as it only had 15,000 miles on it.

The other interesting purchase I made was a 1992 "Typhoon." It's an all-wheel drive GMC mounted on a Jimmy body. It can do 0–60 in 4.1 and would do 169 mph unless you remove the "governor" chip. That removed, it would do 205 mph. It's an amazing piece of work, and I still own it. I had thoughts of giving it to one of my grandchildren until someone talked me out of it because "it was too hot." As it turns out, this was not the only car that I had that could be considered somewhat striking.

One year I was invited to enter one of the Mercedes into the exclusive Concours d'Elegance of the Eastern United States held in Maryland. There were hundreds of cars registered for the event, and 88 in the class with my convertible. Miles and I spent hours preparing it. We removed all of the fuzz from the convertible top with Scotch tape, and even cleaned all of the spots on the motor with toothbrushes! First place went to a 190SL Mercedes, and my car got second! It was a really great honor to earn second place in a concourse of this type.

I have since sold all of the Mercedes because I really cannot take care of them anymore. Plus, when David died, I lost a lot of interest in them. I did have one somewhat interesting sale.

I advertised that Mercedes 280 SE convertible in several publications saying it was the car that Baron Hilton had bought for his wife in 1971. Most of the 30–40 responses I had told me that added no value at all. However, a young man from Sarasota came down to see it, fell in love with it, sold his Ferrari and bought it on the spot. I wanted $100,000 for it, and he gave me $75,000, but I knew I couldn't take care of it any longer and was glad it was gone.

Six weeks later the man read in the newspaper that Paris Hilton had inherited her second $400 million, and he arranged to meet her in Las Vegas. He made the trip and brought along the original letter from her grandfather showing it was the car, along with an album of pictures I had sold with the car. The next day Paris's broker from New York called him and paid him $150,000. I would never have thought about doing what he did.

I still have the Rolls, the 1936 Ford and the Typhoon, although I plan to advertise the Typhoon for sale soon.

⟋ 39 ⟍

Glen Johnson's
Wide World of Sports

FROM THE TIME I was old enough to think about it, even as young as six years old, I really enjoyed trapping. I trapped for muskrats and mink. I found it was best to go hunting alone, rather than with a hunting buddy. We used to get $30–35 for a mink, so if you got the whole amount of money, you did a good job and felt pretty rich. If you had a hunting partner, you had to share the income, and times were tough. Even though it was always fun to have someone with you, most of my mink hunting was alone, with or without a dog.

I would usually drive my Uncle Emil's Model A that had a spotlight, so that I could go out at night. If I was lucky, I could get a couple of mink in a 10-hour period of time. It was more successful, but much harder work, to hunt them with a dog. I would go out along all the ditches and swamps because the mink would make their homes off the ditch banks. The dog would detect them, and I would dig them out. Sometimes it took me six hours simply to get to the end of the burrow. The dog would get the mink as it came out of the hole. I would shoot it and then haul it to the furrier to get paid. I skinned and stretched a few, but I found that the difference in price between one that was skinned and one that was not skinned was very little. Usually the furrier didn't like the way I had skinned them anyway, so it was better to sell them without skinning them.

The most mink I ever got was on a Saturday when I borrowed a dog (a Chesapeake) from Burton Flann and hunted all day. I got four mink, and I received almost 40 dollars apiece for them. That was just incredible! I can still remember hauling all four mink to the furrier, and they were all really large, prime, and dark in color. That's why I got a prime price for them. That kept me in spending money growing up, and was a major source of income for me. In fact, later on it was a bit of income from mink hunting that I used to buy LaVonne's ring when we were married.

Unfortunately, for borrowing his dog, Burton thought I should give him half of the income. I remember giving $25, but certainly not half. I had spent at least 10 hours and dug out every single one of them. There was no way I was going to part with half of the money.

I trapped a lot of muskrats in our little slough, which was west of our place, but there weren't all that many. I probably had five muskrat piles, which meant five muskrat families, and during a good season, I could get from 20–30 muskrats. Pokie and Spike were my two great hunting dogs; Spike was Pokie's son. They were black Labradors.

I also loved to fish from the time I was a youngster. Kandiyohi Lake was just a couple miles from our home, and is where we would go to fish for Walleyes. The lake had frozen out in the 30s when there were droughts, and it didn't come back until 1945 or 1946. The lake didn't have a single boat rental place on it, and people would fish from shore. You could catch your limit of 2-pound Walleyes in as little as half an hour. The fishing really was that good on Kandiyohi Lake.

Once a year we would go north to Fosston, Minnesota, where my uncle and aunt loved to fish for Northern Pike. I would troll for them with a hand line, not even a rod and reel, and would catch a 20-pound Northern on that hand line. It was a very exciting thing to do, and one of my uncles couldn't believe that I could land a big Northern Pike on a hand line.

Once I had gone off to college, I had to wait until I came home to be able to go fishing, even though fishing season had opened by that time. I would go to Green Lake with friends, where the Walleyes were a lot bigger, and if you knew where to catch them, they were just as plentiful.

In spite of having to do loads of work, growing up on the farm had other advantages. I believe I owned my first rifle at age six and my first shotgun when I was eight. As a matter of fact, from that time until I was probably 14, it was my job every night in the fall to go out and shoot five pheasant roosters that Mother would clean, and serve for supper. There was usually a six-week period that we would have pheasant for supper every night. I enjoyed that very much.

My first rifle was a single-shot .22. I would shoot gophers, pheasants, and ducks with it. My cousin had a rifle with a clip on it. He had seven shells in the clip, and his rifle had a peep sight where mine had a v-sight.

My first shotgun is something I will always remember. It was a single shot, bolt action, 410. My father brought it home to me. It cost four dollars, and he bought it in my Uncle Albert's hardware store. The very first time I shot it at pheasants, we were driving down the road, and I just stuck the barrel out the window and shot. Three hen pheasants died with that one shell. I will never forget it because my father just couldn't believe I got three pheasants in one shot.

My father used to shoot the 12-gauge double barrel gun with big curled hammers. It was so "open" that he had to use #4 shot, and everything had to be close if he was going to shoot it.

When I was 10 years old, my cousin Lawrence Julson was drafted into the Army. The day before he left, my dad bought his gun for me. It was a Winchester 16-gauge pump, which I still have to this day. The last time I went out to the farm a couple of years ago; I shot a duck with it. I went pheasant hunting but didn't get any pheasants, although the rest of the guys did.

Hunting really was an enjoyable part of my life, however, there was one terrible thing that happened when I was 10 years old. The incident didn't involve me directly, but the result was that I was a pallbearer at a friend's funeral.

A friend of mine, Donavon Sharp, was also 10 years old. He and his cousin were hunting rabbits. If you know corncribs, you know they are mounted on heavy beams like railroad ties, so that the air can move freely underneath. The rabbit the boys were following took refuge under a corncrib. One of the boys took aim and just as he pulled the trigger, Donavon looked in from the other side. His cousin shot him right between the eyes.

Apparently Donavon was kind of rambunctious, and his pastor talked throughout the whole funeral that he was going straight to hell. It was horrible, and the sermon just went on and on. I'll never forget it, and it really turned me off. From the time that Baptist pastor opened his mouth he claimed this kid had been a real terror. Donavon was only 10. That was the first funeral I was a pallbearer for. I've had that job too many times since.

My friend Donny Hedlin and I had great times hunting together and probably shot more than our quota of pheasants in our lifetime. Of course, we hardly ever missed a shot. It would have been a shame to waste a bullet. That's the way things were. As a matter of fact, when I was 10 years old on opening day of pheasant season, I shot 37 pheasant roosters with my single-shot 410 with 37 shells. That's how good a shot I was. I actually could shoot both ducks and pheasants on a fly with a .22 rifle.

Not only did Donny and I hunt together, but we also worked together. We would use our thrashing machine (separator) to thrash at their place and use our silo filler to fill their silo. As I reflect on times with Donny, I have to say that we not only played together, but we did a lot of hard work together. Those were really good days.

Donny had an older brother by the name of Arnold who was a born mechanic. He fixed up old motorcycles and was constantly riding a motorcycle. Donny had fashioned his own transportation. He rode a scooter that was pulled by his dog Noodles. In fact, Noodles would pull Donny to school in the morning, and then Donny would send him back home. At 3:30 in the afternoon Noodles would actually trot back to school, and the dog would pull Donny the one-mile distance back home. Noodles really was a remarkable little dog.

One event I will never forget was when I was shooting my .22 over at Bud Portinga's place. He said, "Look, I'll throw a quarter up in the air, and you shoot it." I did, and the quarter disappeared. He threw another quarter in the air. I shot it, and that quarter disappeared.

He said, "It's impossible for you to do that." He threw the third quarter in the air, and it disappeared. We looked and looked for the quarters and found one in the cow pasture. The bullet had hit the edge of the quarter. It was phenomenal. At any rate, Bud got tired of throwing quarters in the air, and besides that, he couldn't afford any more. He really thought I was that good. I'd say it was as much luck as it was skill.

I hunted all the years that I lived in places where I could hunt. In time, I found hunting was no longer a simple matter. When we lived in the cities, it became difficult to find time to go hunting.

I decided to try my luck at skeet and trap shooting since I was a member of the Longue Vue Country Club, and they had a great shooting range. It did not take long before I became addicted, and skeet shooting became a real hobby of mine. As a consequence, I have an entire set of "Series-6 Browning Over and Under" skeet guns. I have a 410-gauge, 20-gauge, 28-gauge, and a 12-gauge. Compared to what I paid for them, they are now worth a lot of money. The outcome of the new found passion was that I won my club's skeet championship eight years in a row. One year I won the club trap championship, but that was a total accident.

I have gathered about 50 guns, although I have sold a few. I keep the remainder in a safe at my Florida home. When I stopped shooting I had a lifetime average of 23 ½ out of 25.

A number of years ago there was an event called Marco Days with all kinds of tournaments, such as golf, tennis, soccer, canoe races, swimming, diving, and among other things a skeet shoot at the Port of the Islands Gun Club near Marco. It was a one-day event and I decided I might as well enter. I had shot there very little and knew hardly anyone, but started the competition with a number of people and suddenly realized there were just two of us left. The other guy ran the shooting range for eight years and had shot lots of 25s in his lifetime.

There was a large crowd, all of them cheering for him since they all knew him, and no one had the slightest idea who I was. I told him to shoot first, and when he missed the first shot I knew I had him. I had a perfect round and he missed two more shots along the way, which meant he missed 3 out of 25. I had a perfect round until the last shot, which is where you take the 24th shot over again. I missed that shot, but I got the trophy. That's the only time I shot in competition in Marco. My trophy says 24 out of 25. Although I have had many 25s in my life, most of them were won in skeet shoots at Longue Vue in Pittsburgh and the congressional shoots in Washington.

Every year John Dingell invited me to participate in the Congressional Shoot in Washington. Dingell is still the longest serving congressman from Michigan and a good friend of mine.

The Congressional Shoot consisted of about 30 lobbyists, and about 30 congressmen. I won that shoot five years in a row. That was quite an accomplishment and surprised me.

They didn't want to give the first prize to me since I always won it; so on the sixth year, they held a drawing for the first prize. As it turned out, the winner of the gun was one of the bystanders who had never even shot a firearm in his life.

I used to stop by John's office because we had a great deal of legislation going through the committee that he chaired. On one visit I asked him if he had been hunting lately, and he said he had been hunting turkey in Texas, and while he was there had gone to their championship range in Columbus, Texas. He wanted me to know that he had the highest score ever recorded on the sporting clays

CONGRESSMAN JOHN DINGELL AND GLEN AT THE
ANNUAL CONGRESSIONAL SHOOT, WHERE GLEN
TOOK FIRST PLACE FIVE YEARS IN A ROW.

range. When I informed him he was no longer the leader and that I had beaten him by one the last time I had been in Texas, he could not believe it. When I asked him what else he did in Texas he said he hunted wild turkeys by shooting them in the head with a pistol. I have tried it on several occasions, and it doesn't work, at least for me.

The same people who attended the congressional shoots also attended the congressional golf outings. I attended only one golf outing at Strawberry Falls in Northern Virginia. At the lunch before we teed off, one of the lobbyists and one of the congressmen said, "At least Glen Johnson won't automatically win this contest." That competition at Strawberry Falls is the only time in my life I won a golf match.

I won the golf match by having the lowest handicapped score, and my team won the event hands down. My prize was $500 worth of merchandise in the pro shop. I still have one of the golf shirts from Strawberry Falls, Virginia, as a memento of the good time I had there.

There used to be a standing joke in the bank trust industry that Glen Johnson did not adhere to the 14-club rule (only 14 clubs are allowed in your bag). However, what they really meant was that I belonged to more than 14 country clubs! Obviously, they are all great golf courses, because they were where we entertained our very finest clients throughout the country. The one most worthy of mention is "Burning Tree."

The Burning Tree Club is an all male institution, and until recently, the only time females could go there was two weeks before Christmas to visit the pro shop to purchase gifts for their husbands. It has gotten much better now, because the ladies may drop their spouses off to play golf, however, they are still forbidden to play.

During the pressing times when these activities were being questioned, the owners of the club put it up for sale to see how much it would bring, and informed the members how much they would each receive if it were sold. It was an incredibly high number and 88% of the membership turned it down.

Burning Tree is a very special place, and it's not easy to get in. In fact, you have to be sponsored by a member and seconded by two other members. When I joined, Charlie Moran, our outside lawyer and a long time friend, introduced me. First of all, they put your name out to the membership. If even one member votes no, you're not even considered further. You then must meet with or play golf with every member of the board, particularly those of the membership committee. After a year goes by, you are allowed to sponsor a cocktail party for the members of the board. Sometime after that they let you know whether or not you have been accepted.

Over the course of the next year, all of those things happened. I met with each of the board members, sometimes at their law offices at 6:00 a.m. or on the golf course playing golf. This is not something you can assign to your assistant. You must do it yourself.

It has been a great place to entertain, particularly the members of the Community Bankers Association, an important lobbying arm of Federated. One interesting event occurred just after I'd finished playing golf with the Texas Bankers Association president, his assistant, and his Washington lobbyist. We were having a drink in the bar, and I was playing in a Member/Member Tournament the next morning. An individual came up to our table and asked if Glen Johnson was there. When I identified myself, he said, "I am your partner for tomorrow. I will not be at dinner tonight because I have to be at a dinner for my sister, Faye Dunaway (the movie star). However, I will meet you on the first tee tomorrow morning at 8:00 a.m."

He met me the next morning as planned, and turned out to be an incredibly good golfer. If I remember right, he was a 6-handicap and I was a 22! Everyone was stunned on Sunday morning, when there at the top of the leader board was Glen Johnson and Mac Dunaway. I was shocked when everyone said that as a new member (which I was), you never want to find yourself at the top of the leader board. He played a phenomenal round of golf. I even birdied a couple of holes that I got two strokes on, and my partner birdied some incredible holes as well. But there we were at the top of the leader board.

It all came crashing down on Sunday when we teed of on #10 at 8:00 a.m. and he'd not been to bed. He had been at an all night party and arrived on the first tee barely able to stand up! Needless to say, he and I both had a pretty rough day. However, we still managed to come in second and I have a beautiful silver platter to prove we did it.

I have been kidded ever since that I should never, as a new

member, have been at the top of the leader board. I have played in only one Member/Member Tournament since, and about three Member/Guest events. Mark Blass, one of my Federated associates, won the putting contest out of 96 entrants. He and I took first in our division on that event. It was another memorable affair.

~ 40 ~

I Didn't Leave the Party—
The Party Left Me

NOT ONLY DID I have Democratic friends, but clearly, I was born into a Democratic family, and lived a Democratic life. My father, mother, grandfather, grandmother, aunts, and uncles were all "dyed-in-the-wool" Democrats known as Hoover haters. I attended precinct caucus meetings from the time I was ten years old just to hear what was going on. Before election time, my father would drive the car, and it was my job to jump out and put campaign signs along the road.

As a young man, I went on to be a liberal editor of one of the few liberal weekly newspapers in Minnesota. I ran Democratic congressional campaigns in 1956 and 1958, and Hubert Humphrey's campaign for the senate in the 7th district in 1960. Along the way I was elected secretary of the Minnesota 7th district, and was elected a delegate to Los Angeles in 1960. I could have easily received the nomination to be the Democratic candidate for Congress for Minnesota's 7th district; however, I had just been named state director of the U.S. Savings Bonds Division for the U.S. Treasury. Thus, I let all of the delegates know I could not be a candidate. Instead I campaigned for Alec Olson, who did receive the Democratic nomination and was elected for a couple of terms.

I was a delegate from Minnesota, and later one of only five "super delegates" from the state of Pennsylvania. LaVonne was an alternate delegate in Atlantic City when Hubert Humphrey was chosen as VP to Lyndon Johnson in 1964. I attended the Chicago convention when Humphrey was chosen as the party's presidential candidate. In 1990,

I was named Democrat of the Year in the state of Pennsylvania, and was honored at a dinner of over 500 people, which was at the regular delegates' convention.

With that background you might think I had been indelibly stamped with a "D," but unfortunately that is not the case.

LaVonne and I were invited to the White House (two couples from each state attended), and it happened to be the night the Republicans scored a tremendous landslide and took over the House of Representatives in the 1994 mid-term elections. Bill and Hillary Clinton were absolutely devastated and, while they shook hands with everybody, you could see how badly they were feeling. Clinton almost instantly took the party to the middle of the road, passing numerous Republican aims and goals, including balancing the budget. I voted for him in that second term, and it will go down in history as one of the most economically productive four years in history.

What happened? When Gore received the Democratic Party nomination for President of the United States, he should have been a slam-dunk to be elected after the good (aside from his morals) Clinton years. However, Gore steered the party directly to the left. It became "them and us." His whole campaign was "I'm fighting for you, the underdog." He never once mentioned Clinton in any of his campaigns and literally avoided him altogether. A tragic mistake! When Gore was nominated to be the Democratic candidate, there was no way I could vote for him. He was anti-business and anti-everything that I have always stood for. I have always said that I didn't leave the party; the party left me.

That is why, after most of my life being a Democrat, I am no longer in that column. I certainly don't consider myself a Republican, but I do consider myself a conservative, and I am in support of the capitalistic system. I also favored the renewal of the Bush tax cuts, which were so productive.

No matter what you call it, I certainly consider myself patriotic. I not only love our system, but also am very passionate about it. When they play the *Star Spangled Banner*, I always get a lump in my throat, and when I hear *Taps*, I get a tear in my eye. If my friend, Hubert Humphrey saw what was happening in the Democratic Party today, I believe he would turn over in his grave.

The present administration has certainly lost its way, but in the 2010 mid-term landslide, the voters showed them how far off base they really were. We were headed straight down the line to socialism, but obviously after the shellacking they took in this election, they must find a new course. Thank goodness.

Fourteen months before that 2010 election, I had shared my concerns with my good friend, Congressman John Dingell (D-MI). Over the years he had worked very hard for Federated Investors, and I felt he was a trustworthy sounding board.

Glen R. Johnson
361 Polynesia Court
Marco Island, FL 34145

August 14, 2009

The Honorable John Dingell
2328 Rayburn House Office Building
Washington, DC 20515

Dear John,

I hope you received the letter I sent you most recently, but I wanted to add that I think I am pretty perceptive as to who wins and who loses in politics. In fact, in the elections of four years ago I picked all 435 House races correctly, and all but one Senate seat correctly.

I think the Democrats are off on a very bad tangent. I firmly believe that if they insist on jamming through this health issue as written in the House version, plus cap and trade, plus card check, the Democrats are in real trouble in the next House election. The disturbance among the troops, and the troops being ordinary people, is running very high, and on his present path Obama will be a one-termer.

At any rate, I know you will do what is right. You and I have fought some great battles together, and if they would have listened to us on Glass-Steagall they would not have the huge problem they have today.

Sincerely,

Glen

GLEN SHARES HIS POLITICAL CONCERNS WITH
CONGRESSMAN AND FRIEND JOHN DINGELL.

Part 5

Love of My Family

GLEN AND LAVONNE JOHNSON.

〜 41 〜

My Best Hand was a Full House

POSITIONS MAY COME and go, but *family* is the thread that has woven together more than 60 years of our life's adventures. Of course, family life, and even our homes themselves were certainly influenced by these adventures.

We moved into the Corley's house after our marriage when LaVonne's folks moved to Minneapolis. Her sister Byrma stayed with us for a short time in their house. After that, we moved to the farm and lived for a time in the "summer-kitchen" as it was known. This little three-room, no bathroom abode had served as the place to

THE FARMHOUSE IN MINNESOTA ALONG WITH
THE "SUMMER KITCHEN" CLOSE BY.

323

cook in the summer months to keep from heating up the sleeping quarters in the larger house. We lived there for a very short time. Now it is restored at the farm and holds a collection of antiques, especially old, metal toys.

Early on there was a turkey farm in southwestern Minnesota that I had become aware of during one of my campaigns. The home where the caretakers lived was a 24 × 28 house. We bought that house for $2,500 and moved it to Lake Lillian. We bought the lot, dug a basement, and put the house together. I did most of the wiring and all the plumbing. Basically, I did the whole thing.

Our neighbor, Alton Olson, was the owner of the lumberyard, and he helped me build the fireplace and a patio outdoors. One time, we were planning to roast a turkey in the fireplace. It had an electric spit, and I just kept roasting and roasting that bird. When we finally got ready to eat, there was absolutely nothing left of it; it was light as a feather. We had to go buy hot dogs for dinner because I had cremated the whole turkey. That was my first experience with the fireplace.

The old Metropolitan Building, where I had my first office when I was in the Treasury, was torn down shortly after we bought our house. I bought marble squares that had been in the building for about a nickel each; the last ones I bought were much more expensive. They became very popular. I would haul some of the marble squares home in my car every weekend when I went home from my job. Alton Olson and I built the patio at our house using those marble squares and concrete. Vince Harris, another neighbor, did the metal work for the barbecue.

We lived in that small doll-like house for a while before adding a garage on the place. After our three children were born, we converted the garage into a family room and put the car back outside. We lived in that house for many years until moving to Washington, DC in 1967, the year Vicki was a senior in high school.

It was 90 miles from Lake Lillian to Minneapolis. Every Monday morning I would leave about 5:00 a.m. to be in the office by 8:00 a.m. I would come home on Wednesdays some of the time, and then I'd come home again on the weekends.

One year we borrowed our neighbor's 18-foot metal trailer (the

GLEN AND LAVONNE'S CHILDREN: VICKI, DAVID, AND LORI JOHNSON.

neighbor happened to be the banker in town) and drove it all the way to the Seattle World's Fair. We did a lot of sightseeing along the way, including the Black Hills of South Dakota. The children had never been out of the state of Minnesota, so everything we did was new to them.

I was pulling the heavy trailer with a Ford Fairlane. As was popular in that day, the Fairlane had fins on the back fenders. The first night in the Black Hills, we got caught in a huge rainstorm. So much so, that when we arrived at our intended stopover, we slid all the way to the bottom of the trailer park and parked for the night.

The morning light revealed that the car's tail fins sliced right through the skin of the camper when the trailer jackknifed, as we were sliding down the hill in the dark. After all that rain, I was very concerned that we wouldn't be able to get out the next day due to the mud. However, because of the sandy soil all the water was gone, and we were able to drive right out.

That hole remained there throughout our entire trip, and I had to explain what happened to the owner when we returned. We tried to pay for the damage, but the owners wouldn't accept it.

It was a wonderful trip. We camped in numerous city, state, and national parks along the way. What we enjoyed the most about federal parks was the rangers telling stories around the fire each evening about what we were going to see the next day. It was pretty spectacular, and the children loved every minute of it, especially the bears feeding in trashcans.

We got to Seattle and attended the World's Fair. We parked in a trailer area and moved in and out of there to attend the fair. We camped all along the way on our return as well.

A couple of years later we rented another little camping trailer, which was much lighter, and again we camped in national parks including Yellowstone and Glacier. On this trip we went all the way

GLEN RIDING A DONKEY NAMED CADILLAC, WHEN
HE AND THE FAMILY VISITED A DUDE RANCH IN
ARIZONA (PHOTO BY DEAN "HARPO" ZANEIS).

326

to San Francisco and down to Los Angeles. We took the southern route back through Mesa Verde and the "four corners" where the four states meet in the middle of Indian country. The Southwest was hot, and cars were not air conditioned back then. Instead, we used ice in front of the air vents to cool the ride just a bit. In Death Valley, we tried to cook an egg on some concrete, but it didn't work. We also rode horseback on rough trails, and that scared the daylights out of me.

On a walking tour, we came out of a tunnel, and we discovered we were 800 feet from the ground! The only way to go forward was to go up handmade ladders of logs and trees that were 30 feet long. The children were little, and we had to scramble up. That was a harrowing experience. It was an absolutely incredible time, but one of those times when I really wished we were somewhere else. At any rate, we made it. Those were the only two long trips we took, and they each lasted about two weeks.

After I was appointed to the Treasury in Washington, my home was a hotel room. My family went back to Lake Lillian after the swearing in ceremony, while our older daughter finished her classes. I went back for her graduation from Bird Island High School. After her June graduation, we sold many of our belongings in Minnesota. My father bought our house because my parents wanted to move from the farm.

We rented a six level townhouse on Lake Ann in Reston, Virginia for one year before we bought a "colonial" on the golf course. Vicki, our older daughter, came to Reston with us when we moved, and worked for the District of Columbia. She drove my Mustang to her job. At that time I had the Mustang and another Ford.

David and Lori each went to school in the neighboring town of Herndon. David was in ninth grade, and Lori was one grade behind him at the middle school. We continued to live there until 1974, even after I went to work at Federated Investors in Pittsburgh in 1970.

In 1974 we bought a house on Fernwald Road in Squirrel Hill located in Pittsburgh, Pennsylvania. It was a small house with a nice yard and patio where we did some entertaining. Our children complained that it was too small for them to come home and visit, so we moved.

THE JOHNSON FAMILY: DAVID, LORI, AND
VICKI WITH GLEN AND LAVONNE.

We moved to a house on Northumberland Street where we spent about 14 years. It was a great old house built in 1914 by Barney ("Charley") Dreyfuss, who was a junk dealer and the original founder of the Pittsburgh Pirates. The house had three levels with 11 fireplaces, and a 1,000 BTU steam heat system that burned a lot of gas. The living room had several sets of French doors and the wind had free access. It was situated on about one and one-half acres with a three-car garage.

As time went on, we bought the house that was located behind our property, which had a tennis court. We sold the house and resurrected the tennis court, much to the chagrin of our neighbors, or at least one neighbor in particular.

When I reached the point where I was spending less time in Pittsburgh, we downsized and moved to a townhouse on the corner of Ellsworth and Neville in the Oakland section of Pittsburgh. While we don't spend much time there anymore, we still maintain the property.

Our full-time residence now is the home we built in 1980, on Polynesia Court, in Marco Island, Florida. It is a great location, and we are right on the Marco River and two waterways, so we have the entire point.

THE JOHNSON'S MARCO ISLAND HOME ON THE
MARCO RIVER, THE DIRECT ACCESS WATERWAY
THAT LEADS TO THE GULF OF MEXICO.

GLEN WITH A 42-POUND SNOOK HE CAUGHT FROM THE
DOCK AT THE JOHNSON HOME ON MARCO ISLAND.

329

We still own the farm in Lake Lillian, Minnesota and have restored and enlarged the old farmhouse. In addition, we have a residence that is an old remodeled rooming house that sleeps about 22 people (if they're really cozy), at the Chautauqua Institute in Chautauqua, New York.

THE FARMHOUSE IN MINNESOTA.

ON THE FARM IN MINNESOTA, THE PAINTING ON THE FRONT OF THE BARN WAS COMMISSIONED BY SON, DAVID, AND IS SIMILAR TO THE COVER OF *THE NAKED AND THE DEAD*.

THE JOHNSON'S HOUSE IN CHAUTAUQUA, NEW YORK, WHICH
WAS BUILT IN THE 1880S. IN THE WINTERTIME IT IS DRESSED
UP FOR WINTER BY BEING COMPLETELY ENCLOSED WITH
CANVAS SO THE PORCHES DON'T GET SNOW ON THEM AND FALL
OFF. THEY EXPECT 200+ INCHES OF SNOW EVERY WINTER.
THIS HOUSE SLEEPS 22, AS LONG AS THEY ARE CLOSE!

~ 42 ~

LaVonne

LaVonne Corley Johnson—Love of My Life

LAVONNE'S FAMILY MOVED several times during her childhood to follow work opportunities for her father, Christopher Corley. The resulting impact of those many moves growing up are that LaVonne has never felt geographically tied to a place or a house. With her philosophy that home and heart is where the family is, she adapts easily to new situations. This trait became increasingly beneficial for the future Mrs. Johnson.

In Minnesota, Lake Lillian was home. It was an easy place for children to grow up. People knew and cared for one another. Early in our marriage, LaVonne learned how to be a housewife and a mother, or at least the expectation of the position. She also came to the self-understanding that she should be actively involved in church, school and education, and even expanding beyond our community to the country on a political level. Along with the ordinary duties of a housewife, doing all the cooking, cleaning and laundry, she was also a nurse and a teacher to our children. In addition to all that, she was my faithful helpmate in running the newspaper, taught Sunday school, Bible school, and served on the school board.

Summers are short in Minnesota, so the daily routine started with housework in the morning, followed by a trip to the lake in the afternoon. Juice and snacks were packed, and she was off with the children and other mothers to enjoy the season and take advantage of the sun and warmer water. Our oldest daughter Vicki grew up to be a very normal 5'4" woman, but was always a tiny little girl, like a walking doll of sorts. When she went to first grade, a box for her feet was necessary because her feet didn't touch the floor under her desk. So, although she loved going to the lake with everyone else, it didn't take long for her small frame to get chilly. Her lips would turn blue, and LaVonne would have to rub her with towels until she warmed up.

One day, when David and Lori were toddlers, LaVonne was sitting on the dock with them while Vicki was out in the water playing with the big girls. David managed to fall off the dock, and in an instant, his red straw hat was floating, and he was under the water! Mom jumped in and retrieved him, deciding that from there on out they would wear life jackets. However, the next time they were at the lake LaVonne put on their life jackets, so they could safely play in the shallow water on shore. Surprise! When they waded into the water, in no time at all, they were floating in the life jackets and easily tipped face forward in the water! Safety at the lake meant children must always be in sight, and not far out of reach.

If you compared life in town to life on the farm, life in town was easy. LaVonne always tried to be super-mom, and at times became exhausted, especially with my need to be gone much of the time. Gender clearly defined our roles in those bygone days. Men brought home the money; no matter how many jobs it took. Women stayed home with the children, kept a clean house, clean children, cooked and baked. Clothes were expected to be very white. Thus, no clothes dryer for us, as it was thought that the dryer would yellow the fabrics. The clean laundry was always hung outdoors except in the coldest, stormiest days of winter. On those days, LaVonne would put the basket of wet laundry outdoors to freeze. Then, they were brought in and hung in the basement to dry. Freezing it first both reduced drying time and kept it whiter. There were no wash and wear fabrics back then, and LaVonne hated ironing white shirts and puffed sleeves on the girls' dresses.

When the kids were little, LaVonne drew and painted Disney characters on wood, which I cut out, to decorate their rooms. Although she was good with drawing, LaVonne felt that her sister, Byrma, was the real artist of the family. LaVonne and her friend, Geneva Molenar, drove to Minneapolis to take art lessons. Geneva was an accomplished artist. LaVonne was just learning, and truly loved the trips and the camaraderie with Geneva. Although she decided she would never become a great artist, she appreciated how difficult and demanding it was to do and has remained interested in and supportive of the arts since then. Sadly, her friend Geneva, the real artist of the two, died of breast cancer back in those early years when it was a certain death sentence.

The move to Reston, Virginia in 1967 was a huge change in our lives. The 60s were challenging years, especially with teenagers. Living in the Washington area was also a challenge. We had to learn how to go around the traffic circles, manage heavy traffic, and search for hard to find parking places, all while showing guests around or going about one's business. LaVonne spent an abundance of time chauffeuring David and Lori around. David needed rides to and from baseball practice and the games. Lori kept her mother busy running her to chess practice, chess matches and tournaments, but more than anything, her music lessons. She was a member of the Youth Symphony. It seemed LaVonne was always on the run, and not just for the kids. She took many trips to National Airport (now Reagan National) to drop me off to catch a plane somewhere. She often joked that someday a plane that missed the runway at National, as the planes flew so very low over the road, would hit her car.

In Reston, LaVonne's time was quite routine, except when we had out of town visitors or were attending a White House welcome for a dignitary or attending the ceremony for fallen soldiers on Memorial Day at the Tomb of the Unknown Soldier. It really was thrilling to learn the history of the city, see the historic sites, and think about the founding of our nation and genius of the Founding Fathers.

After I got the job at Federated, LaVonne continued to chauffeur the kids as well as taking me to the airport each Monday and picking me up each Friday. She was certainly keeping busy. However, when Lori was a senior in high school, LaVonne started having problems sleeping and eventually came to realize that she was dreading the empty nest that would be coming soon. To combat this, she and some friends enrolled in W.I.F.E. (Women Interested in Further Education). This led her to enroll in college, which filled her days and left little time to be lonely.

We finally moved to Pittsburgh four years after I went to work there. To make the transition even easier, LaVonne had already enrolled at the University of Pittsburgh where she continued her education and received her undergraduate degree in three years. After receiving her Bachelor of Arts degree from the University of Pittsburgh, she decided that a master's degree was a goal she was interested in. Eventually, she went to work as a planner for Allegheny County and attended classes at night, attaining her Master of Public Administration degree from the University of Pittsburgh Graduate School of Public and International Affairs in three years.

Life in Pittsburgh was very full with LaVonne attending school, serving on boards and other activities at First Lutheran, the church we attended. LaVonne served on the call-committee for a new pastor and helped establish an infant and toddler day care center at the church. Additionally, she served on an advisory board that mentored at-risk children. It was the only center downtown and was a ministry to parents who worked in the area. The downtown area is compact, and parents could come to see their children during the lunch hour if they wished. She also served as chair of Christian Education and served on the church council at various times.

Always with a heart of service, LaVonne contributed in farther reaching arenas as well, serving on the Board of Visitors for the University of Pittsburgh, Graduate School of Public and International Affairs, as well as leading the county as chairwoman for her political party.

During this time, she opened and operated a clothing store for career women with friends Fran Gonzales and Betsy Hastings as partners. Betsy managed the store, while LaVonne and Fran did most of the buying. Of course, this involved plenty of travel as they attended markets in New York. They ran the store for six years, one year longer than originally planned. LaVonne was ready to give up the business by then to spend more time with our grandchildren.

We lived in a big house in Pittsburgh built in the 20s. It had three stories with several French doors, which allowed many drafty, cold winds to blow through the rooms. I suppose that is why there were 11 fireplaces in that house. It sat on about an acre of land with beautiful gardens, including a vegetable garden and a tennis court as well. Pittsburgh is a wonderful city, and we felt very much at home there.

During that time we became acquainted with Naples and Marco Island, Florida. Federated had a few meetings down there, and we ultimately purchased some lots on Marco in the early 70s.

We continued to visit Marco through the decade and always looked at land and houses when we were there. This activity meant our trips to Florida were no vacation. On one trip we bought a lot on the river, and in 1980 we built a small house on it. No more looking at houses or property! In those days it was very easy to travel from our northern home to Miami to connect with a smaller plane that took us straight to Marco. Our dog, Watson, enjoyed the trips with us. As time passed we spent more and more time in Florida, first moving our official residency, then later becoming full time Island residents.

Those first years on Marco were very much family years. We bought the obligatory boats, fished, boated, and became acquainted with the environment and the history of the area. Watson loved to fish and was like a retriever when anyone landed a fish. He would attack them if we didn't get there first.

Eventually, it became obvious that we needed more room if we were to live on Marco full time. We added a bedroom, bathroom, and loft on our original house. As we were enduring this disruption, we decided it made sense to buy the house next door that happened to be for sale, so we could move in rather than live in the midst of the construction in the original house.

LaVonne likes to decorate and design, so we were mulling over how to connect the two houses. She really wanted the final product to look like a Japanese compound. To accomplish this, an architect friend of ours, who had designed and supervised the restoration and expansion of our farmhouse in Minnesota, came to Florida to help us with the project. LaVonne had a book, *Katsura*, which presented a detailed history of the 17th century Imperial Palace in Kyoto, Japan that is a pivotal work of Japanese architecture. She also admired the work of famed American architect and interior designer, Frank Lloyd Wright.

It was out of these influences, that our house was created. The design of the home was intended to unfold as one progresses through the rooms. Clearly the connection and tension between the inside and the beautiful Florida outdoors is felt as you make your way from one space to another. If you look across the property from the upper deck, it does look like a Japanese compound. It has one roof, but it looks like many small buildings with multiple peaks. You would never think you are in Katsura or in a Wright-house, but you might have a sense of serenity and enjoy the attention to line and detail.

LAVONNE AND GLEN WITH GRANDMA
ELPHIE ON HER 100TH BIRTHDAY.

We may be full time residents in Florida, but LaVonne has certainly not retired from her involvement in the visual arts, music, church, and community. Her first priority is family, but she continues to serve on the Arts Advisory Committee for the City of Marco Island, the Endowment Committee of the Art League, and the Foundation Board of Marco Lutheran Church. Other involvements included director and founder of the Bank of Florida, member of the American Association of University Women, and receiving a distinguished Honorary Doctorate of Humane Letters from Gustavus Adolphus College in St. Peter, Minnesota. LaVonne is a natural multi-tasker. In addition to her other areas of interest, she never lets politics out of her sight. She watches Fox and HGTV because she can read at the same time. Since traveling is harder for me now, she attends the Metropolitan Opera in New York with friends, but we are season ticket holders to the Naples Philharmonic and enjoy their programs, as well as those at the Naples Opera, Marco Players, Naples Players, Classic Chamber Orchestra, Town Hall Lecture Series, and other community presentations.

From LaVonne's early days of mother, nurse, linotype operator, press feeder, folder operator, mailer, student, chauffeur, graduate, clothing buyer, fitter, sales person, artist, gardener, and teacher, to even now, LaVonne never lets the grass grow under her feet. She is still the love of my life after 60 years and going strong!

ALFRED AND ELPHIE KETTNER.

FAMILY PICTURE: DEAN (HARPO) ZANEIS, KRISTI LINDGREN, ELPHIE
KETTNER, VICKI (JOHNSON) ZANEIS, MILES AND LORI (JOHNSON)
WALLACE WITH ARIANA AND AIDAN IN FRONT, DAVID JOHNSON,
KATELYN JOHNSON WITH TWINS KORA AND KARI JOHNSON IN FRONT,
SHEILA (BLOCKZYL) JOHNSON, LAVONNE AND GLEN JOHNSON.

GLEN AND LAVONNE WITH GRANDCHILDREN.

**LAVONNE'S MOTHER, "GRANDMA ELPHIE" KETTNER
AND HER 101ST BIRTHDAY CAKE.**

ELPHIE, HER DAUGHTERS BYRMA PAULZINE (BOBBIE)
AND LAVONNE. STANDING IN THE MIDDLE IS LAVONNE
AND BOBBIE'S HALF BROTHER JEFFREY CORLEY.

GLEN AND LAVONNE WITH HER MOTHER ELPHIE.

43

Vicki

Vicki Ann Johnson—October 4, 1949

OUR ELDEST CHILD, Vicki Ann, was born with country in her blood. She loved visiting her grandparents' farm, experiencing all it had to offer, including the extended family that lavished her with unconditional love. Even after the family moved into the town, the farm remained her favorite place with frequent visits and overnight stays for all the years she lived in Minnesota.

As a toddler, Vicki stayed up with LaVonne waiting for me to come home at night. It was typical for us to have a bowl of chili together before she'd head off to bed.

Vicki rode the bus to school in Lake Lillian through the eighth grade. In addition to being on my school bus route, she also liked spending time at the print shop where I published the newspapers and did printing jobs.

Vicki enjoyed childhood life in our small town, riding her bike, building forts, and collecting rocks and butterflies. She always loved outdoor activities and mostly shunned girly play. I built a tree house behind our home where she loved and adored all of her pets, especially the cats.

The small town library was a community resource she frequently utilized. Vicki enjoyed the adventure found in books more than she liked typical schoolwork.

Activities at the First Evangelical Lutheran Church were an important part of social life in our small town. Swimming, fishing, and skating were other favored activities. Bible school in the summertime was something to look forward to each year.

While in high school, she did not excel at her first real job, which was hoeing cucumbers. Being honest, and something of a perfectionist resulted in very little pay for a lot of hard work because the grower paid by the row.

Her next job, working weekends and summers at a nursing home was more to her liking. She made 80 cents an hour pay, but was soon raised to $1 because she did so well working with the residents of the home. She was one of the most popular employees.

Vicki enjoyed singing in the church and school choirs and was a frequent soloist for town or school events. Sometimes she performed musically with siblings David and Lori, accompanying them on the piano while they played their musical instruments.

Vicki graduated from Bird Island High School in 1967, and shortly after the family moved to Reston, Virginia. She was pleased to discover that the South had more than just cotton fields, and she loved the architectural charm and friendly ambiance of our new town.

Before college, she worked in Washington, DC in the accounting portion of President Johnson's Neighborhood Youth Corps. She was also a "Head Start" volunteer.

Vicki attended Gustavus Adolphus College in St. Peter, Minnesota for a year before finding a job with a large plumbing and heating company in Minneapolis.

She was married in 1969 to Darwin Lindgren. After Darwin completed his pharmacy degree, they moved back to Reston, Virginia and enjoyed living close to the rest of the family. She also enjoyed the easy lifestyle of walking to work at an insurance office and later, a real estate firm.

Vicki obtained her real estate license at one point and went into the real estate sales business where she was part owner in the company. Over the years she took several courses at Northern Virginia Community College and the University of Virginia. Art history and civilization were of the greatest interest to her.

Sometimes she would accept a babysitting job when her sister twisted her arm really hard to help out with one of Lori's sitting clients. Lori was not too pleased to learn that for one entire evening, Vicki had failed to change the diaper of one of the small children of one of her best clients, simply because she thought he was old enough to have been potty-trained.

She loved cooking everything from scratch, and over the years had quite a good collection of recipes. She wouldn't even buy ketchup in a bottle, preferring that everything be homemade. When her daughter, Kristianna, was born August 10, 1979, Vicki made all her own baby food.

In the mid 80s, Vicki gradually cut down on the amount of time she spent on her real estate profession. Her client base, due to so many referrals, grew so large that there wasn't enough time to both work and spend time with her young daughter.

In Virginia, she was secretary of her homeowner association board of directors. She had that position for several years and was also secretary on the board of directors at the private school where Kristianna attended and involved in fundraising for the school.

KRISTIANNA,
ONLY CHILD
OF VICKI
AND DARWIN
LINDGREN,
ON HER FIRST
DAY OF FIRST
GRADE.

Vicki threw herself into being a school volunteer in Virginia and Florida after her family relocated to Marco Island. They had previously vacationed in Marco during portions of each winter. Her volunteer efforts with the schools involved working one-on-one with children in need of extra help or with the more gifted children.

After her divorce, she worked in office support for a realty firm.

In 1993, Vicki and her second husband, Dean (Harpo) Zaneis, moved to Central Florida to be closer to the land development project in which he was a partner. Her daughter Kristianna began public high school. They found a lovely farm, but the houses on the property were in need of some remodeling, which was a good project. Harpo built a barn and put up miles of fence, which Vicki painted white.

KRISTIANNA.

KRISTIANNA BECAME QUITE A PROFICIENT RIDER.

She kept horses on her farm and learned a great deal about horse health as their primary caregiver. Kristianna was finally able to have a horse of her own, and continues to enjoy riding and competes in show jumping whenever she can find the time.

In 1995, Vicki began taking lessons to become a safer rider after having previously been somewhat afraid of riding horses when she sustained a head, eye, and facial injury. Eventually, she joined an Arabian drill team and took part in native Arabian, Renaissance, or other types of performances that had costumes for horses. Her talents included sewing her horse's costumes by hand, without the benefit of a sewing machine. Her mother is impressed and amazed since Vicki didn't find sewing to be much fun in high school.

Vicki and her husband became "community activists," fighting against sprawl and in favor of preservation of rural and greenbelt areas. She served on her local county planning agency for three years, meeting frequently as they worked on a new comprehensive plan as well as several new ordinances. The members chose her as their liaison to the Affordable Housing Advisory Committee where she was instrumental in creating improved affordable housing plans for the county.

Vicki believes that it is important to work on preserving and conserving our environmental treasures and natural resources as well as helping those less fortunate.

Having enjoyed many trips to various places around the world, she loves her farm the best of all. She and Harpo enjoy the natural surroundings in the area where they live and are avid Florida Gator fans.

She is pleased to have raised a daughter who will soon take the Florida bar exam and is currently working at a job in conservation. Vicki's husband has two grown sons, both married and college graduates. One son has two young daughters. They are proud of the success of all of the children and enjoy spending time together whenever they can.

Vicki's favorite activity is trail riding and camping out with Lance, her favorite gray Arabian horse.

VICKI JOHNSON ZANEIS.

**VICKI TOOK PART IN MANY RENAISSANCE
PERFORMANCES, SEWING THE COSTUMES BY HAND.**

~∿ 44 ∿~

David

David Glen Johnson
June 4, 1953 –October 17, 2002

OUR SON DAVID was born in Willmar, Minnesota, 18 miles from Lake Lillian when I was the publisher of the local newspaper. LaVonne and I had a small house in town when David was born. Our daughter Vicki was three years old and was looking forward to a playmate.

At a young age, David seemed to exhibit a lot of similar traits that I had as a child. He loved the outdoors, and the times we spent together were like reliving my own childhood in many ways. His eyes lit up when we grabbed our guns or fishing poles and headed for our special hunting spot or fishing hole. I loved telling him stories about when I was growing up, and he loved hearing them.

The wild game in the woods that surrounded our house was plentiful. David was always bringing home some trophy. There was no place he would rather be than outdoors hunting, fishing, and setting traps. Before school each morning, he would head out to check his lines for muskrats, mink, and a number of other small game animals.

One day David brought home a snipe he'd shot and wanted to try eating it. LaVonne soaked it in milk and roasted it. The beagle dog, Snoopy, bayed when she smelled the awful stench! It was not edible, and LaVonne never had to cook another one again.

Having learned to use a gun at a young age, David became quite a good marksman. That skill served him well then, and gave him much pleasure later in his life when he assembled a very fine gun collection.

One tough lesson that happened when David was a youngster

was the loss of Tiny, his Saint Bernard. David could hardly wait to go out every morning and check his trap line, which was about a mile long. One particular morning when David and Tiny left the house, it had snowed a couple of feet during the night. Tiny was 10 years old then and was having a terrible time getting through the soft new snow. This particular morning when David got back home, Tiny was exhausted and went into her doghouse, where she had a heart attack and died. It was so cold that winter that to dig Tiny's grave, we had to hire a man to light a fire just to warm the frozen ground. We were all very sad about losing Tiny, but David was especially affected.

Even though I was busy at the paper, I always tried to be home at mealtime. Sitting around the table together got pretty lively at times. Our daughter Lori was born a year and a half after David. David and Lori were not only close in age, but enjoyed each other's company. We enjoyed numerous birthday celebrations for all the kids, trying to make each special.

David attended kindergarten and grade school in Lake Lillian. For six years, I was the manager of the Little League team when

DAVID WAS A LEFT-HANDED PITCHER. HE
PITCHED FOR RESTON, VIRGINIA HIGH
SCHOOL AFTER PLAYING LITTLE LEAGUE
IN LAKE LILLIAN, MINNESOTA.

David was in grade school. Fathers always had their own children on their team, so David was on mine. I was proud of his talent and dedication to the game. He was a left-hander and a pitcher. Just about every night when I came home from work, he would pitch the ball, and I would catch for him. I could call balls and strikes and the whole nine yards. There were only six teams in all, and our team never lost a ballgame. I attribute much of that to the fact that I played ball as a kid, and knew how to train my team to win. My specialty was showing the team how to slide and steal bases. The other fathers didn't really know much about baseball, but with my prior experience, I was able to ingrain many of the fine arts of playing ball into the team.

David was 14 when we moved to Reston, Virginia in 1967 when I went to work for the Treasury Department in Washington, DC. For one semester when David was still 14, and Lori was 13, we had an exchange student from Chile living with us. Because of that connection, David and Lori, who both spoke very good Spanish, were invited to visit Chile and tour the South American countryside. During the three weeks they were in Chile, Socialist Dictator, Salvador Allende, took power. This resulted in overnight inflation, and cash was almost

A HIGH SCHOOL GRADUATION
PICTURE OF DAVID.

worthless. David was a gun collector of sorts even at that young age. With this sudden turn of events, he had the opportunity to buy an old rifle for $75, which he brought home with him. Today that gun is easily worth 100 times what he paid.

The first year David attended Herndon High School, he played on their baseball team. The high school was located in the neighboring town close to Reston. He was a good pitcher, but there were hundreds of students at the school, and the competition was tough. He just didn't have the same desire to play ball that I did at his age. But he enjoyed school, and especially enjoyed his science classes. After graduating from high school, he attended Robert Morris University in Pittsburgh, Pennsylvania.

When we lived in Reston, David worked at numerous jobs. He strived for perfection in everything he did. He learned electrical work at one job, and helped out with odd jobs at the golf course in town. When it wasn't busy he got to hit a few golf balls around the course. That was in a day and age that if you had one job, it was easy to get another one. There were all kinds of jobs out there if a young person wanted to work, and the pay was good.

David also worked in the Fairfax hospital. One of his duties was to clean up all the needles. We suspect that is where he contracted Hepatitis C. Early in his life he was diagnosed with the virus that affects the liver, and through the years, it continued to get worse and worse. Hepatitis C was almost incurable at that time.

After attending Robert Morris, David moved out west to California for a couple of years working at odd jobs. When he came back from California, we became partners running the farm where he spent so much time as a boy. Since there was not much going on at the farm during the winter, David came to Florida to take a break from the cold, spend time with us, and do some fishing and hunting. Of course, he was back on the farm in plenty of time for the spring planting and fall harvesting. David was an excellent farmer. He kept up with the latest farming techniques, and apart from occasional unforeseen weather, we always had a successful harvest. The man he hired to help run the farm is still running it for me today, and we continue to speak on a weekly basis. This is the first time in 138 years that a member of the family is not running the farm.

Because of his love of nature, David had always wanted to eventually return part of the farmland to a water habitat. We honored that desire after his death by turning 126 acres of the farm into "David's Water Park." It is still used daily by the public as they visit and enjoy the beautiful grounds with wildlife of all kinds. It's full of ducks, pheasant, geese, and deer. The water park is dedicated to Gustavus Adolphus College.

David met his future wife, Sheila Blokszyl, over a friendly game of pool, in which I believe, she won. They were married on June 23, 1984, and the reception was out on the farm. In the years that followed, they gave us three beautiful granddaughters, Katelyn, Kora, and Kari. Kora and Kari are twins, but not identical.

DAVID AND SHEILA WITH DAUGHTERS KATELYN, KORA, AND KARI.

GRANDPA GLEN WITH THE TWINS.

GRANDDAUGHTERS KORA AND KARI JOHNSON.

KORA JOHNSON.

KARI JOHNSON.

KATE JOHNSON.

KATE ON ROGER RABBIT.

From a young age, Katelyn had her father's passion for the outdoors. David taught her to shoot as soon as she was big enough to hold a gun up to her shoulder. Just as I had spent time with David as a boy, Kate loved spending time with her father. When LaVonne and I started to winter in Florida, David would come spend the winter, and occasionally brought friends with him. They would go pig hunting, and of course fishing was a big thing. One time Katelyn was hunting with him in Florida and shot a 500-pound wild boar on a dead run.

David was a world-class trap shooter and rated nationally. In Buffalo, Minnesota he would shoot trap with a sanctioned group that kept track of the scores.

For a number of years, David was a very serious gun collector and read numerous books on the subject. He was so knowledgeable that people who owned or inherited gun collections would come to him

THREE GENERATIONS OF HUNTERS. GLEN (RIGHT)
WITH SON DAVID, AND GRANDDAUGHTER KATELYN,
WHO COULD HUNT WITH THE BEST OF THEM.

to have them appraised. His knowledge of German Lugers was truly outstanding, and he had one of the finest collections, with over 200 rifles, revolvers, and shotguns.

David had another unusual hobby that he took very seriously. He collected German Army uniforms, especially the uniforms of the SS. His collection of 20 complete rare German uniforms is probably one of the finest. The collection still remains in the family.

For years, David realized something in his body was not right when he started feeling fatigued, and couldn't shake it. As his symptoms got worse, we all knew that this was quite serious. The tests confirmed that David needed a new liver. He was placed on the list for a transplant and went on interferon for a year and a half during that time to see if the virus would subside. It did subside for just a short period of time, but then returned. He never fully recovered.

DAVID JOHNSON.

DAVID AND HIS DAD.

At one point during David's battle, there was a ray of hope, albeit bittersweet. Sheila had an uncle who'd fallen down a stairway and was left brain-dead, but still alive. Even in their own pain, Sheila's family decided to donate her uncle's liver to David. A team went to harvest the liver, and we flew with David to meet the transplant team in Pittsburgh. The doctors got him all prepped as we waited for the liver to arrive. We were heartbroken when we got word from the transplant people that the liver was damaged and not fit for transplant. We went back to Florida and waited.

Eventually, while waiting for a viable transplant, David was taken to a hospital in Naples because of bleeding. When I went to see him he was in terrible pain. I don't know on what basis they made their decision, but they dismissed him, suggesting his illness was psychological. Back at the house he continued to get worse. He then went to Cleveland Clinic in Naples for three weeks where he received 21 pints of blood on his first day there. Two days later he started to bleed again, and was finally accepted for a transplant.

We all went to Pittsburgh to prepare for the operation. At the hospital in Pittsburgh, he was on standby to get the next available liver. The next day Sheila called with the words, "Come now!" David was dying. We felt helpless. The whole family was at the hospital the day David passed. It was a very difficult time. He had been through a lot. There are no words to express how much we still miss David and how unfair and cruel life can be at times.

Katelyn was 16, and the twins were 10 when they said good-bye to their father. The younger girls hardly knew their dad any other way, as he'd been sick most of their lives. As a teenager, Kate was her father's closest friend and was his ally for all the years that he was very sick. Once he became bed ridden, you would find Katelyn by his side most all of the time. It was probably the hardest for her when he was gone.

I would be remiss not to mention that I believe politics entered the picture. Congressman Livingston from Louisiana had worked on the legislation that stated that the sickest patients on the transplant list were to get the next available organs. When that bill went into effect, David was number 21 on the transplant list. The ironic thing was that when he got to be the sickest, his body gave out. It has never

KATELYN AND HER DAD WERE BEST FRIENDS.

made sense that a person still healthy enough for a good chance of survival is forced to wait until they are so sick that their chances become almost nil. It was a very unfortunate occurrence for David and our family. That legislation still stands today.

Right after her father's death, Katelyn seemed so lost, as we all were. So after a couple weeks, I suggested to Katelyn that the two of us go out for a day of hunting. We went to David's and her special hunting spot where she shot a 250-pound boar at sunrise and a 10-point buck at sunset on the same day. She enjoyed our time together and knowing how proud her dad would have been of her.

David was just 49 years old. His body is laid to rest in Lake Lillian. This is still so very difficult. I put off talking about it for years because I couldn't face it, but I knew I had to sooner or later. This is the story about our son David.

DAVID GLEN JOHNSON.

FIVE GENERATIONS: LAVONNE WITH HER MOTHER, ELPHIE,
SEATED ON RIGHT. DAVID'S WIFE SHEILA, ON LEFT, WITH
THEIR DAUGHTER KATE, WITH HER SON, DAVID, NAMED
FOR HIS LATE GRANDPA, DAVID GLEN JOHNSON.

KATE'S SON DAVID CARRIES
ON THE FAMILY TRADITION
OF BASEBALL.

KATE'S SON,
DAVID
HUNGRECKER.

KATE'S SON,
CONOR
HUNGRECKER.

FROM LEFT, DAVID'S DAUGHTERS KARI AND KORA JOHNSON,
AND HIS WIFE, SHEILA JOHNSON. SHEILA IS HOLDING
GRANDSON DAVID. GRANDDAUGHTER KATELYN (PREGNANT
WITH CONOR), AND HER HUSBAND ELIOT HUNGRECKER
WITH GRANDMA ELPHIE ON HER 100TH BIRTHDAY.

KATE HOLDS
CONOR IN THE
SAME BAPTISMAL
GOWN PASSED
DOWN THROUGH
THE GENERATIONS.

CONOR'S BAPTISM IN THE CHAPEL NAMED FOR HIS GRANDFATHER.
FROM LEFT, REVEREND DAVID GLEASON, KATE WITH CONOR,
SHEILA, ELIOT, AIDAN, LAVONNE, DAVID, MILES, AND GLEN.

NIGHTTIME SHOT OF THE DAVID JOHNSON MEMORIAL CHAPEL,
ERECTED IN 2003 ON THE GROUNDS OF THIEL COLLEGE.

45

Lori

Lori Susan Johnson
November 15, 1954–January 5, 2006

LORI WAS BORN in the hospital in Willmar, Minnesota. She grew up in Lake Lillian, where she attended grade school until seventh grade. Like all three children, Lori was a good student. She was an avid reader like her older sister Vicki. The series of Nancy Drew books were among her favorites.

To earn spending money for all her pet projects, she made herself available for babysitting. Her sister Vicki, who was quite a bit older than Lori sometimes helped her out in a pinch with her child care jobs. David and Lori were close in age and had a very close relationship. Lori was very proud of her brother and was one of his biggest fans, cheering him on at all his Little League games. Lori and her good friend, Julianne Clarke, spent time together when they weren't busy doing other things.

Because our oldest daughter Vicki had played the clarinet in the school band, we just assumed that Lori would play the clarinet in band too. We were a bit surprised when we found out Lori was playing the French horn, although she continued to play the clarinet also. In the third grade, she stopped playing the clarinet altogether and focused only the horn.

When we moved to Virginia, Lori was in the eighth grade. By

then she was passionate about playing the French horn. About this time she tried out for the Reston Youth Symphony. Drawing from the thousands of students attending school in the Washington area, the leaders were looking for another student to play in the symphony. Lori came home one day and said, "I won the right to be in the Reston Youth Symphony, but I need a new French horn." The horn she had been using up to that point was an inexpensive horn, originally about $300. She explained that she would need something a bit more prestigious.

Lori told me what she needed, I wrote it all down, and began calling music stores. I finally found a store that had ordered instruments for the Navy Band, and they had a French horn. I said, "That's terrific, I'll be right there." I thought that I could just write a check. When I got there, I discovered it was incredibly expensive; it was almost $3,000!

First of all, I was stunned that an instrument could cost that much. Secondly, I had no way to pay cash for it, but somehow we managed to borrow the extra, and she started playing the French horn in the Reston Youth Symphony.

A HIGH SCHOOL GRADUATION PICTURE OF GLEN AND LAVONNE'S DAUGHTER LORI.

Lori continued with the Youth Symphony through her high school years at Herndon. During that time she traveled to Europe and other parts of the world with the group.

One of the more memorable trips we made with Lori was when the Reston Youth Symphony was in worldwide competition in Lausanne, Switzerland. We were there for three weeks with a large number of students and just a few other family members. I was kept busy going to Geneva to replace lost passports, as one student or another seemed to lose one almost every day. It was a great trip, and they did well in competition. We were most gratified to be able to accompany her. After she graduated, Lori was admitted to the School of the Arts in Winston-Salem, North Carolina where she played the French horn.

Somewhere along the way I had received an invitation to take a trip down the Snake River. The Snake River is a major tributary of the Columbia River winding through Wyoming, Idaho, Oregon, and Washington. Lori and I were in the stage of life where we had done a lot of things together, so I assumed she would go with me down the river. Her comment was, "Only if I can take my French horn." What that really meant was that we would never make that trip.

For years she practiced on her French horn six hours a day. She went to the School of the Arts in North Carolina for three years, and spent her senior year at DePaul in Chicago where she graduated with a BA degree in music. She chose DePaul so she could take lessons from the second horn in the Chicago Symphony, while simultaneously pursuing her education.

For a few weeks Lori became a runner on the Options Exchange, which required her to wear a uniform. I believe it was literally her first day on the job, when she misquoted the price of something, and it cost the broker she was running for $2500. It was one of those shocks when it happened, but she continued as a runner at the Exchange while taking lessons from the Second Horn in the Chicago Symphony.

While living in Chicago, Lori tried out for the Tiberius Symphony in Israel, and ended up going to Israel where she was the only Gentile in the symphony. Of course, Israel was at war as they have been most of their years. It was almost impossible to reach her on the phone.

GRANDMA ELPHIE KETTNER, LORI, AND LAVONNE UPON
LORI'S GRADUATION FROM DEPAUL UNIVERSITY IN 1976,
WHERE SHE EARNED A BACHELOR OF ARTS IN MUSIC.

I distinctly remember getting through to her one night, and asked, "What are you doing?"

She said, "I'm sitting on my balcony watching the shells go back and forth over us."

I said, "You have to be kidding, that's dangerous."

Lori said, "Well, I know."

I talked to her a while later, and her musical group had been out at a kibbutz somewhere playing for the troops. They were shooting shells over the top of them, but not at them, because they were there entertaining. After about ten months, the director of the Tiberius Symphony went sort of crazy.

Shortly after she came home, she auditioned for and landed a spot as the First Horn in the Guanajuato Symphony Orchestra in Mexico. Lori moved to Mexico where she had a great job. Musicians in Mexico work for the government, so she had a government salary. She lived in a nice big, but very old house and had a housekeeper.

She even married a Guatemalan musician, but it was a short marriage, and they had no children. We visited her in Mexico a number of times to hear the Symphony play. LaVonne and a friend also went to hear the Symphony. Lori was there for about four years; it was a great experience at the time. When she left that job she moved to the University of Colima where she taught music history in Spanish. While she was teaching in Colima, the peso collapsed. With her salary now almost worthless, she returned to the States.

Lori always enjoyed a challenge. She did something else quite interesting. She attended a class to learn how to be a good speaker. There were perhaps 75 people in her class, including several officers from one of the big Pittsburgh corporations. They were taught how to get up in front of an audience and make a professional presentation. At the end of the class, Lori won an award for being the most efficient at what she did.

Now back in Pittsburgh, Lori was the spokesperson for a group she established, called *Con Spirito*. *Con Spirito* was a five-member woodwind quintet group in residence at Thiel College for a year and then Duquesne University in Pittsburgh for a year.

A friend of mine ran a big restaurant in the Sheraton Hotel. He was so enamored with classical music that *Con Spirito* played in the hotel restaurant every Tuesday night for a year or more. They would fill the place, and we used to go there for dinner and listen to them play.

I often had meetings where I would hire professional musicians to entertain customers, so I always called on Lori's group when I could. Once I had a big meeting at Lincoln Center in New York and had entertainer Crystal Gayle as the lead singer. *Con Spirito* was the opening act that night.

Lori performed one time with the Pittsburgh Symphony. They were looking for a musician for a single performance who could play the horn, and Lori was given the honor. She was very good at what she did and eventually owned three or four French horns.

Con Spirito traveled all over the country. They were booked by a lot of universities like Cornell, Colgate, Ohio, University of

Kentucky, Berea College, and many Lutheran schools in Minnesota and the Midwest.

The group even went to China where they played for the United States Ambassador to China whom they had the privilege of spending some time with. During the three weeks they traveled around China, they performed to absolutely standing room only audiences. They enjoyed their time there very much.

When Lori married Miles Wallace and had her first child, Ariana, she would take a babysitter along on her mini-bus with the five members of *Con Spirito* as they traveled and performed.

A few years later, they traveled to Switzerland and performed in a number of places overseas. When Lori came back from that trip, she decided that she wanted to raise her family before any more performing. In addition to Ariana, Lori now had Aidan, so she put the horn aside for a time.

LORI'S GROUP, "CON SPIRITO" ENTERTAINED AT A WASHINGTON, DC FEDERATED INVESTORS CLIENT SEMINAR JUST PRIOR TO THEIR TRIP TO CHINA. VICE PRESIDENT WALTER MONDALE WAS THE MAIN SPEAKER. BACK ROW: STEVE FRANCISO, CONGRESSMAN BRUCE VENTO, AND MRS. FRANCISO. FRONT ROW: NANCY AMBROSE, ERIC LUDWIG, AND OUR DAUGHTER LORI.

**LORI, WITH HER HUSBAND MILES
WALLACE, ARIANA, AND AIDAN.**

**LORI
AND LAVONNE.**

Lori never smoked a cigarette in her life, yet she began to develop some medical issues with her lungs. I often wondered if a contributing factor could have been related to her time in Mexico. The property where Lori's house was located was along the edge of a silver mine. Colima had an active volcano, which is something else that could have affected Lori's lungs. I was in Pittsburgh the day that Lori had a physical exam, and the doctor called and said that she was perfectly fine. We were rejoicing because we had suspected that there might be something serious going on.

The very next day we got the astonishing phone call that she had inflammatory breast cancer, a very aggressive form of breast cancer that is not usually detected until the later stages. Eventually, they identified that her lung was the primary site, and the cancer spread to her breast from there.

She was in the hospital for a while, but came home where we could all be together. Lori was only 51 years old and lived exactly

LORI JOHNSON WALLACE.

nine months from that diagnosis. We were all in shock as we sat and watched her die so young.

We had now tragically lost two of our children. No parent thinks their children will be gone before them. We remain grateful for all the memories. They are an indelible part of our lives.

ARIANA WON THE ASPCA—MACLAY CHAMPIONSHIP
AGAINST SEVERAL HUNDRED RIDERS.

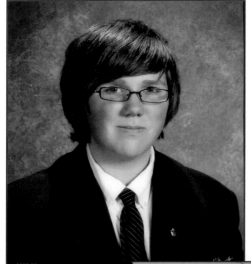

AIDAN WALLACE.

LORI'S CHILDREN, AIDAN AND ARIANA WITH THEIR FATHER, MILES WALLACE, AND GRANDMA ELPHIE AT THE TIME OF HER 100TH BIRTHDAY.

Epilogue

DR. WILLIAM PETIT is the Connecticut doctor who recently survived a gruesome home invasion that claimed the lives of his wife and two daughters. "I don't think there will ever be closure," Dr. Petit told reporters. "Over time, the edges may smooth out a bit, but the holes in your heart . . . are still there."

Grief is a very personal thing, but I agree with Dr. Petit. The hole is always there. Without faith in a loving God and His promise of eternal life, I'm not sure how one can go on. The necessity to get up in the morning, to do any normal thing is almost impossible. LaVonne and I were blessed that both David and Lori had children, extensions of their own lives that were cut short. Our grandchildren needed the family to be strong and to move forward so that they could go on with their young lives. However, when the grandchildren are not physically spending time with us, the reality of death has to be faced over and over. Family, friends, and clergy . . . all were there for us in abundance. Thank God for them. The support system works.

As life slowly began to become more routine, we had to try to stop wondering "Why?" and to do something good in remembrance of them. It is simply amazing how healing it has been to see and hear their names referenced in honorable ways.

Thiel College needed a freestanding chapel. It is a Lutheran school, and it seemed incomplete without a chapel. We joined other donors and helped build the David Johnson Memorial Chapel at Thiel. Other memorials were donated to purchase a processional cross and gospel cover in his memory. There is comfort in this for us.

Lori was a musician and in her memory, Thiel presents free chamber concerts each year. First Lutheran Church also has a new altar cross in Lori's memory. Florida Gulf Coast University has a scholarship in music for prospective teachers. Lori was convinced that children should have a chance for excellent instruction. The Chautauqua Women's Club presents a Lori Johnson Wallace horn scholarship to a college student each season.

Certainly, the memories of David and Lori will always be a part of our family. As long as these efforts continue, David and Lori shall be remembered and even become a blessing to others as well.

There is no answer to "Why?" It just is. But we remember them and are grateful for the memories and the grandchildren that follow after them.

Appendices

Appendix A

Glen R. Johnson Biographic Summary

Vice President, Federated Investors, Inc.
Federated Investors
Federated Investors Tower
1001 Liberty Avenue
Pittsburgh, PA, 5222–3779
Legislative Director

1970 to 1990	President, Multi-Trust Systems, Federated Securities Corp.
1990 to Present	Vice President Federated Securities Corp. (Federated Investors is a $400 billion dollar investment management company).

———

» Born, raised, and educated in Minnesota

» Twelve years as editor and publisher of a Minnesota weekly newspaper, May 1949 through May 1961

» Entered government service as Minnesota Deputy Director, Department of Treasury, U. S. Savings Bonds Division, 1961

» Named Minnesota State Director, Department of Treasury, U.S. Savings Bonds Division, 1962—served in that capacity until 1967

» Appointed National Director and Assistant Secretary, U.S. Treasury Department, Savings Bonds Division, 1967—served in that capacity for two years Under Secretary of Treasury, Henry H. Fowler

» Worked with industry, media, banking, and volunteers; achieved a record breaking 5.5 million new payroll savers and $10 billion in savings bonds sales in a two year period

» Former Chairman, Board of Trustees—Thiel College (14 years on Board of Directors)

» Trustee—Boston University, Morin Center for Banking Law Studies

» Former Member of the Swedish American Royal Round Table

» Former Chairman of the Board—Abraxas Group, Inc.

» Former Member of the Board of Directors—Board of Pensions, Lutheran Church of America

» Former Member of the Board of Trustees—Gustavus Adolphus College

Appendix B

Glen R. Johnson—Honors and Awards

» Graduate of Gustavus Adolphus College—Business Administration Degree

» Honorary Doctor of Letters—Gustavus Adolphus College, 2008

» Honorary Doctor of Laws Degree—Thiel College, Greenville, Pennsylvania, 1988

» Silver Shingle Award for Distinguished Public Service—Boston University School of Law, 1986

» Honorary Member of Minnesota Newspaper Association for outstanding contribution to Minnesota journalism

» Treasury Award of Merit, 1964

» Civil Service "Employee of the Year" in leadership category, chosen from among 16,000 employees in Minneapolis, St. Paul, 1964

» WCCO Radio Good Neighbor Award, 1966

» Lutheran Brotherhood "Distinguished Service Award" for Lutheran of the Year, 1968

» *Who's Who in America*

**GLEN AND LAVONNE RECEIVING HONORARY DEGREES
AT GUSTAVUS ADOLPHUS COLLEGE.**

GLEN ROGER JOHNSON

Doctor of Laws

May 15, 1988

Mr. President,

I present Glen Roger Johnson. Born and raised on a farm, he knows the earth and keeps in close touch with the land and the people he loved as a child. In his early years he learned to listen, to work as a member of a team, and to be direct so as to get to the heart of the matter. He also learned the patience required between seed time and harvest. As a student he developed a fascination with words and the ways humans communicate. Out of college he founded a weekly newspaper and developed it for twelve years, achieving in his thirties honorary membership in the Minnesota Newspaper Association for his outstanding contribution to Minnesota journalism.

Fascinated by a man with a vision for this nation, he entered the world of public service as a campaign manager for Hubert Humphrey and later used his capacity for persuasion to sell U.S. Savings Bonds, so successfully that he was selected from 16,000 civil servants to receive the "Employee of the Year" award in the leadership category. From the position of Minnesota State Director, Department of the Treasury, U.S. Savings Bond Division, he moved in 1967 to become the National Director and Assistant Secretary, U.S. Treasury Department, Savings Bond Division. In public service he came to understand and to honor the sacred trust involved in government "of the people, for the people, by the people," taking inspiration in difficult times from the man who sits in the chair at our nation's capital and looks out from the Lincoln Memorial.

In the Treasury Department he captured the vision of the role of financial institutions in assisting individuals and groups in achieving their potential. He moved to the private sector where his understanding, creativity, drive, tough-mindedness, commitment to reaching tangible goals, and optimism born of faith made possible a major contribution to the phenomenal development of Federated Securities Corporation--now the largest financial institution in the State of Pennsylvania. Throughout the eighteen years he has been with Federated, he has held numerous leadership positions with the company and presently serves as President of Federated MultiTrust Funds. In the industry he is known as the "Dean" of cash management funds as well as other trust funds used by bank trust departments.

Farmer, editor, public servant, business executive--these titles do not exhaust Mr. Johnson's contributions. In the voluntary sector he has been a lifelong churchman, earning the Lutheran Brotherhood Lutheran of the Year award, and is currently an active member of First Lutheran Church in Pittsburgh. As a citizen of Minneapolis he received the WCCO Radio Good Neighbor Award. For his contribution to the banking industry and good government, he received the Silver Shingle Award from the Boston University School of Law. He is a knowledgeable and enthusiastic patron of music and of the visual arts. As Chairman of the Foundation for Abraxas he has played a major leadership role in battling the scourge of illegal drugs.

Mr. President, it is my great privilege and honor to present to you, Glen Roger Johnson, a person distinguished by outstanding achievement in government and finance as well as many other fields, a man of God and a man of the people, a genuine servant of what is good, true and noble. I present him for the degree, Doctor of Laws, Honoris Causa.

**GLEN'S DOCTOR OF LAWS HONORARY DEGREE FROM THIEL COLLEGE
PRESENTED ON MAY 15, 1988 BY THE PRESIDENT OF THIEL COLLEGE.**

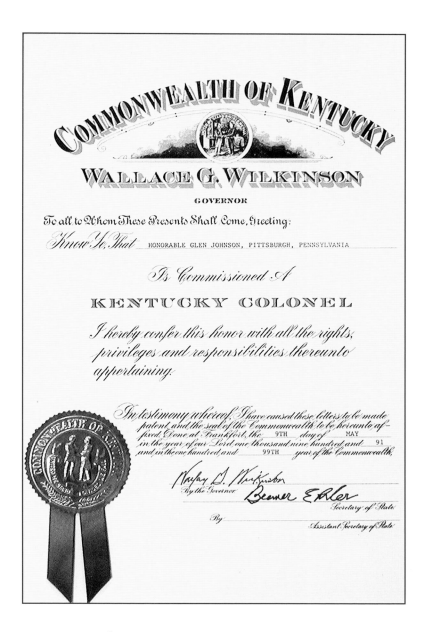

GLEN'S COMMISSION AS A KENTUCKY COLONEL.

HONORARY CITIZEN OF HUNTSVILLE PRESENTED
TO GLEN R. JOHNSON ON OCTOBER 4, 1967.

THE
AMBASSADOR
OF GOOD WILL
FROM THE CITY
OF LOUISVILLE.

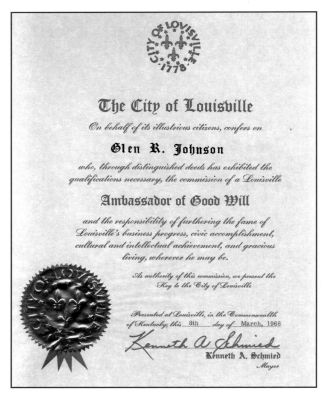

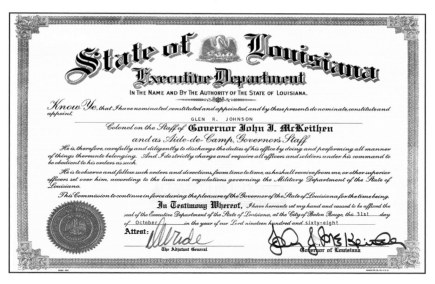

PRESENTATION FROM THE STATE OF LOUISIANA TO GLEN BY
THE GOVERNOR, JOHN MCKEITHEN, OCTOBER 31, 1968.

GLEN WAS PROCLAIMED AN HONORARY CITIZEN
BY THE CITY OF MINNEAPOLIS, JULY 1977.

Appendix C

Glen & LaVonne Johnson—Leaving a Legacy

CHARITABLE REMAINDER TRUSTS ESTABLISHED

» The First Lutheran Church of Pittsburgh, PA: To continue the support of the mission and ministry of the church in the true Lutheran tradition.

» Thiel College: The David Johnson Memorial Chapel in memory of our son David, and the Con Spirito Chamber Series in memory of our daughter, Lori, plus additional support.

» The Johnson Institute for Responsible Leadership at the University of Pittsburgh Graduate School of Public and International Affairs.

» Gustavus Adolphus College: Environmental Studies Program.

OTHER AREAS OF SUPPORT

» Florida Gulf Coast University: Lori Johnson Wallace Memorial Scholarship for Music Pedagogic Excellence.

» Chautauqua Institution: Chautauqua Women's Club Horn Scholarship.

» Seacrest Country Day School: The independent PreK-12th grade school in Naples, Florida attended by four of our grandchildren and now a great-grandchild as well.

Appendix D

by Dr. Louis Almen

GLEN JOHNSON AND THIEL COLLEGE: MEMORIES, PERSPECTIVES, AND APPRECIATION

To properly understand the importance of Glen Johnson to Thiel, it is critical to grasp the fiscal situation of the college from the mid 70s through the early 80s. During the 60s, Thiel College had expanded its facilities with several government loans and grants and had benefited greatly from federal and state scholarship programs.

In the early 70s the fiscal strategies of both the federal and state governments began to shift from grants to loans. As a result, private education became more expensive, and Thiel began to experience a gradual drop in student enrollment and greater difficulty in balancing the budget. This negative shift in funding, combined with other internal problems, led to curricular adjustments to attract more students and to borrowing heavily from its meager $1,800,000 endowment to avoid bankruptcy. That, in turn, threatened its accreditation. In the summer of 1976, after the departure of two presidents in three years, information circulated to the public that Thiel might be forced to close its doors.

This was a low point in Thiel's history, and it was at that time and in that situation that I accepted the presidency of Thiel College. In addition to having been a professor in a Lutheran college for 14 years, I had been a church-wide executive of Lutheran higher education for 10 years during which I had been a member of a four person outside executive committee, which was authorized to make the necessary budget changes to save a Lutheran college from bankruptcy. I had been a member of the Lutheran Church in America's President's Cabinet, which from 1967 onward had been attempting to do more with less money each year. I had applied for the presidency at Thiel because I wished to return to an academic community. I was committed to the importance of Christian higher education, and I thought I had the experience to lead Thiel back to fiscal stability and to the recovery of its character as a Christian liberal arts institution of high quality.

After one year, Thiel managed to balance income with expenditures and did so every succeeding year of my presidency. However, the crisis that followed the shift in political support for higher education was followed by another fiscal crisis. This one was provoked by the increase in the cost of petroleum due to the oil cartel of the late 70s. Plus, the rapid decline in the steel and auto industries caused by the new competition from Japan and South Korea put Western Pennsylvania into a deep recession in the late 70s and early 80s.

It is also important to understand the Western Pennsylvania economy. Over the preceding 100 years Western Pennsylvania and West Virginia had developed great wealth through the production of oil and coal and through the production of steel and steel products. Northern Minnesota iron ore was linked with Pennsylvania and West Virginia coal by the Great Lakes and railroads. Historically, Pittsburgh had been a center of commerce. The Allegheny and Monongahela Rivers merged into the Ohio River. This water-way linked to the Mississippi River and ultimately the Gulf of Mexico, opening up the world. Much of the old wealth of the area was perpetuated for the use of future generations, through foundations and trusts and benefited educational institutions in the area with effective contacts.

The end of WWII diminished the production of oil, and in the late 70s the steel industry was stunned by the imports of cheaper steel from the Far East, leading to dramatic cutbacks in employment and to retooling to remain competitive. Western Pennsylvania entered a decade of deep recession if not economic depression. Some steel mills closed and cut back the number of employees, and several secondary steel related industries also shrunk or moved from the area. The population of Pittsburgh and of many Western Pennsylvania communities declined.

It became clear to me early on that Thiel needed to find new sources of income in addition to tuition, board and room, the alumni giving, which was strong for a college its size, and its grant from the Western Pennsylvania/ West Virginia Synod, which could be counted on but did not grow. Thiel was competing with private colleges, some of which had an endowment over a hundred times greater than Thiel's.

Thiel's need for a decade for leadership was consistent with the need for leadership to set a new course for Western Pennsylvania. To reach out more effectively to the alumni and to the foundations and leading industries in the area, Thiel needed to expand its number of trustees with effective ties to foundations and leading industries, reducing the trustees elected by the Synod to minority status. This was accomplished in the early 80s and made possible the success of the Decade for Leadership Campaign that brought fiscal stability back to Thiel, increased the effectiveness of its development program, and laid the groundwork for strengthening the academic program.

The new wealth that was growing apace in Pittsburgh was located in Federated Investors and in particular its Multi-Trust Systems, Federated Securities of which Glen was the president from 1970 to 1990. It was Glen's experience with the bankers from all over the U.S. as Director of the National Savings Bonds Division in the Treasury Department, his skill in campaigning, his knowledge of the economy, along with his winning personality, and his commitment to be the best at what he does that brought capital from around the United States to be invested in Federated Multi-Trust Funds. The rapid growth in Federated Investors brought capital to Western Pennsylvania for investment in renewing its economy. It was Glen's experience, skills, character, intelligence, and the intensity of his motivation that was ultimately a critical leadership factor for Western Pennsylvania.

To engage Glen Johnson for membership on the Thiel Board and to secure his leadership on Thiel's Decade for Leadership Campaign, along with an alumnus well known in the financial community of Pittsburgh and a local steel company president, was critical to the success of that campaign. By 1990, the Board of Trustees had a dozen or more company presidents, CEOs, or company board chairs as members. It was Glen's record as a leader on the board that led to his election as board chairman in 1993.

It was Pastor Braughler, a member of the Thiel Board and the pastor of First Lutheran Church in Pittsburgh, where Glen and LaVonne Johnson were active members, who first brought Glen Johnson to my attention as a prospect for membership on the Thiel Board. When I went to tender the invitation of the Thiel Board to become one of its members, I was well aware of his potential to make a huge difference to Thiel, but I was also aware of the demands of his job, the depth of his commitment to Abraxas, and importance of its mission, so I was anxious about our chances.

In his usual genial style Glen welcomed me, and soon we were talking about people and places we both knew. One of my high school debate partners had also been a campaigner for Hubert Humphrey and was active in Minnesota politics. We had both been students at Gustavus Adolphus College in St. Peter, Minnesota. My paternal grandfather had been a pioneer pastor in Sacred Heart, Minnesota and later in New London, Minnesota; both were in Kandiyohi County in which his hometown of Lake Lillian was also located. One of my uncles and two of my cousins had also been publishers, editors, and community leaders of small town weekly newspapers. When I left, Glen indicated he was favorably disposed to becoming a member of the Thiel Board, but wanted to clear it with his colleagues as a courtesy. I walked out as if walking on air, and in retrospect, saw the hand of providence in the way things had come together to bring Glen and LaVonne into the Thiel family.

When Glen joined the board, the president was Bishop Kenneth May, an alumnus of Thiel and the Bishop of its supporting Synod. He was pleased to have such a strong Lutheran layman as a board elected trustee, and he appointed Glen as chair of the Investment Committee. Other members of that committee included three bank presidents and a stockbroker. It soon became clear to Glen that the Decade for Leadership Campaign was critical to Thiel's future, and that careful conservative budgeting and close budget management continued to be necessary. Early in his board membership he also spoke clearly and forcefully for 100 percent board support for the annual fund, and when the accreditation team met with the executive committee board in the mid 80s concerned about Thiel's fiscal stability as reported in their message to the college in the mid-seventies, it was Glen's assurance that the situation had turned around that carried the day, especially when they discovered he was president of Federated Multi-Trust System, which at 200 billion dollars was the largest financial institution in Pennsylvania.

Unlike some top executives who serve on college boards and seldom appear at meetings, Glen could be counted on to be present even if he was on the telephone both going and coming and during a break in the meeting. Also, LaVonne came with him and attended the special program to inform board spouses of different aspects of the college program. It soon became apparent that LaVonne was genuinely interested in what was happening at Thiel and shared Glen's growing involvement in advancing Thiel's future and the kind of education Thiel provides. With an undergraduate degree in political science and sociology and a graduate degree in public administration, her commitment to education was clear, and her capacity to make informed evaluations became helpfully apparent.

LaVonne had been deeply interested and supportive of the arts in Pittsburgh including the International Poetry Forum, the Opera Theater of Pittsburgh, the Civic Light Opera, and the Shakespeare Festival and had shown her enthusiasm for Thiel Theatre, the Greenville Symphony, and the Thiel Orchestra and Choir.

As the family's involvement with Thiel grew, their daughter Lori and her woodwind quartet *Con Spirito* became artists-in-residence at Thiel in the

80s. The practice of artists-in-residence on college campuses began at a few nationally recognized colleges in the 60s, and only a few Lutheran colleges had been so privileged during the 70s, but the Johnsons made it possible for Thiel to enjoy that opportunity as well in 1989–90.

Lori, a graduate of DePaul University, had worked as a member of orchestras in Israel and Mexico and had taught music in Colima, Mexico prior to being a founder of *Con Spirito*. They were a great hit with students because of their demeanor and approachability. They were able to engage in discussions with students after class, in the student center, or at receptions following performances. My wife and I remember with great pleasure entertaining the *Con Spirito Quintet* at the president's home at Thiel and listening to their excellent concerts and special appearances.

We had come to love Lori's musicianship and her quiet ways and were saddened by Lori's untreatable illness and early death in 2006. But the Lori Johnson Wallace Music Series at the Memorial Chapel named for her brother David, also taken in mid-life before an organ transplant became available, carries on the gift of music capable of healing souls suffering from anxiety, home sickness, disappointment, failure, self-condemnation, and souls in need of a pick-up of spirit with the music of gaiety, courage, and the wholeness of the beautiful. That was the gift of *Con Spirito,* which is the gift the Johnsons, all of them, have brought to Thiel in different ways.

The source of that Spirit is resident in the spirituality and theology of their Lutheran heritage, whose theology is the theology of the cross. Lutheran theology grasps the reality of physical evil as well as the evils of human willfulness and uncontrolled desires. The Scripture says, "If we say we have no sin, we deceive ourselves and the truth is not in us." But the theology of the cross also calls us to receive the grace of forgiveness and new life with the power to heal. We are united with Christ who though crucified, dead, and buried was raised from death to life and has ascended to the right hand of the Heavenly Father. Baptized into union with Christ in God, and called to a calling of service in His Name in the world, we are to embrace the world as we find it and transform it by wrestling as much love and justice as each situation makes possible. The Christian is to face life with spirit—*con spirito*—with the faith that in this life and in death we are in Christ, united with Him in carrying the burdens of this life and also always being in His Presence. Life in this world is ultimately not to be judged by the number of years we live in this world but by the spirit with which we engage life. In that understanding *con spirito* represents the Christian's calling to bring love, justice, and beauty to what we do best.

Glen has shown that spirit in the earnestness and diligence with which he discharged the duties of his position, giving his very best in service to those who depended on him. His concern for the welfare of others has been revealed by his commitment to Abraxas that worked to keep people away from drugs as well as to help the victims to overcome the habit. Both Glen and LaVonne were committed to helping minority youth in Pittsburgh to get out of the ghetto and to explore opportunities for a better future. They supported a number of youth from the Pittsburgh area to spend several days exploring their future possibilities in a program conducted on the Thiel campus.

One of Glen's habits was to occasionally break away from eating among the financiers who dined at the Duquesne Club or the University Club in order to chat with those who frequented the hot dog and sauerkraut vendors on the street. His humanity embraced the lost and the least as well as the powerful. On a person-to-person basis Glen was a supporter-helper.

Prior to retirement I had to deal with the question of whether I had been faithful to my call to the ministry by spending the last 25 years in the administration of church institutions rather than in preaching or teaching. When I had chosen to enter the Gospel ministry, my father, a Lutheran pastor had challenged me with the admonition—"Remember it is required of a minister that he remains faithful." My father had little appreciation for bureaucracy and administrators. For him the ministry was in the parish. My course of development had been from seminary to parish, to teaching, and then to administration. I felt called to each one, but approaching retirement I became disturbed enough to become choked up in giving the opening prayer for an Executive Committee of the Thiel Board held at the Duquesne Club in Pittsburgh. The next morning it was Glen who called to support the course of action I had taken in my ministry. When I needed a pastor, it was Glen who comforted me, supported me, and who was there for me.

Through hard work and the effective use of his special gifts Glen has become very successful and has achieved an elevated status, but his faith oriented his life around a loving purpose, opened him to the whole world, and in the process enlarged his humanity. *Con Spirito* has characterized the Johnson family in the arts, through their involvement in the church and its institutions, in their professional careers, and in their involvement with and support of their charities.

Over the years their commitment to Thiel has grown, involving almost every area of college life: The Glen Johnson Community Center, the Resident's box in the new stadium, the David Johnson Memorial Chapel, the Lori Johnson Wallace Music Series at the Chapel, scholarships, the Glen and LaVonne Johnson Remainder Trust, membership in the Society of 1966, the Chairman's Circle, contribution to the expansion and renewal of the Howard Miller Center, and to the Thiel Corner Stone.

LaVonne expressed the depth of the Johnson family's connection with Thiel as she thanked friends in 2003 at the groundbreaking of the David Johnson Memorial Chapel, named in honor of their son. She said, "Friends have a way of making the good times more wonderful, and the bad times, when they come, bearable." Thiel and its people have become part of the Johnson's extended family.

When Glen became co-chair of the most challenging third phase of the Decade for Leadership Campaign, the engagement with alumni and friends of the Pittsburgh area happened in the Glen and LaVonne Johnson home in Squirrel Hill, Pittsburgh. A beautiful three-story home on a three-acre site, it had been built by Barney Dreyfus, founder of the Pittsburgh Pirates in 1915. Unique in the midst of a city, it offered a pastoral setting and had the only redwood trees in Pittsburgh. The Johnsons had furnished it elegantly and in keeping with their love of the arts had acquired the works of many of the finest artists including Picasso, Remington, Adams, and Ernst, along with many precious antiques.

Fit for royalty, they made it available for the Thiel campaign and hosted several campaign events to which well over a thousand people had been invited. Thiel alums and friends in the Pittsburgh area could hardly turn down such a rare invitation, and when they saw Glen and LaVonne's enthusiasm for Thiel, any doubts about fiscal instability in the past, that had led some to hold back their support, began to disappear as rapidly as the appearance of the sun evaporates a morning fog. LaVonne herself became a member of the Pittsburgh Campaign Committee and became heavily involved at the Pittsburgh Campaign Inaugural Reception and Dinner at the Vista International Hotel in January of 1989.

Glen had realized early on in his tenure on the Thiel Board that Thiel had been slower than most church-related, private, liberal arts colleges in building its endowment, and even after the campaign of which he was co-chair, pushed for a larger endowment. When Glen was board chair, and subsequently a Trustee Emeritus, Glen and LaVonne hosted estate-planning seminars for key alumni and friends in their beautiful, waterfront home on Marco Island, Florida. These included annual receptions from 1997 to 2002. Thiel has now and in the past had many loyal alumni, but there has been no one more actively involved in building the financial resources for its future than Glen Johnson and his life's teammate and fellow philanthropist, LaVonne Corley Johnson.

In 1988, Thiel recognized Glen's life achievements with an honorary Doctor of Laws degree. The citation describing the basis on which this honor was granted pointed exclusively to Glen's achievements as a person and professional and made no reference to his specific contributions to Thiel. In five paragraphs it summarized major achievements in his career, and stands as a witness to the honor in which he is held not only by the Thiel Community but by the civil and professional community as well. By conferring the degree Thiel not only honored Glen but also honored itself by claiming Glen as one of its own.

PRESENTING TOM RIDGE WITH AN HONORARY DEGREE IN GREENVILLE, PENNSYLVANIA. ON THE LEFT IS THE PRESIDENT OF THIEL COLLEGE, CARLYLE HAALAND, WITH GLEN ON THE RIGHT.

GLEN (STANDING, 4TH FROM RIGHT) PRESENTED TOM RIDGE (SEATED ON COUCH) HIS HONORARY DEGREE FROM THIEL COLLEGE. TOM WAS THE FIRST SECRETARY OF HOMELAND SECURITY.

In 2003 when ground was broken for the David Johnson Memorial Chapel and the Glen Johnson Community Center and was dedicated at the '03 Homecoming, the college granted the Service to Thiel Award to Glen and LaVonne Johnson in recognition of their 20 years of active involvement in support of Thiel, citing the long list of activities and gifts they had shared. This honor was based on recognized leadership in the Thiel Community. It was a corporate expression of gratitude. It said. "You have made the college we all love better, more secure, and capable of greater things. Well done, good and faithful servants. You are all honored members of the Thiel family." It was a public acknowledgement of the loving purpose, which characterizes that which is inspired by God.

THE GLEN JOHNSON COMMUNITY CENTER, DEDICATED
AT THE 2003 THIEL HOMECOMING.

THE DAVID JOHNSON MEMORIAL CHAPEL, ERECTED IN 2003.

THE INSIDE OF THE DAVID JOHNSON MEMORIAL CHAPEL.

Appendix E

by C. Carlyle Haaland
16th President of Thiel College

AS I REMEMBER

Glen Johnson is a person of so many facets that any attempt to document him fully is a challenge. At the same time he is so open in his personality that one finds it is easy to offer at least some description of and narrative about the man.

In seeking to describe Glen, a number of characteristics or traits stand out. These are the elements that have formed his life and made it what it has become. Glen is first and foremost a person of integrity; honest and true in his dealings with people. He is a loyal and dedicated person, particularly toward his family, his church, his business associates, and the two colleges important in his life—Gustavus Adolphus in Minnesota, where he attended, and Thiel College, where he served on the Board of Trustees for 14 years and from which he received an honorary degree. He is a person of thoroughness, of inquiry. In the language of business, he pursues "due diligence" before taking action or giving support. He is insightful, frequently seeing another, more advantageous way to manage an activity or to meet a need or challenge. He is supportive of others, ready to assist those under his care, and especially eager to nurture, mentor, or provide opportunities for young people setting out on a career path. He is generous with his time, abilities, and resources in service to the common good. He is politically and financially astute, attested by multiple careers in both camps. He has a sense of roots, expressed especially in his long-term ownership of the Minnesota farm on which he was raised. Through this, by returning some of the land back to a natural preserve, he also manifests a strong commitment to the stewardship of the land. He has a sense of humor expressed in a quiet way and with a twinkle in the eye. And, he has been blessed and supported along life's way by LaVonne, his wife, who is a person of ability, integrity, good council, generosity, and warmth, as well as achievement in her own right.

To use clichés, Glen is "the salt of the earth." Even with all of his accomplishments he is "down to earth." Of him it can be said, "He is a Minnesota boy who made good." Of him it can be said that he makes it easy to feel like a friend because he has always acted like one.

My first encounter with Glen Johnson was not face-to-face or even direct. I first became aware of him as more than a name in 1990 when I was a candidate for the presidency of Thiel College. As the process unfolded and the list became shorter, reference checks rose in priority. Early in 1990 I received phone calls from some persons who were serving as references. They indicated that an administrative assistant in the office of Glen Johnson had called to do a background check. I found out later that all the references had received similar calls, a thoroughness that was, to say the least, impressive.

When I started service as the 16th president of Thiel College on July 1, 1990, the Vice President for Development, John Hilpert, arranged visits to a number of area trustees. One of them was Glen, then President of Multitrust Funds at Federated Investors in Pittsburgh, Pennsylvania. This was our first face-to-face meeting. It was with a mix of eagerness and trepidation that I walked into his office.

Having found out that he, like I, came from Minnesota, as did our wives, served as a ready icebreaker. So, I asked him how a kid from Lake Lillian, Minnesota migrated to the current position in Pittsburgh, Pennsylvania. He asked what I knew of Lake Lillian, and I said that my wife came from Sacred Heart, not far away. His eyes lit up as he recounted playing in baseball games between these towns in his early years.

Then I asked a question often asked among people with Minnesota roots: "What nationality was behind a name like Johnson?" Swedish, Norwegian, Danish? He replied that he was 100 percent Swedish. I noted in return that I was half-Swedish, and my wife was one-fourth. To this he deadpanned, "Well, that makes you a half-breed." Then the smile broke out. That was the start of a relationship with Glen that was not only professional but also personal.

In 1983, during the very successful presidency of Louis Almen, Glen joined the Board of Trustees, serving on the Investment Committee of which he became the chairman in 1985. He was still serving in that leadership role in 1990 when I became president. He continued to serve in that capacity until the fall of 1993 when he was elected chairman of the board, though he remained a member of this committee as well.

Before the 1990s, many investment committees at small colleges did not distinguish themselves with forward-looking practices. Often they would meet once a year to review the results of very conservative investments and recommend to the full board the expenditure of the total annual earnings on the investments. Little attention was given to fund allocation or emphasis on growth as well as income. One reason for this was that at many institutions, which were financially fragile, oversight of the operating budget was considered to be of a higher priority than managing investments. Fortunately, Thiel started breaking away from this mindset before 1990 with the establishment of the Investment Committee charged with oversight of the endowment, both restricted and unrestricted.

As chairman of this committee, Glen led the way in setting a new direction. First, quarterly meetings with the external fund managers were scheduled and held. Investment allocations and earnings targets, having been set at the beginning of the fiscal year, were reviewed for results. If a fund did not favorably measure up against goals, or was falling out of favor as the market shifted, new directives were issued to the managers.

Beyond this diligence, however, in the early 1990s two very important changes recommended to the committee by the administration were thoroughly studied and then taken to the full board for approval and implementation. One was to move away from spending all of the investment earnings for the year and move to a spending formula that would incrementally, over five years, decrease spending to not more than five percent of the invested fund value averaged over the past twelve quarters.

The second issue involved moving from having one investment firm manage all of the funds to retaining three such companies to manage portions of the investment funds. Their performances were reviewed quarterly, and particularly at the end of the fiscal year. This process not only held the companies responsible for meeting established targets but also created competition due to the built-in comparison of performance results.

These practices, established when Glen led the Investment Committee, did much to increase the value of the endowment by emphasizing the importance of growth through allocation, reinvestment, competition, and limits on spending, and not just through the acquisition of new funds. Consequently, administrators attending Investment Committee meetings looked forward to them with anticipation, not only to see what the outcomes of these management policies and practices were, but also to engage in lively conversations on investment and market strategies.

However, it would be unfair to suggest that during this time Glen Johnson was not attuned to other dimensions of the college. He was. During this time, the college arranged to bring to Western Pennsylvania several groups of Russians embarking on the development of private banking in that country. Glen arranged for meetings at Federated Investors in order to acquaint these visitors with the investment industry.

Second, in order to solicit more broadly and intentionally, from former trustees, from persons unable to serve as trustees, and from supportive alumni and friends, ideas that would be helpful to the college, Glen strongly supported the formation of a Board of Associates. This vehicle became a valuable sounding board in the general locale, providing the college with a clearer sense of how it was perceived in the larger community.

Third, ever the forward thinking board member, Glen supported the early 1990s efforts to develop a long-range plan. This plan focused on six areas: Image, Programs, Faculty and Staff, Physical Plant, Endowment, and Community Building.

Fourth, seeing the immediate need to improve facilities, he encouraged the restoration of historical Greenville Hall, the original campus building dedicated in 1872. It became a Center for the Humanities.

Fifth, he also encouraged a systematic program for refurbishing residential halls and classrooms, and the campus beautification effort undertaken by employees—the *Thiel Grows on Me* program—led by the president's wife.

Sixth, recognizing that many students completed their studies in mid year, moved on to careers, and often moved out of the area, making it difficult to return for commencement each May, he supported the beginning of December commencements.

Seventh, during 1990–1991 he followed with interest and encouraged the yearlong celebration of Thiel's 125th Anniversary.

Finally, he was instrumental in bringing to closure in 1991 the capital campaign begun during the presidency of Louis Almen.

That Glen Johnson was an interested board member was transparent.

When John Mouganis decided that it was time to step down as head of the Board in the fall of 1993, Glen was immediately looked to as the logical successor. By then, he had served on the Board of Trustees for 10 years, giving him a broad exposure to the college. As chairman of the Investment Committee he had also served on the Executive Committee. So, he had an understanding of the working of the board and its relationship to the administrative offices.

As a Lutheran, he was committed to Thiel as a college of the church and its future in higher education, not only as a presence in Western Pennsylvania but also as a magnet for students from many states and other countries. Thus, he had a vision of what the college could continue to become.

As a person with experience in the corporate sector he had an excellent understanding of how a complex organization worked and how its best practices could be applied to a college to address changing times and conditions. Hence, though Glen served as Board leader for just two years, retiring from the board in 1995, these years marked significant change and growth for Thiel.

During this time, the Northeast Ohio/Western Pennsylvania Academic Alliance was formed. A collaborative effort of Lake Erie College, Walsh University, Youngstown State University, and Thiel, it provided for cross-registration between the three smaller institutions and YSU, particularly in the area of science and engineering. This Alliance was funded by a major grant from the Teagle Foundation of New York through the lead efforts of Thiel.

Second, opportunities for groups of faculty to engage in summer study abroad began; places visited included Russia, China, and Latin America. The recruitment of international students expanded, building upon the efforts of the prior decade. Hence, the student international population rose to 45, based on relationships primarily with Asian organizations, agencies, and schools, as well as the Evangelical Lutheran Church in America's efforts to provide education for Namibian youth.

Additionally, Thiel appeared for the first time in the top tier of liberal arts colleges in the Northern Region as ranked by the annual *U.S. News and World Report,* and work began on the self-study for reaffirmation of accreditation by the Middle States Association.

LaVonne's support of Glen and of Thiel was immensely important at this time, too. In addition to graciousness in hosting off campus events, she was one of the spouses of board members regularly on campus at the time of trustee meetings, commencements, and other special events such as Honors Convocation and Founder's Day. During trustee meetings, spouses were offered a special program, arranged by the president's wife and the Director of Special Events, introducing the spouses to aspects of the college and the local community otherwise not encountered. LaVonne was, more often than not, a ready participant on these occasions.

Glen was not only an able manager of board matters and meetings. He also invested himself in a proactive manner in a variety of new efforts. He began the practice that continued for several years of inviting a select group of Thiel junior and senior business majors to the Federated Investors headquarters for a daylong program in the corporate boardroom, offering them an orientation and education experience at which corporate administrators made presentations. This event, which was highly prized, introduced students for the first time to the inner workings of a major financial institution. Then, with his wife LaVonne, the practice of hosting alumni and friends each spring at the Florida home was started. These theme events with buffets were highly appreciated by the many who attended, increasing significantly goodwill toward and support for the college. Frequently, in conjunction with these occasions, the Johnsons would host a private dinner for major and prospective donors, followed by a workshop on estate planning. And keen on raising the prestige and public appearance of the Board at special events, Glen provided the funds to purchase, in college colors, caps and gowns for the members.

Additionally, he engaged Paul Granlund, his long time friend and renowned sculptor at Gustavus Adolphus College in Minnesota, to execute the Thiel Trustee Medallion to be worn on these occasions. One consideration for being a successor board chair was that he or she would be willing to provide additional medallions as needed.

Further, Glen was particularly keen on issues that dealt with compensation and staff. On the first he urged that a portion of dollars budgeted for annual salary increases should be distributed to employees on the basis of merit. On the second, he endorsed and supported an early retirement program for college employees. The first sought to recognize superior work. The second, offered twice, was to assist long-term employees to retire at an age earlier than first anticipated or planned.

Quite possibly, however, one of Glen's most important actions as chair, if not the most important, was when he arranged a two-day board retreat in Pittsburgh in June of 1995.

Since 1990, guided by the Long Range Plan, the college had made strides in refurbishing its buildings and grounds, improving its programs, and securing additional faculty and staff. But the need to add to facilities and improve campus aesthetics and efficiency was increasing. Further, additional resources were being required to fund programs, improve technology, and increase the endowment.

Thus, commitment to developing an updated master plan for the physical campus emerged from this retreat. Subsequently crafted in cooperation with Urban Design Associates of Pittsburgh, it included improvements to the student center (the Howard Miller Center), performing arts space, athletic facilities, driveways and roadways, and pedestrian pathways. It also included a new plaza, entry portals, a bell tower, and chapel. Many of these projects articulating the campus of the future were completed over the next decade, including the David Johnson Chapel, significantly financed by the Johnsons in memory of their son. At the retreat, however, specific commitment was given to renovating and expanding the Howard Miller Center in four phases over a four-year period in order to disrupt the academic years as little as possible. Design work, also with Urban Design Associates, began immediately after the retreat.

To resource physical improvements as well as increase the endowment and support programs, at the retreat a commitment was made to mounting a major fundraising campaign. Known as the *Sharing the Mission* capital campaign, it was developed with the help of Douglas Mason of Gerber Gonser Tinker and Stuhr of Chicago. An early-suggested target of $12,000,000 was shortly increased and authorized at $16,900,000, making it the largest capital campaign at the college up to that time.

Glen put it very well at the end of the retreat when he said that the college must and can bring both the Howard Miller Center project and the capital campaign to successful completion. Both were accomplished as Glen carried the board with him in meeting those commitments, manifesting the resolve so vital in a leader.

When Glen decided to step down as chairman and retire from the board, he was recognized for his years of service with the honorary title of Chairman Emeritus, with the right to receive board information and attend board meetings. Thus, in stepping down he did not step away from the college. Indeed, he remained conversant on the issues facing the college and was a ready counselor, advisor, and confidant to the administration.

Accordingly, by the end of my presidency in December, 1998, Glen had seen the college's accreditation reaffirmed without qualifications, three of the four stages of the renovation and expansion of the Howard Miller Center completed, the dedication of new tennis courts and softball diamond, the dedication of the Center for Women's Leadership and the establishment of the annual Mary Haaland Women's Leadership Forum, the continued high rankings in the *U.S. News and World Report*, and the conclusion of the *Sharing the Mission* campaign with gifts totaling close to $30,000,000, well past the original goal of $16,900,000. The campaign benefited from major corporate and foundation gifts and grants, particularly from the Teagle Foundation in New York, the Buhl Foundation and Phillips Trust in Pennsylvania, and the Kresge Foundation in Michigan. And, Glen was also able to see and enjoy incremental enrollment growth, exceeding 1000 students from less than 800 in 1990.

In addition, he and his wife followed with interest and strongly endorsed the rebirth of the college's choral tradition. Dr. Marlowe Johnson, an alumnus of Concordia College in Minnesota and a choir member there, was the son of the renowned F. Melius Christianson of St. Olaf College and had built this up over the course of 50 years under Paul Christianson. After the retirement of Dr. Johnson, the Thiel College Choir had experienced a decline. But, in the latter 1990s with the appointment of Dr. Michael Bray, the choir began to regain its former status and prestige.

This love of music at Thiel by Glen and LaVonne was reflected in another way as well. Their late daughter, Lori Wallace, an accomplished French horn musician, had formed a woodwind ensemble, *Con Spirito*. This fine instrumental group performed on numerous occasions in the late 1980s and early 1990s on campus, including at my inauguration in the spring of 1991.

Two events during this period, and highly important to the future of the college, deserve special attention. The first involved a visit to the Kresge Foundation as part of the college's application for a grant to support the Howard Miller Center project. This organization looked with particular favor upon institutions from which board leaders took time from busy schedules to accompany the president on a personal visit to its headquarters. The trip could not be made before Glen relinquished his position as chairman of the board, but he wanted to complete this commitment. The visit was made, and shortly thereafter the Kresge Foundation extended a challenge grant in the amount of $650,000. This was the largest corporate or foundation grant the college had received up to that time. Moreover, the value of this grant extended beyond the dollars committed. A grant from Kresge carried much prestige and often opened doors to other foundations because of the reputation and respect Kresge had in the thoroughness with which it investigated the institution submitting the application.

The second issue, an issue of institutional governance, had come up for discussion while Glen was still board chairman, but was concluded thereafter. For a number of years the board had included 45 members with only 40 percent elected by the board itself. The Alumni Association or various Lutheran Church entities chose the rest. Glen pushed for a revised board of 36 members, a more manageable number. Further, he supported the view that all members were to be elected by the board, though a few positions were reserved for representatives of the church entities and the alumni.

Suggestions from these groups for membership were welcomed, but the election of members rested with the board, assuring full board control over its own matters.

All in all, Glen was the consummate board member and leader. He believed that board committees should do their work, that the Executive Committee should function in order to process matters to the full board for dispatch while acting in lieu of the board when necessary, and that the chairperson should facilitate this process. He did not believe in dominating board committees, trusting them to carry out their responsibilities and report faithfully. He also believed that board oversight and review of the administration was essential but that crossing over into management was both bad form and a sign of lack of confidence. Thus, he believed that for the college to advance, grow, and improve, the diverse efforts of many were required, with each "sticking to their knitting" as the saying goes.

Much of the credit for the good things that happen on a campus usually goes to the president. And a president, if candid, will give credit to those on campus who do much of the work, and will also acknowledge that a board with strong members and leadership is a major factor in any success.

Having been associated with more than a dozen board leaders and scores of board members in the 45-year career in higher education, Glen Johnson ranks at the very top by any measure that is applied. And the same applies to his wife LaVonne as board spouse.

And that is how it is with Glen and LaVonne Johnson. It was a privilege to work under Glen. And it was my pleasure as well as Mary's, my wife, to count the Johnsons as friends and to know them as the most significant benefactors that Thiel College has enjoyed up to this time in history.

Appendix F

by Dan Heit

REFLECTIONS OF GLEN JOHNSON:
MENTOR, BUSINESS COUNSEL, AND FRIEND

I first met Glen Johnson in 1978 when I was introduced to him by one of the members of the Pittsburgh chapter of the Family Association for the Youth Services agency I directed. I count that introduction as one of the most fortuitous moments of my life. For 30 years, Glen has been a superlative mentor, business advisor, and caring, generous friend.

Abraxas was started in 1973 as a non-profit organization offering an alternative to incarceration for youthful offenders with drug abuse problems. It was founded in response to a Request for Proposals (RFP) issued by the Pennsylvania Governor's Council on Drug and Alcohol Abuse. A requirement of the RFP was that the programs utilize a then-abandoned

The Arlene Lissner High School

ARLENE LISSNER HIGH SCHOOL, PART OF THE
ABRAXAS FOUNDATION IN PENNSYLVANIA.

U.S. Forest Service Camp located in the Allegheny National Forest. That 90-acre campus, surrounded by forest and located six dirt-road miles from a village of some 600 would be both a blessing and profound challenge to implement a quality treatment program.

I received my Bachelors' degree in Philosophical Psychology from the University of Chicago in 1969. After a few years of fairly random career searching (including trying to start a commune in California, working as a kindergarten teacher, and a sports car mechanic!), I was hired as one of Abraxas' first counselors in 1973. Shortly thereafter, I finished a Master's Degree program offered through a "university without walls" program by the University of California.

Abraxas grew rather quickly, and I was lucky enough to be in the right place at the right time. In 1974 and 1975, halfway houses were started in Erie and Pittsburgh. After a year as a counselor, I was promoted to director of a training center responsible for staff training and offering professional workshops to probation officers (later, Glen would help me understand that was our "market" and we were conducting a value added marketing program). A year later, I was promoted to Program Director (Glen would call this role Chief Operating Officer), responsible for the three facilities.

In 1977 when the founder decided to pursue other interests, I was, to my astonishment, selected to be Executive Director (CEO in Glen-speak). I was 28 years old when I became responsible for a million dollars a year enterprise caring for some 100 youth and employing about 40 people. I didn't set out to be a businessman. I thought I'd work for a couple of years and return to school to get a Ph.D. Instead, I was captivated by the excitement of running a growing organization. To my surprise, I found that creating the environment and system that helped people improve their lives was more satisfying than doing direct counseling myself.

I was 'stuck' in on-the-job training in that role for the next 19 years, but the organization grew beyond any dream I might have had. When I left it in 1996, Abraxas had become one of the largest organizations of its kind in the country and had gained a national reputation of operating innovative effective programs for troubled youth.

The organization's growth and development can be directly credited to the guidance, support, networking, planning, and personal contributions of Glen and his life-mate, LaVonne. On my own strengths, lack of experience and "ready fire aim" management style, I don't think we would have ever reached much farther than Western Pennsylvania, but with Glen's guidance, the program achieved a celebrated quality and reach (albeit still a fraction of enormous success achieved by Glen and the team at his 'day-job' at Federated Investors).

My initial conversation with Glen was held in his elegant office at the old Chamber of Commerce Building in downtown Pittsburgh. I had never been to an investment company and fully expected to see a lot of people running around with buckets full of money. That (sadly) didn't occur, but there was a palpable electric excitement of a group of people constellating a skyrocketing new business.

It had never occurred to me that business could be fun. My only experience with corporate America was as a junior mail clerk at a major life insurance headquarters in mid-town New York. I worked there after graduating high school and before starting college. That was not a fun environment, and any electricity was relegated to the rectangle of florescence that shadowed the rigid workplace. I lasted three weeks before I fled to the adventure of becoming a ride operator at the New York World's Fair.

Glen met me in his business suit, white shirt, and tie (*De rigeur* at Federated but a stricture Glen would eventually happily thumb his nose, or collar, at by wearing blue shirts beneath his Gucci ties!). His office was orderly, the desk and Breuer chairs were elegant, but the Rube Goldberg clock and slot machine (!) in the corner betrayed his own unconventional, humorous, and emphatically human dimension. He joined me at the conversation area in the office and listened intently (a rare skill) to my fumbling explanation of what the program was, how we operated, and the challenges thrown at us as early pioneers in what came to be called public-private partnerships.

Abraxas had the peculiar challenge of working to help young people who didn't particularly want help but viewed the program as an easier place than going to jail. And we were an organization that lived in a complex multi-stakeholder environment where our customers (judges and probation officers) were different and distinct from our regulators and payers. Just to compound the challenge, we had to locate residential facilities in neighborhoods that didn't want us. If there were any neighborhoods longing to invite in a residential facility for delinquent drug addicts, I never found them! Every new facility took a concerted public relations campaign and a sophisticated ability to understand zoning law and its practitioners. Amongst Glen's many contributions were helping me frame the case for how our programs were actually helping improve the neighborhoods we entered.

As we spoke, it was clear that Glen had a deep emphatic understanding of the profound tragedy visited on young people and their families through drug abuse. And as a good businessman and civic-minded person he understood the terrible economic waste and erosion of community values that drug abuse represented.

I've never been courageous enough to ask him, but I suspect he must have taken pity on the young idiot in front of him who was charged with running this important and difficult company (I still thought of it as a 'program'). And I was struck by the Promethean energy of a man who embodied the understanding that 'if you want something done, ask a busy person!' In any case, a couple of hours quickly went by and Glen agreed to visit our main facility several hours away in northwestern Pennsylvania. As I've learned and relearned over the years, when Glen makes a commitment, he keeps it. Within the month, I hosted him in our deteriorating forest camp and introduced him to the clinical and educational aspects of the program.

I was at least smart enough to recognize that Glen was a person who could add enormous breadth and energy to the governance of the program. At the time, there was a very small board of directors comprised entirely of people from within the treatment industry. After that first visit, I asked him if he would be willing to serve on the board, and to my enduring delight, he agreed.

It was a bit of a hard sell to get the founder of the organization (the chairman of the board) and others to agree. Why do we need a businessperson on the board? "Because, he's not just a businessman, he cares, and he knows how to operate growing organizations. And, like it or not, we are growing and face a lot of challenges." So there was a tepid acquiescence, and Glen was elected as a board member. He never missed a meeting, and before long the other directors wondered how we ever got along without him.

As the organization continued to grow, he took on multiple and broad responsibilities to stimulate and guide our efforts. I've heard a business consultant use the term "watershed moment" to describe the Robert Frost-like turn in the road that 'makes all the difference.' There were many of these in the years to come at Abraxas, but one of the first occurred within a year of Glen's joining the board. For the first years of the organization's life, senior management were located at the first treatment program on that remote campus 'in the middle of nowhere.' That came to a severe limitation as the organization grew to locations around Western Pennsylvania and had to regularly deal with regulators in the State Capitol of Harrisburg. Any of these were a full day's round-trip from our wilderness' redoubt.

Another structural challenge was that up to that point in time, Abraxas, despite being a non-profit organization, had never conducted any fundraising. One hundred percent of the organization's funding came from various public entities. In 1978, Proposition 13 in California was the first concerted 'citizen uprising' to control and limit taxes. Across the country quickly spread a consciousness that government could not continue to simply impose more and more burden on taxpayers to fund its myriad responsibilities. We had blithely passed on our increased costs every year, but we were starting to get resistance from the county courts and state agencies that provided funding. It was clear that Abraxas was going to have to find ways to manage its programs in a cost-conscious way and to solicit private aid to offset government limitations.

Not for the first or last time, a solution was evident to Glen that no one else saw: "Why not move your offices to Pittsburgh? You have a facility there, and Pittsburgh is the third largest Fortune 500 headquarters in the country (this would sadly change over the ensuing decades). It has some of the largest foundations in the country and a history of very generous support for children's needs." But other board members said, with the myopic righteousness of those committed to 'that's the way we've always done it': "Our facility in Pittsburgh isn't big enough to accommodate Dan and the controller and other administrative staff PLUS this new fundraiser you're talking about hiring."

"Simple," said Glen, "just rent an office." He continued, "Even though Abraxas is in the business of helping children, it is a business. Administration doesn't have to be on 'the factory floor' to know that good things are going on. One of the things I notice is that the program staff is excellent and really committed. Dan doesn't need to look over their shoulder every minute, and as CEO, he's going to have to spend more time outside the agency, meeting and cultivating donors, dealing with your customers, learning about opportunities, and developing the vision to keep the organization moving forward." Glen was eloquent, succinct, and right. But it was only after several agonizing hours spread over a few meetings that everyone could tolerate his wisdom.

The decision was finally made to move our corporate offices to Pittsburgh. Not only to Pittsburgh, but at Glen's further emphatic suggestion, to the heart of the downtown business community. "The work Abraxas does helps the whole community by reducing crime and drugs. If the corporate sector is going to respond, don't come in as an outsider, be part of them downtown. And being among them will facilitate relationships and lead to surprising opportunities." And then, in a characteristic gesture, Glen made the first (and substantial) donation to our fledgling fund drive and helped offset the costs of the move.

The move of the corporate office to downtown Pittsburgh was truly a watershed moment and led to all of the good things Glen foretold and then some! The move to Pittsburgh also marked the deepening of my personal relationship and then growing friendship with the man I came to think of as the chairman of my personal board of directors.

With the help of a realtor recommended by Glen, Abraxas rented a 1500 square foot office downtown in the "Bank Center," a 15-story office tower adjacent to a small urban mall with shops and restaurants. I found a house in Pittsburgh and became a first-time homeowner. When I told Glen the address, he said in his characteristic delighted tones, "You're kidding!" We were neighbors with just a few blocks between us. That nice touch of ser-endipity contributed to a growing relationship marked by Glen's stopping by with a housewarming gift, invitations to wonderful garden parties, and inclusion in each other's lives.

After the tumult of moving personally and professionally, boxes emptied and rooms organized, I faced the bewildering task of introducing Abraxas to the business and foundation community. Fortunately, Glen had a plan. "Anyone who contributes to an organization wants to feel secure that their money is going to a good cause, one that is well-managed, and that is rec-ognized for doing good work. In order to be successful, it will be necessary for Abraxas to develop public recognition." We had none.

Taking pages out of the book that helped Glen succeed in several busi-ness and government positions, but with no budget, he crafted a series of steps to accomplish our goals. That first year, we set a goal of $25,000 in fundraising revenue, divided between cash and 'in-kind' product contri-butions (to offset items that would otherwise have to be purchased). We raised $21,000. Ten years later, we were raising a million dollars a year and had completed a $5 million dollar capital campaign!

Glen taught me about Public Service Announcements (free!) and all of the local radio and TV shows that were looking for human-interest stories (free!). Of course, an ad agency Glen worked with graciously "volunteered" to produce our public service message. Over the years, there were scores of individuals and companies who stepped up to provide help. Glen was such a believer in what Abraxas did and was such a compelling salesman, that I never felt anyone was resentful of being 'gently encouraged' to donate. They trusted Glen and were convinced by his passionate conviction that this organization was worth helping.

With Glen's instruction, we crafted a message of hope for young drug abusers and a message of understanding for the community that if they supported recovery from drugs, they would be repaid with less crime. The ad agency put in language that hit the mark in 30 seconds, and Abraxas started to be known as an agency that helped children with lots of troubles. And in doing so Abraxas was helping the community. Pittsburgh had proudly received a designation as the country's most livable city, and we worked that theme into our public service message.

Working off Glen's list, I started making the rounds of local radio and TV shows, usually with a few of our clients willing to tell their stories. It was very poignant and impactful to have seemingly 'normal' bright-faced teens describe the horrors they had been through and their challenging efforts to overcome the ravages of drugs. Within six months the fruits of our efforts were acknowledged when I was selected by *Pittsburgh Magazine* as 'one of the 80 people to watch in the 80s'! Glen was the first person I called when I was alerted to this honor, and true to form, he acted like I deserved it and took none of the credit for making it happen.

With Glen's involvement and leadership, Abraxas started to grow in scope and in recognition. We expanded by understanding the needs of the youth we worked with and of the courts and communities that referred them to us.

Organic expansion came from understanding the 'next steps' that would help the youth we worked with succeed. An example of this, is the program I always thought of as "Rhonda's." Rhonda entered our long-term program as barely a 15-year old. She was engaging and bright and did quite well. During the course of the program, she disclosed that her father had abused her, as he had her three sisters. (This pre-dated mandated reporter laws and a more systemic protocol for dealing with abuse. While we did report her disclosure to the authorities, they were not able to do anything).

After a year at our long-term program, Rhonda transferred to our halfway house in Pittsburgh. She hadn't had contact with her parents since entering the program. One day she was walking downtown and saw her mother and sister approaching. Her mother took her sister by the hand and crossed the street without a word to Rhonda.

Rhonda was ready to graduate from the program but had nowhere to go. Sadly, she reached a point of diminishing returns as she was compelled to stay in our halfway house long after her friends and peers were able to move on. Eventually, she ran away and, we didn't hear from her for several years.

In talking with Glen about this sad phenomenon, he wisely counseled to make the system understand its shortfalls and find a way to correct them. He and I visited our local juvenile court judge, who advised writing a proposal to the state agency distributing Federal Justice improvement funds. We wrote the proposal, and we created a new sort of program called Supervised Independent Living. It opened in a small apartment building in the east end of Pittsburgh where youth could have a measured degree of independence but still have the support and supervision of staff.

S.I.L. as we called it had been open a few years, when our receptionist said there was someone asking for me who didn't have an appointment. It was Rhonda. I welcomed her into my office, and she updated me. She had left the state, bounced around for a while, and ultimately found relatives on the West Coast who helped her out. She had attended a community college and was working for a public relations company.

I told her about the Supervised Independent Living facility and that I always called it Rhonda's program. She gave me a great smile and said, "Yes, that would have been perfect for me and would have saved me from a lot of difficulty." When I told Glen the story, he got a tear in his eye and said how proud he was of being part of an organization that could influence and help young people overcome their obstacles.

Glen's tutelage helped me understand the importance of listening to our customers and understanding how to make their work lives simpler or more successful. Our reputation grew as a program that could succeed with tough children and we attracted referrals from around the state. More and more we were used by Philadelphia. In talking to the court officials there, we heard that they needed a halfway house to help bring their youth home. By then, we were getting more adept at researching foundations and at grant writing (at Glen's insistence we had hired our first development officer). We targeted the Pew Foundation for support and went there thinking we'd request (the then unheard of) grant in the amount of $100,000.

We were armed with a new tool that came directly from Glen's wisdom and generosity. As we became more diligent at fundraising, we encountered the difficulty of communicating the intensity and emotionality of our programs. Glen said to me one day, "When you first talked to me, I could tell that you believed passionately in your 'product', and that's always the first thing I look for from a salesman. But, I really couldn't picture the reality of the program, until I took that three hour trip to the facility." He went on to say, "We need a way to give people who won't take the time to make that trip a way to experience it."

Of course, Glen just happened to work with the largest advertising film production company in Pittsburgh. And after a visit with their president, we left with a commitment that they would produce a video, for free, of our primary program. They sent a team of professionals who spent a week at the main facility going everywhere from the gym to the encounter groups.

The filmmakers got caught up in the spirit of the program, and one even announced to me that he had decided to give up drinking!

The week of film was boiled down to a superb 30-minute video that captured the intensity and raw emotionality of youth struggling to overcome their demons. And it was a powerful and 'pump-priming' message to tell prospective donors that the $50,000 cost of the film was entirely given to us.

When we met in the richly appointed offices of the Pew Foundation (over $1 billion in assets), I was a little nervous about how the conservatively dressed program officer would respond to the video. It was replete with the unedited language of the streets. She only nodded when the roughest parts of encounter groups came to the screen. When it was over, she said, "I'm so glad that you didn't attempt to sanitize . . . I can tell that those children are genuine and genuinely working to overcome their problems." She was very positive about the idea of our opening a halfway house in Philadelphia. When she asked what we thought it would cost, she shook her head disapprovingly. I expected our $100,000 request to be drastically cut. Instead, she smiled and said, "I don't think you realize how expensive things can be here." We left agreeing to re-do our budget and make a request for $250,000! Several weeks later she called me to say the board had approved our request and a check for a quarter million dollars would be sent shortly.

After scouring the city for a suitable facility, we found a large home in the Germantown section that had housed a doctor's office and his family upstairs. We made an offer. The realtor returned with a remarkable story. Apparently the doctor had been arrested for selling narcotics prescriptions. His wife was granted the house in their subsequent divorce. She was presented with another offer greater than ours. She decided to accept our offer saying that after all the pain and suffering that drug abuse had brought to her family, she was glad to be able to offer help to those working to overcome it.

For the next decade and a half, while I remained at Abraxas, and with Glen's enthusiastic and committed leadership at corporate governance and fundraising (more below!), the organization continued to grow. Following a model not unlike Federated and their developing a family of funds to meet needs across its market; we developed a broad interrelated continuum of care. By 1995, we had programs operating in six Mid-Atlantic States offering residential programs of varied lengths: a boot camp, several mental health facilities, seven licensed private high schools (including one operated under contract for the State of Pennsylvania's Juvenile Corrections Department), outpatient, and prevention programs.

In total, there were some 35 programs serving nearly 2,000 young people a day and employing nearly 1,000 staff. Our programs were recognized as state-of-the-art, and the organization was receiving interest from states across the country to develop services.

FOUNDATION FOR ABRAXAS

presented to

GLEN R. JOHNSON

In Recognition of Outstanding Leadership

For over 15 years, Glen R. Johnson has served Abraxas, its staff and clients with extraordinary commitment and leadership. With the creation of the Foundation for Abraxas in 1982, he assumed the role of Chairperson and has worked tirelessly on its behalf. Through his efforts, generosity, and leadership, Abraxas has become one of the most successful drug and alcohol treatment programs for young people in the United States. With his creative approach, advocacy and loyalty, with sensitivity and compassion for the needs of others, Mr. Johnson has changed and enriched many lives.

August 12, 1990

Anthony N. Civello
Chairman

Daniel S. Heit
President

CITATION GLEN RECEIVED FROM THE FOUNDATION
FOR ABRAXAS FOR SERVING OVER 15 YEARS IN THE
CAPACITY OF CHAIRMAN OF THE BOARD.

Appendix G

by Milt Klohn

THE MARCO FOCUS GROUP
TIMELINE & REFLECTION

Once upon a time there was a large company called Federated Investors, and there were many small community banks. They had many things in common. Glen Johnson, who had instituted any number of good ideas for Federated, recognized this commonality and invited the staff heads of a number of state community bankers' associations to Marco Island, Florida for a meeting. This is the story of that event and subsequent annual meetings.

Wednesday, the 13th of January 1982, was a cold and stormy night in Washington, DC and Marco Island, Florida. In the early evening, we learned of the Air Florida Flight 90 crash into the icy waters of the Potomac. The tragedy struck home when we later learned that Terry Klaskey, general counsel and secretary of INDEX and former legislative counsel of the IBAA was a passenger on that airplane. *Terry died in that accident . . . on the way to our meeting.* It was a somber beginning to what was to become a joyous adventure.

Breaking new ground at the initial meeting of the Council of Community Bankers Association (CCBA), were Jim Thomas, CO; Walter Law, FL; Ted Arneson and Helge Christianson, WI; Scott Williams, OH; Richard Berglund, IA; Bob Winger, IL; and Richard McFaddin, MO.

Today, only one charter member remains at the helm of this association, Bob Wingert of the Community Bankers Association of Illinois. Host Glen Johnson, along with Bill Kugler, Neal Peterson, and INDEX officers Noel Busch and Milt Klohn rounded out the roster. Although the weather failed to improve over the next three days, our spirits gradually revived . . . spirits from the bar assisting mightily! The participants arrived on Wednesday and Thursday, and the first formal event was dinner on Thursday night at the hotel.

Glen Johnson led off Friday's meeting with the Federated story, followed by the tie-in or synergy between Federated and community banking and ending with his synopsis of the Washington scene. He shared the floor by asking each CCBA questions about the political situation in their particular state. *This was the beginning of a tradition he would carry on for the next 16 years.* Neal Peterson then drew on his long Beltline experience for a no-nonsense appraisal of the banking climate on the Hill. INDEX issues, particularly the Federated AARM program, were discussed at length before the meeting was turned over to the association executives.

Although this was not their first discussion, the CCBA organization that exists today was still in the "idea" stage. The informal sharing of ways to handle the problems of the day seemed enhanced by the environment created by Federated's exceptional hospitality. Seeds were planted that would be watered and fed at subsequent Marco meetings that would produce significant impact on community banking.

The morning meeting adjourned in time for golf, tennis, or fishing. None of the above were options, however, due to wind, rain, and unseasonably cold weather. The first of many splendid dinners (with entertainment) on Friday evening was held at Glen and LaVonne's house on the Marco River. It seemed that each year this event surpassed the year before. Toward the end it became an extremely hard act to follow.

The Saturday morning meeting was turned over to the CCBAs for their own meeting time. This again was the beginning of a tradition, which would endure for the life of the program. The farewell dinner was at the renowned Olde Marco Inn. Norb McCrady first discovered the piano bar that year. He managed to re-discover it each and every year for the next 16 years.

The weather in January 1983 was improved but still cool. The meeting was enlarged to include the CEOs of several bankers' banks including, Ray Campbell, OH; Ed Hennen, MN; Helge Christensen, WI; and Barry Smith, TX. CCBAs in addition to the first year's attendees were Arlene Leingang (Melarvie), ND; Sue Anderson, KS; Paul Nordstrom, SD; Ted Arnesen, WI; Sue Gift, VA; Bruce Senft, PA; and Bob Mathews, LA.

The expanded group gathered at the Marco Marriott on Thursday the 20th. After a splendid dinner at the hotel, a number of us went on to close the lower level piano bar. We were rudely awakened at 7:00 a.m. Friday to the tune of jackhammers working on the hotel's new north wing. Whether the subsequent headaches were due to the construction racket or the previous night's revelry will never be known.

Friday morning's meeting was held at the Marco Lodge in Goodland. Glen's comprehensive remarks once again opened the meeting and were followed by a Federated marketing guru who enlightened the group on some of the services Federated offered. Neal batted cleanup for the morning and lunch preceded golf, fishing . . . or what have you. Glen and LaVonne were consistent in providing outstanding themes, meals, and entertainment on Friday night. Saturday's meeting led to an afternoon of fun that included airboat tours from Everglades City, tennis, fishing or just relaxing on the beach. The latter was reserved for the hardy, hot Florida days had not yet arrived. Dinner at the Olde Marco Inn capped another excellent meeting.

On January 19, 1984, Dorothy and I had a special treat. After a meeting with Glen, Bill Kugler, and others in Pittsburgh, we boarded the Federated company jet and were whisked down to Marco airport . . . faster than a speeding bullet. The weather was clear but still short of sunbathing level. A few new participants were added . . . word of mouth began to spread that this was *the* meeting to attend.

We were billeted at the Quality Inn, next to the marina on the Marco River. The dinner usually held on Saturday was moved up to Thursday at the Olde Marco Inn and after the meeting and Glen and LaVonne's hospitality on Friday, we moved back to the Marriott for Saturday's swan song.

We were on water, but not the beach again in 1985 when we moved just down the street to the Riverside, a huge condominium on the Marco River. After less than tropical weather for our January meetings, the date was moved up to February 8th . . . and it was warmer. As we returned to the Marriott for Thursday's dinner, we noticed construction of a large building just to the South. Glen informed us that this was to be the new Marco Beach Hilton . . . where we would become pampered guests for the next 12 years.

A group from CCBA gathered for a nightcap after dinner at a room on the far end of the Riverside complex. Since our rooms were spread out over a couple of city blocks, I fear we awakened a few residents as we trudged noisily along the balcony walkways in the wee hours of the morning. The meetings were held at the Marco Lodge in Goodland, and again were rewarding to all.

Two milestones were reached in 1986. First, the timing for the meeting was permanently set for the month of March (3-6-86). Second, we christened the brand spankin' new Marco Beach Hilton Hotel. We apparently didn't trust the Hilton chef, being new, because we dined at the Olde Marco Inn on Thursday night. A number of new faces appeared, including Jerry Sage, from MO; Pat Satterfield, from VA; and Early Perry, from KY.

Friday morning began with a sumptuous buffet breakfast with the meeting across the hall. Glen led off with his congressional and regulatory review, and the CCBA led portion of the meeting was enlightening, especially for the new arrivals. Minnesota Congressman Bruce Vento arrived late on Friday. As a member of the House Banking Committee, he gave us the inside story on the progress of banking bills Saturday morning.

Sue Anderson recalled her fishing trip that afternoon. *"Of six fishermen, Gaylord and I caught 33 of the 34 fish netted. When our companions chose not to take any home, Glen offered to take care of them. We were leaving at 6:00 a.m. the next morning. At 5:45 a.m. there was a knock on the door. Glen Johnson was standing there with the frozen fish packed in a cooler with dry ice and taped for shipping. We've never forgotten that special act of kindness. It was so typical of Glen's hospitality and genuineness."*

On March 13, 1987, the first "nationally known" speaker graced our meeting. Former FDIC Director Irving Sprague not only spoke at length at the meeting, he convinced the group that he was solidly on the side of community banking. He set an example that all the other speakers followed; not just giving a speech, but also staying the entire weekend. The ability to talk one-on-one with every speaker was undoubtedly one of the most valuable aspects of the Focus Group meetings. The good Mr. Sprague also autographed a copy of his book *Bailout* for each of us.

After an afternoon of fun in the sun, we bused to the Johnson's residence for another splendid party. Saturday morning found the group describing issues of the day and exchanging ideas for the betterment of the bank members of each association. The Olde Marco Inn was again the scene of the farewell party, and the CCBA departed the Hilton regretfully on a beautiful Sunday in paradise.

Arlene Melarvie described the Johnson home best, *"We were always touched by the warm hospitality of the Johnsons who welcomed us into their home almost as family."* The one exception to this was in 1988. The house had been destroyed . . . not by Mother Nature, but by workmen who would, over the next year plus, create an even more beautiful waterfront home. We dined at the Hilton on the evening of March 14, and repeated the breakfast and meeting Friday morning. The weather was great, and golf, tennis, fishing, and just lying around the pool and beach were the ingredients of a great afternoon. Pat Satterfield had a special memory, *"Jim and I sat on the beach that afternoon and wrote out our wedding invitations and guest list."*

We tooled over to the Blue Heron Inn that night, and most of the beefeaters opted for a savory fish (not heron) dinner.

After a Saturday morning meeting and afternoon of sports or leisure, the group drove to Goodland for another aquatic feast at the Fish House. A few of that day's deep sea fishermen, particularly Bill Kugler, were less than enthused about looking at anything that resembled or came out of the sea.

The Focus Group stayed on a fish diet as we met at the Prawnbroker on March 17, 1989. The Hilton opened its doors to us once again, and the meeting on Friday included Congressman Bruce Vento. Glen and Neal Peterson augmented his appraisal of the status on the Potomac, and the CCBA did the same for their states. The work ethic in Florida must be somewhat poorer than in the northern states because after more than a year, the Johnson house was still under construction. Glen and LaVonne, however, were adamant about having the party back and issued hard-hats to the attendees on Friday night. A number of CCBA expressed fond memories of that night including Jerry Sage who remembered, *"Norb singing from the unfinished landing on the staircase overlooking the kitchen . . . with his mug of green beer held on high!"*

Rumors were flying about a change in ownership for Federated, and Glen promised to let us in on the scoop when and if it became a fact. Faces that had been added by 1989 were Joe Thares, MT; Dave Glomp, WI; Kurt Yost, NE; Frank Pinto, PA; Chris Williston, TX; Julian Hester, GA; and John Pritchard, NY. On the Federated side, Paul Riordan replaced Bill Kugler, and Andy Bonnewell assumed a major role in the company's relationship with CCBA. We returned to the Olde Marco Inn for dinner on Saturday night. The piano player was delighted to have Norb "back at the mic" . . . at least that's what he told us.

The year 1990 ushered in a new era of cooperation between community banking and Federated. On February 8th, the Comptroller of the Currency issued a rule that modified Regulation 9 to deregulate common trust funds. It became immediately apparent to Glen that there were serious ramifications to community banking with the adoption of this rule. By the time the Focus group meeting convened on March 23, he had a synopsis prepared and presented by Washington attorney, Paul Stevens, on the rule's potential harm to trust beneficiaries, community banks, and the public-at-large. Executives representing 14 states heard and gave verbal agreement with the principles involved. Glen announced that Paul Riordan and Milt Klohn would be following up with each of them to gain their grassroots support against the rule.

This was the first issue that had truly substantive common interest for community banking and Federated, and it dominated the discussions at this meeting. Through a concerted effort by all involved, 22 states representing nearly 5,000 community banks had expressed their opposition to the rule by the end of the comment period, May 10, 1990.

On Friday night we viewed the beautiful result of LaVonne's planning for the major remodeling project. Of particular interest were the new sea-view loft and the brass plaque that adorned its stairway landing. It read simply . . . "Norb's Landing." Saturday's meeting was followed by more fun in the sun and the last dinner was at the Olde Marco Inn.

There was joy in Mudville as we gathered on March 14, 1991. Less than a month before, Glen received word from Senator Heinz that the Comptroller of the Currency "has no plans to implement the proposed changes in Regulation 9." This announcement at the opening dinner was greeted with thunderous applause. Once again David had slain Goliath. In this case, David Manning, CB of IL who testified for community banking at the Subcommittee hearing, was identified as "David" while attending his first Marco meeting. Joe DeHaven also made his debut this year.

Glen opened the meeting with a generous introduction of Martin Maher, a well-known and regarded economist and author. Maher gave an impressive talk, took questions, and made himself available for the balance of the weekend. He also autographed copies of his best selling book, *The Greatest Ever Bank Robbery*. His remarks were well timed as the Administration's Brady Bill was poised to fire a thunderous broadside at community banking.

With Regulation 9 on hold, Glen pledged Federated support to defeat all of the onerous provisions of the proposed legislation, not just the repeal of Glass-Steagall. The outstanding hospitality of the Johnsons and Federated had established an incredibly strong bond with the state executives over the years. That bond reached a new level with the cooperative spirit developed during the Regulation 9 battle and the commitment to fight the new Brady banking bill.

A splendid "Cabaret Party" accompanied fine food and drink at Glen and LaVonne's home that evening. Federated CEO, Jack Donahue, greeted the group and thanked them for the important part they played in downing Regulation 9. Don Brockett brought Broadway to Marco with a short song to each CCBA in attendance . . . it was a great show. Once again, the morning meeting and sunshine frolics preceded the last roundup at the Olde Marco Inn on Saturday.

The mood of excitement that characterized the 1991 session carried over into 1992. Although the IBAA took credit for the defeat of the Brady Bill, a few insiders that "worked the halls" throughout the year, know that Glen Johnson's strong relationship and influence with Chairman John Dingell, D-MI, really turned the tide. That said, we must acknowledge the work and cooperation of IBAA, letters from both state community bank associations and many of their bank members, banker visits to key committee members, ads produced and placed by Federated, and countless contacts by Glen, Andy Bonnewell, and myself with members of both houses of Congress. All of these efforts combined to sink a very formidable ship.

After dinner at the Hilton on Thursday, March 12, some lingered in the bar, but all were fast asleep when the fire alarms went off in the wee hours. Is it possible that the sleek, well-dressed men and women who showed up for dinner were the same as the bathrobe clad group that gathered in the lobby at 3:00 a.m.?

We had met a very clever young author when he testified in opposition to the Brady Bill in 1991. Our speaker for this meeting was Stephen Pizzo, co-author of *Inside Job: the Looting of America's Savings and Loans*, a *New York Times* Bestseller. He reiterated his passionate pleas to not repeat the mistakes of the 80s, which were graphically described in the book. Like the others before him, he stayed and autographed copies for everyone in attendance.

Glen had a wealth of "Belt-Line" assistance as he told the Washington story. Congressman Bruce Vento, his chief-of-staff Larry Roman, and Neal Peterson collaborated to assess the Banking Committee's positions on issues important to community banking. There was a lot of meat to this meeting!

Friday night brought fire-eaters, limbo dancers, *and* a surprise for the Johnsons. CCBA, led by Frank Pinto with chorus leader, Norb McCrady, rapped words composed by eminent poet, Dee Peterson. The words were great, but the performance of the tribute to Glen and LaVonne was *"way-off"* Broadway.

After a short Saturday meeting, Dorothy and I played a tennis match with IBAT Mary Lange and husband John. Although the Hilton's clay courts were quite forgiving, Mary assessed my play with, *"Milt, your ineptitude in hitting the ball is only exceeded by your extreme lack of speed afoot."* Mary is *still* one of my favorite people.

The concluding party was held at the Olde Marco Inn. The participants headed for home the next day with gratitude for the substance of the meetings, the fun and games, and the wonderful camaraderie that typified each and every Focus Group meeting.

It was April Fool's Day, 1993, but the chef at the Hilton didn't fool around as he prepared a scrumptious dinner for the Thursday arrivals. On Friday morning, Glen introduced Law Professor Arthur Wilmarth, as the outside speaker for the 1993 session. Since Regulation 9 and elements of the Brady Bill were still smoldering coals lying in wait to be fanned by mega-banks or others, (interstate branch banking in particular) community banking needed all the firemen possible to put out the next blaze. Unfortunately, while we watched for the forest fire, a few grass fires gradually burned up some of the firewalls through regulatory caveat rather than legislative action. When Glass-Steagall was ultimately repealed, it was but a shadow of its former self . . . but we're getting ahead of our story. Mr. Wilmarth was the author of the *Wilmarth Proposal* on interstate branch banking. This "opt-in" proposal was embraced by CSBS initially, and later taken to heart by the IBAA.

Friday night at the Johnsons brought another superb party. After cocktails, hors d'oeuvres, and a fine dinner, we found seats in the courtyard (between the two residences) for some very tricky sleight of hand. The magician didn't saw any of the female guests in half, but did pretty much everything else. He concluded by showing us how some of the tricks were done. I doubt that any of us could perform them . . . even after he shared the secrets.

Saturday dawned with nary a cloud in the sky. With the meeting behind us, some played golf, others went shopping, but the majority lounged around the pool or beach. Scott Williams noted, *"all eyes were on a woman (who we suspect was European) who didn't want any tan lines, so she simply removed her top."* Our complexions had also darkened considerably as we gathered for dinner at the Olde Marco Inn that evening.

March 10, 1994 heralded opening day and the meeting began with a lavish reception and dinner at the Hilton. In the discussion on Friday morning, Glen noted that the Clinton White House seemed to be on both sides of some of our major concerns. On a specific issue, they would agree with community banking on one part and take the big-bank side on another. This wasn't all bad, as we were usually opposed to change and a heaping plateful of ambiguity tasted pretty good.

The affable James Watt, President of CSBS, was our guest speaker, and his major concern was the proposal to establish a "single regulator." He obviously had a vested interest in this issue, as it would eliminate any need for his organization. We had to agree that to put all non-fed member state banks under the thumb of one Federal agency would indeed destroy the dual banking system.

After a spirited meeting Glen called everyone together for an informal lunch at the Hilton. He arose after the meal and announced that a treasure hunt was on tap for that afternoon. Teams of two couples were formed, and deviously written instructions were handed out. *Then the big surprise* . . . car keys were passed out that fit brand-new red convertibles parked randomly throughout the Hilton parking lot. The hitch was that no one knew *which* red convertible *their* keys would fit! The mad scramble that resulted, of course, gave an advantage to those who found their car first. The hunt included a number of stops all over the island and even a mandatory boat ride. The couples that took home the grand prize, a trip to Hawaii, were Richard and Cindy Trammell, AR and Donald and Brenda Holmes, AL. Of all the parties and events over the 17-year run of the Marco Focus Group Meetings, *the 1996 treasure hunt was the most remembered!*

Friday night was special for Dorothy and me. Our daughter, son-in-law, and seven-year-old twin grandsons were invited to the party. The video (did I mention that Glen taped many of the events and supplied each guest with a video tape?) shows Josh and John watching the crab races with eyes wide with wonder. They enter college in the fall, but still remember that night and eating dinner with the Johnson family, including their twin grand-daughters . . . another example of the warm Johnson hospitality.

One of the amazing feats performed by nearly all of us each year was the huge breakfast we put away on Friday and Saturday mornings after eating great hors d'oeuvres and a full dinner the night before. This was by no means a diet program. Meetings over, we again pursued outdoor activities with gusto before cleaning up for the farewell dinner at Olde Marco Inn.

Another special year was 1995. Glen imported some Broadway characters that transformed many of our little group into thespians. March 8th was opening night, and the Hilton provided the stage for an amateur reenactment of the Regulation 9 drama. Under the able direction of Don Brockett, Glen took center stage with assistance from a number of costumed CCBA. Don threw in a couple of pros for good measure.

The theme of the melodrama was, "*Who killed Count Regulation 9?*" The theme song was "*Love Potion No. 9,*" and the mystery concluded on Friday night in the courtyard at Glen and LaVonne's house. Who could forget the performances of Craig Hudson, Sue Anderson, and Jim Pischue?

The following excerpt from the March 21 "INDEX Update" tells it all. "*As the cunning Moe Taxes is extradited to Tallahassee, the Lott sisters, Sella and Wyna, retire to the Midwest. Howie Doing rides the rails to Washington state while Dr. Bill Due polishes his accent for his practice in CA. Owen Everybody wimps his way back to Bear and Bull country, and the gorgeous Robin Plunder sneaks back to the City of Sisterly Love with Share DeWeath. These and other characters created by Don Brockett participated in the demise of the mysterious Count Regulation 9.*

We did take time from our theatrical exercises for meetings and Friday's guest speaker was Banking Commissioner extraordinaire, Sid Bailey of

Virginia. He talked about regulation; the good and bad and the relationship between the Feds and the Staters. Glen held forth with the latest from Federated and the state of the Congress with the changing of the guard. The real meaning and status of Glass-Steagall was discussed, and Glen agreed to put together a concise summary for the CCBA group, their boards, and members.

The weather was ideal, and Saturday afternoon found a rowdy bunch on the beach. More than a few dollops of Long Island Tea had lifted their spirits mightily. Williams, Wingerts, McCradys, Klohns and Pintos were prominent participants in the *happy* beach party.

A fair amount of reminiscing opened the 1996 meeting on March 28. Glen fed us well at the Hilton Thursday night and Friday morning to be sure our strength was up for the meeting. He kicked off with a meaty discussion of the political world and his view on the direction that world was heading in 1996. Jill Ehrenfeld from Federated followed with such an exciting presentation of investment vehicles and strategy that she was invited to make the CCBA convention circuit this year.

Former congressman and Louisiana Governor Buddy Roemer came on next with a brand of charm and wit found only in southern gentlemen. As a Democratic congressman, he made a comment from the house floor, to which Speaker Tip O'Neill replied, *"Yes, that's Buddy Roemer, seldom right, but never in doubt!"* He was so well received; he was booked to speak at a half dozen CCBA conventions later in the year.

The Johnson Friday night party was moved to the glorious paddle wheeler, the *Rosie O'Grady*. After appropriate time to wet our whistles and down a few snacks, a fine dinner was served. But this was more than a dinner-boat ride. From hidden dressing rooms, a Broadway ensemble emerged and sang and danced to *our* heart's content.

A fun Saturday ended with dinner at the Marco Polo and the customary sad faces heading for the airport on an always beautiful, sunny Sunday.

In 1997, the meeting slipped back into February but just barely. Over the last few years, our group had expanded to include such luminaries as Roy Pinnell from IL; Ginger Adams from SD; Ramona Jones from TX; Daryll Lund from WI; Sam (Symantha) from Cook, FL; Tom Miller from NY; Al Olson from MN; and Bud Fliss from MI.

The speaker this year was none other than Benjamin J. Stein, author of a 1991 article in *Barron's* entitled, "You Can Bank on it, Without Glass-Steagall, History Will Repeat." Mr. Stein's credentials also include writing speeches for presidents and playing a beleaguered teacher in *Ferris Bueller's Day Off.* How many actors become famous for reciting just one word? Do you remember, "Anyone? . . . Anyone?" This same Ben Stein was to become more famous for his game show on the Comedy Channel. As a speaker at our meeting on Friday, he played-down his comedic talents and painted a fascinating if somewhat conservative picture of the world, past, present, and future. He stayed for the weekend, and although he had no book to autograph, he was most generous in posing for pictures with everyone. Joe DeHaven recalled, "*A couple of months after Marco, Ben wrote about his experience with us in his column in the 'American Spectator.' He wrote of how nice it was to be around real people who work hard for their constituents. WOW! We made an impression on him!*" Ben Stein made an indelible impression on all of us . . . he was singled out by nearly every CCBA who answered my plea for memories of Marco.

Ah, 1998 . . . it was a good year, but for the fact that it signaled the swan song for the Marco Focus Group meetings. The first (and last) time attendees were Bob Palmer from WV; Joel Gilbertson from ND; Neal McMahon, from LA; Jeff Grady, from FL; and Don Hole, from IA.

After dining at the Hilton on Thursday night, the Friday meeting began with Glen's ever-welcome appraisal followed by Dr. Donald Mullineaux from the University of Kentucky. With some of the potential ramifications of HR10 as a basis, he discussed the future of banking structure with strong participation by the CCBA.

El Nino had some effect on the normally perfect March weather in Marco, but the sun reappeared when necessary to allow outside activities to flourish. We dressed and met for the last time at the Olde Marco Inn on Saturday night.

I don't recall if the celebration included reminiscing about the wonderful years behind us, but Frank Pinto summed up the sentiments expressed with, "*It is impossible to describe your fondest memories of Marco because each memory was more memorable. The experience was exhilarating . . . the education value contagious. What we will miss most is the gracious hospitality and generosity of Glen and LaVonne Johnson. Their legacy has made us all better people.*"

Scott Williams' parting comment was, "*One of the most important facts that will never be known is really how much support Glen and Federated have given to community banking. If only the community bankers of our various states understood what they did for our industry. Yes, we state executives were entertained on this one weekend in March, but Glen and Federated's staff worked for us the year round. Community banking owes a tremendous debt for all of the legislative support it received as well as the financial support Federated contributed to our annual conventions.*"

Virtually everyone who responded to my plea for memories commented on the great Johnson hospitality, the camaraderie developed, the education received, and the major influence on the formation of the formal CCBA organization.

I would add that in my nearly 50 years in and around banking, these meetings and the allied lobbying efforts in Washington with Glen and Andy Bonnewell have been the absolute highlight of my career!

Appendix H

by Milt Klohn

THE GLASS-STEAGALL STORY . . . PART II

The reason this epic tale is entitled "Part II" is that Glen Johnson began this struggle many years before this particular battle. This story reared its ugly head in the spring of 1990, and had its roots in a rule proposed by the OCC regarding the charging of fees on common trust funds by the largest banks known as Regulation 9. This proposal had one thing going for it . . . it was so bad that broad based opposition could be, and was, ultimately assembled. I was contacted in March of that opening year of the decade to meet with Glen and plot strategy to defeat this arguably worst affront to Glass-Steagall since its inception.

You may recall that Glass-Steagall, in addition to establishing the FDIC, separated commercial banking from dealing in securities after the calamitous crash of the stock market in 1929, and the resulting Great Depression.

By 1990, mega banks had poked their nose quite a ways under the G.S. tent and were chasing additional powers like an eagle after a rabbit. They found an agreeable regulator in the OCC, and Regulation 9 was put out for comment on February 16. The substance of this regulation was to permit banks (the big boys) to not only market their own common trust funds to the public, (does this sound like dealing in securities?) but to allow them to assess management fees to those funds including advertising. To say this was the blockbuster of all conflicts of interest is an understatement.

In our strategy discussion, the role of the CCBA would be the centerpiece of our initial effort. The close relationship between Federated and community banking association was crucial. We decided that I would travel to a number of state associations and seek their cooperation in opposing the proposed regulation. Our plan was to begin with the larger (in bank membership) states and after getting a number of them on board, contact the others by mail, e-mail, and telephone.

I compiled a two-page summary of objections to the rule and set off on a whirlwind journey to eight states in a bit over a week. I particularly remember flying to St. Louis then driving to Jefferson City in the morning for a meeting with Jerry Sage's MIBA (Missouri) board. Armed with their approval, I drove back to St. Louis, flew to Atlanta, and paid a visit to Julian Hester that afternoon. It was a long day on April 11, 1990, which was my birthday. There were other double-state days in a whirlwind travel schedule, at the end of which we had eight state community bankers associations committed to fighting Regulation 9. They were: Texas, Illinois, Georgia, Missouri, Ohio, Iowa, Florida, and Minnesota. These associations represented a total of over 3,000 banks. Armed with commitments from these influential states, it was a relatively simple matter to convince another 14 associations to join the fray. I requested and received individual letters from all 22 associations, representing nearly 5,000 community banks, which were forwarded to the Office of the Comptroller of the Currency. In addition to the banking association letters a dozen individual banks voiced their objections to the rule.

The community bank piece completed, we now moved in other directions. Glen gleaned the assistance of Federated's legal council, Gene Maloney, who had a close relationship with former Attorney General Andy Miller of Virginia. He was able to gather attorney generals from seven states to voice their official objections to the rule, and those letters were also sent on to the OCC.

I should mention that each time a new group of opponents became committed to the cause, they added to our arsenal of weapons to enlist others.

Glen and I spent a lot of time in Washington, DC during this period. While there, I met several times with Doyle Bartlett and Robert Richards of CSBS and in late May, they put out a memo to all state banking regulators that stated, *"CSBS will not be filing a comment letter on this rule; however, individual state banking departments may wish to bring the situation in their states to the attention of the Comptroller."* Their memo went on to clearly state why this rule should not be adopted!

Probably the most difficult sell, which took half a dozen meetings with three different staff people over nearly four years, was the consumer Federation of America. It all began with testimony by Peggy Miller in April of 1990 and culminated with a letter to the Comptroller in January of 1994 . . . but I'm getting ahead of the story.

During our time in DC, Glen was busy soliciting support from his many congressional contacts. I joined him occasionally, but he did the heavy lifting. By June of 1990, the following congressional leaders had committed to the fight against Regulation 9: Energy and Commerce Committee Chairman, John Dingell; Subcommittee Chairman, Ed Markey (who lead the fight in hearings of his subcommittee); Banking Committee Chairman, Henry Gonzalez; Subcommittee Chairman, Frank Annunzio; Congressman Bruce Vento, and Stan Parris and Senators Jake Garn, John Heinz, Nancy Kassembaum, David Boren, and Jim Sasser.

Another strong voice answered the call in late May. NASAA (No, not the folks that tool around in space), the North American Securities Administrators Association, the national voice of 50 states, DC, and Puerto Rico securities regulators sent a strong letter to the comptroller.

Now, one would assume that the foregoing would constitute a message powerful enough to cause the national bank chief to back off. It is a fact that the OCC conceded enough to extend the comment period, but they never threw in the towel. Apparently the mega banks applied enough pressure to force them to ignore overwhelming evidence that this rule should never see the light of day . . . so the battle continues!

Glen Johnson had a long and close relationship with the House Energy and Commerce Committee Chairman, John Dingell. Calling on that friendship, in early September, Glen persuaded Dingell to persuade Chairman Ed Markey (this took little persuasion as Markey was a strong advocate of our position) of the Subcommittee on Telecommunications and Finance (Committee on Energy and Commerce) to schedule a hearing on Regulation 9.

The date was set for October 4, 1990, and we then began preparations for the hearing. We asked David Manning, VP of Governmental Relations for the Community Bankers of Illinois, to testify on behalf of all the community bankers who had committed to the cause.

Glen was in contact with the Investment Company Institute, and our friends, Jim McKeown of Oklahoma and Richard Berglund of Iowa, rounded up a congressman to testify in the persons of Michael Synar, Oklahoma and Thomas Tauke, Iowa.

Another lucky break came when Barbara Walker, Colorado State Banking Commissioner (who later became the CEO of the Independent Bankers of Colorado) wrote a dynamite letter trouncing the rule. The break came as she shared the issue with her husband who happened to be the securities commissioner for the state. He also was the upcoming chairman of NASAA (North American Securities Administrators Association). It was his influence that prompted both the strong letter noted above and pivotal testimony by NASAA at the hearing.

The hearing began with a strong opening statement by Chairman Edward Markey. He hit all the bases and emptied them with the following home run: *"Since trust functions must, by law, be performed with the highest degree of fiduciary loyalty, the Comptroller's proposal would appear to set all of this on its head."* He cited investor confusion by branding such funds with the bank's name thereby creating the false impression that they were covered by FDIC insurance. Potential for conflict of interest would create temptation to place the banks own self-interest ahead of that of the trust customers.

Markey concluded with, *"We must work together to craft comprehensive legislation to resolve these issues. Remember, it was the siren call for expanded powers that caused the shipwreck of the S & L industry!"*

Congressman Thomas Tauke from Iowa hit on consumer protection and unfair competition between large and small banks. He also pointed out the huge conflicts of interest this proposal would create.

The next testimony came from, who some would characterize as the "Devil himself," Robert Clarke, Comptroller of the Currency. He began with, *"These are not new powers, and common trust funds have been permissible under law for nearly 50 years. Banks have been able to advertise them as a part of other trust services. An example would be a supermarket could not advertise bananas without advertising all their other products. Sears couldn't advertise a hammer without advertising all their other tools in stock . . . then why shouldn't banks be able to advertise common trust funds separately?"* (What he failed to say here is that the advertising previously allowed was a cost to the trust company itself, not at the expense of trust beneficiaries).

Richard Breeden, Chairman of the Securities and Exchange Commission, was next and he convinced everyone in attendance, except Clarke, that CTF would become the functional equivalent of mutual funds under this rule . . . without the benefit of the regulations under which mutual funds operate. The result would be the loss of the bank exemption from the securities laws of 1933 and 1940.

Oklahoma Congressman Mike Synar kept hitting Clarke with the unfair competitive advantage and the ability of big banks to suck deposits out of smaller communities. *"With no firewalls this proposal is an example of an agency run-amuck!"* The interchange between the two could be labeled contentious.

Next Congressman Thomas Blyley from Virginia gave Mr. Clarke a great deal more than he bargained for. Going right for the jugular, Blyley asked, *"How does this rule benefit the beneficiaries of a trust?"* Clarke foolishly replied, *"It's not the purpose of this rule to benefit beneficiaries of a trust."*

Blyley responded, *"If a widow's trust is in CTF, she will be now charged for this advertising. How does this benefit her?"* Clarke, now digging the hole deeper for himself said, *"It would be the same as a bank charging fees for a checking account."* Blyley hung in there with, *"That's not the same at all . . . the bank is providing a service, the widow is not getting any additional service from this. I repeat, does the beneficiary receive any benefit from this rule?"* Clark hung his head as he said, *"No."*

After submitting a 12-page comment letter in May, Attorney General Don Siegelman testified that, *"Along with several other state attorneys general, I unequivocally oppose this rule. The conflicts of interest in this proposal are so flagrant that I cannot imagine such a proposal seeing the light of day."*

M. Douglas Mays, Chairman of NASAA said, *"The transfer of common trust funds to mutual funds, which this rule would in effect accomplish, without fiduciary responsibility or oversight, would be irresponsible. Securities are not bought . . . they are sold. Sold to an unsophisticated public that will surely believe they are insured deposits."*

There's an old saying, save the best for last. That came in the person of David Silver, President of the Investment Company Institute. He began by explaining the basis of a trust relationship, *"When the grantor of a trust dies, the trust company or department stands in the shoes of that grantor to fulfill his wishes regarding his beneficiaries. That grantor has every right to have his wishes carried out. The trust relationship is the most intense of any fiduciary relationship known to common law. Conversely, in the case of mutual funds, the buyer has a number of choices. If he disagrees with the management of the fund, he may attend a shareholder meeting and vote. That failing, he can voice his disapproval with his feet. There is absolutely no comparison between the mutual fund buyer and the beneficiary of a trust . . . if you don't believe this, just try to change trustees!"*

Chairman Markey closed the hearing with a short summary, and then said, *"Chairman Dingell, Congressman McMillan and I are introducing legislation to deal with this issue tomorrow, and I respectfully request, Mr. Comptroller, that you withhold any implementation of this rule until a legislative solution can be accomplished."*

We left the hearing room with confidence that the arguments against Regulation 9 were compelling enough to put it to rest and caused a cessation in our efforts for the balance of 1990. A vigilant watch was put on the Comptroller's office with any number of spies nosing around for news on Regulation 9. These included members of Congress, lobbyists, lawyers, and possibly Dick Tracy. Just over four months of anxious anticipation preceded an announcement by the Comptroller on February 22, 1991 that, *"the proposed rule was not being adopted at this time."*

That announcement prompted the INDEX Update "Obituary" that opened with *"An obituary is a report of a death—death is usually final!"* It then featured a tombstone inscribed as follows: *"Here lies Regulation 9, Born-1990, Died 1991."* It went on to say, *"Regulation 9 reportedly drew its last breath on 2-22-91, just one year after its birth. But, will it, like Frankenstein's monster, be resurrected should Congress fail to legislate similar powers? Unless concrete assurances can be obtained of the withdrawal of this rule, we must assume that it may rise again . . . "* These words were to become prophetic, as you will see . . . it did indeed, rise again.

OBITUARY?

An obituary is the report of a death -
death is usually final!

**HERE LIES
REG.9
BORN-1990
DIED-1991**

**Reg. 9 reportedly drew its last breath on
February 22, 1991, just over one year after its birth.**

But, will it, like Frankenstein's monster, be resurrected should Congress fail to legislate similar powers? Unless concrete assurances can be obtained of the withdrawal of this rule, we must assume that it may rise again to add risk, unfair competition and inappropriate charges to the banking system and the public.

Reproduced from INDEX's "History of Reg. 9" dated 2-28-91

OBITUARY FOR REGULATION 9.

Meanwhile . . . later in 1991, the winds of change once again threatened the bastion of separation of powers known as Glass-Steagall. On September 9, *The New York Times* featured an article entitled "Regulatory Reform Advancing." It reported that the congress was likely to tear down barriers between banking and securities when they returned from the summer recess. This proposal, with strong backing from the Bush administration, urged both legislative and regulatory action to "modernize" financial services for economic growth and the ability to compete internationally.

The article contained a conflicting statement by a Harvard professor: *"In the 1930s, we assumed that decentralization was the way to prevent mischief . . . now the world has changed fundamentally, through advances in technology and the globalization of the marketplace . . . As a result, the concerns of the 1930s are not on anyone's mine, Washington is acting as if the Great Crash and many of the excesses of the 1920s never existed."*

A bill was put forth and Federated sponsored several hard-hitting ads in *Roll Call* that were endorsed by IBAA and 25 state community bankers associations. After the smoke cleared, IBAA claimed to have shot it to death, but without Glen's influence with Chairman Dingell, it may have won the gunfight.

Fast forward to the spring of 1993 . . . "rumors are flying" about the resurrection of Regulation 9. The hammer didn't fall until November, when mega-bank lobbyists successfully romanced a new OCC Chairman named Eugene Ludwig. We are back with "shoulder to the wheel" and "nose to the grindstone" to once again gather forces to defeat this evil proposal.

The first order of business was to contact community banking through the states associations. We not only requested association letters, but letters from their member banks. I wrote many draft letters for the associations to send to their members as well as letters for the individual banks. The result was a larger body of opposition than we mounted previously. We also went after the other previous objectors to the rule and virtually all of them sent new letters to the new man in charge.

An example of an improvement from 1990 was CSBS. You may recall that they did not send a letter to Clarke but gave details of the objections to their state banking commission members. We had a boost from Barbara Walker, Commissioner of Banks in Colorado and Chair of the CSBS. Her influence tipped the scales, and CSBS officially opposed the rule.

Although Peggy Miller had testified in 1990 briefly on behalf of the Consumer Federation of America, we were unable to get written opposition from them at that time. I began bulldog style campaigning to get a strong show of opposition from the consumer groups. After meeting with Chris

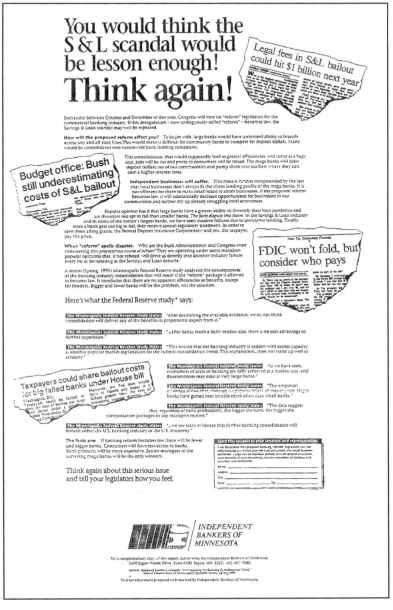

INDEPENDENT BANKERS OF MINNESOTA HELPED THE FIGHT.

Lewis, Director of Banking Policy for the CFA several times, and William Ken Brunette of AARP, the latter suggested a joint letter from the two organizations. One of the most heartfelt victories of this extended campaign was the letter sent to Mr. Ludwig on January 21, 1994 from CFA and AARP, and Ed Mierzwinski, Consumer Advocate for U.S. PIRG (Public Interest Research Group). I believe this group had substantial influence on the decision by a now Democratic OCC Chairman and his boss, Treasury Secretary Lloyd Bentsen.

At last, in May of 1994 William Bowden spoke for the OCC in letters to all objectors, *"The Office of the Comptroller of the Currency has determined not to adopt the proposed (Regulation 9) rule."*

And we breathed a collective, AMEN!

This is the end of the Regulation 9 saga but not Glass-Steagall! In 1995, big bank interests stormed the walls of the GS castle on two fronts. They attacked the front gate with proposed legislation that would grant sweeping new powers while conducting a flank movement toward the regulators to pick away at the new venerable Glass-Steagall. Two conflicting articles appeared in *Business Week* and *Newsweek's* March 13, 1995 editions. The former was entitled, *"It's Time to Guillotine Glass-Steagall."* As the title suggests, it contained every false claim that, as history will affirm, caused not greater economic good, but the disaster of 2007 until who knows when. It did, however, truthfully report the "loopholes" that had been punched in GS over a number of years by regulatory fiat. The latter article, *"Helping Banks Lose Their Bearings"* refuted virtually everything in the first article and author Allan Sloan's concluding remarks were, *"Forgive my skepticism, but I can't help hearing the words 'this time it's different.' Make a fire big enough and hot enough, and the Fed's fire walls will be about as useful as the 'watertight bulkhead' that made the Titanic unsinkable."*

Although perennial Fed Chairman Allen Greenspan gave his usual "on the one hand" and "on the other hand" blessing, the Leach Glass-Steagall Reform Bill failed to see the light of day.

The pressure by the mega banks and securities giants did finally put what was left of the tattered Glass-Steagall Act in its grave in 1999 as it became a featured part of the Gramm-Leach-Bliley Act.

It was a long hard fight . . . that was ultimately lost, but we all became better for staging the battle . . . *and history has proved us right!*

438

Appendix I

Excerpts from Beyond Survival:
How Financial Institutions Can Thrive
in the 1990s *by Michael T. Higgins*

GLEN JOHNSON AND THE PURSUIT
OF A MARKET NICHE

The story of Federated Investors, Pittsburgh, Pennsylvania, serves as a model for banks and thrifts in their quest to compete successfully in a deregulated, highly competitive environment. In less than 18 years, the company grew from a storefront office to become the nation's fourth largest investment firm with approximately $40 billion in managed assets. Today, Federated has business relationships with more than 2,500 financial institutions nationwide.

Federated's brilliant business strategy employed every discipline that bank management teams must master to take their organizations beyond survival.

Federated Investors, founded in 1955, made a business of developing investment products for brokerage firms to market to the public. The company experienced modest success during the subsequent 15 years. By 1970, it managed $200 million in assets. During the next three years, the company continued to succeed, but it became apparent there were opportunities to evaluate and new market segments to serve. In 1973, Federated decided to create a new service: a money market fund for savers, allowing them to achieve money market rates of return for their short-term or savings deposits.

The company believed in the potential of this new service, but it was a first, and one whose success would be achieved only through unparalleled persistence.

This new direction began in 1970 when Jack Donahue, chairman and founder of Federated Investors, hired Glen Johnson to be the company's marketing director. At the time, the company had less than 30 employees.

Three years after Johnson's arrival, Donahue and Johnson had a vision: to create a fund to be invested in short-term bank certificates of deposit (CDs), providing an 8–11% return and marketed directly to consumers or through bank trust departments. If marketed through bank trust departments, the instrument would allow financial institutions to achieve a market rate of return on short-term deposits for their trust clients, would deliver daily dividends, and would have no principal fluctuation. More specifically, the instrument would:

» Significantly improve customers' returns on their trust savings (most trust departments' idle funds were not invested because the instruments available provided only a minimum return to the client and resulted in very high administrative overhead expenses for the bank).

» Eliminate the bank's bookkeeping expenses, which typically exceeded their own spread.

» Provide an adequate fee for the bank.

» Offset Federated's operational overhead expenses.

» Return a good profit to Federated.

To clarify, the return on previously uninvested cash (once it was placed with Federated) was credited to the bank client's account. The bank receives no part of the spread. The fiduciary customer is entitled to the total return. Because the client is already paying the bank a fee for managing the assets, the bank's advantage is that the trust department can perform more effectively with their trust client receiving the revenue benefits.

The most advantageous route to acquiring customers for this new and innovative product was through bank's trust departments. The challenge was that no bank had ever used such an instrument. At the time, bankers regarded mutual funds with suspicion. In particular, bank decision-makers did not look upon funds with variable net asset value favorably.

Because banks were not a sure target, Federated considered marketing its new instrument through brokers. Brokers had dealt with the implications of variable net asset values and had contact with investors. However, investors and savers were two different financial customers, and there were a lot more savers than investors to be served.

Another alternative was to direct Federated's efforts toward attracting the consuming public directly, without going through either banks or brokerage houses. But Federated did not have the distribution system, sales force, or the capital resources to approach that option successfully.

The decision was made to market to banks, but even bankers who were converted saw the new instrument only as an opportunity to improve book-keeping and reporting. When Johnson sold the first account in Boston, the client reduced its staff by 30 people. The operational efficiency, more than the return on client's savings, was what had sold the client.

In a very short period of time, most of the banks unwilling to be the first, jumped on the bandwagon. Banks from New York to California and from Minnesota to Texas soon captured the opportunity.

Not too long thereafter, the regulators started to put pressure on trust departments to invest their idle cash. One big West Coast bank had $30 million in cash that was not invested. This was precisely the opportunity that was driving Johnson. He began to see things happen, and he knew that he was the catalyst.

By 1975, Federated's individual accounts and its banking relationships grew astronomically to $450 million. Then, interest rates dropped, and the return on idle savings decreased from a high of 11.3% to an all time low of 4.15%.

Interestingly, the banks that were clients primarily because of the book-keeping and operational support had a reason for staying, despite the 4.15% rate. The funds had not been invested previously anyway, and the banks had been relieved of a tremendous amount of operational expense. Therefore, when interest rates fell, the banks stayed, but Federated's personal account relationships left.

The light was on; the market segment had been identified. In January 1976, a major decision was made. Federated started a new 45-basis-point "wholesale" fund invested in government securities. The fund was purely institutional—no individual could get into it. The company had decided never again to advertise for a consumer account. The market niche that Federated could best serve was banks, and Johnson and other Federated managers agreed never again to compete with the clientele that had been consistently loyal in the retail world.

In banker's eyes, the perceived value of Federated's fund was that it reduced administrative detail and bookkeeping overhead. Their response to the product line had little to do with client needs or customer service because bankers were not required to think that way. They were driven by operational priorities, not customer priorities. This, unfortunately, is the very challenge the industry still faces today. Operational priorities too often have priority over customer service.

Glen Johnson did not rest, even after he had a respectable list of bank clients. Once, he recalls, he had a meeting at one of Pittsburgh's largest banks. Federated was doing business with a few banks in town, but it had not really penetrated its local market yet. Arriving promptly ahead of schedule, Johnson was ushered into a meeting room in which sat eleven lieutenants without their decision-maker. Precisely 15 minutes after the meeting was scheduled to begin, the decision-maker appeared.

Halfway through the presentation, the decision-maker interrupted, "Mr. Johnson, as you know, our bank is one of the largest and one of the most successful banking organizations in the state of Pennsylvania. It would be very difficult for us to justify a decision to do business with a company the [meager] size of Federated Investors." The meeting was adjourned. The decision-maker departed abruptly. His lieutenants followed.

The ending to the story occurred six years later when Glen Johnson made another appointment at the same Pittsburgh bank. He arrived promptly before the scheduled meeting. Again, on time, the 11 lieutenants appeared and placed themselves quietly around the conference table. Precisely 15 minutes later, the decision-maker appeared. Glen Johnson's opening began with, "Thank you for this opportunity. Now that Federated Investors is the largest financial organization in Pennsylvania, I know that your organization is anxious to learn how we can help you help yourself and help your clientele."

Looking back, why did Federated achieve such success? The key was not the extravagant social events and parties but rather the commitment to effectively serving its customers and overwhelming them with service beyond their expectations. VIP service was Federated's symbol of quality, and it set the company apart from the competition. Moreover, Federated committed to reinforcing that symbol with attentive service before, during, and after the sale.

Glen made a personal commitment to each and every user that, if there was a question or a problem, it would be answered or resolved within 24 hours. If necessary, someone from Federated would be there. He or she would be on the first airplane out, even if Federated lost money, because, the company could be perpetuated only by making good on its commitment to serve unquestionably and beyond anyone's expectations.

By 1978, Federated was on a roll. It grew $1 billion in one 16-day period. It was not long after that it grew another billion in a 13-day period and then another billion in a 10-day period. In one hectic month, Federated added 100 new bank clients to its user list.

The challenge now was not in getting new accounts and building assets. Success had created a new challenge; how to support the operational demands of managing billions of dollars.

I asked Glen Johnson what the one secret was for Federated's success.

We had discussed the product innovation, persistence, differentiation, the commitment to quality, and the extravaganzas. All of those were important, but none was the most important. According to Johnson, the reason Federated was so successful was that Johnson listened to the people in the marketplace. The implications were twofold: one internal, one external.

Early on, Johnson made a commitment to listen to his people. This required him to be with his people in the user regional meetings, the conventions, and the seminars; to be with his people at the extravaganzas and at the sales meetings; to be with his people when they had challenges; and to be accessible to their ideas. "If you accept the role of president of a competitive organization, you accept the role of sales manager," said Johnson. Managing successful sales organizations in a competitive environment requires a very personalized approach to the business. That begins with creating pride.

The excitement and loyalty engendered at Federated are a result of pride the staff now creates for themselves. Just establishing a place to work for someone will not work anymore! You are competing with teams of people who believe in their organization and its purpose. It is belief that sets one organization apart from another, not merely commitment to making a profit. Profit comes from the ability to create belief, which springs from enthusiasm for the organization and its services. Profit is the result of a vision, and the ideas of an energetic management team give life to that vision.

Federated differentiated itself by staying years ahead of the competition. Building internal quality through belief was important in nurturing staff loyalty and enthusiasm and building a satisfied client base. But how did Federated stay ahead of the competition? External listening is the key.

The key is that Federated recognizes that the trust officer is the client. The client is the most important person in the world. "We remind them of it often," Johnson confirms, "and we remind ourselves of it every single day."

Listening and responding is the hook. That is the essence of identifying customer need. Listening and responding is what keeps Federated ahead of the competition. Listening and responding is the prerequisite to differentiation!

Another lesson can be learned from Federated's success. The nature of a successful business in a competitive marketplace demands that management avoid the temptation of thinking that the company can be all things to all people. Glen Johnson confirms this observation when he explains why Federated does not branch out once again beyond the banking industry and sell directly to consumers. "We certainly have the resources now to compete for the individual consumer. But if people call us and want us to put money into a money market fund," he replies, "I send them to their local bank."

Federated's founder and chairman, Jack Donahue, recently reflected on the company's past and future, "We don't accept the norm. If we are going to stay on top in serving our clients, we must continually challenge ourselves not to accept where we are. We see change for what it is. Change has never been a challenge for Federated. Change and managing change is managing opportunity."

The Federated experience serves as an example to bank management because it reveals the critical disciplines that underpin success in a competitive environment. These disciplines are exhibited in any successful operation.

Glen Johnson, President, Federated Investors, Inc., Pittsburgh, Pennsylvania has stated:

Senior management must design, implement, and *be committed to a specific course of action* when pursuing new marketing opportunities, but there is a twist. Instead of setting a goal at the top and selling it "down" to the customer level, it makes more sense today to know what the customer wants and sell that "up" to the senior level.

The new role of bank marketing is to *know customer needs* and communicate them upward to initiate new marketing goals. This approach needs a strong commitment from senior management to follow through on customer preferences. Management must also positively respond to changes brought about by the market-driven approach and reinforce that positive response through a strong commitment to training, as well as an ongoing communication of goals and plans to the customer support staff level.

A closing thought: senior management must adopt the attitude that *there are no marketing problems, only marketing opportunities.*

Appendix J

Excerpts from New Horizons: The Story of Federated Investors

When Glen Johnson joined Federated Investors in 1970, he was the needle in a haystack.

"Dick Fisher handled dealings with the brokers. I handled the affinity groups, and Glen Johnson handled the bank trust departments," Wallander said. "Glen is an extremely talented marketing guy and salesman."

Johnson stood out in the Federated haystack in more ways than one. He grew up a Minnesota farm boy; started and ran his own newspaper for 12 years; spent 18 hours a day for three months driving Hubert Humphrey around in a Ford Falcon campaigning; knew top politicians and Hollywood stars; and, not least, he was a Democrat.

"Basically, we were all very, very conservative," Wallander said of his Federated peers. "But Glen was a Liberal, which made him the apple of the eye of the press, the press basically being fairly liberal. They just loved him—and they gave him lots of publicity."

As a Liberal—and a Humphrey backer—Johnson's career took a sharp turn in 1968 when Humphrey lost the presidential election to Richard Nixon. Johnson described the turn of events as being "Nixonized"—fired by Nixon."

His experience in newspapers, which led him into politics, gave him the opportunity to learn how to communicate with the general public, Johnson said. "That is the key."

Those communication skills were crucial to Federated. "When I went out to sell a Federated fund, I'd go to the newspaper first and get a story about this great product I was selling," Johnson said. "Chances are the guy had been on my national media committee when I was the national director. So he'd write the story."

"Glen Johnson had really good media connections," Jack Donahue said.

"He really was a genius at that. And he's a genius at lobbying. We would often sit and talk, and he was always dreaming up a new idea."

Some of those ideas were clever. When speaking on a radio show, Johnson would blurt out Federated's toll-free Money Market Management telephone number; although he knew many hosts frowned upon the free advertising. All of his tactics worked. By late October 1974, Money Market Management had attracted 23,000 investors and $180 million in assets. It was the hottest financial product of the period.

As Federated's share of the bank trust and mutual fund markets grew, so did the demands placed on the company. Various bank trust departments suggested specialized funds that would simplify business for them. One bank in Ohio, for example, wanted an even "safer" fund, so Federated created the Trust for U.S. Treasury Obligations, which invested only in short-term Treasury bills. Other new funds were developed to meet the specific needs of various institutions. Along the way, Federated was constantly pushing the limits of the industry, fighting numerous legal battles to cut through the miles of red tape that often stood between its clients' needs and the creation of a new type of fund. Federated developed a reputation for dependable management, safe investments, solid returns, and excellent service that would lead to remarkable growth for the company in the coming years.

Appendix K

Forbes Magazine, *February 15, 1982*

"GLEN JOHNSON'S UNLIKELY MONEY MACHINE"
BY BEN WEBERMAN

At the core of every brilliant innovation in the world, there is an essential simplicity. Anything else? Yes: Persistence.

Federated Investors' Glen Johnson will always have a good feeling about Martinsville, Virginia. It was there, back in 1974, that he found the first take for his new money market mutual fund, designed for bank trust departments to put their clients' idle cash balances to work.

Until Martinsville, it had been a hard sell. Most trust departments preferred CDs and the like, where they had an IOU from a well-known name, as things had always been done. "I tried everything," Johnson recalls. "About one banker in five was smart enough to grasp the concept. But nobody wanted to be first."

Today, a scant seven years after the Martinsville breakthrough, Pittsburgh-headquartered Federated is the largest money market operator in the country after Merrill Lynch. With more than 1,350 banks as its customers, it invests over $24 billion. Moreover, Federated has big plans to be the vehicle into the financial supermarket for banks that don't want to do it on their own. It plans to cover everything from IRAs to discount stock brokerage, Glass-Steagall notwithstanding. But Federated is little known, by choice, not by accident, because as a wholesaler of financial services it operates through others without its own brand identification.

Glen Johnson is an unlikely looking tycoon. An affable farm boy from Minnesota, he never graduated from college, but after high school and a local business school he started a weekly newspaper on a borrowed $800. He sold it for $9,000 and was casting around for something else to do when his support from the Hubert Humphrey political machine won him a minor Treasury Department appointment. He soon found himself heading the

U.S. savings bonds drive. If a man could sell those at a time when inflation was way ahead of the interest rate, he could sell anything. In 1969, at age 41, President Nixon, who couldn't conceive of a Humphrey Democrat on his payroll, fired him. A year later he went to work for Federated, then a small-ish mutual fund organization. At first the bankers strongly resisted his idea of a wholesale money market fund; why should they compete with themselves? But he persisted, and when the bankers began losing business on a massive scale to money market funds, they finally grasped Johnson's point.

Johnson, now 52, does not work for Federated directly, but is on the payroll of Federated Securities Corp., its research subsidiary where, as President of Federated Cash Management Funds, he heads institutional funds. But any ego deprivation from being a couple of rungs below Chairman John Donahue is more than made up for by his $675,000 annual compensation. And you get the sense in talking with him that he doesn't have to account overly much to the corporate level for his activities, even though he still owns 143,000 shares (market value $4,862,000) after having sold 45,000 shares.

Why haven't others copied this brilliantly simple idea? The reason is because if the concept has simplicity, the hardware does not. Federated has set up its own $4 million computer system, permitting total automation of bank customer funds. Now, each client bank has a terminal with a screen and printer. With this equipment and the services of Boston's State Street Bank & Trust, all the bank needs to do is dial a local number, and place purchase and sale orders. The printer provides immediate confirmation. "When we have the money before 3 o'clock, the account earns interest that day. If they call us by terminal before noon, they can have the money back in their account that day," says Johnson.

Having convinced bankers that Federated can invest idle cash in trust accounts at lower cost than the banks themselves can do it, Johnson is now doing the same thing with bank checking account balances. So far, he says, he has signed up 300 banks to "sweep up" (one of his favorite phrases) balances of checking account customers over a prearranged amount—say $2,000—at the end of each day and put it to work in a Federated money market fund. Thus the banks can offer checking clients the option of short-term money market vehicles. At the direction of the customer, the money is placed in U.S. Treasury issues, federal agency obligations money funds, tax-exempt money funds, or overnight repurchase agreements.

This service is similar to Merrill Lynch Cash Management Accounts, but is easier on the customer, Johnson contends. "You don't have to carry a check to your broker. It's all done automatically." The customer signs a managed agency agreement and pays a fee, which can range from 0.2 percent of total assets to 15 percent of total income. Merrill Lynch charges a flat $35 a year for its CMA. Like ML, Federated charges a management fee of less than 0.5 percent of total assets on the specific mutual funds used.

With his base firmly in place, Johnson expects to add new services fast. "So far, we serve the bank trust industry," he says. "Now we are using our service to sell the whole Wall Street angle. When a guy walks into a bank and says, 'Can you do what all those brokers are doing?' the bank will be able to answer, 'Yes.'"

For example, "A thousand banks are signing up to offer IRA accounts through us. The bank will be the custodian and charge a fee. We will do all the bookkeeping and file the reports. All they have to do is talk to the client."

Also, he figures, a financial wholesaler like Federated could take over complete management of the investment function of smaller trust departments. "This would be the first step in what I call the nationwide network of common trust companies," he says. One instrument: the Federated "short-intermediate municipal trust, through which cash in individuals trust accounts, can earn tax-free interest. Johnson plans to follow it up with a three-year government securities fund, a CNMA fund and a real estate fund, with trust assets moved "from fund A to B to C back to A according to market trends and client needs."

After that? "Well, says Johnson, Federated could provide discount stock brokerage to commercial bank customers. What about Glass-Steagall Act restraints? No problems, says Johnson: The banks would merely be "agents" for Federated, which would do the actual brokering.

Moving into an allied field, Federated now manages money market mutual funds for stockbrokers, including Edward D. Jones & Co., the midwestern broker, the Milwaukee Co., and Legg Mason of Baltimore. It also runs money market funds for the Lutheran Brotherhood (assets $769 million) and the National Retired Teachers Association of Retired Persons ($3.7 billion).

Federated's earnings did not break through $1 million until 1978, but last year they topped $22 million, or about $4.20 a share on 5.1 million shares outstanding, and Johnson forecasts they will be nearly double that this year. Federated has been sheltering some of this rising income in oil and gas drilling. "We put $10 million into oil and gas last year, including $5 million that would have been paid in taxes," Johnson says.

Federated stockholders who got the point early and kept the faith have reaped a handsome reward. From a low of 1 in 1979 and 2.5 in 1980, Federated's five million shares of non-voting Class B common soared to .34

recently; if Johnson is right and 1982 earnings approach $8 a share, that's still a price/earnings ratio of 4.25.

Not surprisingly, Federated spends much of its time turning down acquisition offers. "We've been the fastest growing financial institution in the country for four years in a row," Johnson says proudly.

You might know that a chap like Johnson would understand clearly the nature of his business and would stubbornly avoid the temptation of thinking he can be all things to all people. You find this out when you ask him why he doesn't branch out into selling directly to consumers. "If someone calls us and wants to put money into a money market fund," he replies, "I ask where they live and send them to the local bank."

Note: *When I was given the opportunity to be interviewed for a major business magazine like* Forbes, *of course I jumped at the chance. I was always looking for ways to promote Federated. I fully expected it to be the Federated Investors story. Imagine my surprise when the story broke, to find that although it alluded to Federated, it was more about Glen Johnson. Not every person in the company was pleased. However, the bottom line was that we received over 800 million dollars from this story alone! (GRJ)*